Group Processes

REVIEW OF PERSONALITY
AND SOCIAL PSYCHOLOGY

Editor: Clyde Hendrick, *Texas Tech University*

Associate Editors:
Susan T. Fiske, *University of Massachusetts*
John H. Harvey, *University of Iowa*
Richard P. McGlynn, *Texas Tech University*
Walter G. Stephan, *New Mexico State University*

Editorial Board

Group Processes

Editor
CLYDE HENDRICK

8
REVIEW of PERSONALITY and SOCIAL PSYCHOLOGY

Published in cooperation with the Society for Personality and Social Psychology
(Division 8 of the American Psychological Association)

SAGE PUBLICATIONS
The Publishers of Professional Social Science
Newbury Park   Beverly Hills   London   New Delhi

For information address:

SAGE Publications, Inc.
2111 West Hillcrest Drive
Newbury Park, California 91320

SAGE Publications Inc.   SAGE Publications Ltd.
275 South Beverly Drive   28 Banner Street
Beverly Hills   London EC1Y 8QE
California 90212   England

SAGE PUBLICATIONS India Pvt. Ltd.
M-32 Market
Greater Kailash I
New Delhi 110 048 India

Printed in the United States of America

Library of Congress Cataloging-in-Publication Data

International Standard Book Number 0-8039-3071-2
0-8039-3072-0

International Standard Series Number 0270-1987

FIRST PRINTING

CONTENTS

Group Processes and Intergroup Relations

EDITOR'S INTRODUCTION

CLYDE HENDRICK

Clyde Hendrick is Professor of Psychology and Dean of the Graduate School at Texas Tech University. He was previously Chairperson of Psychology, University of Miami. His scholarly interests include close relationships, sex roles, and philosophy of science. He has served as Editor for *Personality and Social Psychology Bulletin* and as Acting Editor for *Journal of Personality and Social Psychology*.

Whatever happened to the group in social psychology? Ivan Steiner (1974) posed this question within the context of describing changes in research traditions within social psychology. Several other commentators also noted that the strong emphasis on group research in the 1940s and 1950s had given way to research on individual attitudes, motives, and cognitions in the 1960s. In general, the study of group processes was largely replaced by the study of individual processes. The 1970s saw the full flowering of the "cognitive revolution," and, if anything, the focus on individual processes became even more extreme.

Steiner predicted that the group would rise again, probably in the late 1970s. The prediction, though perhaps delayed by about five years, appears to be in the process of validation. The study of group processes is experiencing a strong resurgence of interest, coming to clear public fruition in the current duo of volumes of the *Review* (Vols. 8 and 9).

The call for chapter proposals for Volume 8 was advertised broadly.

EDITOR'S NOTE: In addition to members of the Editorial Board who reviewed chapters, I am indebted to the following individuals for their reviews of one or more chapters: Eugene Burnstein, Martin M. Chemers, Morton Deutsch, Fred E. Fiedler, Robert House, Michael Hogg, Eric Knowles, Delores Ludwig, Anne Maass, Amnon Rapaport, Stephen G. West, David A. Wilder, and Sharon Wolf. I am also grateful to Charles T. Hendrix, Executive Editor of Sage Publications, for his friendly cooperation in making possible two volumes on group processes and intergroup relations.

Over 40 proposals were received. It was clear that at least two fine volumes could be produced. After hurried consultation among the Editor, members of the Publications Committee of Division 8, and the Executive Editor of Sage, the decision was made to go forward with the two-volume set. The result was 20 chapters, forming Volumes 8 and 9. A great variety of topics is covered in these volumes. From the perspective of an editor, group processes as a field of endeavor now shows amazing vitality after being moribund for a quarter century. A large measure of credit for this revitalization must go to our European colleagues, especially Tajfel, Moscovici, and their collaborators.

The rationale for allocation of the 20 chapters into the two volumes resulted from the chapters' contents and the Editor's intuition. An attempt at justification could be made, but it is expected that each volume will stand on its own merits, thereby foreclosing the need for such justification.

OVERVIEW OF THE CHAPTERS: VOLUME 8

The first two chapters deal with an old issue, conformity. However, conformity can no longer be considered as a single phenomenon, but must be considered in terms of majority influence on a minority as well as minority influence on a majority. Chapter 1, by Levine and Russo, provides a balanced review of both kinds of influence, stressing post-1970 research. This chapter, an invited review, includes many topics: definitions and types of conformity, motivational issues, gender differences, effects of relative size of majority and minority positions, and so forth. Moscovici's conflict perspective, including effects of the minority on the majority, is discussed thoroughly. The importance of minority consistency and rigidity in influencing the majority is noted. The authors propose that understanding minority effects requires a conception of how groups socialize members. A recent model by Moreland and Levine offers one perspective on group socialization. This excellent review and extensive reference list suggests that the study of conformity is alive, well, and prospering.

Chapter 2, by Maass, West, and Cialdini, examines a specific area of conformity, minority influence and conversion. Conversion is defined as changes in private attitude that persist beyond the influence situation. The authors note that majorities may obtain overt compliance but not private attitude change. However, minorities often appear not to effect immediate public change but may induce private attitude change over time. Possible processes mediating such conversion effects are explored in detail. The authors conclude that such minority effects do indeed occur, but that in the wider society effective minorities must be perceived as part of the larger "in-group" that just happens to differ from the rest of the society on the particular issue. The chapter is highly provocative and stimulating.

Chapter 3, by Moreland, deals with a seldom-treated topic, the formation of small groups. This chapter is a broad-ranging review of theories and research from many disciplines that culls and integrates material relevant to group formation. Moreland views group formation as an ongoing process of social integration. There are four major types of social integration. Environmental integration is associated with group formation whenever physical, social, or cultural environments spawn appropriate conditions. Behavioral integration is probably most familiar to personality and social psychologists. It is based on dependency and interdependency in their many forms. Affective integration, the meshing of feelings and emotions, may also serve as a basis for group formation. Cognitive integration promotes group formation whenever people are aware of and share relevant personal characteristics. Moreland provides a valuable service through the erudite scholarship of his chapter. It should stimulate future research on the formation of small groups.

Chapter 4, by Allison and Messick, grapples with two general problems: (1) the extent to which group decisions and actions are veridical with individual cognitive states, and (2) the extent to which observers of group actions infer a correspondence between group behavior and individual preference. The chapter is a masterful review of many phenomena related to these two issues. The old dispute about whether the locus of reality resides in the individual or the group appears in a new guise, and sophisticated arguments may be made in favor of each position. Groups produce decisions that may not correspond to members' preferences, and may have properties that do not characterize any of the individuals. However, groups do exert unique forces on individuals and may affect individual performances (e.g., the phenomenon of social loafing). Combining individual inputs to form a group output is indeed a complex enterprise. However, perceivers of group behavior tend to simplify those complexities. Perceivers tend to make simple correspondent inferences about individuals based on group outcomes. This chapter provides a stimulating discussion of the traditional puzzles involved in considering issues of "the individual" versus "the group."

Chapter 5, by Mackie and Goethals, continues the discussion of individual versus group. The authors present the thesis that groups have goals similar to the goals of individuals, and that groups and individuals are interdependent in goal achievement, despite the fact that groups and individuals are often in conflict about goals. One superordinate goal of intragroup life is achieving an isomorphism between individual action and group behavior so that a given behavior is perceived as satisfying both individual and group goals. Such isomorphism occurs through attainment of three general classes of goals: utilitarian, knowledge, and identity goals. Three classes of behavior promote such goal iso-morphism: social influence, cooperation and competition, and inclusion versus exclusion of individuals with respect to the group. Success in the behavioral enterprise is more probable when the group identity is highly salient to members. How is group identity enhanced? Increase of "unit formation" among individuals and contrast of the group with other groups, especially via intergroup competition, promote a sense of group identity. The chapter provides another worthy and stimulating analysis of the conceptual puzzle of individual versus group.

Chapter 6, by Leary and Forsyth, deals with another facet of group processes, attribution of responsibility for collective endeavors. The authors draw on an extensive literature on attribution of responsibility for individual actions, selecting the subset of articles dealing with group attribution. The point is made that group activity is always accompanied by attributional activity: in coordinating action, arriving at a decision, and in success or failure of a group's endeavors. Major areas of research include diffusion of responsibility and focusing of responsibility with respect to performance-linked attributional biases. Diffusion of respon-sibility is a recurring theme underlying several phenomena: bystander intervention, group polarization, deindividuation, selfishness in social traps, and social loafing. Also, responsibility is focused differently within a group. For example, leaders take more responsibility for group outcomes than do followers, even when the leader is arbitrarily selected. Self-serving biases also occur in groups, such as claiming credit for group success, but disclaiming responsibility for group failure. In addition, attributional biases often occur: in conflicts among group members, negative group processes, status allocation and satisfaction, and the like. This chapter does an excellent job in translating the cognitive social psychology of individuals into a viable perspective on several aspects of group behavior.

Chapter 7, by Kaplan, considers processes of social influence in group decision making. Kaplan refurbishes the traditional concepts of normative and informational influence and makes them central in subsuming other approaches to social influence. Normative influence is construed as a status-seeking/status-setting mechanism within the socioemotional context of group life. Informational influence is construed as processes involved in determining factual states of affairs of the world at large. The two modes of influence differ in the attributes central to social relations, including type of issue, orientation of group members, interaction goals of the group, and the kind of decision rule used in a particular instance. The two types of influence engage different sources, forms, and processes of social motivation. Although Kaplan makes a clear analytic distinction between normative and informational influence, he notes that they are not mutually exclusive in the empirical world. Both types can operate jointly in group decision making. Nevertheless, a strong and interesting case is made for considering the two types of influence as conceptually distinct.

Chapter 8, by Insko and Schopler, provides a detailed examination of Tajfel's assumption that mere categorization into minimal groups cues a bias in favor of one's own group category. The authors have questioned this assumption in a series of published and unpublished articles, suggesting that the results are dependent upon specifics of methodology. For researchers interested in this particular problem, this chapter provides an excellent summary of the issues. For more casual readers, the chapter conveys well the intricacies involved in studying group processes and arriving at definitive conclusions.

The last two chapters deal with leadership, another traditional area in the study of groups. Chapter 9, by Chemers, provides an excellent review of current knowledge about leadership. A brief historical overview suggests the centrality of Fiedler's contingency model. Several recent approaches are also reviewed, including leader-oriented theories that focus on individual differences, exchange theories that focus on leader-follower relations, and cognitive theories that deal with the intrapersonal bases of leadership. Chemers describes his own systems-process theory, an integrative approach to leadership that combines multiple perspectives. The chapter is a state-of-the-art summary, and provides a hopeful reframing of an important area that has sometimes seemed to be in a state of conceptual doldrums.

Chapter 10, by Smith and Fritz, presents a more specialized study than does Chemers's chapter. Previous work by Turner has dealt with conditions of group formation and salience of group membership. The approach is sometimes referred to as depersonalization theory. One component of this approach is an assimilation-contrast model of how group membership affects perceptive/evaluative processes with respect to in-group members and out-group individuals. Smith and Fritz apply depersonalization theory to leadership, and develop what they call a person-niche model of leadership. Several hypotheses are derived concerning leader selection, performance, and evaluation. The chapter is a fine attempt at theorizing and provides an interesting new approach to leadership.

CONCLUSIONS

Collectively, this set of chapters provides broad coverage of several central conceptual areas in the study of group processes. The sense of ferment and new ideas is readily apparent. It has been a privilege to work with the authors, and I have learned much. Clearly, not all relevant topics are covered. However, this set of chapters, in conjunction with Volume 9, covers most of the topical areas that are currently generating considerable research activity.

REFERENCE

Steiner, I. D. (1974). Whatever happened to the group in social psychology? *Journal of Experimental Social Psychology, 10*, 94-108.

1

Majority and Minority Influence

JOHN M. LEVINE
EILEEN M. RUSSO

John M. Levine is Professor of Psychology at the University of Pittsburgh. His major research interests involve small group processes and social comparison. In addition to empirical studies, he has authored and coauthored chapters on reaction to opinion deviance (in P. Paulus's *Psychology of Group Influence*), group socialization (in L. Berkowitz's *Advances in Experimental Social Psychology*), ability comparison in educational settings (in J. Levine and M. Wang's *Teacher and Student Perceptions: Implications for Learning*), and outcome comparison in group contexts (in R. Schwarzer's *Self-Related Cognitions in Anxiety and Motivation*).

Eileen M. Russo is a graduate student in social psychology at the University of Pittsburgh. She is interested in social influence in small groups, particularly the cognitive consequences of disagreement.

The study of interpersonal influence in small groups is one of the most enduring areas of social psychological inquiry. The dominant methodology for investigating such influence uses a laboratory group in which only two distinct positions are represented and a smaller number of individuals holds one position than the other. Researchers have assumed that such bimodal and asymmetrical distributions of opinion are unstable. Even when there is no explicit demand for group consensus, it has been expected that individuals will change their positions in order to produce a more homogeneous distribution of opinion in the group.

Increased opinion homogeneity can be produced in several different ways. Minority members might shift toward majority members, majority members might shift toward minority members, both majority and

AUTHORS' NOTE: Preparation of this chapter was supported by Grant BNS-8316107 from the National Science Foundation and by Grant OERI-G-86-0005 from the Office of Educational Research and Improvement, Department of Education, to the Center for the Study of Learning, Learning Research and Development Center, University of Pittsburgh. We would like to thank the reviewers and editor for their helpful comments on an earlier draft of the chapter.

minority members might shift toward one another, or group composition might change through the departure of some members (Festinger, 1950; Levine, 1980; Moscovici, 1976). During the 1950s and 1960s, work on interpersonal influence in small groups focused almost exclusively on majority-produced influence, usually called *conformity*. The typical conformity paradigm involves exposing a lone subject (minority) to the unanimous disagreement of several peers (majority). Stimulated by the investigations of Asch (1951, 1955, 1956), researchers conducted scores of experiments seeking to clarify the conditions under which individuals who hold a minority position in a group adopt the position held by the majority. Since the early 1970s, increasing attention has been paid to minority-produced influence, usually called *innovation*. The typical innovation paradigm involves exposing several subjects (majority) to the disagreement of one or two peers (minority). Stimulated by the investigations of Moscovici and his colleagues (Moscovici & Faucheux, 1972), many researchers sought to clarify the conditions under which individuals who hold a majority position in a group adopt the position held by the minority. Currently, research attention is shifting from an exclusive focus on either conformity or innovation toward identification of similarities and differences in the antecedents and consequences of these two types of influence.

The goal of the present chapter is to review recent work on majority and minority influence in small groups. We devote attention primarily to empirical and theoretical articles published since 1970. Detailed summaries of older work are widely available (e.g., Allen, 1965; Hollander & Willis, 1967; Jones & Gerard, 1967; Kiesler & Kiesler, 1969; Moscovici & Faucheux, 1972). Our discussion is selective rather than exhaustive and is based primarily on laboratory studies of ad hoc groups. It is divided into two major sections. The first, dealing with work on majority influence, stresses the minority's social and cognitive dependence on the majority. The second, dealing with work on both majority and minority influence, emphasizes conflict negotiation between the majority and minority.

MAJORITY INFLUENCE: THE DEPENDENCE PERSPECTIVE

The dependence perspective on social influence in groups is exemplified by the research of Asch (1951, 1955, 1956), Festinger (1950), Deutsch and Gerard (1955), and many later investigators. This work seeks to identify the major situational and individual variables that affect the propensity of minorities to conform to majorities. In this section, we first review some important issues concerning the definition and measurement of conformity. In so doing, we refer to a number of important distinctions made prior to 1970 that still deserve consideration today. Then we discuss recent research on majority influence conducted within the dependence framework.

Definition and Measurement of Conformity

Conformity can be defined as "behavior *intended* to fulfill normative group expectancies as presently *perceived* by the individual" (Hollander & Willis, 1967, p. 64). Although seemingly straightforward, this definition masks complexities involving movement and congruence conformity, public and private conformity, and motivational deter- minants of conformity.

Movement Conformity and Congruence Conformity

Many authors (e.g., Allen, 1965; Kiesler, 1969) have advocated a movement (i.e., change) definition of conformity. This definition is suggested because a strong inference of conformity can be made when a person who is exposed to perceived majority pressure *changes* position toward the majority position. A major reason for adopting the movement criterion in defining conformity is to differentiate majority influence from behavioral uniformity, which occurs when an individual independently arrives at the majority position without any knowledge of what other group members think or any desire to hold their position.

Although useful in distinguishing conformity from behavioral unifor- mity, the adoption of movement as a *sine qua non* of conformity can sometimes be problematic. Under certain circumstances, the congruence (i.e., similarity) between the individual's position and the majority's position may better reflect conformity (Hollander & Willis, 1967). This would be true, for example, when a person independently agrees with the majority position (uniformity), subsequently is tempted to deviate from this viewpoint, but maintains his or her position because of group pressure (Kiesler & Kiesler, 1969). In such a case, conformity is manifested by *lack* of change. Sorrels and Kelley (1984) have provided a related perspective on the relationship between response inhibition and conformity, distinguishing between "conformity by commission" and "conformity by omission." The former occurs when people perform behaviors because of group pressure that they would not otherwise have performed. The latter occurs when people fail to perform behaviors because of group pressure that they would have performed in the absence of such pressure. Noting that previous work has emphasized conformity by commission, Sorrels and Kelley demonstrated conformity by omission in an autokinetic situation. Subjects who were led to believe that two other participants perceived no autokinetic movement reported seeing less movement than did subjects responding alone.

An additional problem with the movement criterion concerns the temporal relationship between the individual's exposure to majority pressure and his or her response to this pressure. So far, we have implicitly assumed that any movement conformity that is elicited by majority pressure occurs immediately after the pressure is exerted. However, more complex temporal patterns are possible. For example, an individual might expect to receive majority pressure on some issue in the future. The individual might then exhibit *anticipatory conformity* by moving toward the presumed majority position before the actual receipt of pressure (see Cialdini & Petty, 1981; Saltzstein & Sandberg, 1979). Or, an individual might perceive current majority pressure, but be unable or unwilling to conform to this pressure immediately. The individual might then exhibit *delayed conformity* by moving toward the majority position at some time after the receipt of pressure. In both cases, movement toward the majority position occurs, but difficulties arise in detecting the covariation between the individual's exposure to majority pressure and the response to this pressure.

Public Conformity and Private Conformity

In discussing movement and congruence conformity, we restricted our attention to overt responses to majority pressure. A number of investigators have pointed out, however, that majority influence can involve covert responses as well. Two general categories of conformity have therefore been distinguished: public compliance and private acceptance. If conformity is defined as movement, then public compliance refers to an individual's overt behavioral change toward the majority's position, whereas private acceptance refers to an individual's covert attitudinal change toward the majority's position. If nonconformity is defined as lack of movement (independence), then four combinations of public compliance/noncompliance and private acceptance/nonacceptance are possible (Allen, 1965): compliance and acceptance, compliance and nonacceptance, noncompliance and acceptance, and noncompliance and nonacceptance.

Two important questions are raised by the distinction between public compliance and private acceptance. One question, dealt with in the remainder of this section, concerns the measurement of these two forms of influence. The second question, which will be dealt with in a later section, concerns the motivational factors that underlie the occurrence of these two forms of influence.

Although the conceptual distinction between compliance and acceptance is easy to understand, methodological problems arise in demonstrating acceptance empirically (Allen, 1965). One obvious technique is to measure a person's publicly stated opinion in the presence of majority members (Time 1) and then measure the same opinion later when the person is alone (Time 2). If the person agrees with the majority's position at Time 1 but not at Time 2, then we might conclude that public but not private agreement has occurred. However, if the person agrees with the majority at both Time 1 and Time 2, then we might conclude that private acceptance as well as public compliance has occurred. Unfortunately, things are not so simple. For example, the fact that a person privately agrees with the majority at Time 2 does not prove that he or she privately agreed at Time 1. Other factors (e.g., dissonance reduction) might have subsequently produced congruence between the person's public and private responses (see Chaiken & Stangor, 1987, and Higgins & McCann, 1984, for discussions of mechanisms by which public responses can affect private responses). Moreover, the absence of private agreement at Time 2 does not lead to clear conclusions. It is possible that private agreement did occur at Time 1, but has since dissipated. Other techniques for measuring private acceptance are also fraught with problems. For example, asking subjects to recall their private positions during a prior majority pressure situation may elicit intentional distortions or memory errors. Moreover, assessing transfer of majority influence from one topic (e.g., aid to Honduras) to a "related" topic (e.g., aid to Costa Rica) demands detailed knowledge of subjects' perceptions of the relationships between the topics.

An ingenious technique that may prove useful for measuring private acceptance (with or without public compliance) has been suggested by Allen and Wilder (1980). In a study designed to assess whether group pressure can change the meaning of opinion statements, these investigators had subjects read several statements (e.g., "I would never go out of my way to help another person if it meant giving up some personal pleasure.") and then give their interpretations of key phrases in each statement (e.g., "go out of my way"). In one condition, subjects learned that a unanimous group of peers disagreed with their opinions on the statements. In a second (control) condition, no group responses were provided. Allen and Wilder found that subjects interpreted the key phrases differently in the unanimous and control conditions. For example, the phrase "go out of my way" in the above example was interpreted to mean "risk my life" in the unanimous condition and "be inconvenienced" in the control condition. These findings suggest that meaning change, or cognitive restructuring, of stimulus issues may have utility as an index of private acceptance.

A Descriptive Model of Responses to Majority Pressure

Several theorists have offered descriptive models of responses to majority pressure that take into account one or more of the issues discussed above (see review by Nail, 1986). For example, Allen's (1965) fourfold model of public compliance and private acceptance deals explicitly with congruence-noncongruence and compliance-acceptance and deals implicitly with movement-nonmovement. However, Allen's model does not handle the situation of initial agreement between the minority and majority. In another well-known model (Willis, 1963, 1965), four responses to majority pressure are differentiated: conformity (congruence and movement), anticonformity (noncongruence and movement), uniformity (congruence and nonmovement), and independence (noncongruence and nonmovement). This model deals explicitly with congruence-noncongruence and movement-nonmovement and handles the situation of initial agreement between the minority and majority. However, it does not consider compliance-acceptance.

Nail (1986) has offered a "synthetic model" of influence that integrates Allen's (1965) and Willis's (1963, 1965) models. Nail's model uses three factors, each with two levels, to generate eight possible behaviors. The factors are (1) initial agreement-disagreement, (2) final public congruence-noncongruence, and (3) final private agreement-disagreement. The eight possible behaviors are (1) *conversion* (initial disagreement, final public congruence, final private agreement), (2) *compliance* (initial disagreement, final public congruence, final private disagreement), (3) *anticompliance* (initial disagreement, final public noncongruence, final private agreement), (4) *independence* (initial disagreement, final public noncongruence, final private disagreement), (5) *congruence* (initial agreeement, final public congruence, final private agreement), (6) *compliance-2* (initial agreement, final public congruence, final private disagreement), (7) *anticompliance-2* (initial agreement, final public noncongruence, final private agreement), and (8) *anticonversion* (initial agreement, final public noncongruence, final private disagreement).

Nail's model provides a useful framework for describing alternative responses to majority (and, perhaps, minority) pressure. Without some explanatory mechanism to predict when particular behaviors will occur, however, this model is unlikely to generate much empirical work. Neither Allen's (1965) nor Willis's (1963, 1965) model has been notably successful in stimulating research.

Motivational Determinants of Conformity

So far, our discussion of conformity has been at the descriptive level. In this section, we consider explanatory analyses of the motivational and cognitive underpinnings of majority influence. As mentioned above, much of the interest in these issues has been stimulated by a desire to understand better the relationship between public compliance and private acceptance.

Normative and informational influence. The dominant theoretical explanation for the occurrence of conformity has been Deutsch and Gerard's (1955) analysis of normative and informational influence. These investigators defined normative influence as "influence to conform to the positive expectations of another" (p. 629) and informational influence as "influence to accept information obtained from another as evidence about reality" (p. 629). Although Deutsch and Gerard are not alone in proposing a dichotomous model of social and cognitive bases of majority influence (e.g., Kelley, 1952; Jones & Gerard, 1967; Thibaut & Strickland, 1956), their formulation is the best known of these models. Moreover, the normative-informational distinction continues to stimulate new theoretical and empirical work (e.g., Burnstein, 1982; Campbell, Tesser, & Fairey, 1986; Insko, Drenan, Solomon, Smith, & Wade, 1983; Kaplan & Miller, 1983; Stasser, Kerr, & Davis, 1980; Wolf, 1979).

Normative influence is based on the desire to maximize one's social outcomes in the group, coupled with the assumption that majority members will respond more favorably to conformity than to deviance. Evidence indicates that, compared to people who conform to majority consensus, those who deviate anticipate receiving more negative evaluation from other group members (e.g., Gerard & Rotter, 1961). Moreover, there appears to be a realistic basis for this fear of punishment for nonconformity. Many studies indicate that majority members do indeed dislike and reject attitudinal deviates (see Levine,

1980, for a detailed review). Research suggests that normative influence is likely under conditions of public responding (e.g., Deutsch & Gerard, 1955), anticipation of future interaction with other group members (e.g., Lewis, Langan, & Hollander, 1972), and reward interdependence among group members (e.g., Deutsch & Gerard, 1955; Sakurai, 1975).

Informational influence is based on the desire to have accurate beliefs about reality, coupled with the assumption that the majority is more correct or knowledgeable than oneself. A good deal of evidence indicates that people seek to evaluate their beliefs (and abilities, emotions, and outcomes) through social comparison with others (e.g., Festinger, 1950, 1954; Levine, 1983; Levine & Moreland, 1986; Suls & Miller, 1977). According to Allen and Wilder (1977), individuals who desire to evaluate their beliefs are motivated to agree with others, which in turn can produce conformity.[1] In general, the less confident a person is in the validity of a position, the more susceptible that person is to informational influence (Allen, 1965). Confidence, in turn, can be affected by such factors as the ambiguity and difficulty of the stimulus under consideration (Tajfel, 1969).

Deutsch and Gerard (1955) did not discuss the relationship between normative/informational influence and public compliance/private acceptance. Subsequent authors, however, have suggested that normative influence produces compliance but not acceptance, whereas informational influence produces both compliance and acceptance (e.g., Allen, 1965; Kaplan & Miller, 1983; Kiesler, 1969; Nail, 1986). Although this suggestion seems intuitively plausible given how the two forms of influence are defined, it is better viewed as an hypothesis than as a fact, because the motives underlying normative and informational influence (i.e., the desire to maximize one's social outcomes and the desire to gain accurate beliefs about reality, respectively) are rarely measured directly in conformity studies. Instead, investigators either simply assume that their intended operationalizations of normative and informational influence were effective or, worse, make post-hoc judgments that one or the other type of influence was operating on the basis of the results of their study.

Social power. In contrast to Deutsch and Gerard's neglect of the compliance-acceptance issue, other theorists have developed models that deal explicitly with motivational determinants of public and private influence. Although primarily designed to explain influence in dyadic situations, these models are also applicable to conformity and nonconformity in group situations. The social power analysis developed by

Raven and his colleagues (e.g., Collins & Raven, 1969; Raven & Kruglanski, 1970), which subsumes Kelman's (1958, 1961) formulation, is a good example.

Raven posits six types of unilateral social influence. *Reward* influence (based on the desire to obtain majority rewards) produces public conformity and private independence. *Coercive* influence (based on the desire to avoid majority punishments) produces public conformity and private anticonformity. The conformity elicited by reward and coercive influence only continues as long as the individual believes that the majority maintains surveillance of behavior. *Expert* influence (based on the desire to be correct and the perception that the majority has superior knowledge), *referent* influence (based on the desire to identify with an attractive majority), and *legitimate* influence (based on the belief that the majority has a moral right to prescribe one's behavior) all produce both public conformity and private conformity. In order for this conformity to remain stable over time, the individual must continue to view the majority as competent, attractive, or legitimate, respectively. *Informational* influence (based on the desire to be correct and the perception that the majority's position is congruent with one's existing belief and value system) also produces both public conformity and private conformity. However, this conformity persists over time in the absence of any particular perception of the majority or knowledge of majority surveillance.

Although some of Raven's ideas about social influence have not been explicitly tested in group pressure situations, his analysis provides a useful heuristic device for conceptualizing the motivational determinants of public and private conformity. In addition to distinguishing six types of unilateral social influence, Raven considered other issues that are potentially important in group situations, including (a) the impact of influence type on attraction toward and interaction with the influence source, (b) "compounded" influence based on two or more types of unilateral influence, (c) reciprocal influence in which both parties to the interaction (e.g., majority and minority) attempt to exert pressure on one another, and (d) "secondary," or indirect, influence mediated by such processes as cognitive dissonance.

Recent explanations of conformity and nonconformity. Several authors have recently proposed explanations of conformity that emphasize the attributions that individuals make in group pressure situations. Ross, Bierbrauer, and Hoffman (1976) argued that how a person holding a minority position interprets the majority's behavior and expects the majority to interpret his or her behavior will determine the person's level of conformity. They obtained evidence indicating that subjects exposed to majority pressure conformed less and were more confident in their answers when they had an adequate reason for the disagreement and they felt that majority members also had such a reason than when they did not. Arguments for the importance of self- and/or other-attributions in explaining majority influence have also been made by Allen and Wilder (1977) in their discussion of social comparison and conformity, by Duval (1976) in his objective self-awareness interpretation of conformity, and by Santee and Jackson (1982) in their work applying situated identity theory to conformity.

Recent explanations of nonconformity are varied, reflecting the diverse forms that nonconformity can take. Moscovici (1976), whose work will be discussed in more detail later, suggested that a person who is convinced that his or her position is valid will want to gain visibility and social recognition. To do so, the person will confidently assert his or her position (i.e., remain independent) and even try to provoke conflict in the group (see Hollander, 1975; Willis, 1965). Of course, rather than standing firm, a nonconformer might move away from the group's position. Brehm (1966; Brehm & Mann, 1975) argued that a person who believes that behavioral freedom is threatened will feel "reactance," which in turn will cause that person to try to restore the freedom. One way to do this is to anticonform to the majority that is responsible for the reduced freedom. Some attention has also been devoted to why people use partial conformity, or compromise, as a nonconformity strategy. Jones and Wortman (1973), and Schlenker (1980) suggested that an individual who wants to be accepted by a majority may fear that total agreement will be perceived as sycophancy. In order to avoid this negative attribution, the individual may only partially conform. Consistent with this reasoning, evidence indicates that dissenters are viewed more positively than conformers on certain dimensions (e.g., Morris & Miller, 1975b). Finally, it has been suggested that certain individual difference factors, such as private self-consciousness, self-esteem, and depression, may play an important role in stimulating nonconformity (e.g., Santee & Maslach, 1982; Wallace, Becker, Coppel, & Cox, 1983).

Recent Research on Conformity

As the previous section indicates, theorists have suggested several motivational bases for susceptibility and resistance to majority pressure.

The empirical research on majority influence, however, has been more concerned with when conformity occurs than with why it occurs. Investigators have thus devoted their energies to identifying specific variables that increase and decrease the probability of conformity in experimental situations, rather than to testing motivational theories. In this section, we discuss recent research on two factors that have long been viewed as important determinants of susceptibility to majority influence: the sex of minority members, and the relative number of minority members. Our discussion focuses on the determinants of public compliance rather than private acceptance.

Sex of Minority Members

Until the early 1980s, there was a high degree of consensus regarding the relative susceptibility of males and females to majority pressure. A number of reviewers, after examining the empirical work on sex differences in conformity, concluded that females conform more than do males (e.g., Cooper, 1979; Hare, 1976; Nord, 1969; Shaw, 1981). Disagreements have arisen recently, however, regarding the magnitude of this sex difference and the reasons for its occurrence.

It has been suggested that the sex of the researcher is an important determinant of sex differences in conformity. In an extensive review, Eagly and Carli (1981) found that female subjects conform more than male subjects primarily in studies authored by males. In studies authored by females, the two sexes typically conform about equally. Eagly and Carli mentioned several possible reasons why authors' sex may affect conformity. They suggested, for example, that researchers may design experimental settings in which members of their own sex feel particularly self-confident and hence are less susceptible to group pressure than are members of the opposite sex. Although a plausible explanation for greater conformity by females than males in studies authored by males, this interpretation does not account for the absence of greater conformity by males than females in studies authored by females. A second interpretation offered by Eagly and Carli focused on the criteria that researchers use in deciding whether to report null findings. Perhaps female researchers are more likely to report the absence of sex differences in conformity than are male researchers, because females are pleased to disconfirm a traditional feminine stereotype. If so, this tendency could account for the overall pattern of results in Eagly and Carli's review.

Another possible explanation of sex differences in conformity involves the stimulus that subjects are asked to judge (Eagly, 1978; Eagly & Carli, 1981). Some studies that found greater conformity by females used stimuli that were relatively unfamiliar to females. A good deal of evidence indicates that people tend to conform more on difficult or ambiguous stimuli, where their self-perceived competence is low (e.g., Allen, 1965; Endler, Wiesenthal, Coward, Edwards, & Geller, 1975). Therefore, female subjects' higher conformity in certain studies may have been due to their lack of familiarity with the "masculine" stimuli they were asked to judge. Although this informational influence hypothesis is plausible and is supported by the results of several experiments (e.g., Goldberg, 1974, 1975; Karabenick, 1983; Sistrunk & McDavid, 1971), other data reviewed by Eagly and Carli (1981) cast doubt on its usefulness as a general explanation for sex differences in conformity.

Finally, several reviewers (Cooper, 1979; Eagly, 1978; Eagly & Carli, 1981) noted that when sex differences in conformity do occur, they generally involve face-to-face situations in which group members can monitor one another's responses. Eagly (1978) suggested that females may be more concerned than males with maintaining group harmony and cohesiveness. To test this idea, Eagly, Wood, and Fishbaugh (1981) assessed the conformity of male and female subjects in situations involving either surveillance or no surveillance by a group. Results indicated that women did conform more than men in the group surveillance condition. However, women showed equal conformity in the surveillance and no surveillance conditions, whereas men conformed less in the former than in the latter condition. Eagly et al. interpreted their findings as indicating that, rather than females exhibiting heightened conformity under surveillance in order to maintain group harmony, males exhibit reduced conformity in this situation, perhaps to fulfill gender role expectations of independence.

Relative Number of Minority Members

In a group containing *n* members in which only two distinct positions are represented and a smaller number of individuals holds one position than the other, minority size can vary from a low of 1 to a high of $(n/2) - 1$. A substantial amount of research has investigated the impact of relative minority size on conformity.

Minorities of one member. Looking first at research on how one-person minorities react to disagreement from majorities of different sizes, we find a rather confusing picture. Asch (1951) reported that conformity increased until the majority reached three persons, at which point influence leveled off. Some later studies confirmed the existence of a ceiling effect in conformity (e.g., Rosenberg, 1961; Stang, 1976), but other experiments either indicated that conformity increased as majority size increased (e.g., Carlston, 1977; Gerard, Wilhelmy, & Conolley, 1968) or revealed no significant relationship between size and conformity (e.g., Goldberg, 1954; Kidd, 1958). In order to resolve some of the ambiguities in earlier studies, recent research has sought to determine a precise mathematical relationship between majority size and conformity and to clarify the psychological basis of this relationship.

Latane and Wolf (1981; Wolf & Latane, 1985) offered an analysis of majority size and conformity based on Latane's (1981; Latane & Nida, 1980) social impact theory. These investigators argued that individuals are affected by the mere presence of other people and that the amount of majority influence in a group situation is a multiplicative function of the strength (e.g., status), immediacy (e.g., physical closeness), and number of people holding the majority position. In regard to the impact of majority size, Latane and Wolf (1981) reported a study by Latane and Davis in which college students were asked to give their opinions on several related questions. Subjects were exposed to the unanimous responses of 1, 2, 3, 6, or 12 persons on each question. Latane and Wolf found that conformity was related to majority size by a power function. That is, conformity increased as group size increased, but each succeeding majority member produced a smaller increment in conformity than the preceding member. In a reanalysis of results from the Gerard et al. (1968) experiment, Latane and Wolf found that a power function also described the relationship between group size and conformity in that study. Similar data have been obtained by Wolf and Latane (1983) and Wolf (in press).

Tanford and Penrod (1984) presented a social influence model of the relationship between majority size and conformity that differs from Latane and Wolf's social impact model in several ways, most notably by predicting that the second and third influence sources have more impact than the first source and that total influence eventually reaches some asymptote. Tanford and Penrod argued that the relationship between majority size and conformity is not a power function, but rather an S-shaped growth (*Gompertz*) curve. On the basis of a meta-analysis of a large number of studies, Tanford and Penrod concluded that their social influence model does a better job of accounting for data on majority size and conformity than does the social impact model.

Mullen (1983) offered yet another alternative to the social impact model. He argued that conformity varies positively as a function of the *other-total ratio,* (O / O + S), where S = number of people in the individual's own subgroup and O = number of people in the other subgroup. On the basis of a meta-analysis of 12 studies, Mullen concluded that the other-total ratio accurately predicts conformity. He suggested that while his model is similar to the social impact model in some ways (e.g., in predicting a negatively accelerating relationship between the number of influence sources and their impact), it is superior in other ways. The most important of these advantages is the provision of a theoretical explanation for the impact of majority size on conformity. (It is important to note that such an explanation is missing from Tanford and Penrod's—as well as Latane and Wolf's—model.) Mullen's explanation for the majority size effect assumes that individuals become more self-attentive as the relative size of their subgroup decreases, that increased self-attention leads to greater efforts to match behavior to salient standards (Carver & Scheier, 1981), and that the salient standard in a group pressure situation is the majority position. As Wolf (in press) argues, however, this last assumption is open to question because Mullen's analysis suggests that the minority's position, rather than the majority's position, is the focus of attention for all group members. This in turn might cause the minority's viewpoint to become the salient standard.

As mentioned earlier, several authors have suggested that an individual's conformity to majority pressure is influenced by his or her interpretation of majority members' responses (e.g., Ross et al., 1976). If so, it seems plausible that the impact of majority size on conformity may also be affected by these perceptions. Consistent with this reasoning, Wilder (1977) argued that perhaps conformity did not increase with majority size in some prior studies because majority members were viewed as nonindependent sources of information. That is, subjects may have viewed the majority as a single entity rather than as an aggregate of independent individuals, which in turn caused subjects to suspect that majority members influenced one another's judgments (Wilder, 1978b). This line of reasoning led Wilder to hypothesize that conformity will not vary with the simple number of majority members adhering to a position. Instead, conformity will increase as a function of the number of distinct (i.e., independent) social entities espousing the majority position, regardless of whether the entities are groups or individuals.

Wilder (1977, 1978a) confirmed this hypothesis in several studies. Taken as a whole, Wilder's findings suggest that if a subject is opposed by an unanimous majority, conformity will vary directly with majority size only if majority members are viewed as having arrived independently at their common position. This conclusion is quite consistent with an informational influence interpretation of conformity.

Minorities of two or more members. In turning to the question of how minorities larger than one person react to disagreement from majorities, we again see the important generative role of Asch's early work. To determine whether one-person and two-person minorities respond differently to majority pressure, Asch (1951) had a confederate dissent from erroneous majority consensus and agree with the subject on visual perception stimuli. The presence of this social supporter reduced conformity dramatically, compared to a condition in which the subject was confronted by a unanimous majority. Asch (1955) next sought to determine if the supporter's effectiveness was due to (a) merely breaking group unanimity, or (b) providing an answer with which the subject privately agreed. To test the relative importance of these two factors, Asch had a confederate dissent from majority consensus by answering even more incorrectly than the erroneous majority. He found that this extreme dissenter reduced conformity almost as much as the social supporter, suggesting that the supporter's effectiveness was based on simply breaking group unanimity, rather than agreeing with the subject's private judgment.

More recent research suggests that Asch's conclusion, although correct for simple perceptual judgments, is not valid when subjects are asked to respond to other kinds of stimuli. Allen and Levine (1968, 1969) compared the effectiveness of social support and extreme dissent in reducing conformity on both visual perception and opinion items. They found, consistent with Asch, that both types of dissenters reduced conformity on visual items. However, on opinion items only the social supporter was effective. Thus, in order to reduce conformity on matters of opinion, a dissenter must agree with the subject's private judgment.

A number of additional studies have been conducted to determine the generality of the social support effect and to clarify the mechanisms underlying it. Most of this work has been carried out by Allen and his colleagues (see Allen, 1975). Regarding the generality of social support, it has been found that the presence of a partner decreases conformity for many different types of people, including male and female adults and normal and mentally retarded children. Moreover, under certain circumstances, the resistance to majority pressure conferred by social support continues even after the partner physically leaves the situation. This outcome occurs, for example, when the same type of stimulus is judged on both occasions and the supporter never repudiates his or her dissenting position.

Two major explanations have been proposed for why social support reduces conformity. One explanation is based on the partner's ability to reduce the subject's fear of majority retaliation for deviance. Evidence indicates that a subject who deviates alone from group consensus anticipates rejection and that the presence of a partner who publicly agrees with the subject reduces this fear (Allen, 1975). This decreased fear of majority retaliation may occur because the subject believes that the majority will "divide" its hostility between the supporter and the subject. In addition, the subject may assume that if he or she has a partner, the majority will be less likely to attribute nonconformity to a personal idiosyncrasy, which in turn will reduce the majority's anger at nonconformity. It should be noted, however, that if the subject believes that the majority particularly dislikes the supporter (e.g., because of race), the subject will be reluctant to agree with the supporter (Boyanowsky & Allen, 1973). This outcome occurs because a disliked supporter may increase, rather than decrease, the amount of punishment that the majority directs to the subject.

Besides protecting the subject against majority punishment, a social supporter also provides information about the stimulus object. Research indicates, for example, that a supporter who is allegedly competent on the group task is more effective in reducing conformity than is an incompetent supporter (Allen & Levine, 1971b). In addition to the supporter's competence, the timing of agreement is important. A supporter who responds first in the sequence of group members is most effective in reducing conformity, presumably because the early supporter reinforces the subject's initial judgment and thereby prevents uncertainty from arising when subsequent group members disagree with the subject's position (Allen & Levine, 1971a; Morris & Miller, 1975a). In addition, there is evidence that a supporter who answers after all the majority members have responded also reduces conformity substantially, perhaps because late support reduces a high level of uncertainty (Morris, Miller, & Sprangenberg, 1977). Finally, Allen and Wilder (1980) discovered yet another way in which social support provides information about the stimulus object. In addition to finding that unanimous group pressure produces cognitive restructuring of stimulus material, these investigators found that the presence of a social supporter *prevents* such restructuring.

In discussing the operation of social support, we have focused on how one-person versus two-person minorities react to disagreement from majorities. Of course, minorities can have more than two members. The issue of how larger minorities respond to majority pressure has been addressed by several theorists already mentioned. Latane and Wolf (1981; Wolf & Latane, 1985) argued that individuals holding a minority position in a group are in both a multiplicative and a divisive force field. The pressure that these individuals feel to adopt the majority position varies positively with the strength, immediacy, and number of people in the majority and varies negatively with the strength, immediacy, and number of people in the minority (i.e., pressure and majority impact/minority impact).[2] Tanford and Penrod (1984) also took minority size into account in their social influence model. They used transition matrices borrowed from the DICE model of jury decision making (Penrod & Hastie, 1980) to specify the likelihood that a member of a minority faction of a given size will be influenced by a majority faction of a given size at a particular point in time. And, although Mullen (1983) did not explicitly discuss the impact of minority size on conformity, his other-total ratio can deal with variations in minority as well as majority size.

The work of Davis and his colleagues on influence processes in decision-making groups provides another theoretical perspective on the relationship between majority/minority size and conformity (see Stasser, Kerr, & Davis, 1980). In most of the studies described so far, interaction among group members is severely limited, there is no explicit pressure to arrive at a joint decision, and individual opinion change is the major dependent variable. In contrast, Davis and his colleagues are interested in decisions reached by freely interacting groups seeking to reach a consensus. These investigators study the process as well as the outcomes of group discussion and explicitly recognize that reciprocal influence can occur between majorities and minorities (see Penrod & Hastie, 1980). Three complementary mathematical models of group decision making have been developed: the social decision scheme (SDS) model (Davis, 1973), the social transition scheme (STS) model (Kerr, 1981, 1982), and the social interaction sequence (SIS) model (Stasser & Davis, 1981). These powerful models clarify many aspects of social influence in groups, including opinion changes at the individual as well as the group level and the role of task type and member status in decision making (Kirchler & Davis, 1986). In regard to the impact of majority/ minority size on conformity, Davis and his colleagues have found that members of minority factions are more likely to change their positions than are members of majority factions and that the power of the majority increases as a function of its size (e.g., Davis, Stasser, Spitzer, & Holt, 1976; Kerr, 1981). Moreover, recent evidence suggests that this majority effect is based on informational rather than normative influence (Stasser, Stella, Hanna, & Colella, 1984).

MAJORITY AND MINORITY INFLUENCE: THE CONFLICT PERSPECTIVE

As described above, the dependence perspective on social influence in groups views the minority as a target but not a source of influence and explains conformity (majority influence) in terms of the minority's social and cognitive dependence on the majority. Within the last 15 years, an alternative to this approach has been developed by Moscovici. His model of social influence views the minority as a source as well as a target of influence and explains both conformity and innovation (minority influence) in terms of conflict and behavioral style (Moscovici, 1974, 1976, 1980, 1985a, 1985b; Moscovici & Faucheux, 1972; Moscovici & Mugny, 1983; Moscovici & Nemeth, 1974).

Moscovici believes that his approach supplants rather than supplements traditional thinking about social influence. He exemplifies his theoretical ideas about minority influence by taking a rather combative position and thereby provoking conflict with other theorists. For example, in introducing a summary of recent work by Ross et al. (1976), Allen and Wilder (1980), and Latane and Nida (1980), Moscovici (1985b) stated that "even after anomalies have begun to pile up alarmingly and even after a new theoretical paradigm has emerged, normal science continues to advance and prosper in the traditional direction, just as nature in the fall brings to full bloom flowers that are doomed to wither in a matter of hours once the first frost appears" (p. 382).

In this section, we first summarize Moscovici's comparison of the dependence and conflict models of social influence. Then we present research on majority and minority influence stimulated by the conflict perspective. Finally, we discuss how innovation is affected by the group context in which the majority and minority interact.

Overview of Moscovici's Position

Moscovici states that the dependence position emphasizes asymmetrical influence, in which minorities are potential targets (but not sources) of influence and majorities are potential sources (but not targets) of influence. In this framework, minority disagreement is treated as obstinate refusal to conform rather than an as active challenge to the majority. In contrast, the conflict position emphasizes symmetrical influence in which both minorities and majorities can be sources and targets of influence. Minorities are likely to be influential, according to Moscovici, when they are "nomic" (i.e., strongly committed to their position) rather than "anomic" (i.e., uncommitted to their position). Related to the distinction between asymmetrical and symmetrical influence is Moscovici's contention that the dependence position emphasizes only social control, whereas the conflict position also emphasizes social change.

In regard to the psychological mechanisms that mediate influence, Moscovici states that the traditional perspective focuses on dependence relations and the need to reduce uncertainty, whereas his own perspective focuses on conflict and behavioral style. In criticizing the dependence model, Moscovici argues that neither dependence nor uncertainty is an important determinant of majority or minority influence (see Levine, 1980, for a detailed critique of the empirical and logical basis of this argument). In defending the conflict model, Moscovici argues that influence is directly related to the production and resolution of conflict. He suggests that disagreement produces both interpersonal and intrapersonal conflict and that the essence of influence is conflict negotiation. Conflict is affected by such variables as the discrepancy between the majority and minority positions, the nature of the response alternatives (categorical versus variable), individuals' commitment to their positions, and the possibility of excluding the minority. Moscovici views behavioral style, which involves the organization, timing, and intensity of responses, as the most important determinant of both majority and minority influence. Of the five behavioral styles that he originally identified (investment, fairness, autonomy, consistency, rigidity), only the last two have received systematic research attention. Consistency, defined as maintenance of a position over time and modality, is assumed to enhance influence. Rigidity, a variant of consistency in which the influence source is perceived negatively (e.g., as inflexible and dogmatic) rather than positively (e.g., as self-confident and committed), is assumed to reduce influence.

Moscovici contrasts the dependence and conflict models in terms of the norms that underlie influence and the forms that influence can take. The dependence model only considers the objectivity norm (i.e., pressure to hold an objectively correct position). In contrast, the conflict model considers the objectivity norm, the preference norm (i.e., tolerance for a variety of different positions), and the originality norm (i.e., pressure to hold a novel position). Regarding the forms of influence, the dependence model recognizes only conformity. In contrast, the conflict model recognizes conformity (i.e., majority influence that reduces conflict), normalization (i.e., reciprocal influence that avoids conflict), and innovation (i.e., minority influence that creates conflict). According to Moscovici, conformity occurs when the majority is nomic and the minority is anomic, normalization occurs when there is no clear consensus and group members are relatively uncommitted to their positions, and innovation occurs when the minority is nomic and the majority is either nomic or anomic. Finally, Moscivici argues that majority influence generally produces overt but not covert response change, whereas minority influence generally produces covert but not overt response change.

Several criteria must be considered in evaluating a new theory. One criterion is the degree to which the new perspective stimulates empirical work on neglected problems. According to this standard, Moscovici's theory clearly deserves credit for focusing attention on the importance of minority influence and stimulating research on this issue. A second criterion is the theory's ability to account for data obtained by researchers working within other paradigms. By this standard, Moscovici's analysis is problematic. His efforts to discredit dependence interpretations of prior studies and to reinterpret these studies in his own terms are often based on selective citations and questionable inferences (see Doms, 1984; Levine, 1980). Finally, a new theory must be evaluated in terms of the precision and testability of its predictions and the degree to which these predictions are empirically confirmed. According to these standards, Moscovici's position has both strengths and weaknesses. Although his model suggests many interesting hypotheses, it is stated in very general terms and fails to specify with precision the psychological mediators of majority and minority influence. Moreover, although a number of studies have provided data consistent with the model, other studies have yielded ambiguous or nonsupportive findings.

Research on Minority and Majority Influence

Given its relatively recent introduction, Moscovici's model has stimulated a substantial amount of research. Detailed summaries of this literature are available (Levine, 1980; Maass & Clark, 1984; Tanford & Penrod, 1984; Moscovici, 1976, 1985b), and therefore our coverage is restricted to an overview of the two most active lines of inquiry: (a) how minority consistency and rigidity affect minority influence, and (b) how the source of influence (majority versus minority) affects the outcome of influence (compliance versus conversion).

Minority Consistency

A major premise of Moscovici's model is that minority consistency is a necessary (though not a sufficient) condition for minority influence. In an early test of this idea, Moscovici and his colleagues (Moscovici & Lage, 1976; Moscovici, Lage, & Naffrechoux, 1969) exposed a four-person majority to a two-person minority that expressed either consistent or inconsistent disagreement with the majority's judgments on a simple perceptual task. As predicted, results revealed that majority members were influenced by the consistent, but not by the inconsistent, minority. Subsequent research has found that consistent minorities are influential under a variety of conditions (Maass & Clark, 1984).

In spite of this evidence, however, other data suggest that minority consistency does not operate in a simple manner. For example, using a different experimental paradigm than that favored by Moscovici and associates, Levine and his colleagues found that, on attitudinal issues, consistency is *not* a crucial determinant of minority influence (Levine & Ranelli, 1978; Levine, Saxe, & Harris, 1976; Levine, Sroka, & Snyder, 1977). Their findings indicate, for example, that a person who shifts from the majority position to a minority position is much more influential than a person who consistently espouses a minority position. Additional research demonstrates that the impact of minority consistency is importantly constrained by other variables, including: (a) the size of the minority (e.g., Moscovici & Lage, 1976; Nemeth, Wachtler, & Endicott, 1977), (b) the extremity, content, and assumed reason for the minority's position (e.g., Levine & Ranèlli, 1978; Levine & Ruback, 1980; Paicheler, 1976, 1977), (c) the normative context in which majority/minority interaction occurs (e.g., Maass, Clark, & Haberkorn, 1982; Moscovici & Lage, 1978; Paicheler, 1976, 1977), and (d) the amount of social support available to the majority (Doms, 1984; Doms & Van Avermaet, 1985).

Two important conceptual issues regarding the relationship between minority consistency and influence have also been raised. One issue involves confusion regarding the definition of "consistency," particularly as it relates to "rigidity" (Maass & Clark, 1984). The second issue concerns precisely why consistency increases influence. Attributional explanations of the relationship between consistency and influence were offered by Moscovici and Nemeth (1974) and Maass and Clark (1984). Chaiken and Stangor (1987) criticized both of these explanations for their emphasis on attributions regarding the minority's underlying dispositions (e.g., certainty). They suggested that attention should be given instead to attributions regarding the validity of the minority's message (see Eagly & Chaiken, 1984). Chaiken and Stangor also sounded a note of caution regarding the utility of any attributional model as a complete explanation of minority influence, arguing that such models are relevant primarily when majority members are motivated to maximize the validity of their opinions.

Minority Rigidity

Rigidity has been extensively studied by Mugny and his colleagues, who extended Moscovici's model by proposing a "psychosociological" theory of minority influence (Mugny, 1982, 1984b; Papastamou, 1984; Papastamou & Mugny, 1985). This theory, which embeds minority influence within large institutional contexts, emphasizes the importance of social categories and ideology. Mugny distinguished three social entities linked by three relationships. Regarding the entities, the *power* dictates norms and rules within an institution or society, the *population* submits to the power's domination and accepts (to a greater or lesser extent) the power's ideology, and the *minority* actively challenges the power. Regarding the relationships between entities, the power and the population are linked by domination, the power and the minority are linked by antagonism, and the minority and the population are linked by influence. According to this analysis, the power seeks to maintain its domination over the population while weakening or destroying the minority, and the minority implacably opposes the power while trying to influence the population to adopt its position.

Mugny argues that, in order to win the population, the minority must be perceived as consistent and unyielding vis-à-vis the power, but as willing to negotiate with the population. He therefore suggests that behavioral style (consistency/inconsistency) defines the antagonistic relationship between the minority and the power, whereas negotiation style (flexibility/rigidity) defines the influence relationship between the minority and the population. A rigid negotiating style, which refuses to make any concessions to the population, is unsuccessful because the population will perceive the minority's consistency as dogmatism. This perception, in turn, makes it likely that the population will attribute the minority's position to some stable, idiosyncratic characteristic and will view the minority as an out-group. These negative perceptions of the minority are encouraged by the power as part of its efforts to maintain domination.

Mugny and his colleagues have conducted a number of studies to test these and related ideas about the impact of rigidity on minority influence. Most of their experiments used a paradigm in which subjects who believed that industry was only partially responsible for pollution read a statement that placed total blame on industry. According to Mugny, this statement represented a minority position in relation to power. The rigidity/flexibility of the minority was operationalized in terms of the extremity of the sanctions recommended for industrial polluters (e.g., rigid: shutdown of manufacturing; flexible: monetary fines). After reading the statements, subjects expressed their views about the causes of pollution on both direct items (that were explicitly presented in the statement) and indirect items (that were implied in the statement). These studies provided suggestive evidence that flexible minorities produce more direct influence than do rigid minorities; that the influence of rigid minorities increases if subjects are prevented from attributing the minority's position to idiosyncratic personal characteristics and if subjects view themselves as members of the same social category as the minority; and that flexible minorities produce similar levels of direct and indirect influence, whereas rigid minorities produce more indirect influence (see reviews by Mugny, 1982, 1984b; Papastamou, 1984; Papastamou & Mugny, 1985).

Mugny (1982) argued that, in evaluating an interrelated series of studies such as his own, it is inappropriate to criticize individual experiments; instead, the studies should be evaluated as a total set. Although there may be merit in this suggestion, its application in this case leads to a mixed evaluation. On the positive side, Mugny and his colleagues made a bold effort to explain minority influence in societal contexts and offered a number of intriguing hypotheses. On the negative side, there was sometimes slippage between Mugny's conceptual and operational definitions, as when rigidity/flexibility was operationalized as extremity. In addition, the most complete review of this research (Mugny, 1982) reveals that findings often failed to replicate from study to study and complex *a posteriori* interpretations were needed to make sense of the data. This lack of clarity may stem in part from the inherent difficulties of testing molar-level theories in laboratory settings.

Majority/Minority Influence and Compliance/Conversion

Moscovici (1980, 1985a, 1985b) argued that majority influence and minority influence are qualitatively different processes. Although conflict is aroused in both cases, the manner in which it is resolved differs. Majorities induce a *comparison* process, in which minority attention is focused on the social implications of the majority-minority disagreement. In order to hold the correct opinion and to be accepted, the minority often exhibits manifest (public) change toward the majority's position. However, because the minority does not engage in active information processing about the issue in question, it is unlikely to experience latent (private) influence. In contrast, minorities induce a *validation* process, in which majority attention is focused on the issue underlying the disagreement. This focus causes the majority to engage in active information processing about the issue, which in turn often produces latent change toward the minority's position. Manifest change is unlikely to occur, however, because the majority does not want others to view it as deviant. According to this line of reasoning, majorities are more likely to produce "compliance" than "conversion," whereas minorities are more likely to produce conversion than compliance.

A number of experiments have assessed the impact of majority and minority influence on compliance and conversion. These studies have used a range of stimulus issues (e.g., perceptual, opinion) and a variety of dependent measures (e.g., public and private, immediate and delayed, direct and indirect). A recent review of this literature (Maass & Clark, 1984) suggests that majorities and minorities do indeed have different effects. Majorities are more likely than minorities to produce compliance, whereas minorities are more likely than majorities to produce conversion. Moreover, majorities rarely produce conversion in the presence of compliance, whereas minorities produce conversion even in the absence of compliance. Although there are exceptions to these generalizations (e.g., Doms & Van Avermaet, 1980; Mugny, 1984a;

Personnaz, 1981; Sorrentino, King, & Leo, 1980; Wolf, 1985), the bulk of available evidence suggests that majorities have their primary impact at the manifest, or public, level, and minorities have their primary impact at the latent, or private, level.

Since Moscovici first distinguished between compliance and conversion, several perspectives have been offered regarding the mediators of majority and minority influence. To the question, "Are majority and minority influence mediated by qualitatively different processes?", three answers have been proposed: no, yes, and sometimes.

One negative answer has been given by Latane and Wolf (1981; Wolf & Latane, 1983, 1985) and Tanford and Penrod (1984). These theorists argued that a single process is responsible for both majority and minority influence and that these two forms of influence differ in quantitative rather than qualitative terms. (Mullen's, 1983, formulation has not been applied to minority influence, but is also consistent with a single-process interpretation.) Given their ability to account for substantial variance in previous studies, the social impact and social influence models must be taken seriously. Nevertheless, because they fail to specify a *psychological* process underlying majority and minority influence, their adequacy as explanatory models is open to question. Moreover, these models do not deal explicitly with evidence, discussed above, that majorities typically produce public influence, whereas minorities typically produce private influence.

In contrast to the social impact and social influence models, other single-process explanations of majority and minority influence do posit underlying psychological mechanisms. Wolf (1979, in press) argued that minority influence, like majority influence, is mediated by dependence. According to this analysis, majorities, because of their numerical superiority, often elicit both normative and informational dependence (Insko, Smith, Alicke, Wade, & Taylor, 1985; Stasser et al., 1980). Minorities, in contrast, derive whatever strength they possess primarily from their ability to elicit informational dependence. Although these suggestions are plausible, it is questionable whether they really constitute a single-process explanation of majority and minority influence, because somewhat different mechanisms are assumed to operate in the two cases.

A related proposal has been made by Doms (1984; Doms & Van Avermaet, 1985). Like Wolf, Doms suggested that informational dependence may mediate both majority and minority influence. In addition, Doms asserted that social support (Allen, 1975) is a crucial determinant of the impact of minorities as well as majorities. According to this analysis, just as majority influence is affected by whether minority members have support from others who hold their position, so minority influence is affected by whether majority members have similar support. Doms's research indicated that majorities and minorities operating under identical social support conditions produce similar levels of public influence. By failing to deal with private influence, however, Doms's analysis only partially addresses the question of whether majority and minority influence are mediated by a single process.

In addition to single-process models of majority and minority influence, dual-process models have also been proposed. For example, Nemeth (1985, 1986, in press) extended Moscovici's (1980) analysis by suggesting that disagreement from majorities and minorities has different effects on attention, thought, and problem solving. Nemeth asserted that majorities produce a narrow focus on the position that they advocate, whereas minorities produce a broader focus on new information and alternative positions. This difference presumably occurs because individuals exposed to majorities are more likely to feel stress, assume that the influence source is correct, and resolve the disagreement-induced conflict quickly. According to Nemeth, majority and minority disagreement have different consequences for problem solving. Minorities tend to produce divergent, creative solutions, while majorities tend to produce convergent, uncreative solutions (e.g., Nemeth & Kwan, 1985; Nemeth & Wachtler, 1983).

A related dual-process interpretation of majority and minority influence has been proposed by Maass, West, and Cialdini (this volume). These authors offered a thought-provoking analysis of the cognitive processes underlying conversion and the characteristics of minorities that trigger these processes. Maass et al. argued that, compared to majorities, minorities are more likely to focus attention on the stimulus under consideration (e.g., Personnaz & Guillon, 1985) and produce intense cognitive activity regarding this stimulus (e.g., Maass & Clark, 1983). In addition, they suggested that these effects are mediated by such minority characteristics as distinctiveness, credibility, capacity to produce arousal, and resistance to social pressure.

In contrast to the single-process and dual-process explanations, Chaiken and Stangor (1987) suggested that *multiple* cognitive processes (e.g., heuristic processing, attributional reasoning, message- and issue-relevant thinking) may underlie *both* majority and minority influence.

These authors asserted that the motives (e.g., reward, referent, informational) that operate in majority and minority settings constrain the cognitive processes that produce influence in these settings. Chaiken and Stangor hypothesized that when different motives operate in the two types of settings, qualitative differences in influence processes are likely. In contrast, when the same or similar motives are operative in both settings, quantitative differences are probable. Although Chaiken and Stangor did not attempt to present a complete account of the processes underlying majority and minority influence, they made a valuable contribution by emphasizing the importance of motivational as well as cognitive factors.

Group Context of Innovation

As the previous section indicates, a good deal of theoretical and empirical attention has been devoted to the cognitive mediators of minority influence in laboratory groups. In contrast, relatively little effort has been made to clarify how innovation operates in natural groups (Chaiken & Stangor, 1987; Maass & Clark, 1984). This state of affairs is somewhat surprising, since Moscovici frequently bolsters his arguments with historical references to consistent minority groups that triumphed over powerful majorities.

Although a systematic analysis of how the group context affects innovation is not yet available, several theorists have examined the impact of group factors on minority influence. As discussed previously, Mugny (Mugny 1982, 1984b; Papastamou, 1984; Papastamou & Mugny, 1985) has developed a psychosociological theory of minority influence dealing with the relationships between powers, populations, and minorities. Deconchy (1985) has analyzed the role of orthodox minorities within the Roman Catholic church, arguing that, although minority positions are "doctrinally unthinkable and functionally impossible" in orthodox systems, such systems often find minority positions useful and hence foster their existence. Gerard (1985), in analyzing why dissident minorities in real-world settings adopt consistent behavioral styles, has suggested the importance of such factors as external threat, minority distinctiveness, and social projection. Allen (1985) has argued that social interaction can be construed at different levels (infragroup, intragroup, intergroup) and that minority influence may be mediated by a different mechanism at each level.

A crucial characteristic of many natural groups is that, unlike laboratory groups, they exist for considerable periods of time (months, years, decades). The group's expectations and behavior regarding an individual, and the individual's expectations and behavior regarding the group, often vary as a function of how long the individual has been a group member. These temporal changes in the relationships between natural groups and their members can have important consequences for the amount and type of innovation that occurs.

To understand innovation, then, it is necessary to employ a conceptual model that reflects two critical aspects of group life: (a) that the group (or majority) and the individual (or minority) exert reciprocal influence on one another, and (b) that over time important changes occur in the relationship between the group and the individual. Moreland and Levine (1982) developed a model of group socialization that fulfills both of these criteria. It is meant to apply primarily (but not exclusively) to small, autonomous, voluntary groups whose members interact on a regular basis, have affective ties with one another, share a common frame of reference, and are behaviorally independent.

Socialization in Groups

The group socialization model incorporates three processes: evaluation, commitment, and role transition. It is assumed that a group and an individual continuously evaluate the rewardingness of their relationship. On the basis of these evaluations, feelings of commitment develop between the group and the individual. Levels of commitment change over time, rising or falling to previously established decision criteria. When a decision criterion is reached, a role transition takes place, and the individual enters a new phase of group membership. Evaluation proceeds, producing further changes in commitment and subsequent role transitions. In this way, the individual passes through five consecutive phases of group membership (investigation, socialization, maintenance, resocialization, remembrance), separated by four role transitions.

Initially, the group and the individual go through an *investigation* phase, during which the group looks for people who are likely to contribute to the attainment of group goals and the individual looks for groups that are likely to contribute to the satisfaction of personal needs. If the group's and the individual's commitment levels rise to their respective entrance criteria, then the individual enters the *socialization* phase. In this phase, the group attempts to change the individual so that he or she can make greater contributions to group goal attainment, and the individual attempts to change the group so that it can better satisfy his or her personal needs. If the commitment levels of both parties rise to their respective acceptance criteria, then the individual enters the *maintenance* phase. Here, the group seeks to find a specialized role for the individual that maximizes his or her contributions to the attainment of group goals, and the individual attempts to define a specialized role that maximizes the satisfaction of personal needs. To the extent that the parties regard their relationship as rewarding, their commitment levels will remain high. However, if the group's and the individual's commitment levels fall to their respective divergence criteria, then the person enters the *resocialization* phase. In this phase, the group and the individual seek to make their relationship satisfactory once again. If the commitment levels of both parties rise to their respective divergence criteria, then a special role transition occurs and the individual reenters the maintenance phase. In contrast, if the group's and the individual's commitment levels fall to their exit criteria, then the individual leaves the group and enters the *remembrance* phase. Here, the group and the individual engage in retrospective evaluations of their past relationship and ongoing evaluations of one another.

Socialization and Innovation

Levine and Moreland (1985) recently used their group socialization model to analyze innovation. They defined innovation broadly to include any significant change (intentional or unintentional) that the individual produces in the structure, dynamics, or performance of the group. They suggested that each of the five membership phases in the group socialization model provides special opportunities for innovation.

During investigation, several factors can affect the ability of a prospective member to influence the group. The lower the number of prospective members relative to the number of "open" positions, the higher the commitment each of those persons will elicit from the group. The more commitment a prospective member elicits, the more that person will be able to change the group. The number of prospective members that a group attracts can also affect how current members are treated. For example, groups that have many prospective members may change their divergence and exit criteria to expel current members who are performing poorly. The characteristics of prospective members are also likely to influence their ability to produce innovation. If a prospective member possesses abilities or traits that the group particularly admires, then the group's commitment to the person may be higher than his or her commitment to the group, and the person will be able to "demand" that the group change.

During socialization, newcomers can produce innovation both unintentionally and intentionally. The mere presence of newcomers alters the distribution of members' characteristics and thereby influences various aspects of group life. Newcomers also produce unintentional innovation by affecting the effort that other group members must devote to socialization activities. The greater this effort, the less members will be able to work on other group tasks. In regard to intentional innovation, newcomers are typically anxious about being accepted and hence reluctant to demand that the group accommodate to them. This diffidence may be overcome, however, if newcomers feel that they have been deceived about the rewards of group membership, particularly if they receive social support from other newcomers who also feel victimized.

During maintenance, full members elicit high commitment from others in the group and hence have substantial leverage in producing innovation. Moreover, full members are often given positions of leadership that provide special opportunities for changing the group. A leader who is especially powerful can sometimes force innovations on fellow members, but the typical leader requires the cooperation of others in order to produce change. To gain this cooperation, the leader must build coalitions by promising rewards and threatening punishments. The coalition-building process may itself alter the group by raising the commitment of those who join the coalition, lowering the commitment of those who do not, and reducing the group's productivity through the consumption of critical resources. Finally, in some cases, leaders may be required, rather than simply allowed, to alter the group's structure, dynamics, or performance. This is likely to occur if the group is having difficulty achieving its goals and views the leader as possessing special skills.

During resocialization, marginal members can produce unintentional changes in the group by causing others to engage in resocialization activities. If the group must devote time and energy to rehabilitating the marginal member, then it will have fewer resources to expend in trying to achieve its goals. The need to engage in resocialization activities may also elicit conflict among group members regarding how the marginal member should be treated. In other cases, marginal members may desire to produce innovation. Such innovation is often difficult to produce because the group's commitment to marginal members is relatively low. Therefore, marginal members must use special strategies, such as reminding others of their previous contributions to the group and downplaying their current shortcomings. Under certain circumstances (e.g., when the group is short of members and the likelihood of obtaining new members is low), a marginal member's threat to leave the group may increase his or her ability to produce innovation.

During remembrance, innovation is sometimes related to the group's memories of how an ex-member behaved before leaving the group. If remembered positively, the ex-member may be used as a model in developing normative expectations for current members. In contrast, an ex-member who is remembered negatively may elicit just the opposite response. Innovation during remembrance is not always related to memories of how the ex-member behaved previously. That the person has merely left the group can produce changes in group performance, status relationships between members, and opportunities for upward mobility. Innovation can also be influenced by the conditions surrounding the ex-member's exit from the group and the degree to which the group and the individual have been successful since exit occurred. For example, groups are likely to accept innovation attempts from an ex-member if (a) the individual left the group at an appropriate time (e.g., graduation), (b) the individual has been successful since exit, and (c) the group has been unsuccessful since exit. In contrast, groups are unlikely to accept innovation attempts from an ex-member if (a) the individual left the group at an inappropriate time (e.g., expulsion), (b) the individual has been unsuccessful since exit, and (c) the group has been successful since exit.

Although many of these ideas regarding the relationship between innovation and group socialization are speculative, they nevertheless suggest the importance of investigating minority (and majority) influence in natural groups that have a past and a future. Such research should provide a useful counterweight to atemporal studies using laboratory groups.

CONCLUDING COMMENTS

Based on the sheer number of cited articles, it is clear that the topic of social influence in group contexts is attracting substantial theoretical and empirical attention. Moreover, this work is paying dividends in terms of increased understanding of both majority and minority influence. In spite of Moscovici's urging, the dependence model does not seem likely to be discarded in the near future. Normative/informational influence remains a useful explanatory construct, and the dependence model, broadly defined, continues to generate interesting work. Nevertheless, it is also true that the conflict model is having a major impact on the way investigators conceptualize and study influence. Innovation is currently receiving as much attention as conformity, and vigorous debates are being waged concerning the mediators and consequences of these two forms of influence.

The major task for investigators in the years ahead is to clarify the processes that underlie majority and minority influence. One approach is to focus on the cognitive processes of individuals, using theories and methods borrowed from the attitude change and social cognition literatures. Several current explanations of majority/minority influence make assumptions about attention, information processing, and learning, but little direct evidence is available regarding how these processes operate in group influence situations. Research on such intrapersonal processes is likely to yield interesting information. We feel little need to encourage such work, however, given social psychology's current emphasis on cognitive explanations of individual behavior.

Instead, we argue for increased attention to interpersonal and intergroup factors. In order to understand majority and minority influence, it is essential to understand the social processes that occur within and between majorities and minorities. Although some suggestions have been made regarding these processes (e.g., Allen, 1985; Deconchy, 1985; Gerard, 1985; Levine & Moreland, 1985; Mugny, 1982), much remains to be learned.

In most studies of majority and minority influence, interaction between group members is severely restricted. The experimenter controls the responses of the source of influence (majority members in majority influence studies, minority members in minority influence studies), and the recipients of influence are not allowed to interact freely either with the source or with one another during the group session. Therefore, very little is known about the interactions that occur between majority members, between minority members, and between majority and minority members. In the following paragraphs, we offer hypotheses regarding these three types of interactions in natural groups.

A minority's presence may affect interactions between majority members in several ways (Levine, 1980). For example, in seeking to achieve consensus regarding the reason that the minority espouses its position, majority members may engage in mutual social influence involving conformity, bargaining, coalition formation, and group polarization. Attainment of group consensus may be complicated by the fact that the minority's behavior often must be interpreted while the minority is physically present, thereby inhibiting open exchange among majority members. One outcome of the effort to attain consensus may be the discovery that certain majority members are themselves deviates by virtue of their nonmodal interpretation of the minority's behavior. In some cases, these newly discovered deviates may cause more concern to other group members than does the original minority. Once majority members decide why the minority espouses its position and what impact this position will have on group goal attainment, they must decide on appropriate treatment for the minority. This decision may be constrained by group norms concerning how deviates should be handled. If such norms do not exist or are difficult to apply in a particular case, majority members may attempt to achieve consensus regarding appropriate treatment for the minority. In the course of the ensuing discussion, conflict may arise regarding the most effective way to alter the minority's position (e.g., persuasive communications versus threats) and the selection of an "enforcer" to deal with the minority. Finally, if the behavior decided on by the majority does not have the intended effect, there may be recriminations toward those who suggested the behavior or carried it out.

The presence of a majority may also substantially affect interactions between minority members. In minorities that exist for relatively long periods of time, power struggles may arise between different factions that wish to lead the minority to its struggle against the majority. Whatever their origin, these struggles are often couched in ideological terms, with each faction claiming that its position is closer to the central core of minority beliefs. These struggles often become quite heated, escalating from claims that the other faction is in error to charges that the other faction is betraying the minority cause, to a disintegration of the original minority. In extreme cases, one of the factions may even ally with the majority against its former compatriots. Such minority conflict may increase cohesiveness among faction members and produce more commitment to their position (see Gerard, 1985). It may also stimulate efforts to gain converts to the faction in order to increase its strength and reassure members about the validity of their position. As competition increases, the factions may adopt more hierarchical power structures and may prefer more authoritarian leaders. These changes may further exacerbate tensions between factions and decrease the probability of forming coalitions against the majority. Although not validated in laboratory settings, these ideas seem consistent with the bahavior of many political and religious minorities.

Finally, some suggestions can be offered regarding interactions between majority members and minority members. The initial behavior of the minority toward the majority may set a tone that influences their interaction for some time. For example, a minority that publicly challenges a central tenet of the majority's position will probably elicit a more defensive and hostile reaction than a minority that privately challenges a peripheral aspect of the majority's position (Levine, 1980). This may occur because the former minority is seen as bent on destruction, whereas the latter minority is viewed as seeking reform. The majority's reaction to the minority's initial presentation may in turn affect the minority's subsequent decision to surrender, compromise, or fight to the finish. Of course, this decision may be affected by other factors, including the minority's commitment to its position, access to resources (e.g., printing presses, bombs), and perception of the majority's long-term strength. Whether majorities and minorities view themselves as members of the same or different groups may also have important implications for their interactions (Aebischer, Hewstone, & Henderson, 1984; Allen, 1985; Gerard, 1985; Maass et al., 1982). Organizations provide an interesting context in which to study how intragroup/intergroup perceptions affect interactions between majorities and minorities. When the organization as a whole feels threatened, majorities and minorities within the organization may view their disagreement in intragroup terms, which in turn may produce amicable relations and the tendency for compromise. In contrast, when the organization as a whole feels secure, majorities and minorities may view their disagreement in intergroup terms, which in turn may produce hostile relations and the tendency for polarization. These hypotheses are constrained, of course, by the hierarchical relationship between the majority and the minority. Interaction between a low-status minority and a high-status majority is likely to be quite different from that between a low-status majority and a high-status minority.

In conclusion, the future seems bright for research on majority and minority influence. Many interesting questions remain to be answered, theoretical controversy abounds, and investigators with divergent interests (e.g., cognitive processes, intergroup relations) are attracted to the area. Given this fertile soil, many flowers are likely to bloom.

NOTES

1. It should be noted that sometimes the desire for belief validation is stronger than the desire for belief evaluation and sometimes dissimilar others are preferred to similar others for social comparison (Levine, 1980).

2. See Mullen (1985, 1986) and Jackson (1986) for a critical discussion of the role of strength and immediacy in social impact theory.

REFERENCES

Aebischer, V., Hewstone, M., & Henderson, M. (1984). Minority influence and musical preference: Innovation by conversion not coercion. *European Journal of Social Psychology, 14,* 23-33.

Allen, V. L. (1965). Situational factors in conformity. In L. Berkowitz (Ed.), *Advances in experimental social psychology* (Vol. 2, pp. 133-175). New York: Academic Press.

Allen, V. L. (1975). Social support for nonconformity. In L. Berkowitz (Ed.), *Advances in experimental social psychology* (Vol. 8, pp. 1-43). New York: Academic Press.

Allen, V. L. (1985). Infra-group, intra-group, and inter-group: Construing levels of organization in social influence. In S. Moscovici, G. Mugny, & E. Van Avermaet (Eds.), *Perspectives on minority influence* (pp. 217-238). Cambridge: Cambridge University Press.

Allen, V. L., & Levine, J. M. (1968). Social support, dissent and conformity. *Sociometry, 31,* 138-149.

Allen, V. L., & Levine, J. M. (1969). Consensus and conformity. *Journal of Experimental Social Psychology, 4,* 389-399.

Allen, V. L., & Levine, J. M. (1971a). Social support and conformity: The effect of response order and differentiation from the group. *British Journal of Social and Clinical Psychology, 7,* 48-58.

Allen, V. L., & Levine, J. M. (1971b). Social support and conformity: The role of independent assessment of reality. *Journal of Experimental Social Psychology, 7,* 48-58.

Allen, V. L., & Wilder, D. A. (1977). Social comparison, self-evaluation, and conformity to the group. In J. M. Suls & R. L. Miller (Eds.), *Social comparison processes: Theoretical and empirical perspectives* (pp. 187-208). Washington, DC: Hemisphere.

Allen, V. L., & Wilder, D. A. (1980). Impact of group consensus and social support on stimulus meaning: Mediation of conformity by cognitive restructuring. *Journal of Personality and Social Psychology, 39,* 1116-1124.

Asch, S. E. (1951). Effects of group pressure upon the modification and distortion of judgments. In H. Guetzkow (Ed.), *Groups, leadership, and men* (pp. 177-190). Pittsburgh, PA: Carnegie Press.

Asch, S. E. (1955). Opinions and social pressure. *Scientific American, 193*, 31-35.

Asch, S. E. (1956). Studies of independence and submission to group pressure: I. A minority of one against a unanimous majority. *Psychological Monographs, 70*, No. 9 (Whole No. 417).

Boyanowsky, E. O., & Allen, V. L. (1973). Ingroup norms and self-identity as determinants of discriminatory behavior. *Journal of Personality and Social Psychology, 25*, 408-418.

Brehm, J. W. (1966). *A theory of psychological reactance.* New York: Academic Press.

Brehm, J. W., & Mann, M. (1975). Effect of importance of freedom and attraction to group members on influence produced by group pressure. *Journal of Personality and Social Psychology, 31*, 816-824.

Burnstein, E. (1982). Persuasion as argument processing. In H. Brandstatter, J. H. Davis, & G. Stocker-Kreichgauer (Eds.), *Group decision making* (pp. 103-124). London: Academic Press.

Campbell, J. D., Tesser, A., & Fairey, P. J. (1986). Conformity and attention to the stimulus: Some temporal and contextual dynamics. *Journal of Personality and Social Psychology, 51*, 315-324.

Carlston, D. (1977). Effects of polling order on social influence in decision-making groups. *Sociometry, 40*, 115-123.

Carver, C. S., & Scheier, M. F. (1981). *Attention and self-regulation: A control-theory approach to human behavior.* New York: Springer-Verlag.

Chaiken, S., & Stangor, S. (1987). Attitudes and attitude change. In *Annual review of psychology* (Vol. 38, 575-630).

Cialdini, R. B., & Petty, R. E. (1981). Anticipatory opinion effects. In R. E. Petty, T. M., Ostrom, & T. C. Brock (Eds.), *Cognitive responses in persuasion* (pp. 217-235). Hillsdale, NJ: Lawrence Erlbaum.

Collins, B. E., & Raven, B. H. (1969). Group structure: Attraction, coalitions, communication, and power. In G. Lindzey & E. Aronson (Eds.), *The handbook of social psychology* (Vol. 4, 2nd ed., pp. 102-204). Reading, MA: Addison-Wesley.

Cooper, H. M. (1979). Statistically combining independent studies: A meta-analysis of sex differences in conformity research. *Journal of Personality and Social Psychology, 37*, 131-146.

Davis, J. H. (1973). Group decision and social interaction: A theory of social decision schemes. *Psychological Review, 80*, 97-125.

Davis, J. H., Stasser, G., Spitzer, C. E., & Holt, R. W. (1976). Changes in group members' preferences during discussion: An illustration with mock juries. *Journal of Personality and Social Psychology, 34*, 1177-1187.

Deconchy, J. (1985). The paradox of "orthodox minorities": When orthodoxy infallibly fails. In S. Moscovici, G. Mugny, & E. Van Avermaet (Eds.), *Perspectives on minority influence* (pp. 187-200). Cambridge: Cambridge University Press.

Deutsch, M., & Gerard, H. B. (1955). A study of normative and informational social influences upon individual judgment. *Journal of Abnormal and Social Psychology, 51*, 629-636.

Doms, M. (1984). The minority influence effect: An alternative approach. In W. Doise & S. Moscovici (Eds.), *Current issues in European social psychology* (Vol. 1, pp. 1-33). Cambridge: Cambridge University Press.

Doms, M., & Van Avermaet, E. (1980). Majority influence, minority influence and conversion behavior: A replication. *Journal of Experimental Social Psychology, 16*, 283-292.

Doms, M., & Van Avermaet, E. (1985). Social support and minority influence: The innovation effect reconsidered. In S. Moscovici, G. Mugny, & E. Van Avermaet (Eds.), *Perspectives on minority influence* (pp. 53-74). Cambridge: Cambridge University Press.

Duval, S. (1976). Conformity on a visual task as a function of personal novelty on attributional dimensions and being reminded of the object status of self. *Journal of Experimental Social Psychology, 12,* 87-98.

Eagly, A. H. (1978). Sex differences in influenceability. *Psychological Bulletin, 85,* 86-116.

Eagly, A. H., & Carli, L. L. (1981). Sex of researchers and sex-typed communications as determinants of sex differences in influenceability: A meta-analysis of social influence studies. *Psychological Bulletin, 90,* 1-20.

Eagly, A. H., & Chaiken, S. (1984). Cognitive theories of persuasion. In L. Berkowitz (Ed.), *Advances in experimental social psychology* (Vol. 17, pp. 267-359). Orlando, FL: Academic Press.

Eagly, A. H., Wood, W., & Fishbaugh, L. (1981). Sex differences in conformity: Surveillance by the group as a determinant of male nonconformity. *Journal of Personality and Social Psychology, 40,* 384-394.

Endler, N. S., Wiesenthal, D. L., Coward, T., Edwards, J., & Geller, S. H. (1975). Generalization of relative competence mediating conformity across differing tasks. *European Journal of Social Psychology, 5,* 281-287.

Festinger, L. (1950). Informal social communication. *Psychological Review, 57,* 271-282.

Festinger, L. (1954). A theory of social comparison processes. *Human Relations, 7,* 117-140.

Gerard, H. B. (1985). When and how the minority prevails. In S. Moscovici, G. Mugny, & E. Van Avermaet (Eds.), *Perspectives on minority influence* (pp. 171-186). Cambridge: Cambridge University Press.

Gerard, H. B., & Rotter, G. S. (1961). Time perspective, consistency of attitude and social influence. *Journal of Abnormal and Social Psychology, 62,* 565-572.

Gerard, H. B., Wilhelmy, R. A., & Conolley, E. S. (1968). Conformity and group size. *Journal of Personality and Social Psychology, 8,* 79-82.

Goldberg, C. (1974). Sex roles, task competence, and conformity. *Journal of Psychology, 86,* 157-164.

Goldberg, C. (1975). Conformity to majority type as a function of task and acceptance of sex-related stereotypes. *Journal of Psychology, 89,* 25-37.

Goldberg, S. C. (1954). Three situational determinants of conformity to social norms. *Journal of Abnormal and Social Psychology, 49,* 325-329.

Hare, A. P. (1976). *Handbook of small group research* (2nd ed.). New York: Free Press.

Higgins, E. T., & McCann, C. D. (1984). Social encoding and subsequent attitudes, impressions, and memory: "Context-driven" and motivational aspects of processing. *Journal of Personality and Social Psychology, 47,* 26-39.

Hollander, E. P. (1975). Independence, conformity, and civil liberties: Some implications from social psychological research. *Journal of Social Issues, 31,* 55-67.

Hollander, E. P., & Willis, R. H. (1967). Some current issues in the psychology of conformity and nonconformity. *Psychological Bulletin, 68,* 62-76.

Insko, C. A., Drenan, S., Solomon, M. R., Smith, R., & Wade, T. J. (1983). Conformity as a function of the consistency of positive self-evaluation with being liked and being right. *Journal of Experimental Social Psychology, 19,* 341-358.

Insko, C. A., Smith, R. H., Alicke, M. D., Wade, J., & Taylor, S. (1985). Conformity and group size: The concern with being right and the concern with being liked. *Personality and Social Psychology Bulletin, 11,* 41-50.

Jackson, J. M. (1986). In defense of social impact theory: Comment on Mullen. *Journal of Personality and Social Psychology, 50,* 511-513.

Jones, E. E., & Gerard, H. B. (1967). *Foundations of social psychology.* New York: John Wiley.

Jones, E. E., & Wortman, C. (1973). *Ingratiation: An attributional approach.* Morristown, NJ: General Learning Press.

Kaplan, M. F., & Miller, C. E. (1983). Group discussion and judgment. In P. B. Paulus (Ed.), *Basic group processes* (pp. 65-94). New York: Springer-Verlag.

Karabenick, S. A. (1983). Sex-relevance of content and influenceability: Sistrunk and McDavid revisited. *Personality and Social Psychology Bulletin, 9,* 243-252.

Kelley, H. H. (1952). Two functions of reference groups. In G. E. Swanson, T. Newcomb, & E. Hartley (Eds.), *Readings in social psychology* (rev. ed., pp. 410-414). New York: Holt.

Kelman, H. C. (1958). Compliance, identification, and internalization: Three processes of attitude change. *Journal of Conflict Resolution, 2,* 51-60.

Kelman, H. C. (1961). Processes of opinion change. *Public Opinion Quarterly, 25,* 57-78.

Kerr, N. L. (1981). Social transition schemes: Charting the group's road to agreement. *Journal of Personality and Social Psychology, 41,* 684-702.

Kerr, N. L. (1982). Social transition schemes: Model, method and applications. In H. Brandstatter, J. H. Davis, & G. Stocker-Kreichgauer (Eds.), *Group decision making* (pp. 59-79). New York: Academic Press.

Kidd, J. S. (1958). Social influence phenomena in a task-oriented group situation. *Journal of Abnormal and Social Psychology, 56,* 13-17.

Kiesler, C. A. (1969). Group pressure and conformity. In J. Mills (Ed.), *Experimental social psychology* (pp. 233-306). New York: Macmillan.

Kiesler, C. A., & Kiesler, S. B. (1969). *Conformity.* Reading, MA: Addison-Wesley.

Kirchler, E., & Davis, J. H. (1986). The influence of member status differences and task type on group consensus and member position change. *Journal of Personality and Social Psychology, 51,* 83-91.

Latane, B. (1981). The psychology of social impact. *American Psychologist, 36,* 343-356.

Latane, B., & Nida, S. (1980). Social impact theory and group influence: A social engineering perspective. In P. B. Paulus (Ed.), *Psychology of group influence* (pp. 3-34). Hillsdale, NJ: Lawrence Erlbaum.

Latane, B., & Wolf, S. (1981). The social impact of majorities and minorities. *Psychological Review, 88,* 438-453.

Levine, J. M. (1980). Reaction to opinion deviance in small groups. In P. B. Paulus (Ed.), *Psychology of group influence* (pp. 375-429). Hillsdale, NJ: Lawrence Erlbaum.

Levine, J. M. (1983). Social comparison and education. In J. M. Levine & M. C. Wang (Eds.), *Teacher and student perceptions: Implications for learning* (pp. 29-55). Hillsdale, NJ: Lawrence Erlbaum.

Levine, J. M., & Moreland, R. L. (1985). Innovation and socialization in small groups. In S. Moscovici, G. Mugny, & E. Van Avermaet (Eds.), *Perspectives on minority influence* (pp. 143-169). Cambridge: Cambridge University Press.

Levine, J. M., & Moreland, R. L. (1986). Outcome comparisons in group contexts: Consequences for the self and others. In R. Schwarzer (Ed.), *Self-related cognitions in anxiety and motivation* (pp. 285-303). Hillsdale, NJ: Lawrence Erlbaum.

Levine, J. M., & Ranelli, C. J. (1978). Majority reaction to shifting and stable attitudinal deviates. *European Journal of Social Psychology, 8,* 55-70.

Levine, J. M., & Ruback, R. B. (1980). Reaction to opinion deviance: Impact of a fence straddler's rationale on majority evaluation. *Social Psychology Quarterly, 43,* 73-81.

Levine, J. M., Saxe, L., & Harris, H. J. (1976). Reaction to attitudinal deviance: Impact of deviate's direction and distance of movement. *Sociometry, 39,* 97-107.

Levine, J. M., Sroka, K. R., & Snyder, H. N. (1977). Group support and reaction to stable and shifting agreement/disagreement. *Sociometry, 40,* 214-224.

Lewis, S. A., Langan, C. J., & Hollander, E. P. (1972). Expectation of future interaction and the choice of less desirable alternatives in conformity. *Sociometry, 35,* 440-447.

Maass, A., & Clark, R. D., III (1983). Internalization versus compliance: Differential processes underlying minority influence and conformity. *European Journal of Social Psychology, 13,* 197-215.

Maass, A., & Clark, R. D., III (1984). Hidden impact of minorities: Fifteen years of minority influence research. *Psychological Bulletin, 95,* 428-450.

Maass, A., Clark, R. D., III, & Haberkorn, G. (1982). The effects of differential ascribed category membership and norms on minority influence. *European Journal of Social Psychology, 12,* 89-104.

Maass, A., West, S. G., & Cialdini, R. B. (in press). Minority influence and conversion. In C. Hendrick (Ed.), *Review of personality and social psychology.*

Moreland, R. L., & Levine, J. M. (1982). Socialization in small groups: Temporal changes in individual-group relations. In L. Berkowitz (Ed.), *Advances in experimental social psychology* (Vol. 15, pp. 137-192). New York: Academic Press.

Morris, W. N., & Miller, R. S. (1975a). The effects of consensus-breaking and consensus-preempting partners on reduction of conformity. *Journal of Experimental Social Psychology, 11,* 215-223.

Morris, W. N., & Miller, R. S. (1975b). Impressions of dissenters and conformers: An attributional analysis. *Sociometry, 38,* 327-339.

Morris, W. N., Miller, R. S., & Sprangenberg, S. (1977). The effects of dissenter position and task difficulty on conformity and response conflict. *Journal of Personality, 45,* 251-266.

Moscovici, S. (1974). Social influence I: Conformity and social control. In C. Nemeth (Ed.), *Social psychology: Classic and contemporary integrations* (pp. 179-216). Chicago: Rand-McNally.

Moscovici, S. (1976). *Social influence and social change.* New York: Academic Press.

Moscovici, S. (1980). Toward a theory of conversion behavior. In L. Berkowitz (Ed.), *Advances in experimental social psychology,* (Vol. 13, pp. 209-239). New York: Academic Press.

Moscovici, S. (1985a). Innovation and minority influence. In S. Moscovici, G. Mugny, & E. Van Avermaet (Eds.), *Perspectives on minority influence* (pp. 9-51). Cambridge: Cambridge University Press.

Moscovici, S. (1985b). Social influence and conformity. In G. Lindzey & E. Aronson (Eds.), *The handbook of social psychology* (Vol. 2, 3rd ed., pp. 347-412). New York: Random House.

Moscovici, S., & Faucheux, C. (1972). Social influence, conformity bias, and the study of active minorities. In L. Berkowitz (Ed.), *Advances in experimental social psychology* (Vol. 6, pp. 149-202). New York: Academic Press.

Moscovici, S., & Lage, E. (1976). Studies in social influence III: Majority versus minority influence in a group. *European Journal of Social Psychology, 6,* 149-174.

Moscovici, S., & Lage, E. (1978). Studies in social influence IV: Minority influence in a context of original judgments. *European Journal of Social Psychology, 8,* 349-365.

Moscovici, S., Lage, E., & Naffrechoux, M. (1969). Influence of a consistent minority on the responses of a majority in a color perception task. *Sociometry, 32,* 365-380.

Moscovici, S., & Mugny, G. (1983). Minority influence. In P. B. Paulus (Ed.), *Basic group processes* (pp. 41-64). New York: Springer-Verlag.

Moscovici, S., & Nemeth, C. (1974). Social influence II: Minority influence. In C. Nemeth (Ed.), *Social psychology: Classic and contemporary integrations* (pp. 217-249). Chicago: Rand-McNally.

Mugny, G. (1982). *The power of minorities.* New York: Academic Press.

Mugny, G. (1984a). Compliance, conversion, and the Asch paradigm. *European Journal of Social Psychology, 14,* 353-368.

Mugny, G. (1984b). The influence of minorities: Ten years later. In H. Tajfel (Ed.), *The social dimension: European developments in social psychology* (Vol. 2, pp. 498-517). Cambridge: Cambridge University Press.

Mullen, B. (1983). Operationalizing the effect of the group on the individual: A self-attention perspective. *Journal of Experimental Social Psychology, 19,* 295-322.

Mullen, B. (1985). Strength and immediacy of sources: A meta-analytic evaluation of the forgotten elements of social impact theory. *Journal of Personality and Social Psychology, 48,* 1458-1466.

Mullen, B. (1986). Effects of strength and immediacy in group contexts: Reply to Jackson. *Journal of Personality and Social Psychology, 50,* 514-516.

Nail, P. R. (1986). Toward an integration of some models and theories of social response. *Psychological Bulletin, 100,* 190-206.

Nemeth, C. (in press). Style without status expectations: The special contributions of minorities. In M. Webster & M. Foschi (Eds.), *Research on expectation status.* Palo Alto, CA: Stanford University Press.

Nemeth, C. (1985). Dissent, group processes, and creativity: The contribution of minority influence. In E. Lawler (Ed.), *Advances in group processes* (pp. 57-75). Greenwich, CT: JAI Press.

Nemeth, C. (1986). Differential contributions of majority and minority influence. *Psychological Review, 93,* 23-32.

Nemeth, C., & Kwan, J. L. (1985). Originality of word associations as a function of majority vs. minority influence. *Social Psychology Quarterly, 48,* 277-282.

Nemeth, C., & Wachtler, J. (1983). Creative problem solving as a result of majority vs. minority influence. *European Journal of Social Psychology, 7,* 15-27.

Nemeth, C., Wachtler, J., & Endicott, J. (1977). Increasing the size of the minority: Some gains and some losses. *European Journal of Social Psychology, 7,* 15-27.

Nord, W. R. (1969). Social exchange theory: An integrative approach to social conformity. *Psychological Bulletin, 71,* 174-208.

Paicheler, G. (1976). Norms and attitude change I: Polarization and styles of behaviour. *European Journal of Social Psychology, 6,* 405-427.

Paicheler, G. (1977). Norms and attitude change II: The phenomenon of bipolarization. *European Journal of Social Psychology, 7,* 5-14.

Papastamou, S. (1984). Strategies of minority and majority influence. In W. Doise & S. Moscovici (Eds.), *Current issues in European social psychology* (Vol. 1, pp. 33-83). Cambridge: Cambridge University Press.

Papastamou, S., & Mugny, G. (1985). Rigidity and minority influence: The influence of the social in social influence. In S. Moscovici, G. Mugny, & E. Van Avermaet (Eds.),

Perspectives on minority influence (pp. 113-136). Cambridge: Cambridge University Press.

Penrod, S., & Hastie, R. (1980). A computer simulation of jury decision making. *Psychological Review, 87,* 133-159.

Personnaz, B. (1981). Study in social influence using the spectrometer method: Dynamics of the phenomena of conversion and covertness in perceptual responses. *European Journal of Social Psychology, 11,* 431-438.

Personnaz, B., & Guillon, M. (1985). Conflict and conversion. In S. Moscovici, G. Mugny, & E. Van Avermaet (Eds.), *Perspectives on minority influence.* Cambridge: Cambridge University Press.

Raven, B. H., & Kruglanski, A. (1970). Conflict and power. In P. Swingle (Ed.), *The structure of conflict* (pp. 69-109). New York: Academic Press.

Rosenberg, L. A. (1961). Group size, prior experience, and conformity. *Journal of Abnormal and Social Psychology, 63,* 436-437.

Ross, L., Bierbrauer, G., & Hoffman, S. (1976). The role of attribution processes in conformity and dissent: Revisiting the Asch situation. *American Psychologist, 31,* 148-157.

Sakurai, M. M. (1975). Small group cohesiveness and detrimental conformity. *Sociometry, 38,* 340-357.

Saltzstein, H. D., & Sandberg, L. (1979). Indirect social influence: Change in judgmental process or anticipatory conformity? *Journal of Experimental Social Psychology, 15,* 209-216.

Santee, R. T., & Jackson, S. E. (1982). Identity implications of conformity: Sex differences in normative and attributional judgments. *Social Psychology Quarterly, 45,* 121-125.

Santee, R. T., & Maslach, C. (1982). To agree or not to agree: Personal dissent amid social pressure to conform. *Journal of Personality and Social Psychology, 42,* 690-700.

Schlenker, B. R. (1980). *Impression management: The self-concept, social identity, and interpersonal relations.* Monterey, CA: Brooks-Cole.

Shaw, M. E. (1981). *Group dynamics: The psychology of small group behavior* (3rd ed.). New York: McGraw-Hill.

Sistrunk, F., & McDavid, J. W. (1971). Sex variable in conforming behavior. *Journal of Personality and Social Psychology, 17,* 200-207.

Sorrentino, R. M., King, G., & Leo, G. (1980). The influence of the minority on perception: A note on a possible alternative interpretation. *Journal of Experimental Social Psychology, 16,* 293-301.

Sorrels, J. P., & Kelley, J. (1984). Conformity by omission. *Personality and Social Psychology Bulletin, 10,* 302-305.

Sorentino, R. M., King, G., & Leo, G. (1980). The influence of the minority on perception: A note on a possible alternative interpretation. *Journal of Experimental Social Psychology, 16,* 293-301.

Stang, D. J. (1976). Group size effects on conformity. *Journal of Social Psychology, 98,* 175-181.

Stasser, G., & Davis, J. H. (1981). Group decision making and social influence: A social interaction sequence model. *Psychological Review, 88,* 523-551.

Stasser, G., Kerr, N. L., & Davis, J. H. (1980). Influence processes in decision-making groups: A modeling approach. In P. B. Paulus (Ed.), *Psychology of group influence* (pp. 431-477). Hillsdale, NJ: Lawrence Erlbaum.

Stasser, G., Stella, N., Hanna, C., & Colella, A. (1984). The majority effect in jury deliberations: Number of supporters versus number of supporting arguments. *Law and Psychology Review, 8,* 115-127.

Suls, J. M., & Miller, R. L. (Eds.). (1977). *Social comparison processes: Theoretical and empirical perspectives.* Washington, DC: Hemisphere.

Tajfel, H. (1969). Social and cultural factors in perception. In G. Lindzey & E. Aronson (Eds.), *The handbook of social psychology* (Vol. 3, 2nd ed., pp. 315-394). Reading, MA: Addison-Wesley.

Tanford, S., & Penrod, S. (1984). Social influence model: A formal integration of research on majority and minority influence processes. *Psychological Bulletin, 95,* 189-225.

Thibaut, J. W., & Strickland, L. H. (1956). Psychological set and social conformity. *Journal of Personality, 25,* 115-129.

Wallace, J. E., Becker, J., Coppel, D. B., & Cox, G. B. (1983). Anticonformity aspects of depression in mild depressive states. *Journal of Personality, 51,* 640-652.

Wilder, D. A. (1977). Perception of groups, size of opposition, and social influence. *Journal of Experimental Social Psychology, 13,* 253-268.

Wilder, D. A. (1978a). Homogeneity of jurors: The majority's influence depends upon their perceived independence. *Law and Human Behavior, 2,* 363-376.

Wilder, D. A. (1978b). Perceiving persons as a group: Effects on attributions of causality and beliefs. *Social Psychology, 41,* 13-23.

Willis, R. H. (1963). Two dimensions of conformity-nonconformity. *Sociometry, 26,* 499-513.

Willis, R. H. (1965). Conformity, independence, and anticonformity. *Human Relations, 18,* 373-388.

Wolf, S. (in press). Majority and minority influence: A social impact analysis. In M. P. Zanna, J. M. Olson, & C. P. Herman (Eds.), *Social influences: The Ontario Symposium* (Vol. 5). Hillsdale, NJ: Lawrence Erlbaum.

Wolf, S. (1979). Behavioral style and group cohesiveness as sources of minority influence. *European Journal of Social Psychology, 9,* 381-385.

Wolf, S. (1985). Manifest and latent influence of majorities and minorities. *Journal of Personality and Social Psychology, 48,* 899-908.

Wolf, S., & Latane, B. (1983). Majority and minority influence on restaurant preferences. *Journal of Personality and Social Psychology, 45,* 282-292.

Wolf, S., & Latane, B. (1985). Conformity, innovation and the psychosocial law. In S. Moscovici, G. Mugny, & E. Van Avermaet (Eds.), *Perspectives on minority influence* (pp. 201-215). Cambridge: Cambridge University Press.

2

Minority Influence and Conversion

ANNE MAASS
STEPHEN G. WEST
ROBERT B. CIALDINI

Anne Maass is Assistant Professor at the University of Padova, Italy. She was previously Assistant Professor at the University of Kiel, West Germany, and during the past year was Visiting Assistant Professor at Arizona State University. Her major research interests are in the areas of minority influence and psycholegal research, particularly eyewitness identification. She is the author of a chapter on minority influence in D. Frey and M. Irle's *Theorien der Sozialpsychologie* (Vol. 2).

Stephen G. West is Director of the Graduate Training Program in Social Psychology at Arizona State University. He is currently Editor of the *Journal of Personality* and Associate Editor of *Evaluation Review*. He has research interests in a number of basic and applied issues in social psychology, personality, and methodology. He is coauthor of *A primer of social psychological theories* and *Psychotherapy and behavior change: Social, methodological and cultural perspectives* (in press), is coeditor of *Evaluation studies review annual* (Vol. 4), and is editor of special issues of the *Journal of Personality* on "Personality and prediction: Nomothetic and idiographic approaches" and "Methodological developments in personality research."

Robert B. Cialdini is Professor of Psychology at Arizona State University where in 1985 he was named Graduate College Distinguished Research Professor. He has held visiting faculty appointments at Ohio State University, the University of California at San Diego, and the University of California at Santa Cruz, as well as at the Annenberg School of Communications in Los Angeles. His current research interests include social influence, altruism, and image management. He is the author of *Influence,* chapters on compliance in J. Matarazzo et al.'s *Behavioral health: A handbook of health enhancement* and M. Zanna et al.'s *Social influence: The Ontario symposium* (Vol. 5.), and a chapter on attitudes and attitude change in the *Annual Review of Psychology* (1981).

Group research has demonstrated a variety of influences of groups on individual behaviors, ranging from judgments of the length of lines

AUTHORS' NOTE: Anne Maass was supported by a special stipend from the Dean, College of Liberal Arts and Sciences, Arizona State University, during the writing of this chapter. We thank Jennifer Campbell, John Levine, Charlan Nemeth, Richard Petty, Norbert Schwarz, Sharon Wolf, Clyde Hendrick, and two anonymous reviewers for their comments on an earlier version of this chapter.

(Asch, 1956) to the size of tips left in restaurants (Freeman, Walker, Borden, & Latane, 1975). Sometimes, such as when a unanimous majority of group members presents a viewpoint not consistent with the individual's position, changes in public behavior are not accompanied by corresponding changes in the individual's privately held judgments, attitudes, and values (Asch, 1956). In other situations, groups elicit parallel effects on both the observable behaviors and privately held attitudes of individual members, as in cases in which the majority consists of an important reference group (Newcomb, 1943) or in which the stimulus is highly ambiguous (Sherif, 1935). Finally, one intriguing line of research (Moscovici, Mugny, & Van Avermaet, 1985) has typically led to the paradoxical effect that active minorities within groups fail to produce any change in the individual's public statements in the group context, yet such minorities can produce conversions— changes in the individual's privately held opinions and judgments that appear to persist beyond the experimental situation.

The purpose of the present chapter is to examine a series of cognitive and motivational processes that may help distinguish between majority and minority influence and account for the repeated finding that conversion is more likely to be obtained in minority than in majority influence.

PRIVATE ACCEPTANCE VERSUS PUBLIC COMPLIANCE: DIFFERENTIAL OUTCOMES OF SOCIAL INFLUENCE

Conversion

With few exceptions (e.g., Doms & Van Avermaet, 1980; Wolf, 1985), research on minority influence has demonstrated that minorities tend to produce profound and lasting changes in attitudes and perceptions that generalize to new settings and over time. Such change has been termed the conversion effect by Moscovici (1980). Conversion implies a modification of the individual's abilities, opinions, or values, which is more likely to be manifested in private rather than public responses. Indeed, these changes apparently occur in some cases without reaching the subject's direct awareness. In contrast, compliance, in which the individual yields to a powerful influence source without modifying his or her basic attitudes on the issue, is more likely to occur in public than in private. In general, minorities have been found to produce conversion, whereas majorities are more likely to elicit compliance that is confined to the original influence setting (for overviews, see Chaiken & Stangor, 1987; Maass & Clark, 1984; Maass, West, & Clark, 1985).

Research Paradigms

In the standard minority influence paradigm, a group of several subjects (the majority) is exposed to one or two consistent and unyielding confederates (the minority). Throughout the discussion, the confederate(s) advocate an extreme position that is contrary to the subjects' beliefs or perceptions. At the end of the discussion, all subjects are asked to state their position in public. Later, each subject completes a second measure of opinion that is taken in private (see Mugny, 1974-75, 1976) or which refers to a new, ostensibly unrelated task (see Moscovici & Lage, 1976). Thus the basic elements of the standard minority influence paradigm are one or two consistent and unyielding confederates who advocate a position contrary to that of the more numerous majority subjects, reversing the roles of the majority and minority in the familiar Asch conformity paradigm.

In line with Houts, Cook, and Shadish's (1986) plea for the investigation of phenomena under a variety of method choices, the potential effects of minority influence have been explored using several different variants of the basic paradigm and multiple operationalizations of the independent and dependent variables. Variants of the paradigm have ranged from largely unstructured group interactions to highly structured influence situations (see Tanford & Penrod, 1984), and from face-to-face interactions between subjects and confederates (e.g., Maass, Clark, & Haberkorn, 1982) to written counterattitudinal messages, the authors of which are described as minorities or majorities (e.g., Mugny, 1982). Further, minority influence experiments have utilized a wide variety of experimental tasks, including both *objective* items (e.g., Moscovici & Personnaz, 1980; Personnaz, 1981; Mugny, 1974-75, 1976) and *opinion* items (e.g., Maass & Clark, 1983). Minority influence researchers have also used subject samples drawn from diverse industrialized countries in Europe and North America.

Recently, researchers have started to compare minority and majority influence by using both Moscovici's and Asch's paradigms within the same experiment (see Maass & Clark, 1984; Moscovici, 1985). In these experiments some of the subjects are exposed to minority influence, whereas others are exposed to majority influence. Maass and Clark (1983, 1986) have also utilized a within-subject version of this approach, *simultaneously* exposing individuals with moderate or undecided positions on an issue to both a minority and a majority, with one side taking an extreme pro and the other an extreme anti position on the issue.

Yet, a complete test of Moscovici's conversion notion requires not only exposure to majority and minority sources, but also direct measurement of both publicly expressed and privately reported attitudes. If conversion occurs, private attitude change should be greater than public attitude change; the opposite pattern should occur for compliance. In past research, a wide range of dependent variables has been used to assess conversion versus compliance suggesting that conversion embraces a wide spectrum of interrelated phenomena. The measurement of conversion has ranged from private attitude measures (e.g., Maass & Clark, 1983; Martin, 1985; Mugny, 1974-75, 1976) over delayed assessments (Moscovici et al., n.d., reported in Moscovici, 1980) and indirect item procedures (Mugny, 1982) up to subtle, unobtrusive procedures that disguise the connection between the minority's or majority's influence attempt and the dependent measure (Moscovici & Lage, 1976; Moscovici & Personnaz, 1980; Personnaz, 1981; Nemeth & Kwan, 1985, 1987; Nemeth & Wachtler, 1974). Although all techniques are intended to measure the same basic concept, namely conversion versus compliance, they do differ on at least four critical dimensions: time (immediate versus delayed influence), specificity (influence specific to the message versus influence beyond the message), privacy (private versus public responding) and awareness of the connection between influence situation and dependent variable.

With the possible exception of the chromatic complementary afterimage measure (e.g., Doms & Van Avermaet, 1980; Moscovici & Personnaz, 1980),[1] the different experimental paradigms, operationalizations, and sources of experimental subjects have almost always produced equivalent results. In comparison to majorities, minorities have a longer-lasting impact (e.g., Moscovici et al., n.d., reported in Moscovici, 1980), are more likely to induce private attitude change (e.g., Maass & Clark, 1983, 1986; Mugny, 1974-75, 1976), are more likely to have an impact *beyond* the advocated position (e.g., Moscovici & Lage, 1976), and may even modify the unconscious aspects of the target's behavior (e.g., Nemeth & Kwan, 1985). The question then arises as to which psychological mechanisms may be responsible for these different facets of minority influence. What are these processes and what is it about the minority that triggers them? What characteristics of the minority enable it to have such a striking advantage over the more powerful majority in producing internalized change? It is the purpose of this article to present different theoretical hypotheses about the processes underlying the conversion effect and to evaluate these hypotheses in light of existing research evidence.[2]

DIFFERENTIAL COGNITIVE PROCESSES AND THEIR MEDIATING FUNCTION

In his original formulation of conversion theory, Moscovici (1980) proposed two distinctly different processes to account for minority and majority influence. According to Moscovici, majorities elicit a "comparison" process in which the divergent opinions are compared with each other without further attention to the issue in question. In contrast, consistent minorities trigger a "validation" process in which the person actively thinks about the issue. Moscovici also hypothesized that the two processes differ on two related dimensions, namely *attentional focus* and *cognitive activity*. In majority influence, attention is directed toward the other group members; in minority influence, it is focused on the task or stimulus. Consequently, people are more likely to raise issue-relevant arguments and counterarguments when the influence source is a minority. Thus cognitive activity would be expected to be greater in minority than in majority influence.

Attention: Interpersonal vs. Stimulus Focus

A number of studies have provided indirect support for the idea that minorities and majorities elicit differential attentional focus. Guillon and Personnaz (1983) videotaped group discussions in which subjects were either confronted with a minority or with a majority. Subsequently they were asked to view segments of the videotaped discussion and to express their thoughts on each segment. A content analysis revealed that subjects in the majority influence condition experienced an increasing *interpersonal* conflict during the discussion, whereas subjects in the minority influence condition reported an increasing *cognitive* conflict. Although attentional focus was not directly observed in this study, the results are perfectly in line with Moscovici's hypothesis.[3]

Additional indirect support for the idea of differential attention comes from studies employing recall measures (Moscovici et al., n.d., reported in Moscovici, 1980; Nemeth & Mayseless, 1986). In these studies, minorities produced higher recall rates than majorities for (a) the stimulus material (Nemeth & Mayseless, 1986), (b) the content, and (c) the source of the message (Moscovici et al., n.d., cited in Moscovici, 1980). Although the exact mechanisms of these recall differences (e.g., encoding, rehearsal, depth of processing, decoding) are still awaiting empirical examination, one clear possibility is that the superior recall in the minority influence paradigm is a function of greater attention.

The limited data reviewed here suggest that attention is enhanced under minority influence. This conclusion, however, should be treated with caution for two reasons. First, all of the above studies have employed indirect measures of attention that are open to alternative interpretations. Second, the focus of attention remains ambiguous. Do minorities increase attention to the stimulus material, to the message content, to the influence source and/or to other issue-relevant features (see Moscovici, 1980; Nemeth, 1986, for a discussion)? Conversely, do majorities increase self-focused attention, particularly when there is no easy resolution to the conflict between the individual's and the majority's positions (Duval & Wicklund, 1972, chap. 4; Mullen, 1983)? Although systematic comparisons of different experimental tasks are still waiting, we suggest that minorities are likely to enhance the amount of attention focused on the stimulus information at the center of the disagreement between majority and minority group members. In simple perceptual tasks (color judgments) the attentional focus should be on the colored stimulus whereas in paradigms involving opinions the attentional focus should be on the message presented by the minority.

Cognitive Activity

As noted above, Moscovici (1980) has argued that "a judgment expressed by a minority is more likely to raise arguments and counterarguments than the ones expressed by a majority" (p. 214). To this point, there are only a few studies that have assessed people's cognitive activity in social influence situations.

Maass and Clark (1983) made the first attempt to measure the cognitive activity of people who were simultaneously exposed to a minority and a majority. Adopting a methodology from the literature on the cognitive response approach to persuasion (see Petty, Ostrom, & Brock, 1981), subjects were asked to list their thoughts in response to both the minority's and majority's arguments. Contrary to the predictions of conversion theory, subjects were not found to generate more thoughts when the source of influence was a minority than when it was a majority. That is, there was no indication of *quantitative* differences in cognitive activity.[4]

Yet, a separate analysis of arguments (thoughts that support the viewpoint of the influence source) and counterarguments (thoughts that oppose the viewpoint of the influence source) revealed interesting *qualitative* differences in the reaction to minorities and majorities. Compared to majorities, minorities were more likely to elicit arguments and less likely to evoke counterarguments. These findings suggest that the two influence sources do not trigger differential amounts, but rather qualitatively different types of cognitive activity. In particular, majorities seem to elicit a more self-protective type of information processing than minorities.

This idea of *qualitatively* different forms of cognitive activity has received further support in three recent experiments by Nemeth and her coworkers (see Nemeth, 1986). In the first experiment (Nemeth & Wachtler, 1983), subjects were instructed to find an embedded figure in a series of comparison figures. A majority or minority discovered an embedded figure in two of the six comparison figures. When confronted with a majority, subjects generally adopted the majority's solutions without discovering additional embedded figures. In contrast, when confronted with a minority, subjects were less likely to name the two figures that had been identified by the minority. Rather, they correctly identified additional embedded figures that had not been reported by the confederates. Interestingly, this effect was obtained independently of whether the minority was correct or incorrect. These results suggest that minorities may stimulate creative problem solving, leading to the detection of novel correct solutions.

A similar pattern of results emerged in a second study by Nemeth and Kwan (1987) in which subjects were asked to identify three-letter words from a string of five letters (e.g., tDOGe). A majority or a minority consistently used backward sequencing of the capitalized letters to form the three-letter words (e.g., "GOD"). Subsequently subjects were instructed to form all possible words from each of 10 letter strings within a give time period. Subjects who had previously been confronted with a minority found more correct solutions. More important, they were more likely to alternately use all possible word construction strategies, namely forward, backward, and mixed sequencing of letters. Those who had been confronted with the majority performed more poorly because of their predominant use of backward sequencing at the expense of other strategies.

Finally, Nemeth and Kwan (1985) used an intriguing variant of the traditional color perception paradigm to demonstrate the differential thought processes engendered by minority and majority influence. During the social influence phase of experiment, blue slides were labeled "green" either by an ostensible minority or majority. Then subjects were instructed to form word associations to the words "green" and "blue." Subjects who had previously been exposed to a minority gave more original, (i.e., statistically infrequent) associations, whereas those exposed to a majority formed more conventional (i.e., statistically frequent) associations.

Taken together, the three studies by Nemeth and her coworkers suggest that minorities and majorities evoke qualitatively different thought processes. Compared to majorities, minorities trigger more creative, original, and divergent cognitive activity, leading to the detection of novel, correct solutions. Not surprisingly, these results have motivated Nemeth to offer an extension to Moscovici's original theory. According to Nemeth's (1986) reformulation, people confronted with a majority viewpoint engage in message-relevant, convergent thinking; their attentional focus is narrow, since they only reflect upon the majority's position without considering further alternatives. This convergent thinking limits the influence of the majority on the individual to producing immediate adoption of the proposed viewpoint. In contrast, people exposed to a minority do not engage in more thinking about the minority message as proposed by Moscovici (1980). Rather, they engage in more issue-relevant, divergent thinking that goes well beyond the minority's message. These divergent thought processes will tend to lead to the discovery of more creative solutions and to broader changes in individual's attitudes and cognitive structures.

The above experiments (Maass & Clark, 1983; Nemeth & Wachtler, 1983; Nemeth & Kwan, 1985, 1987) all demonstrate that minorities elicit qualitatively different thought processes than majorities. They trigger less defensive and more divergent thinking. Yet, in order to explain fully the conversion effect described in the first section of this paper, an additional assumption is needed: Cognitive activity must be assumed to influence private or latent attitude change without necessarily surfacing on the public or manifest level.

Cognitive Activity and Level of Influence

Moscovici's conversion theory predicts that the thought-intensive "validation process" in minority influence produces latent attitude change that will endure over time, whereas the relatively shallow "comparison process" in majority influence is more likely to produce temporary modifications of attitudes. This notion bears strong resemblance to the more general elaboration likelihood model by Petty and Cacioppo (1981, 1986). According to their model, a message can either be processed by a central or a peripheral route, depending on the person's ability and motivation to process the communication. Only the central route involving issue-relevant thinking will lead to enduring attitude change.

Strong evidence for the link between cognitive activity and level and persistence of influence comes from the persuasion literature. Central information processing involving the generation of arguments has generally been found to produce enduring attitude change and to be predictive of subsequent behavior, whereas peripheral processing has been found to be associated with short-lived persuasion effects (for overviews of the relevant literature, see Cialdini, Petty, & Cacioppo, 1981; Chaiken, 1987; Petty & Cacioppo, 1981, 1986).

Although the link between cognitive activity and influence has been investigated frequently in the persuasion literature, relevant studies within the social influence framework are rare. Richardson (1985) has provided indirect support for the idea that cognitive activity mediates minority but not necessarily majority influence. Using a perceptual task, he found that minority influence occurred only if the subject was allowed the opportunity to attend to the stimulus material after exposure to the minority opinion. In contrast, the impact of the majority was not contingent upon the opportunity to scrutinize the stimulus material.

Maass and Clark (1983, Exp. 2) have investigated the mediating function of cognitive activity using a process-oriented methodology. They showed that measures of cognitive activity associated with the position advocated by the majority or minority accounted for a significant portion of the variance in private but not in public attitude change. This result is consistent with the hypothesis that the private acceptance of the minority position is mediated by the generation of arguments and counterarguments, whereas public compliance is unrelated to the amount and direction of cognitive activity (see Baron & Kenny, 1986).

The research reviewed so far indicates that people exposed to a minority engage in different thought processes than people exposed to a majority. Those exposed to the minority (a) are more likely to focus on the stimulus, (b) engage in more divergent and less defensive thinking, and (c) are more likely to show private/latent rather than public/manifest attitude change. These observations, however, do not explain *why* a minority elicits such diverse cognitive processes. What is it about the minority that allows it to induce nondefensive and divergent thinking?

Although *consistency* has repeatedly been demonstrated to be a necessary condition for minority influence to occur, it alone cannot account for the conversion effect. One can easily imagine majorities that defend their position with equal stubbornness, as is the case for certain prominent religions persistently upholding traditional doctrine despite new societal challenges. In fact, it appears likely that people in real life settings are usually exposed to both, uncompromising minorities *and* majorities. For example, in the post-Chernobyl climate of concern about the safety of nuclear power, residents of the United States are confronted with a strong pronuclear minority as well as a strong antinuclear majority that may be just as uncompromising and consistent as the minority. In order to investigate such simultaneous influence attempts, Maass and Clark (1983) developed an experimental paradigm in which subjects are exposed to influence attempts from both the minority and majority. Studies using this paradigm (Maass & Clark, 1983, 1986) have shown that the predictions of conversion theory are supported even under simultaneous social influence. People move toward the minority in private but toward the majority in public, even when they are exposed *simultaneously* to a consistent majority and a consistent minority.

These observations suggest that the same consistent behavior may take on a different *meaning* when it is shown by a minority rather than a majority. In the following sections of the paper we will examine a number of hypotheses about the distinguishing features of minorities and majorities that may explain why consistency may have a greater impact on people's cognitive activity when it is displayed by a minority rather than a majority.

MINORITY CHARACTERISTICS
FACILITATING COGNITIVE ACTIVITY

The minority intrinsically differs from the majority on a number of important dimensions. First, minorities are by definition more salient and distinct. Second, the minority is a priori a less credible source of influence since "correctness" is usually associated with high levels of consensus. Therefore, everything else (e.g., competence, status) being equal, the minority is the less valid source of informational influence (see Deutsch & Gerard, 1955). Third, the minority is more likely to be exposed to social pressure. This third difference is where consistency becomes a critical factor. From an attributional perspective, a minority's consistency is likely to provide information about its true beliefs whereas the equally consistent behavior of a majority member is attributionally more ambiguous, reflecting either true beliefs or compliance to group pressure (Maass et al., 1985). We examine each of these characteristics below.

Distinctiveness

The first and most obvious characteristic of the minority is its greater salience both in terms of numbers and of category membership. Since Schachter's (1951) early work we know that much of the total attention of the group is directed toward deviant member(s). The same is true for minorities from distinct social categories, such as solo women in predominantly male groups or solo blacks in predominantly white groups. Taylor's (1981) work on relative distinctiveness clearly indicates that "solos" are perceived as more prominent and evaluated more extremely than group members belonging to the majority. Thus, due to its greater salience, the minority will automatically draw more attention to its message than will a majority. Not surprisingly, minority messages are also better retained in memory (Nemeth & Mayseless, 1986; Moscovici et al., n.d., reported in Moscovici, 1980; Taylor, 1981).

Since distinctiveness does increase the attention to and the recall of the minority's message, it may play an important role in minority influence. In particular, distinctiveness may facilitate long-term attitude change (Moscovici et al., n.d., reported in Moscovici, 1980). Yet, distinctiveness may neither be a sufficient nor a necessary condition for conversion since conversion effects have also been observed in experimental paradigms that do not render the minority salient (Mugny, 1982). In such settings, characteristics other than distinctiveness must account for the minority's unique capacity to produce conversion.

Credibility

Credibility of a message source has been repeatedly stressed in theoretical writings as an important factor. In general, an opinion is more likely to be perceived as correct the larger the number of people who share it. Therefore, the viewpoint of a majority is a priori more credible than the viewpoint of a minority. Although some authors (e.g., Kelman, 1958) have claimed that high source credibility is associated with high internalization, Moscovici (1980) proposed that the *reverse* relationship holds. He argued that people process the message of a low credibility source more carefully and internalize it more readily than the message of a high credibility source. In particular, a less credible source motivates people to focus more carefully on the stimulus. Since the majority is a more reliable source of information, there is less need to scrutinize the stimulus. To put it in social comparison terms (Festinger, 1954), people exposed to a majority are more inclined to rely on social comparison information, whereas those exposed to a minority are more motivated to evaluate their opinions and perceptions through "objective," nonsocial means.

Credibility and cognitive processing. While Moscovici (1980) mainly stressed the connection between source credibility and attentional focus, Nemeth (1986) elaborated the link between a priori credibility and divergent versus convergent thinking. Since people are inclined to find the majority opinion true, they are mainly concerned about the majority viewpoint without considering other alternatives. When confronted with the less credible minority, they are more likely to consider other alternatives as well.

There is suggestive evidence that people do, in fact, expend more energy on processing the message of a less credible source. Further, low credibility facilitates divergent thinking and conversion. The persuasion literature generally shows that people engage in more thinking when confronted with a source of low rather than high credibility, except in cases of high ego involvement or high prior knowledge (Petty & Cacioppo, 1981; Heesacker, Petty, & Cacioppo, 1983). In the minority influence literature Nemeth and Wachtler (1983) reported evidence that low credibility facilitates divergent thinking. In this experiment, the influence source (either a minority or a majority) proposed either a correct or an incorrect solution. Independently of whether or not the minority was correct, subjects exposed to minority influence discovered a number of novel, correct solutions. Those exposed to majority influence were more likely to detect novel solutions when the majority was *incorrect*. Thus the poorest performance was shown by subjects exposed to the most credible source of influence investigated, a correct majority.

Similar results emerged from a recent study by Mugny (1985) who found that low credibility was associated with a high degree of conversion in the Asch paradigm. In this study, students were least likely to comply publicly with a majority of younger students who were perceived to have lower ability on the task. Yet it was this low credibility group that exerted the greatest latent influence. Along the same line, Martin (1985) found that the depreciated out-group minority had the greatest impact on the subjects' attitudes at the private level while the more credible in-group majority was more influential on the public level.

Taken together, these results suggest that divergent thinking and conversion are more likely to occur when the influence source has limited credibility.[5] Interestingly, this is true both for a low status or low competence minority and for a low status or low competence majority. Thus differential credibility may not only account for difference between the two paradigms (minority versus majority influence) as typically implemented, but it may also explain *intra-paradigm* differences. However, the reader should keep in mind that differential credibility constitutes a post hoc explanation of the results of the studies reviewed here. In particular, none of the minority influence experiments included an explicit manipulation of credibility or even a manipulation check assessing the subjects' perceptions of source credibility.

Further, most of these studies have involved issues of low to moderate personal relevance. Research results in the persuasion literature suggest that low credibility is associated with greater cognitive activity only for issues of low involvement. On highly involving issues, high credibility sources are more likely to induce cognitive activity (Heesacker et al., 1983; Petty & Cacioppo, 1981, 1986). Thus it is possible that a highly credible majority source may elicit greater thought and conversion when the issue is very ego-involving.

Credibility and heuristic processing. A cognitive explanation for the differential credibility findings may be derived from Chaiken's (1987) heuristic model of persuasion. According to her approach, people frequently use simple decision rules such as "more arguments are better arguments" when assessing the validity of a message. Rather than processing the *content* of the message, people often prefer to rely on heuristics that require little cognitive effort. Applying this idea to the social influence situation, a person in the conformity paradigm who is confronted with a unanimous majority may simply utilize a consensus heuristic of the type "if everybody agrees on this issue, they must be right." However, in the presence of one or more consistent minority members the use of such a heuristic is precluded, so that subjects are more likely to process the message content systematically. A similar interpretation can be offered for Mugny's (1985) and Martin's (1985) results: People may have relied on a liking-agreement heuristic when confronted with a peer or in-group influence source, whereas such a heuristic would be unlikely to be used when the influence source is an out-group member.

The heuristic model further predicts that only systematic processing will lead to enduring attitude change; heuristic processing is expected to produce only temporary agreement with the influence source. Thus the model can also account for the fact that conversion effects are unlikely to occur in situations that facilitate the use of consensus or liking-agreement heuristics. Although Chaiken's (1987) heuristic model has yet to be tested in the majority/minority influence paradigm, it offers an intriguing post hoc explanation for the finding that highly credible influence sources are less likely to induce conversion than their less credible counterparts.

Credibility and arousal. In light of the current zeitgeist in social psychology to focus on cognitive explanations of social phenomena, it is important to explore whether other, noncognitive explanations may also provide adequate accounts of the observed findings (see Houts et al., 1986). From the perspective of research on stress and arousal, for example, it is not particularly stressful to be in disagreement with minorities since they are typically assumed to be wrong. It is far more upsetting to be in the position of a lonely outsider defending one's position against an overwhelming, presumably correct majority. Consistent with this analysis, psychological and physiological observations do, in fact, indicate that people experience considerable stress when exposed to an opposing majority (see Allen & Wilder, 1978).

It has long been known that people perform best at moderate levels of arousal (Yerkes-Dodson law), at least on tasks of intermediate difficulty. In fact, subjects in Nemeth and Wachtler's (1983) study reported fairly high levels of stress when exposed to a majority but only moderate amounts of stress when confronted with a minority. They also experienced more stress when the influence source was correct than when it was incorrect. Since subjects also performed considerably better when exposed to a minority or an incorrect majority, it is likely that the interaction with the consistent minority or with the less credible (incorrect) majority provided an "optimal" level of arousal. The highly stressful exposure to the credible (correct) majority may have hampered the subjects' cognitive abilities.

Easterbrook (1959) offered an attentional account of the Yerkes-Dodson law. According to his cue utilization hypothesis, arousal narrows the attentional field. With increasing arousal, people tend to focus on central cues at the expense of peripheral cues. In general, the narrowing of the attentional field will initially improve performance since irrelevant peripheral cues are no longer processed. Beyond a certain (optimal) level of arousal, however, the attentional field becomes so limited that important cues are no longer processed (Bacon, 1974). Nemeth (1986) used the cue utilization hypothesis to account for her findings that people exposed to a minority perform better and consider a wider range of alternatives. The Easterbrook hypothesis can also explain why recall improves under minority influence (presumably associated with moderate arousal) but deteriorates under majority influence (associated with high arousal) as compared to a no-influence control group (Nemeth & Mayseless, 1986). Finally, assuming that disagreement with others becomes more stressful the more credible they are, the Easterbrook hypothesis can also explain why people show greater conversion in the Asch paradigm with a less credible majority (Mugny, 1985).

To summarize thus far: Although the processes underlying source credibility effects are not yet well understood, studies on minority/majority influence do in general suggest that less credible influence sources produce more divergent thinking and greater conversion. Various explanations have been outlined in the previous section based on social comparison, Chaiken's heuristic model of persuasion, and the Easterbrook hypothesis. Although all of these explanations can account for the differential credibility findings reported above, none of them can explain the findings obtained from the *simultaneous influence paradigm* (Maass & Clark, 1983, 1986). That is, none of them can convincingly explain why people who are simultaneously exposed to a minority and a majority move toward the minority in private but toward the majority in public.

Resistance to Group Pressure

Besides salience and credibility, a third characteristic of the minority position, consistency, may be important in the context of social influence, but has received surprisingly little attention in the literature. By definition, a minority can be identified only with reference to a majority. This banal idea has one important implication: If the minority consistently defends a given viewpoint, it does so *against* a considerably more numerous and more powerful majority. In a situation of high social pressure, the minority's consistency signifies certainty, conviction, and even courage because the minority is risking the disapproval of the majority. The same consistent behavior on the part of a majority may take a completely different meaning because the majority is not exposed to a similar degree of social pressure (Maass et al., 1985).

Considered in this way, consistency becomes a crucial variable. Although the minority viewpoint may initially be perceived as incorrect, the minority's resistance to group pressure may soon enhance its credibility. In fact, there are numerous historical examples of minorities that were victims of repression and persecution and that were highly influential in the long run (e.g., Galileo).

The traditional distinction between "knowledge" and "reporting bias" (Eagly, Chaiken, & Wood, 1982) assumes that source credibility is determined by two largely independent factors. On one hand, communicators may be biased because their knowledge on a given issue is limited or idiosyncratic. On the other hand, they may very well possess complete and correct knowledge, but report on it in a biased manner. Applying this distinction, the majority may be perceived as possessing unbiased knowledge, but the minority may be perceived as more credible in terms of the reporting bias. Maass and Clark (1984) have argued that, compared to a majority, a minority may be perceived as more convinced of and committed to its position because it is resisting considerable group pressure from members of the majority in their attempt to reach group consensus. This argument is in line with Kelley's (1971) augmenting principle, that the attribution of an event (consistent behavior of the influence source) to a facilitative cause (conviction and commitment to a given position) will be more likely when an inhibitory cause (social pressure against the advocated position) is also present. At the same time, an increase in social pressure makes reaching a public agreement with the minority more difficult. Thus, as the social pressure increases (e.g., with increasing size of the majority against which the minority is defending its position), people should become more likely to attribute certainty and commitment to the consistent minority. They should be increasingly motivated to process the minority message and thus more likely to change their private attitudes toward the minority opinion. Yet, with increasing social pressure, people should become less likely to adopt the minority opinion in public. Thus social pressure should facilitate conversion while impeding compliance. This social pressure hypothesis can explain why consistent minorities produce more conversion than majorities, but have a smaller public impact. Surprisingly little research has been done to investigate the role of relative social pressure in majority and minority influence.

As pointed out elsewhere (Maass & Clark, 1984; Maass et al., 1985), the relative social power of the majority may not only serve as an augmenting cue for the minority but also as a discounting cue for the majority. The behavior of any given majority member is attributionally ambiguous. It may either indicate belief in the advocated position or yielding to social pressure.

Some indirect evidence for augmenting/discounting as a function of majority pressure comes from a study by Wilder (1978). Subjects in this study observed an actor who either agreed or disagreed with the remaining group members. The actor's disagreement was attributed to dispositional cause whereas agreement was attributed to situational factors (social pressure). Interestingly, this pattern of attribution was not found when the actor was perceived as merely part of an aggregate rather than a group.

Additional evidence for the link between social pressure and the perception of certainty comes from a study by Nemeth, Wachtler, & Endicott (1977). In line with the augmenting principle, minorities were found to be perceived as increasingly certain (but less competent) as the number of minority members decreased. Nemeth et al., however, increased the number of minority members holding the size of the majority constant rather than holding the size of the minority constant and varying the social pressure put on the minority. Further, neither Nemeth et al. nor Wilder distinguished between private and public attitude change. Thus a systematic investigation of the role of social pressure in minority influence is needed.

The same discounting cue (social pressure) may also affect the subject's self-inference of an attitudinal position. From the perspective of self-perception theory (Bem, 1972), if subjects agree publicly with a powerful majority, they will be unlikely to infer that their true private attitudes are consistent with their statements. Note, however, that the self-perception analysis is applicable "to the extent internal cues are weak, ambiguous, or uninterpretable" (p. 2), circumstances that do not characterize most minority influence research paradigms, although they may characterize many real-world minority-influence settings. To this point, we have considered various minority characteristics that may explain why minorities attract greater attention and elicit deeper cognitive processing. In particular, we have argued: (a) Minorities are more *distinct,* therefore they draw more attention, they are evaluated more extremely, and their message is remembered longer and more accurately. (b) Minorities have a *lower a priori credibility;* because they are assumed to be wrong, people seem to have greater motivation to attend to the stimulus for nonsocial validation of their opinion. Finally, disagreement with a low credibility source is less stressful. Because people are only moderately aroused, they attend to a wider range of relevant cues. (c) Minorities are exposed to considerable *social pressure* from the majority; if they are consistent despite group pressure, people are motivated to give careful consideration to their message. Thus social pressure seems to facilitate conversion while impeding compliance.

WHEN DOES CONVERSION SURFACE IN PUBLIC?

In general, minority-induced conversion is not manifest in the group situation. Yet, from an applied point of view, it is often the public or manifest behavior that is most relevant. The impact of an anti-Contra minority has little political relevance as long as it is limited to private attitudes. Along the same line, a feminist minority would hardly be satisfied if its influence were to remain latent. Thus, from an applied point of view, it is important to understand when conversion effects will surface on the public level.

Maass and Clark (1984) proposed that people may refuse to agree publicly with the minority position in order to save face in front of majority group members. Considering the low a priori credibility of the deviant minority, it is hardly surprising that people do not want to be associated with it. Such self-presentational motivations have been widely investigated in the persuasion literature. People seem to be very sensitive to potential evaluations by the persuasive agent and/or by independent observers, and often monitor the public expression of their attitudes so as to produce positive evaluations from others. For example, they dissociate from disliked others by expressing strongly dissimilar attitudes (e.g., Cooper & Jones, 1969). They may yield in the presence of the influence source, but resist persuasion attempts when independent observers are present who are expected to derogate yielders (e.g., Braver, Linder, Corwin, & Cialdini, 1977).

Although the role of self-presentational strategies in minority influence has not yet been investigated systematically, it is likely that these motivations are an important determinant of whether or not private attitude change will surface in public. Suggestive evidence comes from four areas of research. First, several investigations have demonstrated that minority influence is facilitated when the normative context stresses originality rather than objectivity (Moscovici & Lage, 1978) or when the zeitgeist favors the minority position (e.g., Paicheler, 1976, 1978). Second, it has generally been observed that subjects are more likely to yield to a deviant minority after the minority has left the influence setting. Thus people seem to avoid being identified with the minority, thereby assuming majority status (Moscovici, 1980; Mugny, 1982). Third, public agreement is facilitated when the deviant minority offers a compromise at the very last minute (Nemeth & Brilmayer, 1987). Fourth, people seem particularly reluctant to agree with out-group minorities. Various studies have found that out-group minorities belonging to a distinctly different social category (e.g., different gender, sexual preference, school) have considerably less impact on people's public attitudes than in-group minorities (Maass et al., 1982; Mugny, Kaiser, & Papastamou, 1983). Interestingly, this is not true for *private* attitudes. Out-group minorities may actually have a greater indirect impact than in-group minorities (Aebischer, Hewstone, & Henderson, 1984; Martin, 1985). Taken together, these results suggest that people are reluctant to admit persuasion effects in public when the minority is a member of a derogated out-group. Conversion effects are more likely to become public when in-group minorities are involved, when the minority is absent altogether, or when the normative context facilitates agreement with the minority.

METHODOLOGICAL CONSIDERATIONS

In closing, a methodological comment seems warranted. Although new, creative research designs have emerged in recent years (e.g., Nemeth, 1986), the area is still characterized by a number of shortcomings that may hamper theoretical development (see Maass & Clark, 1984).

First, experimental tasks vary widely from uninvolving perceptual tasks (e.g., finding word strings, labeling colors) to moderately involving discussions of social issues (e.g., death penalty, gay rights, pollution). Some of these tasks are concerned with performance (e.g., discovering hidden figures, Nemeth & Wachtler, 1983), others with opinions (e.g., are individual consumers or industry to be blamed for pollution, Mugny, 1982). On the dependent variable side, conversion has been operationalized in diverse ways. Although the similarity of results across paradigms and dependent measures is certainly encouraging, it may lead to the questionable assumption that the wide array of findings results from equivalent processes. Persuasion research suggests that people engage in different thought processes depending on their level of ego-involvement (see Petty & Cacioppo, 1981). Along the same line, three decades of research on social comparison informs us that people turn to different individuals for comparison depending on whether they are evaluating performance-related abilities or opinions (see Suls, 1977; Goethals & Darley, 1977). Thus it is very well possible that the different facets of conversion operate by different mechanisms.

This argument is closely related to our second criticism, namely the continuing omission of process-oriented research. Although it seems intuitively convincing that minorities produce conversion-specific thought processes because of their distinctiveness, low a priori credibility, and resistance to group pressure and that these cognitive processes are, in turn, responsible for the conversion effect, there is little empirical evidence for the causal relations among these factors. To this point, only a few causal links have been investigated (e.g., between nondefensive thinking and conversion, Maass & Clark, 1983). Other hypothesized processes have not been supported. As a case in point, Richardson and Cialdini (1983) found that attributions of confidence and changes in judgment were independent effects of minority influence; attributions of confidence did not mediate changes in judgment. We strongly believe that process-oriented research is needed to probe the numerous mechanisms now hypothesized to underlie conversion. Such research needs to include both direct manipulation of factors that are expected to affect the proposed causal processes and careful measurement of indicators of those processes. Through the application of techniques from causal modeling (Kenny, 1979; Baron & Kenny, 1986), the success of each of the competing theoretical perspectives in accounting for the data from the full array of minority influence paradigms can be compared. In the long run, this approach will help winnow the number of theoretical accounts that are competing as potential explanations of minority influence and conversion.

NOTES

1. Studies using the chromatic complementary afterimage measure have yielded two successful demonstrations (Moscovici & Personnaz, 1980; Personnaz, 1981) and two

clearly unsuccessful demonstrations (Doms & Van Avermaet, 1980; Sorrentino, King, & Leo, 1980) of minority influence effects. Two speculative methodological explanations of the lack of robustness of the afterimage effects may be offered. First, the perceived hue of afterimages is known to be dependent on such variables as the amount of adaptation time, the luminance of the original stimulus, and the luminance of the projection field (Brown, 1965; Cornsweet, 1970). These factors have been poorly controlled in minority influence research to date. The likelihood of successful minority influence in this paradigm may be increased as the ambiguity of the hue of the stimulus being judged (i.e., the afterimage) increases. Second, the two successful demonstrations of minority influence have both used French-speaking subjects. Like trait terms (John, Goldberg, & Angleitner, 1984), judgments of color may differ as a function of nationality and language, making it necessary to recalibrate the stimulus parameters to demonstrate the afterimage effect with English-speaking subjects.

2. In this chapter we will focus exclusively on dual process approaches that assume that different processes underlie majority and minority influence. Single process models have also been proposed (Latané & Wolf, 1981; Tanford & Penrod, 1984; Wolf, in press); these are reviewed elsewhere in this volume (Levine & Russo, 1987). Comparisons of the single and dual process approaches can be found in Maass and Clark (1984), and Chaiken and Stangor (1987).

3. Further suggestive evidence comes from a study by Tesser, Campbell, and Mickler (1983) in which subjects were found to pay somewhat more attention to the stimulus when exposed to one rather than three others insisting on a deviate viewpoint. However, these findings are only tangentially relevant since the exposure to a single source of influence does not exactly resemble the minority influence paradigm.

4. Note, however, that cognitive processing of the minority versus majority position was assessed as a within-subjects variable. As pointed out by Chaiken & Stangor (1987), quantitative differences in cognitive activity may be better tested in a between-subjects design.

5. Note that source credibility may also explain why people process the majority message in a more defensive way than the message of the less credible minority (Maass & Clark, 1983). Since majorities are assumed to be correct, disagreement with them requires greater justification. Therefore, people will expend more effort to discount the arguments of the majority than those of a minority.

REFERENCES

Aebischer, V., Hewstone, M., & Henderson, M. (1984). Minority influence and musical performance: Innovation by conversion not coercion. *European Journal of Social Psychology, 14,* 23-34.

Allen, V. L., & Wilder, D. A. (1978). Social comparison, self-evaluation, and group conformity. In J. M. Suls & R. L. Miller (Eds.), *Social comparison processes* (pp. 187-208). New York: Halstead Press.

Asch, S. E. (1956). Studies of independence and conformity: A minority of one against a unanimous majority. *Psychological Monographs, 70* (9, Whole No. 416).

Bacon, S. J. (1974). Arousal and the range of cue utilization. *Journal of Experimental Psychology, 102,* 81-87.

Baron, R. M., & Kenny, D. A. (1986). The moderator-mediator distinction in social psychology: Conceptual, strategic and statistical considerations. *Journal of Personality and Social Psychology, 51,* 1173-1182.

Bem, D. J. (1972). Self-perception theory. In L. Berkowitz (Ed.), *Advances in experimental social psychology* (Vol. 6, pp. 1-62). New York: Academic Press.

Braver, S. L., Linder, D. E., Corwin, T. T., & Cialdini, R. B. (1977). Some conditions that affect admissions of attitude change. *Journal of Experimental Social Psychology, 13,* 565-576.

Brown, J. L. (1965). Afterimages. In C. H. Graham (Ed.), *Vision and visual perception* (pp. 479-503). New York: John Wiley.

Chaiken, S. (1987). The heuristic model of persuasion. In M. Zanna, J. Olson, & C. P. Herman (Eds.), *Social influence: The Ontario Symposium* (Vol. 5, pp. 3-39). Hillsdale, NJ: Lawrence Erlbaum.

Chaiken, S., & Stangor, C. (1987). Attitudes and attitude change. *Annual Review of Psychology, 38,* 575-630.

Cialdini, R. B., Petty, R. E., & Cacioppo, J. T. (1981). Attitudes and attitude change. *Annual Review of Psychology, 32,* 357-404.

Cooper, J., & Jones, E. E. (1969). Opinion divergence as a strategy to avoid being miscast. *Journal of Personality and Social Psychology, 13,* 23-30.

Cornsweet, T. N. (1970). *Visual perception.* New York: Academic Press.

Deutsch, M., & Gerard, H. B. (1955). A study of normative and informational social influences upon individual judgment. *Journal of Abnormal and Social Psychology, 51,* 629-636.

Doms, M., & Van Avermaet, E. (1980). Majority influence, minority influence and coversion behavior: A replication. *Journal of Experimental Social Psychology, 16,* 283-292.

Duval, M., & Wicklund, R. A. (1972). *A theory of objective self awareness.* New York: Academic Press.

Eagly, A. H., Chaiken, S., & Wood, W. (1982). An attribution analysis of persuasion. In J. H. Harvey, W. Ickes, & R. F. Kidd (Eds.), *New directions in attribution theory and research* (Vol. 3, pp. 37-62). Hillsdale, NJ: Lawrence Erlbaum.

Easterbrook, J. A. (1959). The effect of emotion on cue utilization and other organization of behavior. *Psychological Review, 66,* 183-201.

Festinger, L. (1954). A theory of social comparison processes. *Human Relations, 7,* 117-140.

Freeman, S., Walker, M. R., Bordon, R., & Latané, B. (1975). Diffusion of responsibility and restaurant tipping: Cheaper by the bunch. *Personality and Social Psychology Bulletin, 1,* 584-587.

Goethals, G. R., & Darley, J. M. (1977). Social comparison theory: An attributional approach. In J. M. Suls & R. L. Miller (Eds.), *Social comparison process: Theoretical and empirical perspectives* (pp. 259-278). New York: Halstead Press.

Guillon, M., & Personnaz, B. (1983). Analyse de la dynamique des representation des conflits minoitaire et majoritaire. *Cahiers de Psychologie Cognitive, 3,* 65-87.

Heesacker, M., Petty, R. E., & Cacioppo, J. T. (1983). Field dependence and attitude change: Source credibility can alter persuasion by affecting message-relevant thinking. *Journal of Personality, 51,* 653-666.

Houts, A. C., Cook, T. D., & Shadish, W. R., Jr. (1986). The person-situation debate: A critical multiplist perspective. *Journal of Personality, 54,* 52-105.

John, O. P., Goldberg, L. R., & Angleitner, A. (1984). Better alphabet: Taxonomies of personality-descriptive terms in English, Dutch, and German. In H. Bonarius, G. van Heck, & N. Smid (Eds.), *Personality psychology in Europe: Theoretical and empirical developments* (pp. 83-100). Lisse: Swets & Zeitlinger.

Kelley, H. H. (1971). Causal schemata and the attribution process. In E. E. Jones, D. E. Kanouse, H. H. Kelley, R. E. Nisbett, S. Valins, & B. Weiner (Eds.), *Attribution: Perceiving the causes of behavior* (pp. 151-174). Morristown, NJ: General Learning Press.

Kelman, H. C. (1958). Compliance, identification, and internalization: Three processes of attitude change. *Journal of Conflict Resolution, 2,* 51-60.

Kenny, D. A. (1979). *Correlation and causality.* New York: John Wiley.

Latane, B., & Wolf, S. (1981). The social impact of majorities and minorities. *Psychological Review, 88,* 438-453.

Levine, J. M., & Russo, E. M. (1987). Majority and minority influence. In C. Hendrick (Ed.), *Review of Personality and Social Psychology* (Vol. 8). Newbury Park, CA: Sage.

Maass, A., & Clark, R. D., III (1983). Internalization vs. compliance: Differential processes underlying minority influence and conformity. *European Journal of Social Psychology, 13,* 197-215.

Maass, A., & Clark, R. D., III (1984). Hidden impact of minorities: Fifteen years of minority influence research. *Psychological Bulletin, 95,* 428-450.

Maass, A., & Clark, R. D., III (1986). Conversion theory and simultaneous majority/minority influence: Can reactance offer an alternative explanation? *European Journal of Social Psychology, 16,* 305-309.

Maass, A., Clark, R. D., III, & Haberkorn, G. (1982). The effects of differential ascribed category membership and norms on minority influence. *European Journal of Social Psychology, 12,* 89-104.

Maass, A., West, S. G., & Clark, R. D., III (1985). Soziale einflusse von minoritaten in gruppen. In D. Frey & M. Irle (Eds.), *Theorien der Sozialpsychologie* (Vol. 2, pp. 65-91). Bern: Huber.

Martin, R. (1985). *Minority influence and social categorization: An intergroup explanation.* Paper presented at the Small Group Meeting on "Minority Influence: The Conversion Effect," Geneva, Switzerland (November).

Moscovici, S. (1980). Toward a theory of conversion behavior. In L. Berkowitz (Ed.), *Advances in Experimental Social Psychology* (Vol. 13, pp. 209-239). New York: Academic Press.

Moscovici, S. (1985). Social influence and conformity. In G. Lindzey & E. Aronson (Eds.), *Handbook of Social Psychology* (Vol. 2, 3rd ed., pp. 347-412). New York: Random House.

Moscovici, S., & Lage, E. (1976). Studies in social influence III: Majority vs. minority influence in a group. *European Journal of Social Psychology, 6,* 149-174.

Moscovici, S., & Lage, E. (1978). Studies in social influence IV: Minority influence in a context of original judgments. *European Journal of Social Psychology, 8,* 349-365.

Moscovici, S., Mugny, G., & Van Avermaet, E. (1985). *Perspectives on minority influence.* New York: Cambridge University Press.

Moscovici, S., & Personnaz, B. (1980). Studies in social influence V: Minority influence and conversion behavior in a perceptual task. *Journal of Experimental Social Psychology, 16,* 270-282.

Mugny, G. (1974-75). Majorite et minorite: Le niveau de leur influence. *Bulletin de Psychologie, 28,* 831-835.

Mugny, G. (1976). Quelle influence majoritaire? Quelle influence minoritaire? *Revue Suisse de Psychologie, 4,* 255-268.

Mugny, G. (1982). *The power of minorities.* New York: Academic Press.

Mugny, G. (1985). Direct and indirect influence in the Asch paradigm: Effect of "valid" or "denied" information. *European Journal of Social Psychology, 15,* 457-461.

Mugny, G., Kaiser, C., & Papastamou, S. (1983). Influence minoritaire, identification et relations entre groups: Etude experimental autour d'une votation. *Cahiers de Psychologie Sociale, 19,* 1-30.

Mullen, B. (1983). Operationalizing the effect of the group on the individual: A self-attention perspective. *Journal of Experimental Social Psychology, 19,* 295-322.

Nemeth, C. (1986). Differential contributions of majority and minority influence. *Psychological Review, 93,* 23-32.

Nemeth, C., & Brilmayer, A. G. (1987). Negotiation vs. influence. *European Journal of Social Psychology.*

Nemeth, C., & Kwan, J. (1985). Originality of word associations as a function of majority vs. minority influence. *Social Psychology Quarterly, 48,* 277-282.

Nemeth, C., & Kwan, J. (1987). Minority influence, divergent thinking and detection of correct solutions. *Journal of Applied Social Psychology, 17.*

Nemeth, C., & Mayseless, O. (1986). *Enhancing recall: The contributions of conflict, minorities and consistency.* Manuscript submitted for publication.

Nemeth, C., & Wachtler, J. (1974). Creating perceptions of consistency and confidence: A necessary condition for minority influence. *Sociometry, 37,* 529-540.

Nemeth, C., & Wachtler, J. (1983). Creative problem solving as a result of majority vs. minority influence. *European Journal of Social Psychology, 13,* 45-55.

Nemeth, C., Wachtler, J., & Endicott, J. (1977). Increasing the size of the minority: Some gains and some losses. *European Journal of Social Psychology, 7,* 15-27.

Newcomb, T. (1943). *Personality and social change: Attitude formation in a student community.* New York: Holt, Rinehart & Winston.

Paicheler, G. (1976). Norms and attitude change: I. Polarization and styles of behavior. *European Journal of Social Psychology, 6,* 405-427.

Paicheler, G. (1978). Norms and attitude change: II. The phenomenon bipolarization. *European Journal of Social Psychology, 7,* 5-14.

Personnaz, B. (1981). Study in social influence using the spectrometer method: Dynamics of the phenomena of conversion and covertness in perceptual responses. *European Journal of Social Psychology, 11,* 431-438.

Petty, R. E., & Cacioppo, J. T. (1981). *Attitudes and persuasion: Classic and contemporary approaches.* Dubuque, IA: W. C. Brown.

Petty, R. E., & Cacioppo, J. T. (1986). The elaboration likelihood model of persuasion. In L. Berkowitz (Ed.), *Advances in experimental social psychology* (Vol. 19, pp. 123-205). New York: Academic Press.

Petty, R. E., Ostrom, T. M., & Brock, T. C. (1981). Historical foundations of the cognitive response approach to persuasion. In R. E. Petty, T. M. Ostrom, & T. C. Brock (Eds.), *Cognitive responses to persuasion* (pp. 5-29). Hillsdale, NJ: Lawrence Erlbaum.

Richardson, K. D. (1985). *Social change in groups: The influence of deviant minority factions.* Unpublished doctoral dissertation, Arizona State University.

Richardson, K. D., & Cialdini, R. B. (1983). *Factors related to social change: Shifts in group judgments induced by deviant minorities.* Unpublished manuscript, Arizona State University.

Schachter, S. (1951). Deviation, rejection, and communication. *Journal of Abnormal and Social Psychology, 46,* 190-207.

Sherif, M. (1935). *The psychology of social norms.* New York: Harper & Row.

Sorrentino, R. M., King, G., & Leo, G. (1980). The influence of the minority on perception: A note on a possible alternative explanation. *Journal of Experimental Social Psychology, 16,* 293-301.

Suls, J. M. (1977). Social comparison theory and research: An overview from 1954. In J. M. Suls & R. L. Miller (Eds.), *Social comparison processes: Theoretical and empirical perspectives* (pp. 1-19). New York: Halstead Press.

Tanford, S., & Penrod, S. (1984). Social influence model: A formal integration of research on majority and minority influence processes. *Psychological Bulletin, 95,* 189-225.

Taylor, S. E. (1981). A categorization approach to stereotyping. In D. Hamilton (Ed.), *Cognitive processes in stereotyping and intergroup behavior* (pp. 83-114). Hillsdale, NJ: Lawrence Erlbaum.

Tesser, A., Campbell, J., & Mickler, S. (1983). The role of social pressure, attention to the stimulus, and self-doubt in conformity. *European Journal of Social Psychology, 13,* 217-234.

Wilder, D. A. (1978). Perceiving persons as a group: Effects on attributions of causality and beliefs. *Social Psychology, 1,* 13-23.

Wolf, S. (1985). Manifest and latent influence of majorities and minorities? *Journal of Personality and Social Psychology, 48,* 899-908.

Wolf, S. (in press). Majority and minority influence: A social impact analysis. In M. P. Zanna, J. M. Olson, & C. P. Herman (Eds.), *Social Influences: The Ontario Symposium* (Vol. 5). Hillsdale, NJ: Lawrence Erlbaum.

3

The Formation of Small Groups

RICHARD L. MORELAND

Richard L. Moreland is an Associate Professor in the Social/Personality Program of the Psychology Department at the University of Pittsburgh. A general interest in small groups has led him to study some of the changes that inevitably occur in such groups over time. These changes include the formation, development, and termination of small groups, and socialization processes within small groups.

Although many social psychologists are interested in small groups, few of them have studied how and why such groups form. This neglect is unfortunate, because research on the formation of small groups could yield important benefits. At a theoretical level, a better understanding of group formation could help to clarify many other phenomena that occur in small groups, since the conditions surrounding a group's formation often affect its subsequent development (see Back, 1951). At an applied level, a better understanding of group formation could also help those who rely on small groups for the improvement of their own lives or the lives of others (see Katz, 1981). If these persons knew more about how to successfully create small groups, or about how to accurately predict the natural formation of such groups, then their goals could be accomplished more easily. Clearly, more research on group formation is needed.

The purpose of this chapter is to generate greater interest among social psychologists in studying the formation of small groups. My approach is to provide an integrative review of previous theoretical and empirical work on group formation. Because group formation is poorly understood at present, I have conceived of it in very broad terms. Materials for the chapter were thus gathered from a wide variety of sources representing nearly all of the social sciences. At least some of those materials did not involve group formation at all, but focused instead on other topics (e.g., the initiation of close personal relationships

AUTHOR'S NOTE: My thanks go to Celia Brownell, Sam Gaertner, John Levine, David Wilder, and Nancy Moreland for their helpful and supportive comments during the writing of this chapter.

or the founding of business organizations) that seemed relevant. This emphasis on breadth of coverage may have limited the depth of my analysis; I certainly have no comprehensive "theory" of group formation to offer. But such a theory may be premature when so little about the formation of small groups is really known. For now, it seems more useful to simply summarize what *is* known about group formation and offer whatever insights I can into that phenomenon.

GROUP FORMATION THROUGH SOCIAL INTEGRATION

An analysis of group formation raises several complex issues. One such issue involves the meaning of the term "group." In order to determine whether a group has formed, someone must be able to specify what a group is. Unfortunately, there is little agreement among social psychologists about the "essential" characteristics of small groups (see DeLameter, 1974). And it seems unlikely that anyone will produce a definitive listing of those characteristics anytime soon. Perhaps we should abandon these efforts to distinguish groups from nongroups and consider instead a hypothetical dimension of "groupness" that is relevant to every set of persons. Group formation could then be regarded as a *continuous* phenomenon involving the movement of a set of persons along that dimension, rather than as a *discontinuous* phenomenon involving the transformation of a nongroup into a group. A second and related issue involves the meaning of the term "formation," which suggests a special *event* that occurs at some particular place and time. Although some artificial groups may arise in this way, most natural groups do not. Perhaps we should analyze the "forming" of small groups rather than their formation and thereby acknowledge that group formation is a *process* that unfolds over time. What is that process? I believe that it involves "social integration," or a strengthening of the bonds among persons.

Sociologists have long been interested in social integration and have provided many insightful analyses of it. Some theorists (e.g., Durkheim, 1893/1964; Gross, 1956) have argued that social bonds are based on either shared beliefs or the need for cooperative effort. Other theorists (e.g., Feldman, 1968; Hagstrom & Selvin, 1965; Lott & Lott, 1965) have noted that social bonds can also be based on feelings of interpersonal attraction. My own reading of the literature suggests that there are at least four types of social integration involved in the formation of small groups: *environmental integration, behavioral integration, affective integration,* and *cognitive integration.* Because group formation is a continuous process rather than a discrete event, these different types of social integration should not be regarded as *causes* for the formation of small groups. They are instead *aspects* or varieties of group formation. One might say that a small group has formed insofar as environmental, behavioral, affective, and cognitive integration have taken place.

Environmental Integration

Sometimes small groups form through the environmental integration of their members. This can occur whenever the environment provides the resources (e.g., people, money, time) necessary for a group to form. Most research on environmental integration has focused on the *physical environment*, which can affect the formation of small groups in several ways. One such effect involves propinquity; people who live or work in close proximity to one another often become friends. Festinger, Schachter, and Back (1950), for example, performed a classic study on the formation of friendships among married students living in a university apartment complex. Because these students were assigned to their apartments randomly, those who lived closer together were not especially similar to one another, nor were they more likely than others to be prior acquaintances. Yet when asked to name their closest friends within the apartment complex, the students were more likely to name people who lived closer to them than those who lived farther away. Similar studies performed in other settings have produced analogous results; a review of this work can be found in Stokols (1978).

Of course, small groups can form even among people who do not live or work together. Some settings contain special sites where people tend to congregate, and the resulting interaction can forge friendships among persons who might otherwise have little contact with one another. Willsie and Riemer (1980), for example, described the role of campus bars in the formation of college student groups. These bars attract students because they provide a variety of benefits, including goods, services, entertainments, and chances for social contacts. The pleasantness of a setting can also affect the formation of small groups, regardless of how many people occupy that setting. People who meet in more pleasant settings are more likely than others to become friends. Environmental psychologists have identified several factors that can affect the pleasantness of a setting (see Russell & Ward, 1982). These factors include temperature, noise level, air quality, and the degree of crowding. Settings that people find more interesting, or that offer people a greater sense of personal control, also seem to promote feelings of attraction.

Just as people live and work within a physical environment, they also inhabit a *social environment* that can have effects of its own on the formation of small groups. Research on the social environment has focused primarily on "social networks." A social network is a pattern of relationships among one's relatives, friends, and acquaintances. Many descriptive studies of social networks have been conducted (see Boissevain, 1974; Feger, 1981) and several important characteristics of such networks have been identified. These characteristics include the total size of the network, its composition, the frequency, duration, and type of interactions that occur among network members, the network's "density" (ratio of actual to potential relationships among members), and so on. When the networks of two or more people are compared, their degree of "overlap" can also be measured. This overlap among social networks often leads to group formation (see Kerckhoff, 1974; Milardo, 1986).

There are two major ways in which social networks can affect the formation of small groups. First, social networks generate opportunities for contacts among persons. The more friends and acquaintances people share, the more likely they are to interact and thereby become friends. Although there is some anecdotal evidence for this first effect (e.g., Kravetz, 1978), it has not yet been investigated thoroughly. Second, social networks develop, communicate, and enforce norms about who should interact with whom. The more social support there is for the formation of a group, the more likely it is to form. Several researchers have investigated this second effect, primarily as it influences romantic relationships. Two especially interesting studies of this sort were performed by Lewis (1973) and by Parks, Stan, and Eggert (1983).

Lewis studied the influence of "reflection" and "labeling" by social network members on the development of college students' romantic relationships. Dating couples were asked how often their relatives, friends, and acquaintances treated them like a couple (reflection) or referred to them as a "couple" (labeling). Several months later, the strength of each couple's relationship was assessed. Couples who initially reported more reflection and labeling by their social networks had stronger relationships later on than couples whose social networks were less supportive. Parks, Stan, and Eggert studied more direct forms of social support for the romantic relationships of college students.

Dating couples were asked to describe the composition of their social networks, their contacts with and attitudes toward the members of those networks, and the degree to which network members actively encouraged their romance. The strength of each couple's romantic relationship was also assessed. Couples who received more support from their social networks had stronger relationships than couples whose social networks were less supportive. Although the couples in both of these studies were already dating, the potential relevance of the results to the formation of romantic relationships seems clear.

Another area of research on social networks that seems relevant to group formation involves relationships among people who are in the same profession or who work for the same organization. Research on professional relationships has focused on the "invisible colleges" that seem to form among scientists in many fields (see Crane, 1972). Unfortunately, researchers have been less interested in discovering how or why such groups form than in analyzing their effects on the scientific process. It is interesting to note, however, that invisible colleges are usually dominated by a single person who serves as an advocate for some special viewpoint (often unorthodox) shared by other members of the group. The possible role of such leaders in the formation of invisible colleges deserves further study. Research on the relationships among coworkers has focused on the "cliques" that seem to form within every organization (see Payne & Cooper, 1981). These cliques often reflect the simple effects of propinquity; people who work together interact frequently and thus are likely to become friends. But cliques can also form among coworkers who are similar to one another in important ways (e.g., age, sex, race, job classification), or who share some basic need (e.g., social support, career advancement, access to information) that membership in the clique can satisfy. In either case, both the number and types of cliques that arise within an organization should depend on such factors as its size and complexity, the characteristics of its workers, and the kinds of problems that they face on the job. Although some theorists have speculated about these matters (e.g., Tichy, 1973), little evidence has yet been gathered.

Finally, some of the most interesting research on social networks involves the study of groups with shared members (e.g., Alba & Kadushin, 1976). Research on these shared memberships is relevant to group formation in at least two ways. First, people who belong to many of the same groups can be regarded as an emergent group themselves. One might study why these persons share so many memberships, whether they are aware of that fact or not, and how (or if) they use those memberships to their own advantage. Second, people who belong to the same groups are more likely than others to form new groups reflecting their common interests. For example, Curtis and Zurcher (1973) studied the emergence and growth of community antipornography groups. Members of those groups were asked to name any other community groups to which they belonged. Their responses revealed that people who belonged to the same antipornography group often shared other group memberships as well, and that at least one antipornography group was formed when people who belonged to a community service group began to discuss the need for family-oriented films in local theaters.

Although the effects of the physical and social environments on group formation have received more research attention, the *cultural environment* within which people live and work may also be important. Several studies have shown that both the number and the types of groups to which people belong can vary considerably from one country to another within the same time period (e.g., Bennett, 1979), and from one time period to another within the same country (Thomson, 1985). These results suggest that cultural factors may play a role in the formation of small groups. One such factor is urbanization. Urban environments generally contain a greater number and variety of small groups than do rural environments, but the reasons for this effect are unclear. Wirth (1938) argued that the size, density, and heterogeneity of cities not only produce feelings of alienation among residents, but also weaken their relationships with family members and friends. City dwellers thus form other kinds of groups as a means of coping with their loneliness. Although these arguments seem plausible, the available research evidence does not support them (Korte, 1980). People who live in large cities, for example, get along with their friends and relatives just as well as people who live in small towns, and friends and relatives often recruit people into small groups. The level of empirical support for other theories about the effects of urbanization on social behavior is somewhat better, but still weak. The real cause for those effects is not yet known.

Another cultural factor that might affect the formation of new groups is the presence of old groups. Groups that coexist must compete to some extent for both the acquisition of new members and the commitment of old members (McPherson, 1983). This competition should inhibit the formation of new groups, especially when the number of old groups is large. However, most people probably belong to fewer groups than they could, given the time, energy, and other resources available to them. And specialization can allow new groups to form even when the competition among old groups is severe. The inhibiting effects of competition among old groups on the formation of new groups may thus be minimal in many settings. There are several ways in which old groups might even facilitate the formation of new groups (see Stinchcombe, 1965). First, people who belong to small groups and appear to be satisfied with them may serve as models for those who have not yet become group members. Second, people who are satisfied with their current group memberships may be more willing and able to later form (or join) other groups. Third, the more small groups people join, the more likely they are to belong to some of the same groups; these shared memberships can (as noted earlier) lead to the formation of new groups. Finally, some small groups may help others to form if their members share common goals.

A final cultural factor that might affect group formation is freedom. In order to form small groups, people must be free to do so. All too often, that freedom is lacking. For example, in authoritarian societies there are often laws that prohibit the formation of groups with certain political or religious orientations. Even in democratic societies, there are often norms that discourage contacts among people from different social strata. And in any society, poverty, ignorance, and physical or social isolation can prevent people from forming groups by limiting their awareness of one another. All of this serves as a reminder that group formation can depend as much on opportunity as it does on motivation.

As a closing note, the physical, social, and cultural environments are clearly related to one another in complex ways. It thus may be possible to develop a more general theory of how environmental factors affect social behavior. Several ambitious attempts along these lines have already been made (see Micklin, 1984). Most of this work is based on ecological concepts borrowed from the biological sciences. Pennings (1980), for example, showed how the ecological analysis of an urban area could be useful in understanding changes in the growth of new industrial organizations there. As analyses of this sort become more sophisticated,they may yield valuable insights into the formation of small groups.

Behavioral Integration

Sometimes small groups form through the behavioral integration of their members. This can occur whenever people become dependent on one another for the satisfaction of their needs. The behavioral integration of group members is so compelling that many theorists have regarded it as the key to group formation (see Turner, 1985). Several different theoretical perspectives on behavioral integration have been offered, each providing its own unique answers to the questions of how and why small groups form. They suggest that a variety of important needs can be satisfied through memberships in small groups.

Some social scientists have taken an *evolutionary perspective* on behavioral integration. Advocates of this perspective (e.g., Alexander, 1979) argue that membership in small groups enhances "inclusive fitness," or the ability of a person to pass his or her genetic heritage on to another generation. The potential advantages of group membership in this regard are clear. Group members are healthier and stronger than solitary persons, enjoy greater access to sexual partners, and are safer from predators. Because of these and other advantages, the process of natural selection favors people who are group members. The cumulative result of that process, over a long period of time, is the development of social instincts that lead people to form or join small groups.

Research arising from this evolutionary perspective has focused on a variety of interesting issues. One such issue is whether people really are drawn instinctively to small groups. Recent work by developmental psychologists shows that even infants behave in ways that seem designed to foster relationships with other people, and that these behaviors become increasingly sophisticated with age (Hartup, 1983). By the end of their first year, children develop a propensity to "attach" themselves to specific persons (Bowlby, 1979). Parents play an important role in the formation of these early attachments and children whose early attachments are stronger have more success at establishing and maintaining other social relationships later on (LaFreniere & Sroufe, 1985). Finally, both deprivation and satiation effects involving social approval have been observed among children of many ages (Eisenberger, 1970). Children who are deprived of social interaction become more responsive to the approval of others, whereas children who are satiated with social interaction become less responsive to that approval. These and other findings suggest that social instincts indeed exist, and that they can have a strong influence on behavior.

Another interesting issue is whether social instincts could ever have been produced by natural selection. Consider the problems that might be faced by a sociable and cooperative person surrounded by unsociable and competitive others. How could that person survive, let alone prosper? An intriguing attempt to answer these questions was made by Axelrod and Hamilton (1981), who programmed a computer to play the Prisoner's Dilemma Game. The computer created several "players" and then conducted a "tournament" among them. Each player used a unique game "strategy." These strategies varied not only in complexity, but also in their emphasis on cooperation or competition. As it turned out, the winning player used a strategy called "Tit for Tat," which involved cooperation on the first move of each game and then copying the moves of its opponent thereafter. This was one of the simplest and most cooperative strategies used in the tournament. Subsequent tournaments provided further evidence for the viability of this cooperative strategy, even within largely competitive environments. Of course, the external validity of simulations like these must be considered carefully, but their results suggest that social instincts could have evolved through natural selection.

A final issue is whether the same environmental pressures that made group membership so valuable in the past still lead people to join small groups today. The available evidence (see Boissevain, 1974; Gottlieb, 1983) suggests that modern groups are indeed used for a variety of purposes, including courtship, career advancement, and social support. The use of small groups as a tool for coping with stress and anxiety has received the most research attention. A classic experiment by Schachter (1959) illustrated this phenomenon. Subjects in that experiment believed that they would be participating in a physiological study of human responses to electrical shock. While waiting for the study to begin, everyone was given a choice between waiting alone or with other people. Those who expected to receive strong shocks preferred to wait with other people, whereas those who expected to receive mild shocks preferred to wait alone. Schachter argued that his results reflected a greater need among the more anxious subjects to determine whether their anxiety about participating in the study was justified. A subsequent experiment, in which anxious subjects chose to wait with others only when those persons also expected to receive electrical shocks, seemed to support this argument. But later research (see Cottrell & Epley, 1977) indicated that the effects of stress on affiliation were not so simple. Rofé (1984) recently offered an elegant analysis of those effects, proposing a "utility" theory of stress and affiliation. He argued that people under stress only seek out others when they believe that those persons will help them to cope with that stress. A similar point was made by Stein (1976) regarding the effects of external threats on group cohesiveness. He argued that an external threat increases the cohesiveness of a group only when its members believe that they can overcome that threat by working together. So the evidence suggests that people are not drawn together automatically by feelings of stress and anxiety, but affiliate only when they can be of some use to one another.

A *social exchange perspective* on behavioral integration has been taken by social scientists from many different disciplines. Advocates of this perspective (e.g., Homans, 1961; Kelley & Thibaut, 1978; Thibaut & Kelley, 1959) argue that social behavior is analogous to economic behavior. Every social relationship involves an "exchange" of behaviors that generate "rewards" and "costs" for the participants. People want to "profit" as much as possible from their relationships with others, so they seek relationships in which the rewards are high and the costs are low. The relevance of these considerations to the formation of small groups is clear. Groups that maximize the rewards and minimize the costs for their members are more likely to form. Any factor that might influence the rewards and costs of group membership should thus affect group formation as well. For example, large groups should form less often than small groups, because the latter are less costly to form and more likely to be rewarding. Heterogeneous groups should form less often than homogeneous groups for the same reasons.

The social exchange perspective has generated a great deal of research, much of it involving coalition formation (see Murnighan, 1978). Research on coalition formation involves situations in which several persons are striving for a goal that can be achieved by anyone possessing sufficient resources. Unfortunately, no single person has the resources needed to achieve that goal, so each person must consider the utility of forming a coalition with one or more of the others. Several theories of coalition formation have been developed, but bargaining theory (Komorita & Chertkoff, 1973) has received the best support. Bargaining theory is based on two general propositions. First, preferences for coalition partners depend not only on their ability to help a person achieve the goal, but also on their anticipated demands regarding the distribution of any rewards associated with goal achievement. People who possess more resources contribute more to a coalition's success, but also tend to demand more in return and may thus seem unattractive as potential coalition partners. Second, people who would like to form a coalition with one another bargain together about how to distribute any rewards associated with their achievement of the goal. Each person's bargaining power depends not only on the resources that are possessed, but also on the other coalitions that might be joined. A person with many options may bargain more confidently, and command greater respect from others, than someone whose options are fewer.

Attempts to study the formation of small groups from a social exchange perspective raise some interesting issues. One such issue involves the complexities of social exchange among several persons. Most social exchange theorists have focused their attention on dyadic relationships. Recently, however, some innovative efforts have been made to develop theories of social exchange "networks" (e.g., Emerson, 1972). One important aspect of such a network appears to be the level of "balance" among its participants. A balanced network is one in which each participant is equally dependent on all of the others. A network becomes imbalanced when patterns of differential dependency among participants arise. Consider, for example, a network that revolves around a single person. He or she generates many rewards and few costs for the other participants, but they generate few (or perhaps no) rewards or costs for one another. More complicated patterns of differential dependency among the participants in a social exchange network can also be imagined. Theorists interested in such networks have concentrated on the effects of imbalance on power, conformity, bargaining, and so on. But it seems clear that imbalance might have important effects on group formation as well.

Another issue worth noting involves the notion of fairness. In the process of forming a group, people often suffer a variety of costs. Time, energy, and money may all be required, and a certain amount of friction among members may occur. As a result, the costs of group membership often exceed its rewards at first. People are willing to make that sacrifice, but only if they can be assured of recouping their investment someday. Each person must believe that he or she will eventually enjoy rewards commensurate with the costs already suffered. This is only possible, however, when the rewards of belonging to a group can be divided among its members. Many rewards are indeed divisible, but others are not. Insofar as the rewards of a group are indivisible, no one may be willing to help form the group. They will be tempted instead to take advantage of efforts by others and to avoid letting others take advantage of them. Economists (e.g., Buchanan, 1965; Olson, 1965) are fascinated by this problem. Olson, for example, has argued that groups whose rewards are indivisible will not form at all unless (a) there are external forces pressuring people to form the group, (b) the group is so small that even indivisible rewards justify the minimal costs of its formation, (c) the "marginal costs" of forming the group are small, or (d) divisible rewards can be created and distributed among group members. Of course, problems can also arise in groups whose rewards are divisible when there are disagreements among members about how those rewards should be divided.

Some of these same issues have recently concerned sociologists who study social movements. Many theories regarding the origins of such movements have been developed. Initially, most of these theories focused on the role of shared grievances, such as feelings of relative deprivation, status inconsistency, or alienation, in the formation of social movements. Subsequent research, however, raised serious doubts about the adequacy of these theories. More recent theories have focused on the role of "resource mobilization" in the formation of social movements (e.g., McCarthy & Zald, 1977; Oberschall, 1973). According to these theories, shared grievances among the members of a social movement are less important than the ability of those members to mobilize whatever resources (e.g., labor, money, publicity) are necessary for the movement's success. Unfortunately, resource mobilization can be a costly business, and the rewards generated by a successful social movement are often indivisible. Under these conditions, it is surprising that such movements ever arise at all. What makes them possible is a social and/or cultural environment in which the costs of resource mobilization are low enough to justify whatever rewards a successful social movement will bring. Several environmental factors that facilitate the mobilization of resources have been identified. These factors include the existence of prior relationships among group members (to facilitate bloc recruiting), the help of leaders who are experienced organizers, support from other groups with similar goals, and a permissive attitude on the part of authorities.

Some social scientists have taken a *social evaluation perspective* on behavioral integration (e.g., Pettigrew, 1967). Advocates of that perspective argue that membership in small groups provides people with valuable information about themselves and the world around them. Many aspects of life are confusing, so people form or join small groups to resolve some of this confusion. Within such groups, a social rather than personal evaluation of the world can be made. These social evaluations often are (or seem to be) more accurate than those a person can make on his or her own.

The social evaluation perspective has generated two distinct lines of research. One can be found in social psychology and the other in sociology. Social psychological research on social evaluations began with the work of Festinger (1954), who believed that people are motivated to evaluate their abilities and opinions. The accuracy of these self-evaluations is important, so people base them on objective information whenever possible. When objective information is unavailable, people base their self-evaluations on subjective information instead, comparing their own abilities and opinions to those of other people. These "social comparisons" can be very informative, especially when they involve similar others. Festinger argued that a desire for social comparison information is responsible for the formation of most small groups.

Social comparison has been studied extensively (e.g., Suls & Miller, 1977). Some of those studies are relevant to group formation, because they involve the effects of uncertainty about abilities or opinions on a person's desire to affiliate with others. For example, Singer and Shockley (1965) asked subjects to perform a perceptual task and then gave them feedback about their own scores on that task. Some subjects were also given feedback about the scores of their fellow participants. During a subsequent pause in the procedure, all of the subjects were given a choice between waiting alone or together in a nearby room. Subjects who knew only their own scores were more interested in waiting together than were subjects who knew the scores of all participants. An analogous study was performed by Radloff (1961), who asked subjects for their opinions about the proper role of the government in educational funding. After expressing their own opinions on this issue, his subjects were given either no information about the opinions of others or (false and standardized) information about the opinions of people whose knowledge about the issue seemed inferior, equal, or superior to their own. All of the subjects were later given a chance to form small groups in which the issue of government funding for education could be discussed. Subjects who knew nothing about the opinions of others showed the greatest interest in forming such groups. Interest among the remaining subjects varied inversely with the perceived quality of the opinions about which they were informed.

In both of these studies, the importance of the subjects' self-evaluations was held constant while their uncertainty about those evaluations was varied. As that uncertainty increased, so did the subjects' desire to affiliate with others. These results suggest that any factor associated with the uncertainty of self-evaluations, such as a person's intelligence or access to objective evaluative criteria, might also affect the formation of small groups. Another approach might be to vary the importance of subjects' self-evaluations while holding their uncertainty about those evaluations constant. As the importance of evaluating their abilities or opinions increases, the subjects' desire to affiliate with others should increase too. This suggests that any factor associated with the importance of self-evaluations, such as situational pressures for accuracy, might affect the formation of small groups as well. Finally, if social comparisons with more similar persons lead to more accurate self-evaluations of abilities and opinions, then the desire of subjects to affiliate with others should vary directly with their actual or perceived similarity. Any factor that brings similar people together (e.g., housing, jobs) or leads people to regard one another as more similar (e.g., stereotypes, false consensus effects), should thus promote the formation of small groups.

A second line of research reflecting the social evaluation perspective can be found in sociology. Sociological research on social evaluations was stimulated by the work of Merton (1976) and others on "reference groups." A reference group is a set of persons used to "orient" oneself to the world. Reference groups can serve both a normative and a comparative function. That is, they can (a) set and enforce attitudinal and behavioral standards, and (b) provide standards for self-evaluations. The latter process is similar, of course, to social comparison, except that people can use a reference group to make self-evaluations without actually belonging to it. Because people need not and often do not belong to their reference groups, most sociologists have ignored how such groups are "formed," focusing instead on how they are "selected" by people for the purpose of self-evaluation (see Stryker & Serpe, 1982). Although this work is interesting, it seems more relevant to cognitive than to behavioral integration.

A major contribution of sociological research on social evaluations has been to broaden our awareness of how useful such evaluations are and how often they are made. Research on reference groups, for example, shows that they can affect self-evaluations of many different personal characteristics, including health, wealth, and happiness. People also use reference groups to evaluate the characteristics of others or of the social system in which they live and work. Equity theory, for example, involves social evaluations of "fairness" based on comparisons between one's own outcomes and the outcomes of others. Finally, some sociologists claim that most or all of our knowledge about the world is derived in some way from social evaluations. All of this serves to emphasize how important social evaluations are and how often small groups are probably formed so that such evaluations can be made.

Finally, a *psychodynamic perspective* on behavioral integration has been taken by some social scientists. Advocates of this perspective (e.g., Jacques, 1976) argue that small groups serve an important therapeutic function for their members. No one enjoys perfect psychological health; everyone relies on psychological defenses of various sorts to control their feelings of neurotic anxiety. Many of these defenses are easier to conduct within small groups or can only be conducted there. People thus form or join such groups as a conscious or (usually) unconscious means of coping with personality conflicts.

Lindt and Pennal (1962) have suggested that group membership is especially helpful in resolving three types of personality conflicts. First, many people experience feelings of separation anxiety from time to time. Some of these feelings may reflect early childhood experiences, such as the trauma of birth or the problem of achieving independence from parents during infancy. Adolescents also experience feelings of separation anxiety as they enter adulthood and spend less time at home and more time at school and work. Finally, feelings of separation anxiety can arise at any age whenever close relationships with others are broken or lacking altogether. In order to defend against such feelings, people become group members. A small group can serve as a nurturant "mother" (Scheidlinger, 1964) or a warm and caring "family" for its members. People who belong to such a group receive the reassurance that they are indeed loved by others. This reassurance allays their feelings of separation anxiety and thus promotes their psychological adjustment.

A second type of personality conflict that can be resolved through memberships in small groups involves the problem of personal identity. Many psychologists (e.g., Erikson, 1968) believe that personal identity is essential for psychological adjustment; people must have clear and consistent images of themselves as persons. There are several ways to develop a personal identity, but one of the most common is to form or join small groups. People who belong to such groups acquire a "social identity" (see Tajfel & Turner, 1979) that allows them to describe (to themselves and to others) who they really are. Some people derive most or all of their personal identity from the groups to which they belong.

Although a social identity can be reassuring, it can also be threatening when people identify too strongly with a single group. Several psychologists (e.g., Dipboye, 1977) have described the fears of "engulfment" that arise in such situations. One way to cope with these fears is to form or join many different small groups. This tactic allows a person to feel close to the members of each group without losing his or her sense of individuality. As the number and variety of groups to which a person belongs increase, his or her sense of individuality will grow, since the chances of anyone else belonging to those small groups are less (Snyder & Fromkin, 1980). People who belong to more small groups are indeed happier and better adjusted than others (Thoits, 1983), perhaps for this reason. Of course, multiple group memberships can lead to other kinds of problems. For example, people who belong to a variety of groups may have trouble reconciling the various social identities available to them. Special tactics, such as focusing one's attention on the similarities rather than on the differences among the members of the various groups, may be required so that a sense of personal unity or integrity can be maintained (Wong-Rieger & Taylor, 1981).

Some people have a clear personal identity but are dissatisfied with it. These people may form or join small groups in order to improve their self-image. An interesting series of studies by Cialdini and his associates (Cialdini, Borden, Thorne, Walker, Freeman, & Sloan, 1976) seems relevant to this use of small groups. They found that college students identified more strongly with their universities when the football teams from those schools were winning rather than losing games. This tendency was stronger among students with poorer self-esteem. Apparently those students hoped to "bask in the reflected glory" of their teams. Of course, these efforts may reflect the need for a positive public image as much as a private one. But in either case, the research suggests that small groups are more likely to form when people are dissatisfied with themselves and have the opportunity to affiliate with others who seem "better" in some way.

Finally, impasse represents a third type of personality conflict that can be resolved through memberships in small groups. Impasse is a feeling of anxiety that occurs when psychological development has halted and someone is no longer making any progress toward self-actualization. Such a person may form or join small groups as a way of enhancing personal growth. No direct evidence on this use of small groups has been gathered. However, the plethora of groups devoted to self-actualization and personal growth (see Katz, 1981) has convinced many observers that it is quite common.

Affective Integration

Sometimes small groups form through the affective integration of their members. This can occur whenever people develop shared feelings. Theorists vary widely in their beliefs about the kinds of feelings that can lead to group formation and the ways in which those feelings are shared among group members. The most popular point of view (see Lott & Lott, 1965; Thibaut & Kelley, 1959) is that groups form through what might be called a "chaining" process. This process begins with a single pair of people who are attracted to one another. Those two people can, of course, be regarded as a small group in their own right. Any factor that produces interpersonal attraction can thus lead to the formation of such groups. But what about larger groups—how do they form? Perhaps larger groups really consist of many such dyads all linked together by feelings of attraction. If that is the case, then the same factors that produce dyads should also lead to the formation of larger groups.

This viewpoint suggests a need for at least two sorts of research. First, research on interpersonal attraction is needed to understand how and why people form dyadic relationships with one another. Fortunately, extensive research of this sort has already been conducted (see Berscheid, 1985). The evidence suggests that propinquity, physical attractiveness, competence, similarity, and reciprocity are all major factors in producing interpersonal attraction. If dyadic relationships are the foundation of larger groups, then these same factors should also promote the formation of such groups. Only a few studies relevant to this issue have been performed, but their results are generally supportive. For example, Gilchrist (1952) studied the role of competence in group formation. The subjects in his study first worked singly and then in pairs on various tests of reasoning ability. All of them then received (false and standardized) feedback about their own test scores and those of their partners. Later on, the subjects were asked to choose new partners to work with on similar tests. Subjects who earned higher test scores earlier in the study were chosen as partners more often than those whose test scores were lower. Good and Good (1974) studied the role of similarity in group formation. The subjects in their study were first asked to express their personal opinions about several topical issues. A few days later, they were given (false and standardized) information about the opinions held by members of a local fraternity or sorority on those issues. These opinions were either similar or dissimilar to the subjects' own opinions. The subjects were then asked to evaluate that fraternity or sorority and indicate their interest in joining it. Subjects who believed that fraternity or sorority members shared their own opinions evaluated that group more positively and indicated a greater interest in joining it than did subjects who believed that their own opinions were not shared by the group's members.

Although it is important to understand the sources of attraction within dyads and larger groups, another sort of research is also needed. This research should focus on how and why dyadic relationships become linked with one another. Unfortunately, little research of this sort has been conducted. Anecdotal accounts of chaining can be found (e.g., Boissevain, 1974), but their validity is difficult to assess. Several studies of social networks are also available (e.g., Salzinger, 1982), providing rich descriptive data on the relationships among and between the members of existing friendship groups. These studies show that people who belong to the same group are often bound together by strong feelings of mutual attraction, whereas people who belong to different groups are usually less attracted to one another. This pattern of relationships is at least consistent with the notion that small groups form through a chaining process, but it hardly represents conclusive proof. After all, several other patterns of relationships would also be consistent with that notion, and the observed pattern of relationships could have been produced by several other processes.

More convincing evidence might be obtained through careful observations of changes in a social network over time. A classic study by Newcomb (1961) produced such observations. Newcomb convinced a number of unacquainted college students to live together in a rooming house for a year and serve as subjects in a longitudinal study of the acquaintance process. At the beginning of the study, the students were asked to complete a battery of tests measuring their attitudes and values. At the end of the first week and at various times throughout the following year, their feelings toward one another were also assessed. Many pairs of students became friends with one another during the course of the study. Propinquity was the major factor in producing these friendships at first, but similarity became a more important factor later on. Larger groups of friends also formed as time passed. Newcomb found that these groups almost always grew out of dyadic relationships. Apparently, chaining is indeed a process that can lead to the formation of small groups.

Another point of view on the affective integration of group members involves their feelings toward the group itself. Perhaps small groups form because people become attracted to group membership rather than to one another. Several aspects of group membership might engender such feelings. First, a group's activities might prove attractive to people. Some activities, such as team sports, can only be conducted in groups. Other activities may simply be more enjoyable when conducted in groups (see Marks, 1959; Panelas, 1983). People might also become attracted to a group's goals. Ideological commitment, for example, seems to be an important factor in the formation of political and religious groups (Zurcher & Snow, 1981). Finally, a group might be attractive because people believe that membership in it will be useful in other social contexts. For example, college students often join fraternities and sororities because they believe that such groups are prestigious and can lead to better jobs or more active social lives (Willerman & Swanson, 1953). Many studies have shown that people who already belong to a group enjoy its activities, believe in its goals, and capitalize on its prestige whenever possible. Unfortunately, few researchers have studied the influence of these factors on the actual formation of small groups.

A third and final viewpoint on the affective integration of group members involves a process that might be called "crystallization." Freud (1922/1959) was the first person to describe this process. He noted that many groups have strong leaders who are loved and respected by their followers. Freud speculated that these feelings reflect the identification of group members with their leaders. According to Freud, identification with a leader might occur for two reasons. First, everyone has used identification in the past to resolve some of the crises associated with psychosexual development. Boys generally learn to identify with their fathers, whereas girls learn to identify with their mothers. These childhood experiences later affect behavior outside the family as well, so that when people come together in small groups, they are prone to identify with those (leaders) who seem stronger and wiser than themselves. Second, everyone possesses unconscious memories of a distant past when small tribal groups struggled for survival. These early groups were dominated by leaders whose abilities determined whether their followers lived or died. As time passed and experiences in such groups accumulated, people developed a natural propensity to identify with their leaders.

Although Freud's ideas about group formation are interesting, few of them have been tested and the available evidence is not very supportive (see Billig, 1976). For example, leaders are not always loved and respected by their followers, and some groups seem to get along without any leaders at all. If identification with the leader is based on early childhood experiences, then people should be more satisfied with leaders of their own sex, but that does not seem to be the case. Finally, there is no evidence that group cohesiveness depends solely (or even largely) on the identification of group members with their leaders. All of this suggests that crystallization probably does not occur for the reasons that Freud described. His major contribution may have been to interest others in the crystallization process.

Redl (1942) became interested in crystallization and collected several fascinating case studies of its role in group formation. His work revealed that crystallization need not always involve feelings of attraction for the leader of a group. Other feelings, such as guilt or anger, can also be involved. Moreover, those feelings need not be directed toward the group's leader. Other "central" persons can also serve as targets. Finally, Redl argued that many psychoanalytic processes besides identification could lead to the crystallization of a group. Other psychoanalysts (e.g., Flescher, 1957; Money-Kyrle, 1950) later concurred.

Sociologists have recently become interested in group formation through crystallization as well. For example, Lofland (1981) analyzed the emotional bases of collective behavior, distinguishing among groups based on feelings of fear, hostility, and joy. His analysis proved useful in classifying many different examples of collective behavior and revealed some interesting aspects of the crystallization process. For instance, Lofland discovered that finer distinctions could often be made among groups experiencing the same general emotions. Fearful groups could thus be divided into those experiencing panic, terror, dread, and so on. Lofland also noted that other general emotions besides fear, hostility, and joy might sometimes lead to the formation of small groups. Perhaps *any* emotion, if it is strong enough, could draw people together into a group. Many of the examples that Lofland analyzed also seemed to involve emotions directed toward targets other than persons. Objects, places, and events all seemed to be capable of producing feelings strong enough for groups to form. All of this suggests that crystallization is a highly versatile process worthy of further research attention.

Cognitive Integration

Sometimes small groups form through the cognitive integration of their members. This can occur whenever people realize that they share important personal characteristics. Of course, members of small groups often think alike, viewing their world through the same frame of reference. But cognitive integration involves more than mere similarity among persons. It also involves an awareness on their part that they are similar to one another. This awareness is an important and perhaps essential aspect of membership in any group. There is a sense in which a group forms whenever people begin to think of themselves as a group.

The potential importance of cognitive integration for the formation of small groups is suggested by recent work in the area of intergroup relations (see Wilder, 1986). Many researchers in that area have used a "minimal groups" paradigm to study the influence of cognitive factors on prejudice and discrimination. A prototypical study of this sort was performed by Tajfel, Billig, Bundy, & Flament (1971). They invited a number of young boys to participate in a study of artistic tastes. The boys first evaluated several paintings by Klee and Kandinsky shown to them on slides. These evaluations were then "reviewed" by the researchers, who provided the boys with (false) feedback about their artistic preferences. Some boys were told that they preferred the paintings of Klee, whereas others learned that they preferred the paintings of Kandinsky. Each boy knew his own artistic preference but not the preferences of others. Later in the study the boys were given an opportunity to distribute small cash prizes to one another through the use of special payoff charts. Each chart offered several options for the payment of prizes to boys who were identified only in terms of their artistic preferences. No one was able to use these charts to affect his own prize. The choices that the boys made on these charts revealed clear evidence of systematic bias. In general, each boy tended to favor those who shared his own artistic preference and disfavor those whose preference was different. The results of this study are remarkable because the "groups" to which the boys belonged were so minimal. Apparently, the mere fact that they shared the same artistic preference was enough to convince some boys that they ought to behave like good group members and help one another.

These results suggest that small groups can indeed form through the cognitive integration of their members. But when does such integration occur? In most minimal group studies, subjects are reminded by researchers of groups to which they already belong or are informed by researchers that they belong to new groups. Although this kind of "external designation" (Cartwright & Zander, 1968) probably occurs in the real world as well, people there more often become aware of group memberships on their own. Many psychologists have speculated about the kinds of factors that might affect this natural awareness of group memberships (e.g., Brewer, 1979; Campbell, 1958; Heider, 1958; Higgins & King, 1981; Stryker & Serpe, 1982; Turner, 1985; Wegner & Giuliano, 1982). A review of their work suggests that both personal and situational factors can be important.

At the personal level, there are three factors that might affect someone's awareness of membership in a group. The first factor is whether the person was aware of that membership before. The more often someone acknowledges group membership, the easier it becomes. A second factor is whether the person was aware of that membership recently. Someone who acknowledged group membership recently is likely to do so again. Finally, a third factor is whether an awareness of group membership was useful to the person in the past. Acknowledging membership in a group can be useful if it helps someone to better understand the world or provides that person with a stronger and/or more positive social identity. The more useful group membership has been in the past, the more likely someone is to acknowledge it in the future.

At the situational level, there are also three general factors that might affect someone's awareness of membership in a group. The first factor is whether the person is reminded of his or her group membership or not. As noted a moment ago, people sometimes label one another as group members. The more often someone is told by others that he or she belongs to a group, the more likely that person is to acknowledge group membership. Sometimes people do not actually label one another as group members, but treat one another like group members instead. The more often someone is treated by others like a group member, the more likely that person is to acknowledge group membership. Finally, even rather subtle cues can sometimes remind people of their membership in a group. Wilder and Shapiro (1984), for example, placed students in rooms that were either undecorated, decorated with items relevant to their schools, or decorated with irrelevant items. The subjects performed two tasks in those rooms, a memory task involving words that were relevant or irrelevant to their schools and a self-description task requiring them to list their most important personal characteristics.

Subjects who worked in rooms decorated with cues reminding them of their schools learned more of the words that were relevant to those schools and gave greater emphasis to those schools in their self-descriptions than subjects who worked in undecorated rooms or rooms decorated with irrelevant cues.

A second situational factor that can affect someone's awareness of membership in a group is whether that person believes that group membership is relevant to personal outcomes. Several studies have shown that as personal outcomes become more dependent on the success or failure of a group, the group becomes more salient to its members. Rabbie and Horwitz (1969), for example, assigned subjects arbitrarily to meaningless groups and then asked them to evaluate one another. When there were no outcomes associated with group membership, the subjects evaluated one another fairly. But when a prize was randomly awarded to one of the groups, subjects evaluated members of their own groups more positively than members of the other group. This bias was displayed by all of the subjects, whether they won the prize or not. Brewer (1979) provided an excellent review of research on the effects of cooperation and competition on the behavior of subjects in minimal groups. She found that competition between such groups strengthens the tendency of those subjects to favor members of their own group and disfavor members of other groups.

A third and final situational factor that can affect someone's awareness of membership in a group is whether that person's group is distinctive or unusual in some way. The more distinctive a group is, the more likely a person is to acknowledge membership in it. Sometimes groups are distinctive because their members are rare (see Mullen, 1983). McGuire, McGuire, Child, and Fujioka (1978), for example, interviewed school children of many different ages and asked them to describe themselves. Their responses were later analyzed to determine how often each child mentioned his or her ethnic group. Ethnic groups that were mentioned more often were assumed to be more salient to their members. School records were also consulted to determine what proportion of each child's class belonged to his or her ethnic group. Comparisons between these data sources revealed a direct relationship between the rarity of an ethnic group and its salience in the minds of group members.

Groups can also be distinctive because their members are similar to one another and/or different from those who belong to other groups. Allen and Wilder (1975), for example, asked subjects to express their opinions on a variety of topical issues and then to evaluate several paintings by Klee and Kandinsky shown to them on slides. After "reviewing" those opinions and evaluations, the researchers provided the subjects with (false) feedback about their similarities and dissimilarities. Some subjects were told that they preferred the paintings of Klee, whereas others learned that they preferred the paintings of Kandinsky. Subjects' beliefs about how similar their own opinions were to those of people who shared their artistic preferences, and to those of people whose artistic preferences were different from their own, were also manipulated independently. Later in the study, all of the subjects had an opportunity to distribute small cash prizes to one another using special payoff charts (see Tajfel et al., 1971). Their choices on those charts revealed the usual tendency to favor the members of one's own group and disfavor the members of other groups. But this tendency was modified by the subjects' beliefs about how similar their opinions were to the members of those groups. Subjects were more biased when they believed that their own opinions were similar rather than dissimilar to those of their fellow group members. However, subjects' beliefs about the similarity or dissimilarity of their own opinions to those of people in other groups had little effect on their behavior.

To summarize briefly, both personal and situational factors can affect the awareness of group membership and thereby influence the formation of small groups. Research on personal factors suggests that small groups will form when people (a) have acknowledged their shared characteristics before, or (b) have done so recently, or (c) have found it useful to think of themselves in that way. Research on situational factors suggests that small groups will form when (d) people are reminded of shared characteristics, or (e) their outcomes seem to depend on those characteristics, or (f) the characteristics that they share are unusual in some way.

CONCLUSIONS

Social psychologists need to learn more about the formation of small groups. The purpose of this chapter was to stimulate interest in group formation by providing an integrative review of theoretical and empirical work on that topic. I conceived of group formation as a *continuous process* of *social integration*. Several types of social integration were identified and their apparent effects on group formation were considered. *Environmental integration* was found to produce small groups whenever the physical, social, or cultural environments provided the resources necessary for group formation. *Behavioral integration* was found to produce small groups whenever people became dependent on one another for the satisfaction of their needs. *Affective integration* was found to produce small groups whenever people developed shared feelings. Finally, *cognitive integration* was found to produce small groups whenever people became aware of shared personal characteristics.

Many interesting issues regarding the formation of small groups were not considered because of time and space constraints. At least two of those issues are important enough, however, to be discussed briefly. The first issue is how the different types of social integration work together to produce small groups. Do they operate simultaneously or in some special order? At an intuitive level, it seems likely that environmental integration creates the potential for behavioral integration, which leads in turn to affective and cognitive integration. But intuitions are often wrong, and one can imagine situations in which any type of social integration might lead to any other. Which type of social integration plays the most important role in group formation? The most popular viewpoint among social psychologists has been that behavioral integration is the key to group formation, but Turner (1985) has recently offered a different point of view. He argues that cognitive integration is more important for group formation, and that a group can form even among persons who are negatively interdependent, so long as they regard themselves as a group. To support this argument, Turner and his colleagues (e.g., Hogg & Turner, 1985a, 1985b; Turner, Sachdev, & Hogg, 1983) have performed several innovative studies. The results of those studies are complex and difficult to interpret, but they suggest that group formation may indeed depend more on the cognitive than the behavioral integration of group members.

Another important issue involves the similarities and differences among forming, joining, and creating small groups. This chapter focused on the formation of natural groups, whose members come together freely and often unintentionally. But one might also study how and why people join groups that already exist. Although forming and joining small groups may involve similar psychological processes, they are *not* the same phenomenon. People who are joining a group usually know more about it, and may actually be recruited by its members (Moreland & Levine, 1982). As a result, they are probably much more deliberative about becoming group members. One might also study how and why artificial groups are created. The creation of small groups is a fascinating phenomenon in itself. Sometimes a group is created by a single person (see Schein, 1983), who must rely on his or her own power, charisma, or persuasiveness to bring group members together. And sometimes one group is created by another group. A large group, for example, may create smaller subgroups for the purpose of performing special tasks (e.g., Payne & Cooper, 1981), or break down into smaller subgroups because of conflicts among members (e.g., Gustafson, 1978). A successful group may produce "spin-offs" (e.g., Garvin, 1983), whereas an unsuccessful group may undergo a radical transformation or collapse completely to be "reborn" later (e.g., Sussman, 1956). Finally, new groups are sometimes created through mergers among old groups (e.g., Marks & Mirvis, 1986). Many of the same factors that affect the formation of natural groups are probably important in the creation of artificial groups as well, but a more careful analysis of this and other issues must await another day.

REFERENCES

Alba, R. D., & Kadushin, C. (1976). The intersection of social circles: A new measure of social proximity in networks. *Sociological Methods and Research, 5,* 77-102.

Alexander, R. D. (1979). Natural selection and social exchange. In R. L. Burgess & T. L. Huston (Eds.), *Social exchange in developing relationships* (pp. 197-221). New York: Academic Press.

Allen, V. L., & Wilder, D. A. (1975). Categorization, belief similarity, and intergroup discrimination. *Journal of Personality and Social Psychology, 32,* 971-977.

Axelrod, A., & Hamilton, W. D. (1981). The evolution of cooperation. *Science, 211,* 1390-1396.

Back, K. (1951). Influence through social communication. *Journal of Abnormal and Social Psychology, 46,* 9-23.

Bennett, D. (1979). The cultural variable in friendship and group formation. *Economics and Sociology Review, 10,* 123-145.

Berscheid, E. (1985). Interpersonal attraction. In G. Lindzey & E. Aronson (Eds.), *Handbook of social psychology* (Vol 2., pp. 413-484). New York: Random House.

Billig, M. (1976). *Social psychology and intergroup relations.* New York: Academic Press.

Boissevain, J. (1974). *Friends of friends: Networks, manipulators and coalitions.* Oxford: Basil Blackwell.

Bowby, J. (1979). *The making and breaking of affectional bonds.* London: Hogarth.

Brewer, M. B. (1979). In-group bias in the minimal intergroup situation: A cognitive-motivational analysis. *Psychological Bulletin, 86,* 307-324.

Buchanan, J. M. (1965). An economic theory of clubs. *Economica, 32,* 1-14.

Campbell, D. T. (1958). Common fate, similarity and other indices of the status of aggregates of persons as social entities. *Behavioral Science, 3,* 14-25.

Cartwright, D., & Zander, A. (1968). Groups and group membership: Introduction. In D. Cartwright & A. Zander (Eds.), *Group dynamics: Research and theory* (pp. 45-62). New York: Harper & Row.

Cialdini, R. B., Borden, R. J., Thorne, A., Walker, M. R., Freeman, S., & Sloan, L. R. (1976). Basking in reflected glory: Three (football) studies. *Journal of Personality and Social Psychology, 34,* 366-375.

Cottrell, N. B., & Epley, S. W. (1977). Affiliation, social comparison, and socially mediated stress reduction. In J. M. Suls & R. L. Miller (Eds.), *Social comparison process: Theoretical and empirical perspectives* (pp. 43-68). Washington, DC: Hemisphere.

Crane, D. (1972). *Invisible colleges: Diffusion of knowledge in scientific communities.* Chicago: University of Chicago Press.

Curtis, R. L., & Zurcher, L. A. (1973). Stable resources of protest movements: The multi-organizational field. *Social Forces, 52,* 53-61.

DeLameter, J. (1974). A definition of group. *Small Group Behavior, 5,* 33-41.

Dipboye, R. L. (1977). Alternative approaches to de-individuation. *Psychological Bulletin, 84,* 1057-1075.

Durkheim, E. (1964). *The division of labor in society* (G. Simpson, Trans.). New York: Free Press (Original work published 1893).

Eisenberger, R. (1970). Is there a deprivation-satiation function for social approval? *Psychological Bulletin, 74,* 255-275.

Emerson, R. M. (1972). Exchange theory, Part II: Exchange relations and network structures. In J. Berger, M. Zelditch, & B. Anderson (Eds.), *Sociological theories in progress* (Vol. 2, pp. 58-87). Boston: Houghton Mifflin.

Erikson, E. H. (1968). *Identity, youth, and crisis.* New York: W. W. Norton.

Feger, H. (1981). Analysis of social networks. In S. Duck & R. Gilmour (Eds.), *Personal relationships: Studying personal relationships* (pp. 91-105). New York: Academic Press.

Feldman, R. A. (1968). Interaction among three bases of group integration. *Sociometry, 31,* 30-46.

Festinger, L. (1954). A theory of social comparison processes. *Human Relations, 7,* 117-140.

Festinger, L., Schachter, S., & Back, K. (1950). *Social pressures in informal groups.* New York: Harper.

Flescher, J. (1957). The economy of aggression and anxiety in group formation. *International Journal of Group Psychotherapy, 7,* 31-39.

Freud, S. (1959). *Group psychology and the analysis of the ego* (J. Strachey, Trans.). New York: W. W. Norton (Original work published in 1922).

Garvin, D. A. (1983). Spin-offs and the new firm formation process. *California Management Review, 25,* 3-20.

Gilchrist, J. C. (1952). The formation of social groups under conditions of success and failure. *Journal of Abnormal and Social Psychology, 47,* 174-187.

Good, L. R., & Good, K. C. (1974). Similarity of attitudes and attraction to a social organization. *Psychological Reports, 34,* 1071-1073.

Gottlieb, B. H. (1983). Social support as a focus for integrative research in psychology. *American Psychologist, 38,* 278-287.

Gross, E. (1956). Symbiosis and consensus as integrative factors in small groups. *American Sociological Review, 21,* 174-179.

Gustafson, J. P. (1978). Schismatic groups. *Human Relations, 31,* 139-154.

Hagstrom, W. O., & Selvin, H. C. (1965). Two dimensions of cohesiveness in small groups. *Sociometry, 28,* 30-43.

Hartup, W. (1983). Peer relations. In P. H. Mussen (Ed.), *Handbook of child psychology* (Vol. 4, pp. 103-196). New York: John Wiley.

Heider, F. (1958). *The psychology of interpersonal relations.* New York: John Wiley.

Higgins, E. T., & King, G. (1981). Accessibility of social constructs: Information processing consequences of individual and context variability. In N. Cantor & J. F. Kihlstrom (Eds.), *Cognition, social interaction, and personality* (pp. 69-121). Hillsdale, NJ: Erlbaum.

Hogg, M. A., & Turner, J. C. (1985a). Interpersonal attraction, social identification, and psychological group formation. *European Journal of Social Psychology, 15,* 51-66.

Hogg, M. A., & Turner, J. C. (1985b). When liking begets solidarity: An experiment on the role of interpersonal attraction in psychological group formation. *British Journal of Social Psychology, 26,* 267-281.

Homans, G. C. (1961). *Social behavior: Its elementary forms.* New York: Harcourt, Brace & World.

Jaques, E. (1976). Social systems as a defense against persecutory and depressive anxiety. In G. S. Gibbard, J. J. Hartmann, & R. D. Mann (Eds.), *Analysis of groups: Contributions to theory, research, and practice* (pp. 277-299). San Francisco: Jossey-Bass.

Katz, A. H. (1981). Self-help and mutual aid: An emerging social movement? In R. H. Turner & J. F. Short (Eds.), *Annual review of sociology* (Vol. 7, pp. 129-155). Palo Alto, CA: Annual Reviews.

Kelley, H. H., & Thibaut, J. W. (1978). *Interpersonal relations: A theory of interdependence.* New York: John Wiley.

Kerckhoff, A. C. (1974). The social context of interpersonal attraction. In T. L. Huston (Ed.), *Foundations of interpersonal attraction* (pp. 61-78). New York: Academic Press.

Komorita, S. S., & Chertkoff, J. M. (1973). A bargaining theory of coalition formation. *Psychological Review, 80,* 149-162.

Korte, C. (1980). Urban-nonurban differences in social behavior and social psychological model of urban impact. *Journal of Social Issues, 36,* 29-51.

Kravetz, D. (1978). Consciousness-raising groups in the 1970's. *Psychology of Women Quarterly, 3,* 168-186.

LaFreniere, P. J., & Sroufe, A. L. (1985). Profiles of peer competence in the preschool: Interrelations among measures, influence of social ecology, and relation to attachment theory. *Development Psychology, 21,* 56-69.

Lewis, R. A. (1973). Social reaction and the formation of dyads: An interactionist approach to mate selection. *Sociometry, 36,* 409-418.

Lindt, H., & Pennal, H. A. (1962). On the defensive quality of groups: A commentary on the use of the group as a tool to control reality. *International Journal of Group Psychotherapy, 12,* 171-179.

Lofland, J. F. (1981). Collective behavior: The elementary forms. In M. Rosenberg & R. H. Turner (Eds.), *Social psychology: Sociological perspectives* (pp. 411-446). New York: Basic Books.

Lott, A. J., & Lott, B. E. (1965). Group cohesiveness as interpersonal attraction: A review of relationships with antecedent and consequent variables. *Psychological Bulletin, 64,* 259-309.

Marks, J. B. (1959). Interests and group formation. *Human Relations, 12,* 385-390.

Marks, M. L., & Mirvis, P. H. (1986, October). The merger syndrome. *Psychology Today,* pp. 36-42.

McCarthy, J. D., & Zald, M. N. (1977). Resource mobilization and social movements: A partial theory. *American Journal of Sociology, 82,* 1212-1241.

McGuire, W. J., McGuire, C. V., Child, P., & Fujioka, T. (1978). Salience of ethnicity in the spontaneous self-concept as a function of one's ethnic distinctiveness in the social environment. *Journal of Personality and Social Psychology, 36,* 511-520.

McPherson, M. (1983). An ecology of affiliation. *American Sociological Review, 48,* 519-532.

Merton, R. K. (1957). *Social theory and social structure.* Glencoe, IL: Free Press.

Micklin, M. (1984). The ecological perspective in the social sciences: A comparative overview. In M. Micklin & H. M. Choldin (Eds.), *Sociological human ecology: Contemporary issues and applications* (pp. 51-90). Boulder, CO: Westview.

Milardo, R. M. (1986). Personal choice and social constraint in close relationships: Applications of network analysis. In V. J. Derlega & B. A. Winstead (Eds.), *Friendship and social interaction* (pp. 145-166). New York: Springer-Verlag.

Money-Kyrle, R. (1950). Varieties of group formation. In G. Roheim (Ed.), *Psychoanalysis and the social science* (Vol. 2., pp. 313-329). New York: International Universities Press.

Moreland, R. L., & Levine, J. M. (1982). Socialization in small groups: Temporal changes in individual-group relations. In L. Berkowitz (Ed.), *Advances in experimental social psychology* (Vol. 15, pp. 137-192). New York: Academic Press.

Mullen, B. (1983). Operationalizing the effect of the group on the individual: A self-attention perspective. *Journal of Experimental Social Psychology, 19,* 295-322.

Murnighan, J. K. (1978). Models of coalition formation: Game theoretic, social psychological, and political perspective. *Psychological Bulletin, 85,* 1130-1153.

Newcomb, T. M. (1961). *The acquaintance process.* New York: Holt.

Oberschall, A. (1973). *Social conflict and social movements.* Englewood Cliffs, NJ: Prentice-Hall.

Olson, M. (1965). *The logic of collective action.* Cambridge, MA: Harvard University Press.

Panelas, T. (1983). Adolescents and video games: Consumption of leisure and the social construction of the peer group. *Youth and Society, 15,* 51-65.

Parks, M. R., Stan, C. M., & Eggert, L. L. (1983). Romantic involvement and social network involvement. *Social Psychology Quarterly, 46,* 116-131.

Payne, R., & Cooper, C. L. (Eds.). (1981). *Groups at work.* Chichester: John Wiley.

Pennings, J. M. (1980). Environmental influences on the creation process. In J. R. Kimberly & R. H. Miles (Eds.), *The organizational life-cycle: Issues in the creation, transformation, and decline of organizations* (pp. 135-160). San Francisco: Jossey-Bass.

Pettigrew, T. F. (1967). Social evaluation theory: Convergences and applications. In D. Levine (Ed.), *Nebraska symposium on motivation* (Vol. 15, pp. 241-311). Lincoln: University of Nebraska Press.

Rabbie, J. M., & Horwitz, M. (1969). Arousal of ingroup-outgroup bias by a chance win or loss. *Journal of Personality and Social Psychology, 13,* 269-277.

Radloff, R. (1961). Opinion evaluation and affiliation. *Journal of Abnormal and Social Psychology, 62,* 578-585.

Redl, F. (1942). Group emotion and leaders. *Psychiatry, 5,* 573-596.

Rofe, Y. (1984). Stress and affiliation: A utility theory. *Psychological Review, 91,* 235-250.

Russell, J. A., & Ward, L. M. (1982). Environmental psychology. In M. R. Rosenzweig & L. W. Porter (Eds.), *Annual review of psychology* (Vol. 33, pp. 651-688). Palo Alto, CA: Annual Reviews.

Salzinger, L. L. (1982). The ties that bind: The effects of clustering on dyadic relationships. *Social Networks, 4,* 117-145.

Schachter, S. (1959). *The psychology of affiliation: Experimental studies of the sources of gregariousness.* Stanford, CA: Stanford University Press.

Scheidlinger, S. (1964). Identification: The sense of belonging and of identity in small groups. *International Journal of Group Psychotherapy, 14,* 219-296.

Schein, E. H. (1983). The role of the founder in creating organizational culture. *Organizational Dynamics, 3,* 13-28.

Singer, J. E., & Shockley, V. L. (1965). Ability and affiliation. *Journal of Personality and Social Psychology, 1,* 95-100.

Snyder, C. R., & Fromkin, H. L. (1980). *Uniqueness: The human pursuit of difference.* New York: Plenum.

Stark, R., & Bainbridge, W. S. (1980). Networks of faith: Interpersonal bonds and recruitment to cults and sects. *American Journal of Sociology, 85,* 1376-1395.

Stein, A. A. (1976). Conflict and cohesion: A review of the literature. *Journal of Conflict Resolution, 20,* 143-172.

Stinchcombe, A. (1965). Social structure and organizations. In J. G. March (Ed.), *Handbook of organizations* (pp. 142-193). Chicago: Rand McNally.

Stokols, D. (1978). Environmental psychology. In M. R. Rosenzweig & L. W. Porter (Eds.), *Annual review of psychology* (Vol. 29, pp. 253-295). Palo Alto, CA: Annual Reviews.

Stryker, S., & Serpe, R. T. (1982). Commitment, identity salience, and role behavior: Theory and research example. In W. Ickes & E. S. Knowles (Eds.), *Personality, roles, and social behavior.* New York: Springer-Verlag.

Suls, J. M., & Miller, R. J. (1977). *Social comparison processes: Theoretical and empirical perspectives.* Washington, DC: Hemisphere.

Sussman, M. B. (1956). The "Calorie Counters": A study of spontaneous group formation, collapse, and reconstitution. *Social Forces, 34,* 351-356.

Tajfel, H., Billig, M. G., Bundy, R. P., & Flament, C. (1971). Social categorization and intergroup behavior. *European Journal of Social Psychology, 1,* 149-178.

Tajfel, H., & Turner, J. C. (1979). An integrative theory of intergroup conflict. In W. G. Austin & S. Worchel (Eds.), *The social psychology of intergroup relations* (pp. 33-47). Monterey, CA: Brooks-Cole.

Thibaut, J. W., & Kelley, H. H. (1959). *The social psychology of groups.* New York: John Wiley.

Thoits, P. A. (1983). Multiple identities and psychological well-being: A reformulation and test of the social isolation hypothesis. *American Sociological Review, 48,* 174-187.

Thomson, I. T. (1985). From other-direction to the me decade: The development of fluid identities and personal role definitions. *Sociological Inquiry, 55,* 274-290.

Tichy, N. (1973). An analysis of clique formation and structure in organizations. *Administrative Science Quarterly, 18,* 194-208.

Turner, J. C. (1985). Social categorization and the self-concept: A social cognitive theory of group behavior. In E. J. Lawler (Ed.), *Advances in group process* (Vol. 2, pp. 77-122). Greenwich, CT: JAI Press.

Turner, J. C., Sachdev, I., & Hogg, M. A. (1983). Social categorization, interpersonal attraction, and group formation. *British Journal of Social Psychology, 22,* 227-239.

Wegner, D. M., & Giuliano, T. (1982). The forms of social awareness. In W. Ickes & S. Knowles (Eds.), *Personality, roles, and social behavior* (pp. 165-198). New York: Springer-Verlag.

Wilder, D. A. (1986). Social categorization: Implications for creation and reduction of intergroup bias. In L. Berkowitz (Ed.), *Advances in experimental social psychology* (Vol. 19, pp. 291-355). New York: Academic Press.

Wilder, D. A., & Shapiro, P. N. (1984). Role of out-group cues in determining social identity. *Journal of Personality and Social Psychology, 47,* 342-348.

Willerman, B., & Swanson, L. (1953). Group prestige in voluntary organizations. *Human Relations, 6,* 57-77.

Willsie, D. A., & Riemer, J. W. (1980). The campus bar as a "bastard" institution. *Mid-American Review of Sociology, 5,* 61-89.

Wirth, L. (1983). Urbanism as a way of life. *American Journal of Sociology, 44,* 3-24.

Wong-Rieger, D., & Taylor, D. M. (1981). Multiple group membership and self-identity. *Journal of Cross-Cultural Psychology, 12,* 61-79.

Zurcher, L. A., & Snow, D. A. (1981). Collective behavior: Social movements. In M. Rosenberg & R. H. Turner (Eds.), *Social psychology: Sociological perspectives* (pp. 447-482). New York: Basic Books.

4

From Individual Inputs to Group Outputs, and Back Again

GROUP PROCESSES AND INFERENCES ABOUT MEMBERS

SCOTT T. ALLISON
DAVID M. MESSICK

Scott T. Allison is currently a doctoral candidate in social psychology at the University of California, Santa Barbara. His research has focused on how people make decisions in groups, and on how people draw inferences about group members on the basis of group decisions.

David M. Messick received his Ph.D. in social psychology from the University of North Carolina at Chapel Hill. He is the author of numerous articles on decision making, attributions, and fairness biases. He is currently Professor of Psychology at the University of California, Santa Barbara.

Thirty years ago, sociologists Ralph Turner and Lewis Killian (1957) wrote a review of research on collective behavior in which they noted several problems associated with drawing an analogy between individual behavior and group behavior. One of these problems they described as the tendency "to impute to the individual members of the group the motives and attitudes that would explain the action of the total group— [as] if it had been the action of an individual" (p. 14). With this statement Turner and Killian, in effect, raised two important questions. First, to what extent do group actions and decisions reflect the "motives and attitudes" of members? Second, to what degree do *observers* of group actions infer a correspondence between those actions and members' motives and attitudes? The purpose of this chapter is to propose some answers to each of these questions.

AUTHORS' NOTE: The preparation of this chapter was supported by NSF Grant BNS83-02674 to David M. Messick. The authors are indebted to Clyde Hendrick, Ken Gergen, and two anonymous reviewers for their discerning comments on an earlier version of this work.

To place these issues in a broader context, we begin with a brief excursion through history. Questions addressing the meaning of group action, and whether it is appropriate to look to individuals to explain the actions of a group, have been asked repeatedly by social scientists throughout the past century. Rarely, though, has there been much consensus in the answers to these questions. Following this historical overview, we will review theoretical work that has addressed the processes by which individuals combine their efforts or preferences to form a group product. The purpose of this review is to illustrate the fact that group products are rarely a simple manifestation of the inputs of members. The third section of the chapter then examines the cognitive end of the group-individual relation. Specifically, we will describe recent research bearing on the degree to which people *perceive* that group outcomes reflect members' preferences. The conclusion we reach is that people tend to believe that a group's decision is representative of its members' attitudes even when information is available that suggests otherwise.

HISTORICAL ROOTS OF THE PROBLEM

A review of the history of sociology and psychology reveals that issues concerned with the degree to which group actions mirror members' attitudes have been around as long as the disciplines themselves. Scholars of the late nineteenth and early twentieth centuries adopted one of two philosophical positions. Either they espoused the notion that the group was the true unit of analysis in the study of social behavior and that collective reality superseded the reality of individuals; or they believed that the individual was the proper unit of study and that phenomena that arose at the individual level could adequately explain collective action.

The most vociferous advocate of the collective reality doctrine was, of course, Emile Durkheim. His first fundamental rule of sociological methods was to "consider social facts as things" (1898, p. 14). The passage for which he is most noted is the following:

> The group thinks, feels, and acts quite differently from the way in which its members would were they isolated. If, then, we begin with the individual, we shall be able to understand nothing of what takes place in the group. Consequently, every time that a social phenomenon is directly explained by a psychological phenomenon, we may be sure that the explanation is false. (p. 104)

Durkheim acknowledged that individuals have attitudes, but he insisted that these attitudes did not determine social life. He justified this position by his observation that "even when society is reduced to an unorganized crowd, the collective sentiments which are formed in it may not only not resemble, but may even be opposed to, the sentiments of the average individual" (p. 106).

This latter statement is important because it illustrates the great preoccupation that the early social scientists had with crowd behavior. In fact, the crowd was considered by many to be prototypical of all groups. Gustave LeBon's classic work, *The Crowd* (1903), stressed the emergence of a dominant "collective mind" in a crowd, a mind that contained properties quite different from the minds of the individuals who composed the crowd. In 1908, E. A. Ross released the first social psychological textbook, *Social Psychology*, which focused almost entirely on the pernicious nature of crowd behavior. Ross described mobs and crowds as the lowest forms of human association, evil and irrational entities, subject to extremes, of which individuals are helpless members. This idea of helplessness in groups illustrated the impact of Durkheim's collective reality doctrine on the theoretical ideas of many of the early social psychologists, particularly those with a sociological bent.

But sociologists were not the only scholars who downplayed the role of individual-level phenomena in group life; most anthropologists, too, clung to this position. Of this group, Leslie White (1947) was perhaps the most outspoken on the group-individual issue. He believed that all behavior is culturally determined and that it is foolhardy to explain group behavior from a psychological perspective. White maintained that drawing conclusions about the citizens of a country on the basis of what that country does is a serious error. His diatribe of psychological explanations for social behavior included the following classic passage:

> Polls of opinion are sometimes interpreted psychologically, i.e., upon the assumption that what "the people" think and desire determines the behavior of a nation. This is one of the illusions of democracy: "the people rule." But what the people think and feel, in concrete and specific terms, is determined not by themselves, but by the socio-cultural magnetic field in which they are but articulate, protoplasmic iron filings. (p. 691)

Ironically, then, White's position was that the proper study of human behavior is not humans, but culture: "The most realistic and scientifically adequate interpretation of culture is one that proceeds *as if* human beings did not exist" (p. 694, italics in original).

Not all of the early social scientists readily attributed reality to group phenomena. As psychologists grew in number, they began to challenge the positions held by Durkheim and White by insisting that true reality resided only in individuals and that the word "group" was merely a convenient linguistic term used to describe a collection of individuals. Eventually, from these two opposing factions—one advocating group reality, the other individual reality—grew social psychology, the study of behavior as the intersection of both group and individual forces. Ironically, though, the emergence of social psychology early in this century not only failed to extinguish the controversy, it actually inflamed it.

Perhaps no one was more responsible for further extending the group-individual debate than was William McDougall. One of the first self-proclaimed social psychologists, McDougall embraced a Durkheimian position in his 1920 book, *The Group Mind.* This work, especially its title, failed to endear McDougall to other mainstream psychologists, who were skeptical of group reality and who were only willing to attribute reality to individuals. McDougall no doubt ruffled a lot of psychological feathers with his thesis that society, a group, or any organized collectivity "has a mental life which is not the mere sum of the mental lives of its existing independent units" (p. 10). Groups, it seemed to McDougall, were not only real, but actually had a separate life of their own.

This position, of course, met with fierce resistance from other social psychologists. Floyd Allport (1924) was especially biting in his attack on McDougall's thesis, claiming that "there is no psychology of groups which is not essentially and entirely a psychology of individuals" (p. 4). Allport was puzzled why a "consciousness" and a "mind" were being attributed to groups when clearly only individuals with central nervous systems could possess such properties. He believed that McDougall was the victim of a literary illusion: "When we say that a crowd 'feels,' 'wills,' or 'is emotional,' the language we use establishes the illusion" (p. 7) that groups are live entities. Later, in his 1933 book *Institutional Behavior,* Allport again attacked the notion of group domination over individuals. He wrote that "it is a fallacy . . . to think of men in democratic countries as slaves to institutions over which they have no control, unless we accept the premise that men have no control over themselves" (p. 137).

Allport made it clear that he wished the study of collective behavior to be conducted at the individual level, and his ideas furnished the young crop of social psychologists in the 1920s and 30s with the atmosphere to do just that.

It was not long after Allport's critique of Durkheim and McDougall that the scientific dialogue on the group-individual problem quieted considerably. Depending on whom one read, the debate was either resolved or unresolvable. For most social psychologists, experimentally studying how people behaved in groups was deemed a more important undertaking than speculating from one's armchair what exactly groups were. For Allport, however, this lack of closure on the group mind problem was hindering research on group processes and compromising group theory. As late as 1962, he asserted that there were still a number of important questions relevant to the group-individual relation that remained unanswered, the most important of which was this: What do we mean when we say that a group decides, thinks, or acts? Allport believed that the act of "deciding" is a cognitive process that only an individual can engage in, and that using language such as "group decision" was inaccurate and attested to the imprecision that plagued the terminology of the social sciences. So strong was his conviction that group action and individual action should not be confused that he claimed that the question of what group behavior means represented the *master problem* of social psychology (Allport, 1962).

In summary, throughout the history of the social sciences there has been a division in theoretical perspective between those who believe that the group is the primary reality in social life, and those who maintain that true reality resides only in the individual. Those who have endorsed the group reality position have believed that there is typically very little correspondence between group actions and members' preferences. Those advocating the individual reality position have acknowledged the role of group influences on the individual but have maintained that it is the individual who controls his or her own behaviors and, more importantly, that it is the individual who directs the course of a group's actions. Allport, the spokesperson for the individualist position, grappled with issues pertaining to the definition of group action and group decision making throughout his career. It is to the nature of the group decision making process, as we understand it today, that we turn next.

THE ROCKY ROAD FROM
INDIVIDUAL INPUTS TO GROUP OUTPUTS

On April 15, 1986, more than two dozen American war planes took off from Lakenhearth air base in Great Britain to attack Libya for its alleged involvement in international terrorism. The most direct flight path to Libya from Britain involved crossing French airspace; however, French president Francois Mitterand refused to allow the United States to use this airspace. As a result, American planes were forced to circumvent the Iberian peninsula, thus doubling their flight length to Libya. In the aftermath of these bombing raids, Americans were heard grumbling about French attitudes while praising British loyalty to noble American intentions. However, a Newsweek magazine poll conducted shortly after the military raid revealed that only 30% of Britons but 61% of the French approved of the raid ("A Poll," 1986).

In this example, there was a clear disjunction between the actions of two groups—in this case nations—and the attitudes of the individuals who composed the groups. There was a tendency, moreover, for observers of these actions to overlook this disjunction and assume that the groups' behaviors were correspondent with members' desires. People, it seems, treat the decisions that are made by collectivities in the same way that they treat the decisions that are made by individuals. They observe the actions of a group or individual, and they assume that these actions come about as a direct result of the attitudes held by the group or individual. This tendency to evaluate a group's decisions as those of an individual is reflected in the following statement that appears in a recent book by Swap et al. (1984) on collective decision making:

> Groups clearly . . . can act and can be thought of for many purposes as persons who are responsible for their actions . . . It is plausible, therefore, to analyze and evaluate a group's decisions as those of a unitary—if highly complex and often conflicted—actor. (p. 18)

Although this statement acknowledges that decision making at the group level is more complicated than at the individual level, the passage does imply that it is convenient to view a group's decision as sharing much in common with that of an individual. But earlier in the same book, Swap et al. make the following remark about the individual-group comparison:

The study of individual decision making has limited utility in understanding how groups make decisions. Group processes are not simply extensions and elaborations of the processes that characterize individuals. (p. 9)

The above two passages, taken from the same volume on group decision making, illustrate the lingering confusion between phenomena that characterize individuals and those that are unique to groups. Swap et al. do not contradict themselves with these two statements; rather, the authors underscore two conflicting perceptions of group life. On the one hand, it is tempting to view collective decision making as simply an analog of decision making that occurs at the individual level. Individuals usually mean what they say, and logic demands that groups, too, should produce actions that correspond with their members' attitudes. But as we shall illustrate shortly, drawing this type of analogy between an individual and a group can lead to serious inferential errors.

In this section we review a number of phenomena that obscure the correspondence between group products and members' inputs. We draw from several areas of research both within and outside of social psychology.

Social Psychology and Group Decision Making

In discussing the reasons why group products often do not correspond to the inputs of members, it is convenient to distinguish between instances of noncorrespondence that result from the changes that people undergo when they are in a group setting, and instances of noncorrespondence that result from the nature of the interdependence in a group. An example of the first type of noncorrespondence occurs when individuals fail to pull as hard on a rope when they are in a group as when they are alone, a finding that Ringlemann (1913) so aptly demonstrated. To explain why this type of group action is a distorted representation of members' inputs, one must examine social influence processes that occur in groups.

The second type of noncorrespondence occurs when members are constrained by the interdependence structure of their group or by the formal decision rule that the group uses to arrive at a decision. In this type of situation, individual preferences need not shift at all to produce a distorted collective outcome. Britain's and France's roles in the American bombing raid on Libya are classic examples of this kind of noncorrespondence. When Mitterand refused American entrance into French airspace, the opinions of French citizens apparently did not enter into his decision. Similarly, England's prime minister Margaret Thatcher did not appear to take her constituents' attitudes into account when she approved America's use of Lakenheath air base. If these leaders had acted in a manner consistent with their citizens' attitudes, the bombing raid may never have occurred, or if it had, it may have originated from France rather than from Britain.

Below we review several areas of research in social psychology that bear on the distinction between noncorrespondence that results from social influence processes, and noncorrespondence that results form structural constraints that are placed on group members.

Noncorrespondence Resulting From Social Influence Processes

Social loafing. The early rope-pulling study conducted by Ringlemann (1913) was among the first to illustrate the dubiousness of using an additive model of individual inputs to arrive at an estimate of a group product. Ringlemann found that the amount of force that eight-person groups applied to a rope was roughly equivalent to the sum of the forces exerted by *four* individuals pulling alone. Although he attributed the decrement in group performance to coordination loss among the members, recent studies have shown that the decrement is the result of *social loafing,* a loss in individual motivation that occurs in groups (Harkins, Latane, & Williams, 1980). Other, more recent studies have replicated Ringlemann's results using rope-pulling, cheering, and hand-clapping procedures (e.g., Ingham, Levinger, Graves, & Peckham, 1974; Latane, Williams, & Harkins, 1979).

Group polarization. Prior to 1960, group decisions were believed by many to be safer, wiser, and more reliable than individual decisions. This presumed superiority of groups to individuals is reflected in the literature reviews of Shaw (1932), Faust (1959), and Lorge, Fox, Davitz, and Brenner (1958). But in the early 1960s, it was discovered that group members often hold riskier beliefs following a group discussion than they do prior to the discussion (Stoner, 1961; Wallach, Kogan, & Bem, 1962). Later it was discovered that the mean attitudinal position of a group, whether risky *or* conservative, tends to become more extreme as a result of group discussion. This extremity of belief that results from group discussion has been called *group polarization* (Lamm & Meyers, 1978).

Several explanations have been proposed to account for the group polarization phenomenon. One explanation, based on social comparison theory, is that once people discover the normative position in a group, their desire to be evaluated favorably leads them to adopt an attitude that is more extreme than the norm (Goethals & Zanna, 1979). Another explanation posits that attitudes become polarized because the exchange of information that occurs during group discussion leads people to consider facts in support of their position that they had not previously considered (Vinokur & Burnstein, 1974). A more recent approach to group polarization, based on social identity theory, assumes that people perceive groups, including their own, in terms of extremes; they then shift their attitudes to conform to the extremitized group norm (Mackie, 1986). Regardless of whether all three processes are operative, or whether one is particularly important, the net result is the same: One cannot use a simple additive or averaging model of individuals' attitudes to estimate the decision that these individuals will make as a group.

Groupthink and the abilene paradox. It is perhaps ironic that cohesive groups sometimes reach decisions that are poorer in quality than groups that lack cohesiveness. Pressures toward uniformity in a cohesive group often prevent members from considering alternative courses of action, from accurately assessing the riskiness of choices, and from considering minority viewpoints within the group. Irving Janis (1972) has called this suboptimal form of collective decision making *groupthink.* When a group succumbs to groupthink, it reaches a decision that none of the members would have reached alone and that all members later regret having made. Groupthink is said to have affected John F. Kennedy's 1961 decision to invade Cuba at the Bay of Pigs, Lyndon Johnson's decision to escalate American involvement in the Vietnam War in the late 1960s, and perhaps NASA's decision to launch the Challenger space shuttle in 1986.

Another similar instance of flawed group decision making has been described by organizational psychologists as the *abilene paradox* (Harvey, 1974). The paradox describes the tendency for people to accede to a group decision because they think that everyone else in the group favors the decision. When no one speaks against the proposal in the belief that all others support it, the content of the discussion will be primarily positive and supportive, convincing listeners of the popularity of the idea. This type of pluralistic ignorance, in which each person believes him or herself to be unique in opposing the group consensus, allows group decisions to be made that reflect the desires of none of the members. Thus, as we have seen in examples of social loafing, group polarization, and groupthink, the abilene paradox illustrates a situation in which the psychological effects of being in a group produce a group action that does not accurately reflect members' inputs or preferences.

Noncorrespondence Resulting From Interdependence Structures

We have seen that in many group decision making situations, the consequences of social interaction are such that a decision is reached that differs from one that would have been reached had members not interacted. However, this does not mean that a complete correspondence between members' preferences and group outcomes can be achieved when social influence processes are held in check. Indeed, there are many situations in which social influence does not occur and yet collective products still fail to correspond to members' inputs. We discuss these situations below.

Social dilemmas. In *The Wealth of Nations*, Adam Smith (1976) noted one important virtue of capitalism, a virtue that has since been called the *invisible hand* doctrine. According to this principle, citizens who successfully pursue their own best individual economic interests are also bound to further society's best economic interests. There is, in other words, a correspondence between the attainment of individual and collective well-being. For a number of years, however, social psychologists have known that there are forms of interdependence in which individual and group goals are in direct conflict. This knowledge is reflected in the enormous experimental literature on decision making in the Prisoner's Dilemma (PD) Game. When two individuals are in a PD situation, they find that they are worse off behaving in an economically rational fashion than behaving in an irrational fashion. In other words, the joint outcome of two optimal choices is poorer than the joint outcome of two sub-optimal choices.

By the 1970s, social psychologists recognized that this conflict between individual and common interest was not limited to two-person settings. This realization was made possible, in part, by Garrett Hardin's (1968) essay, *The Tragedy of the Commons*. Hardin's article focused on the overpopulation problem, and the "tragedy" he described was simply a multiperson extension of the social interdependence that characterized the PD game. Hardin's thesis was that, although it is usually in people's best interest to beget many children, the pursuit of this rational course of action in an overpopulated world is certain to produce disastrous global consequences. This collective version of the PD that Hardin described has since been called a *social dilemma* (Dawes, 1980; Messick & Brewer, 1983).

As in a PD, when individuals in a social dilemma make the best choice for themselves, a group outcome is created that is neither intended nor desired by any of the individuals. In addition to the overpopulation problem, there are many other large-scale social dilemmas that retain the properties of the PD, including problems of pollution, animal poaching, election turnout, and the use of natural resources. People choose the selfish choice in social dilemmas for a variety of reasons. Some do so because they cannot delay gratification (Cross & Guyer, 1980). Others fail to cooperate in a social dilemma because they wish to compete with others or to avoid falling behind (Messick & Thorngate, 1967). Still others fail to cooperate because they lack knowledge of the cooperative choice and cannot discern the damaging consequences of their selfish actions (Allison & Messick, 1985a). Social dilemmas are a pernicious form of noncorrespondence between individuals' desires and collective outcomes that social scientists are only beginning to investigate.

Group decision rules. Groups, like individuals, are often subject to external constraints that shape their behavior. The most important of these external constraints on group action are the formal *group decision rules* by which groups may be bound. A group's decision, then, is often determined not only by the the preferences of its members, but also by the specific decision rule that the group uses to map those preferences into a collective choice.

Among the first social psychologists to study the effects of decision rules on group behavior were Smoke and Zajonc (1962). In this important article, Smoke and Zajonc examined the ways in which various rules for combining individual judgments influenced the probability that a group judgment was correct as a function of the probability that the individual judgments were correct. Figure 4.1 displays the relationship between the probability of a correct group judgment, *A*, and correct individual judgment for the seven decision rules that they explored.

In Figure 4.1, we assumed that there are five people in the group. The independent function merely represents a case in which the group will choose *A* with probability .50 regardless of the likelihood that the individuals are correct. The minimal quorum means that the group will decide *A* if at least one person in the group does so. Likewise, the

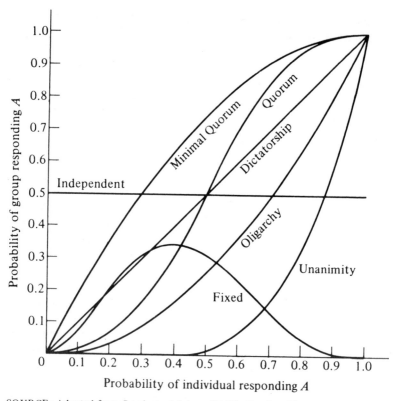

SOURCE: Adapted from Smoke and Zajonc (1962). Reprinted by permission.

Figure 4.1 Probability of a Group Choosing *A* Given the Probability That a Member
Chooses *A* for the Seven Decision Rules

quorum rule requires the group to choose *A* if at least two people do.
The dictatorship rule means that the group decides *A* if one predesignated person in the group chooses it, and the oligarchy rule specifies that
the group chooses *A* if both of two predesignated members do so.
Unanimity, of course, means that the group selects *A* if and only if all
members do so, and the fixed rule means that the group makes the *A*
choice if exactly two members do.

We will not discuss when these different rules might be appropriate
for a group to use. The important principle that Figure 4.1 illustrates is
that each rule defines a different relationship between individual and
group probability of choice. Two of the group decision rules, indepen-

dent and fixed, fail to afford the group an increasing chance of choosing *A* as the probability of an individual choosing *A* increases. They are consequently very unrepresentative of the individual propensity. The other rules all imply a monotonic increasing relationship between the group and the individual probability of choice. Of these, unanimity makes the probability of group choice minimal, and the minimal quorum maximizes it for all levels of individual propensity between 1 and 0. Neither of these rules is representative of the tendencies of the typical member, however. The most representative rule of all is, of course, the dictatorship rule, in which the group is represented by a single member.

Important research by Davis (1973) and his collaborators has explored these and related ideas. In one study, for instance, Nagao and Davis (1980) report that in the three years from 1973 to 1976, college students' likelihood of responding to a standard prerecorded rape trial with a predeliberation judgment of guilty increased about 16%. How, they ask, might one expect this change to affect research on the effects of jury size? Using plausible group decision schemes, assumptions relating the probability of a jury reaching a guilty verdict to the number of jurors favoring guilty prior to deliberation, they show that 12-person juries might be either more or less likely than 6-person juries to convict the defendant, depending on the likelihood of predeliberation guilty judgments. Thus conflicting experimental results about jury behavior could be anticipated as a function of a more or less continuous change in individual inputs.

Economics, Political Science, and Group Decision Making

One important line of research that is directly relevant to the question of the relationship between individual inputs and group outputs, and one that has been largely ignored by social psychologists, goes under the rubrics of collective choice, social choice, and public choice. These refer to the analysis of the characteristics of the rules or institutions that we can use to reach collective decisions. This research has been conducted by economists, political scientists, game theorists, and mathematicians. It is often mathematically sophisticated and that is possibly why it is frequently disregarded by psychologists studying group decision making. The field is at least 200 years old, dating back to the famous essay by Condorcet (1785), and while we only have space to note a few highlights, we will try to convey the relevance of this work for our general point and for social psychology more broadly. Accessible treatments of different aspects of this research area may be found in Chechile (1984), Colman (1982), Brams and Fishburn (1983), Fishburn (1973), McKay (1980), Schelling (1978), and Sen (1970), to mention just a few sources.

The basic approach is to assume that each member of a group that can range in size from very small (n = 3) to very large, has a set of fixed preferences for some collection of options, alternatives, or candidates. The group must make an evaluation of these options, alternatives, or candidates and this evaluation can take the form of choosing one, choosing a subset, or rank ordering them. There are different methods, of course, that the group can use to map the individual preferences into a group evaluation, and the basic question is which of these methods are good ones, and what does that mean? Another key question is what does the group evaluation tell one about the collection of individual preferences? We will describe seven examples of the collective choice approach in this section, four theoretical ones and three empirical ones.

Condorcet Paradox

Imagine a committee of three social psychologists having to decide which of three Ph.D. dissertations is the best. Imagine further that all three members of the committee have read all three dissertations and have recorded their rankings. Suppose the rankings are those given in Table 4.1, where a ranking of "1" means best. Thus Dr. X thinks that Dr. A's dissertation was the best of the lot and that Dr. C's dissertation was the poorest. If the Chair of this committee were to propose that the winner be selected by having members vote, using majority rule, first between Dr. A and Dr. B, and then between the winner and Dr. C., Dr. C would emerge victorious. Dr. A would be selected in the first round, being preferred by both X and Y, and Dr. C would win the second round, being preferred by Y and Z.

If the order of the vote had been different, however, the outcome would also have changed. If the initial vote had paired Drs. B and C, B would have won, only to be defeated by A in the second round; and if the first pair had been A and C, B would have been the ultimate winner. Thus, holding the preferences of the evaluators fixed, the award winner will depend on the agenda, the order in which the votes are taken.

The reason for this anomalous outcome is that, while each evaluator has a simple preferences order, the group does not. Using majority rule, the group "preference" is intransitive. A is preferred to B, and B is

TABLE 4.1
Rank Orders by Three Evaluators of Three Dissertations
Displaying the Condorcet Paradox

	Dissertations		
Evaluators	A	B	C
X	1	2	3
Y	2	3	1
Z	3	1	2

preferred to C, but C is preferred to A. This simple illustration shows how group choices may have qualitatively different properties from those of any of the group members. In this case, the property is the transitivity of preference.

Voting Paradoxes

A number of unusual and paradoxical properties of voting systems have been discovered by collective choice theorists (Brams, 1976; Fishburn, 1974). In the example described here, taken from Fishburn (1974), we show how a group can reverse its ranking of a set of candidates when the least preferred candidate decides to withdraw from the race.

Imagine an election with seven voters, T through Z, and four candidates, A through D. In this case, suppose the voters have decided to use a Borda voting system in which each voter's most preferred candidate gets three points, the next more preferred two points, and so on with the least preferred getting zero points. The winner is the candidate receiving the most points. In Table 4.2, we present the Borda points that each voter gives to each candidate. Note that in this case, unlike the last one, the most preferred candidate gets the largest number.

Clearly, with the four-candidate slate, the group rank order is ADCB, with A emerging as the winner. The situation for B is bleak, being least preferred, so if B could foresee this outcome, he might well save himself the time and trouble and remove his name from the slate. Were he to do so, there would be a three-person election involving A, C, and D. The voters' points for these candidates are presented in Table 4.3. No rank orders have changed, only the numbers of points have been adjusted for the three-person election. When the points for this three-person slate are accumulated, *the winner is not A but C.* Moreover, the group rank order

TABLE 4.2
Borda Points Given by Seven Voters
to Each of Four Candidates

Voters	Candidates			
	A	*B*	*C*	*D*
T	3	2	1	0
U	2	1	0	3
V	1	0	3	2
W	0	3	2	1
X	3	2	1	0
Y	2	1	0	3
Z	1	0	3	2
Totals	12	9	10	11

NOTE: The winner is the candidate receiving the most points, in this case candidate A.

is CDA, whereas when B was a candidate, the rank order of these three were ADC. B's withdrawal reversed the group ranking.

Arrow's Impossibility Theorem

Without a doubt, the single most important discovery made by collective choice researchers was the impossibility theorem of Arrow (1963). Arrow tried to discover an "ideal" voting system that would convert any set of individual rankings of three or more candidates or options into a group ranking. The "ideal" system would satisfy four conditions that appear to be desirable, if not necessary, for a system to be considered democratic, that is, representative in some meaningful sense of the preferences of the participants. One of the conditions, for instance, is *nondictatorship*, which is to say that there ought not to be a person in the group whose preference ranking is always exactly like the group ranking, no matter what the other people in the group prefer. A second condition called *citizen's sovereignty* simply means that for any pair of options, there is some configuration of individual preferences that will lead to the group ranking one member of the pair over the other. In other words, there is no pair in which the group prefers one to the other regardless of the preferences of the group members.

The remaining two conditions, rather imprecisely, require that an alternative not be penalized if that alternative moves up in one or more person's rank orders (*positive association*), and that the group ordering of a subset of the alternatives not depend on what other alternatives are being evaluated (*independence of irrelevant alternatives*). This latter

TABLE 4.3

**Borda Points Given by the Same Seven Voters as in Table 4.2
to the Remaining Three Candidates after Candidate B Withdraws**

		Candidates	
Voters	A	C	D
T	2	1	0
U	1	0	2
V	0	2	1
W	0	2	1
X	2	1	0
Y	1	0	2
Z	0	2	1
Totals	6	8	7

NOTE: Unlike the result in Table 4.2, the winner in this election is candidate C.

condition is violated in our previous example of a voting paradox.

Arrow (1963) mathematically proved that there can be no scheme that has these four desirable properties. The search for ideal democratic procedures must come to grips with the realization that perfection of the sort sought by Arrow is impossible to achieve.

Sophisticated Voting

Social psychologists have traditionally been concerned with the relationship between inner qualities, like attitudes or personality dispositions, on the one hand, and behavior on the other. While most social choice analyses had assumed that people would vote in strict accordance with their true preferences, Farquharson (1969) noted that voting systems sometimes create incentives for people to misrepresent their true preferences. Sophisticated voting, strategically misrepresenting one's real preferences, can sometimes yield outcomes that are higher on one's true preference ordering than sincere voting.

Suppose in our earlier example that we had seven judges evaluating the dissertations rather than three. Suppose further that the committee had agreed to use a Borda procedure rather than a pair-wise majority rule system and that the points given to each to the three dissertations are as shown in Table 4.4. Four of the evaluators rank the dissertations ABC, and the other three rank them BAC. The Borda procedures give A the award with 11 points over B with 10. However, if the three judges who preferred B misrepresented their relative preferences for A and C and stated their orders as BCA, they would give no points to A, and B would emerge as the winner with 10 points to 8 points for A and 3 for C. The first four judges can prevent this coup, however, by voting strategically themselves and by expressing their preferences as ACB, thereby giving their four second-place votes to C rather than B. Dr. A now emerges as the winner with eight points, C takes second place with all seven second-place votes, and B gathers only six points. The group ranking that results from this pattern of sophisticated voting is ACB, although all of the group members agree that Dr. C did the poorest dissertation.

The analysis of sophisticated voting not only uncovers one more way in which group outputs may be seriously at odds with individual inputs, it also illuminates two other principles of social psychological interest. First, it points to the possibility that there may be a disagreement between true preferences and votes, suggesting yet another rock on the road from dispositions to acts. Second, this analysis hints at another possible process involved in intergroup polarization. In terms of their true preferences, the two groups of judges disagree only about which of two candidates is the best. They are in complete agreement about who is last. However, in terms of their expressed (sophisticated) preferences, they are in complete disagreement. Sophisticated voting results in differences in expressed preferences that are greater than the differences in the true underlying preferences. Rapoport, Felsenthal, and Maoz (1986) report a study that shows that people engage in sophisticated voting when it benefits them to do so.

Approval Voting

Sophisticated voting refers to the tendency to misrepresent one's real preferences in order to attain one's real preferences. Brams and Fishburn (1983) have argued that the commonly used practice of plurality voting, the system in which each voter casts a single vote and the winner is the candidate receiving the largest number of votes, can reward strategic voting, especially in multiperson elections. In the 1980 presidential election, a large group of voters whose most preferred candidate for the presidency was John Anderson voted instead for Carter or Reagan on the belief that Anderson could not win and that a vote for him would have been a "wasted" vote. Anderson's political strength was therefore underestimated by his popular vote due to strategic voting.

In a democracy, it is disturbing to consider that the result of a free and open election might not depend so much on *vox populi* as on the

TABLE 4.4
Borda Points Given to Three Dissertations
by Each of Seven Evaluators

| | Dissertations | | |
Evaluators	A	B	C
T	2	1	0
U	2	1	0
V	2	1	0
W	2	1	0
X	1	2	0
Y	1	2	0
Z	1	2	0
Totals	11	10	0

NOTE: There is an incentive for both the A supporters and the B supporters to pretend to prefer C to their true second choice.

particular type of voting procedure that is used. Yet this is precisely the claim made by Brams and Fishburn regarding plurality voting. Plurality voting not only rewards the strategic misrepresentation of preferences, but, when there are more than two candidates, it also creates the possibility that the winner might not have been able to defeat one of the losing candidates in a two-person election. To illustrate this problem, Brams and Fishburn refer to the 1980 United States Senate election in New York State. The winner of this election was Alphonse D'Amato, who won with 45% of the vote over Elizabeth Holtzman, with 44%, and Jacob Javits, with 11%. Exit polls apparently indicated that over twice as many Javits supporters would have supported Holtzman as D'Amato in a two-person race, and, if so, the approximately 52% of the voters in New York who would have preferred her to D'Amato have been deprived of their representation by the system of plurality voting.

Such problems would not arise with approval voting according to Brams and Fishburn. With approval voting, each voter may vote for, or approve of, as many of the candidates as he or she wishes. The candidate gaining the most votes is declared the winner. With this system, it is not necessarily to the detriment of one candidate to have another candidate from the same side of the political spectrum on the ballot. The vote from that side need not be split since voters may approve of both candidates. Brams and Fishburn imply that had the New York election been held with approval voting instead of plurality voting, Holtzman would have been the winner. Moreover, an empirical demonstration of the superiority of approval voting to plurality voting has been provided by Felsenthal, Maoz, and Rapoport (1985).

APA Elections

If the kinds of problems that we illustrated with our first four examples never occur in real situations,, then they might be interesting as logical gimmicks but not as social problems. A study by Coombs, Cohen, and Chamberlain (1984) indicates that some of these problems arise in the presidential elections of the American Psychological Association (APA). Coombs et al. studied five presidential elections of the APA. While they did not analyze all the votes cast in these elections, the data that they report with regard to the roughly 40% of the ballots that gave complete rankings of all five candidates for the office may be characteristic of patterns to be expected with the complete vote.

Coombs et al. used five different methods for aggregating from 5,000 to 6,000 complete ballots in these elections to determine, among other things, the extent to which the "group" ordering changed as a function of the voting method used. Three of the systems studied were relatively common ones—plurality voting, the Borda system, and the Hare system—while two were relatively unusual—the Kemeny (1959) system and one devised by Coombs.

The most general of the findings was that in none of the elections did the five different methods lead to the same group ranking. Moreover, in each of the five years the number of distinct group rankings was either three or four out of a possible five. Worse yet, in only two of the five elections did the five methods agree on who the winner was. In the other three years the person elected APA president would have depended on the election system that was used *even though individual inputs are held constant.* In these three years, the "choice of the members" would have depended on more than the members' choices. Finally, in every election, there is evidence that independence of irrelevant alternatives was not the case.

Gerrymandering

Gerrymandering is the drawing of boundaries of voting districts so as to favor the party that is doing the drawing. As an intentional strategy to maximize the number of seats the party can occupy in a legislative body, gerrymandering represents an effort to render *vox populi* more mellifluous to party officials. Gerrymanderers rarely confess, however, and it is up to the Supreme Court to determine what constitutional guarantees, if any, gerrymandering violates (Schneider, 1985).

What is of interest to us are the facts that have been presented as evidence of gerrymandering. As a rule, the basic fact is a sizable disparity between the proportion of votes cast in favor of a party's candidates and the fraction of seats won by that party. In the case of Davis v. Bandemer, a case that the U.S. Supreme Court has agreed to hear, the complaint is that the redistricting plan approved by the Republican majority in the Indiana legislature blatantly protects Republican seats. In the 1982 legislative election in Indiana, Democrats won 52% of the votes for the Indiana House of Representatives, but only 43 of the 100 seats in the House (Schneider, 1985). The Wall Street Journal (1985) editorializes against Democratic gerrymandering by pointing out that in the 367 races that both parties entered in the 1984 national congressional election, Republicans received 500,000 more votes than the Democrats, but the latter ended up with 30 more seats in the House than their opponents.

Arguments based on the vote-seat disparity assume that there should be close agreement between the proportion of votes and the proportion of seats won. In legislatures built around proportional representation, like those of Israel, The Netherlands, or Norway, for instance, this should indeed be the case. In the United States, legislatures are not built on the idea of proportional representation, and if the proportions of seats and votes are close, it is more or less accidental (e.g., Grofman, 1982). If in 100 congressional races, one party won by a 51-49 split in all districts, that party would have won 100% of the seats with 51% of the votes. It was in this way that Ronald Reagan won 91% the electoral votes in his 1980 "landslide" victory over Carter and Anderson with only 51% of the popular vote (Boller, 1984).

In the political system of the United States, the relationship between seats won and votes cast is not simple. Some of the simplest ideas—for example, that there could be a uniform winning percentage in all districts and that the percentage of seats won by a party would equal the percentage of votes cast for that party—are mathematically impossible. The relationship is further complicated by differential voter turnouts in different districts, as Cain (1984) and Ornstein (1985) have shown. It is easy to demonstrate how this latter phenomenon can lead to an outcome in which the party receiving the most votes also receives the fewest seats. Ornstein (1985) makes precisely this argument regarding the outcome of the 1984 U.S. congressional elections.

Gerrymandering certainly happens, but Cain (1984) argues that it is as much a part of the political process as log-rolling and that its consequences are probably exaggerated. The mere fact that a vote-seat discrepancy exists is not in and of itself evidence of gerrymandering. The conversion of votes into seats in the U.S. political system is more complicated than we generally assume.

THE ROAD FROM
GROUP OUTPUTS TO INDIVIDUAL INPUTS

In the previous section we illustrated in a variety of ways the complexity of the process of combining individual inputs into a group output. This complexity is not only important to understand in and of itself, it also provides the backdrop for the major point of the present section, namely, that people tend to ignore that complexity and assume that a group decision or choice is an accurate indicant of the preferences or desires of the group members. This is what we have called the *group attribution error* (Allison & Messick, 1985b).

The Group Attribution Error

The group attribution error refers to people's tendency to assume a direct correspondence between a group decision, choice, or evaluation, and the preferences or attitudes of the members of the group. We have called this phenomenon the group attribution error to highlight its similarity to the *fundamental attribution error* (Ross, 1977), more recently called the *correspondent inference bias* (Gilbert & Jones, 1986).

This latter error or bias refers to people's tendency to make correspondent inferences about individuals on the basis of their behavior regardless of the external constraints that are placed on that behavior. The data of Jones and Harris (1967) provide a classic illustration of this tendency. The subjects in their study read either pro- or anti-Castro essays that they believed were written by others who were either given a choice to do so or who were compelled to do so. The subjects were then asked to draw inferences about the essay writers' attitudes toward Castro. According to correspondent inference theory, subjects should have made correspondent inferences only under those conditions in which the writers voluntarily chose to endorse a particular essay position. Jones and Harris found, however, that subjects tended to make attributions in the direction of the essay position regardless of whether the writers were permitted to select that position. Numerous studies have since replicated this result (e.g., Jones, Worchel, Goethals, & Grumet, 1971; Snyder & Jones, 1974; Yandrell & Insko, 1977).

The fact that people often fail to take into account external constraints that are placed on individuals suggests that they may fail to do so for groups as well. If so, group members may be seen as holding attitudes that are consistent with their group's behaviors, even if evidence is available to the contrary. Thus we hypothesized that one type of external constraint on the group decision—the group decision rule—would tend to be disregarded by subjects as they made inferences of members' attitudes from group decisions. We tested this idea in a recent series of five studies (Allison & Messick, 1985b).

The paradigm we used to explore group attributions consisted of presenting subjects with a vignette that described a group decision. After reading about the decision, subjects were asked to indicate the degree to which they believed that the average member of the group held an attitude that was consistent with that decision. In one study (Allison & Messick, 1985b, Exp. 4), we gave subjects a scenario that contained three items of information relevant to a recall election in Montana. Subjects read that (a) either 35%, 50%, or 65% of the voters were required to favor the recall for it to be successful; (b) either 43% or 57% of Montana's voting citizens subsequently voted in favor of the recall; and (c) the recall either succeeded or failed, depending on the configuration of the above two facts. After reading the vignette, subjects were asked, as manipulation checks, to remember the percentage of votes needed for the recall to succeed as well as the actual percentage of voters who did favor the recall. Subjects were then asked to estimate on a 1 (not at all in favor of the recall) to 7 (completely in favor of the recall) scale the attitude of the typical Montana citizen concerning the recall issue.

An analysis of the manipulation check questions revealed that virtually all of the subjects recalled all of the facts pertinent to the recall election. In examining subjects' attributions about the typical citizens of Montana, we found evidence that while subjects' judgments were influenced by the percentage of citizens favoring the recall, they were also significantly affected by the success or failure of the recall. Table 4.5 presents these attributions. As the table shows, the three conditions in which there was a successful outcome produced the three greatest attributed preferences for the recall. Despite remembering the precise number of citizens in favor of the recall, subjects tended to draw a correspondent inference between the ultimate success or failure of the

TABLE 4.5

**Mean Attitude Attributions as a Function of Decision Rule
and the Proportion of Voters in Favor of the Recall
in Allison and Messick's (1985b) Experiment 4**

| | *Percentage in Favor* | | |
Decision Rule	*43%*	*57%*	*Mean*
35%	4.75 (success)	5.19 (success)	4.97
50%	3.81 (failure)	5.13 (success)	4.47
65%	3.38 (failure)	4.19 (failure)	3.78
Mean	3.98	4.83	4.41

NOTE: The higher the number, the greater the attributed preference for the recall. The success or failure of the recall is in parentheses.

election and citizens' attitudes. We have obtained this same result in a number of other studies that have varied both the type of group that arrives at a decision (e.g., city, state, jury, nation) and the attributional measure (e.g., typical member, a randomly selected member, and the group in general).

It is clear, of course, that the tendency to infer a correspondence between attitudes and behavior is not always an error. What we are proposing is that, when drawing inferences about a group or an individual, people focus an inordinate amount of their attention on behavior, whether that behavior is an individual's or a group's, and focus too little attention on environmental forces that shape or influence the behavior. People, it seems, use the *heuristic* of assuming that an individual's or a group's behavior reflects the attitudes of these entities. Whether the use of this heuristic leads to errors depends on whether there are environmental constraints on an individual's actions and on the type of collective choice rule that a group uses to arrive at a decision. It is also clear that an awareness of these external constraints on individual and group behavior is not enough to prevent an attribution error from occurring. Jones and Harris's (1967) subjects *knew* that the essay writers had no choice in the selection of the essay position, and yet they still made correspondent inferences. Similarly, our subjects *knew* of the decision rule that influenced the outcome of the Montana recall election, and yet they still inferred a correspondence between that outcome and Montana's citizens' attitudes.

An additional question that we wished to answer was whether the correspondent group attributions that we demonstrated were limited to circumstances in which a person is a passive observer of decision made by other people. In other words, would a person commit the error if he or she were an active participant in the group decision making process? To test this idea, we conducted another study in which subjects participated in a mock jury task (Worth, Allison, & Messick, 1986). In this experiment, subjects were told that their jury was to determine the innocence or guilt of a fictitious defendant. They were presented with the facts pertinent to the case and were asked to decide, individually and without the benefit of deliberation, whether the defendant was innocent or guilty. After making their individual decisions, subjects were given false feedback about the number of other jurors voting guilty, the decision rule by which their jury was bound, and, of course, the final group decision. Subjects' attitude attributions revealed a pattern that was consistent with the data reported by Allison and Messick (1985b). When the final decision was guilty, subjects tended to believe that their fellow jurors were in favor of guilt; and when the final decision was innocent, the average other juror was believed to be in favor of innocence. This finding suggests that the group attribution error may not only arise in our perceptions of other groups' decisions, but may also arise in our perceptions of our *own* group's decisions.

Why the Error Occurs

The fact that people commit the same attributional error at the group level (the group attribution error) as they do at the individual level (the fundamental attribution error) suggests that a person and a collectivity may be interpreted as similar entities. Behavior that is displayed by the individual or collective entity is assumed to be diagnostic of underlying attitudes. There is a growing body of evidence that, in fact, people do perceive a group as a unit not unlike an individual. Political scientists have long known that there is a tendency among both lay people and government officials to view the actions of nations as those of individuals (e.g., Allison, 1971; Morgenthau, 1966; Wolfers, 1959). As a result of this group personification, the citizens of a given country are believed to be responsible for, and have attitudes consistent with, the actions of that country's government.

What evidence is there in social psychology that a group is perceived as a single unit or entity similar to an individual? Although the idea has been brought up in numerous theoretical pieces (e.g., Campbell, 1958; Steiner, 1972), the first empirical demonstrations that people perceive a group as a unit were published by Knowles and Bassett (1976) and by Wilder (1977). Knowles and Basset conducted a study in which confederates were placed at the entrance of a library while varying the extent to which these confederates were physically similar to one another. Passers-by were then filmed as they walked toward and around this collection of individuals. The authors reported that people were more likely to walk around confederates who were similar to one another, and who thus looked like a group, than around confederates who were dissimilar. In another study, Knowles, Kreuser, Haas, Hyde, and Schuchart (1976) found that passers-by not only physically distanced themselves from groups, but that the larger the group, the larger the distance passers-by left between it and themselves.

In another study demonstrating a similar effect, Wilder (1977) addressed the issue of whether individuals and groups were equally powerful in exerting influence on a person. He proposed that social influence varies with the number of social entities present rather than with the number of individuals present. To test this idea, Wilder exposed subjects to a tape recorded persuasive message spoken by each of four persons. Some subjects were informed that these persons constituted a group of other "subjects who were here yesterday." Other subjects were told that they were to listen to two tapes, one a recording of two subjects who were in the laboratory the previous morning, the other a recording of two subjects present the previous afternoon. Wilder found that subjects were more persuaded by the message when they were exposed to the opinions of two groups of two persons each than when they heard the opinions of one group of four persons. These data, along with those reported by Knowles and Bassett (1976), indicate that people perceive a group of individuals as a social unit in the same sense that they perceive an individual as a social unit.

Given that people unitize groups, it does not seem surprising that they commit an attribution error at the group level that is similar in structure to one that they commit at the individual level. If groups and individuals are perceived as similar entities, moreover, then the etiology of the group attribution error may have much in common with the etiology of the fundamental attribution error. According to current theory, the fundamental error arises simply from the tendency of an actor's behavior to "engulf the field" of an observer (Heider, 1958). This explanation is, of course, a perceptual one, as it relies on the tendency for behavior to be more salient in one's visual field than the situational factors that may have given rise to that behavior.

While the principle of behavior engulfing the field may adequately explain correspondent inference biases at the individual level of behavior, it appears to have limited applicability in the domain of group decisions. In the vignette method that we (Allison & Messick, 1985b) employed, information about the group decision cannot be any more perceptually "engulfing" or salient than information about the decision rule or information about the proportion of members favoring the decision.

Perhaps a better explanation for the group attribution error is that it involves the use of the representativeness heuristic (Kahneman & Tversky, 1972). As these authors note, a judgment of representativeness can refer to the relation between a value and a distribution, an instance and a category, a sample and a population, and an effect and a cause. The case that we are dealing with, the relation between a group judgment, choice, or ranking and the attitudes, choices, or preferences of the group members, has similarities to both the sample-population and the value-distribution cases. People expect that the sample of political representatives will have roughly the same party composition as the electorate, although as we noted earlier, there is no scientific basis for this expectation. A successful recall election is more representative of voters who are opposed to their elected officials than an unsuccessful election, and we demonstrated that estimates of the typical attitude of the voters change as a function of the success or failure of the recall even when the percentage of voters favoring the recall is held constant (Allison & Messick, 1985b).

In the domain of statistical reasoning, the representativeness heuristic implies that judgments about samples should be relatively insensitive to sample size, prior probability, and other features that have to do with the generation of the sample from the population. In the same way, we have shown that judgments about group outcomes tend to be insensitive to the decision rules that are used to generate the decision (Allison & Messick, 1985b).

A related type of overgeneralization regarding group judgments has been reported by Hamill, Wilson, and Nisbett (1980). They gave subjects characterological information about a single member of a group. The information was said to be either typical or atypical of all group members in general. The authors found that subjects made generalizations to the population on the basis of the single sample *regardless of the sample's typicality*. We propose that the group attribution error reflects a process similar to the one uncovered by Hamill et al. (1980). When people learn of a group's decision, they use the representativeness heuristic to infer that the decision is representative of those attitudes.

The use of judgmental heuristics means that such judgments can be made quickly, and with little thought. At the individual level of inference, there is some evidence that people who witness a behavior arrive at a correspondent inference *spontaneously* and *automatically*, without intention, awareness, or control (Winter, Uleman, & Cunniff, 1985). This evidence has prompted Hamilton (1987) to draw a distinction between a correspondent trait inference and what social psychologists have traditionally referred to as a "causal attribution." According to Hamilton, an attribution requires a thoughtful analysis of information that leads to an assessment of the cause of some behavioral event. A correspondent inference, on the other hand, precedes that causal analysis and may actually dictate whether an internal or external causal attribution is made. Although we have no data supporting the idea that trait inferences are also made automatically at the group level, we believe that this automaticity may indeed occur for judgments about groups as well as for judgments about individuals.

CONCLUDING REMARKS

We began this chapter with a brief overview of the historical origins of the group-individual relation. For more than a century scholars have debated the appropriateness of looking to individuals to explain the actions of a group. One faction, led by sociologists and anthropologists, maintained that the group was the true reality and that it was a mistake to use individual-level phenomena to explain group actions. Psychologists composed the opposing faction, asserting that only by looking to individuals could one truly achieve an understanding of groups. Our review of the group decision making literature suggests that both factions may be correct. Groups, as we have shown, can and do produce decisions that fail to correspond to members' preferences. More than that, we have also seen that group decisions may have properties that do not characterize any of the individuals. Group preferences may be intransitive when all the group members have transitive preferences, group rankings may not be independent of irrelevant alternatives when the individual ones are, and sophisticated voting may result in group preferences that are shared by none of the members.

Groups, on the other hand, do exert unique forces on individuals. Only in groups do people need to consider sophisticated voting, the strategic misrepresentation of their preferences. The polarizing effect of group interaction influences individual as well as group judgments. The deterioration of group performance that accompanies social loafing or the groupthink phenomenon can be attributed to changes in individual actions induced by others.

The complexities involved in combining individual inputs to form a group product are reflected in the heading of that section of the chapter, where we borrowed from Jones's (1979) "rocky road" metaphor to describe the difficulty in attaining a correspondence between individual preferences and group outcomes. The roughness of this road has been aptly summarized by Thomas Schelling (1971) in his discussion of micromotives and macrophenomena: "There is no universal teleology relating individual adaptations to collective results, neither a beneficent teleology nor a pernicious one" (p. 89).

The second road, the inferential one from group outputs to individual inputs, is far from rocky. It describes the path that perceivers take when they must judge whether a correspondence exists between a group product and members' preferences. The smoothness of this road is illustrated by the tendency of perceivers of collective action to overlook the complexities of the group decision making process and infer that collective products are representative of individual inputs. There are indications, moreover, that the tendency to make correspondent trait inferences at both the individual and at the group levels may be done automatically, with little attributional work performed at all.

REFERENCES

A poll: Europe vs. the U.S. (1986, April 29). *Newsweek*, p. 22.

Allison, G. T. (1971). *Essence of decision: Explaining the Cuban missile crisis.* Boston, MA: Little, Brown.

Allison, S. T., & Messick, D. M. (1985a). Effects of experience on performance in a replenishable resource trap. *Journal of Personality and Social Psychology, 49,* 943-948.

Allison, S. T., & Messick, D. M. (1985b). The group attribution error. *Journal of Experimental Social Psychology, 21,* 563-579.

Allport, F. H. (1924). *Social psychology.* Boston, MA: Houghton Mifflin.

Allport, F. H. (1933). *Institutional behavior.* Chapel Hill, NC: University of North Carolina Press.

Allport, F. H. (1962). A structuronomic conception of behavior: Individual and collective I. Structure theory and the master problem of social psychology. *Journal of Abnormal and Social Psychology, 64,* 3-30.

Arrow, K. J. (1963). *Social choice and individual values* (2nd ed). New Haven, CT: Yale University Press.

Boller, P. F., Jr. (1984). *Presidential campaigns.* New York: Oxford University Press.

Brams, S. J. (1976). *Paradoxes in politics: An introduction to the nonobvious in political science.* New York: Free Press.

Brams, S. J., & Fishburn, P. C. (1983). *Approval voting.* Boston, MA: Birkhauser.

Cain, B. P. (1984). *The reapportionment puzzle.* Berkeley, CA: University of California Press.

Campbell, D. T. (1958). Common fate, similarity, and other indices of the status of aggregates of persons as social entities. *Behavioral Science, 3,* 14-25.

Chechile, R. A. (1984). Logical foundations for a fair and rational method of voting. In W. C. Swap and associates (Eds.), *Group decision making* (pp. 97-114). Newbury Park, CA: Sage.

Colman, A. M. (1982). *Game theory and experimental games: The study of strategic interaction.* Oxford: Pergamon.

Condorcet, M.J.A.N.C. Marquis de (1785). Essai sur l' application de l'analyse a la probabilite des decisions rendues a la pluralite des voix. In M.J.A.N.C. Marquis de Condorcet, *Oeuvres Completes.* Paris.

Coombs, C. H., Cohen, J. L., & Chamberlain, J. R. (1984). An empirical study of some election systems. *American Psychologist, 39,* 140-157.

Cross, J. G., & Guyer, M. J. (1980). *Social traps.* Ann Arbor, MI: University of Michigan Press.

Davis, J. H. (1973). Group decision and social interaction: A theory of social decision schemes. *Psychological Review, 80,* 97-125.

Dawes, R. M. (1980). Social dilemmas. *Annual Review of Psychology, 31,* 169-193.

Durkheim, E. (1898). *The rules of sociological method.* New York: Free Press.

Farquharson, R. (1969). *Theory of voting.* New Haven, CT: Yale University Press.

Faust, W. L. (1959). Group versus individual problem-solving. *Journal of Abnormal and Social Psychology, 59,* 68-72.

Felsenthal, P., Maoz, A., & Rapoport, A. (1985). *Comparing approval with plurality voting in genuine elections* (IPDM Report NO. 21). Haifa, Israel: University of Haifa.

Fishburn, P. C. (1973). *The theory of social choice.* Princeton, NJ: Princeton University Press.

Fishburn, P. C. (1974). Paradoxes of voting. *American Political Science Review, 68,* 537-546.

Gilbert, D. T., & Jones, E. E. (1986). Perceiver-induced constraint: Interpretations of self-generated reality. *Journal of Personality and Social Psychology, 50,* 269-280.

Goethals, G. R., & Zanna, M. P. (1979). The role of social comparison in choice shifts. *Journal of Personality and Social Psychology, 37,* 1469-1476.

Grofman, B. (1982). For single member districts random is not equal. In B. Grofman, A. Lijphaut, R. B. Mackay, & H. A. Scarrow (Eds.), *Representation and redistricting issues* (pp. 55-58). Lexington, MA: D. C. Heath.

Hamill, R., Wilson, T. D., & Nisbett, R. E. (1980). Insensitivity to sample bias: Generalizing from atypical cases. *Journal of Personality and Social Psychology, 39,* 578-589.

Hamilton, D. L. (1987). Causal attribution viewed from an information processing perspective. In D. Bar-Tal & A. Kruglanski (Eds.), *The social psychology of knowledge*. Oxford: Cambridge University Press.

Hardin, G. (1968). The tragedy of the commons. *Science, 162*, 1243-1248.

Harkins, S. G., Latane, B., & Williams, K. (1980). Social loafing: Allocating effort or taking it easy? *Journal of Experimental Social Psychology, 16*, 457-465.

Harvey, J. B. (1974). The abilene paradox: The management of agreement. *Organizational Dynamics, 3*, 63-80.

Heider, F. (1958). *The psychology of interpersonal relations*. New York: John Wiley.

Ingham, A. G., Levinger, G., Graves, J., & Peckham, V. (1974). The Ringlemann effect: Studies of group sizes and group performance. *Journal of Experimental Social Psychology, 10*, 371-384.

Janis, I. L. (1972). *Victims of groupthink*. Boston, MA: Houghton Mifflin.

Jones, E. E. (1979). The rocky road from acts to dispositions. *American Psychologist, 34*, 107-117.

Jones, E. E., & Harris, V. A. (1967). The attribution of attitudes. *Journal of Experimental Social Psychology, 3*, 1-24.

Jones, E. E., Worchel, S., Goethals, G. R., & Grumet, J. F. (1971). Prior expectancy and behavioral extremity as determinants of attitude attribution. *Journal of Experimental Social Psychology, 7*, 59-80.

Kahneman, D., & Tversky, A. (1972). Subjective probability: A judgment of representativeness. *Cognitive Psychology, 3*, 430-454.

Kemeny, J. (1959). Mathematics without numbers. *Daedalus, 88*, 577-591.

Knowles, E. S., & Bassett, R. L. (1976). Groups and crowds as social entities: Effects of activity, size, and member similarity on nonmembers. *Journal of Personality and Social Psychology, 34*, 837-845.

Knowles, E. S., Kreuser, B., Haas, S., Hyde, M., & Schuchart, G. (1976). Group size and the extension of social space boundaries. *Journal of Personality and Social Psychology, 33*, 647-654.

Lamm, H., & Myers, D. G. (1978). Group induced polarization of attitudes and behavior. In L. Berkowitz (Ed.), *Advances in experimental social psychology* (Vol. 11, pp. 145-195). New York: Academic Press.

Latane, B., Williams K., & Harkins, S. (1979). Many hands make light the work: The causes and consequences of social loafing. *Journal of Personality and Social Psychology, 37*, 822-832.

LeBon, G. (1903). *The crowd*. London: Unwin.

Lorge, I., Fox, D., Davitz, J., & Brenner, M. (1958). A survey of studies contrasting the quality of group performance and individual performance, 1920-1957. *Psychological Bulletin, 55*, 337-372.

Mackie, D. M. (1986). Social identification effects in group polarization. *Journal of Personality and Social Psychology, 50*, 720-728.

McDougall, W. (1920). *The group mind*. New York: Putnam.

McKay, A. F. (1980) *Arrow's theorem: The paradox of social choice*. New Haven, CT: Yale University Press.

Messick, D. M., & Brewer, M. B. (1983). Solving social dilemmas: A review. In L. Wheeler & P. Shaver (Eds.), *Review of Personality and Social Psychology* (Vol. 4, pp. 11-44). Newbury Park, CA: Sage.

Messick, D. M. , & Thorngate, W. B. (1967). Relative gain maximization in experimental games. *Journal of Experimental Social Psychology, 3*, 85-101.

Morganthau, H. (1970). *Politics among nations.* New York: Academic Press.

Nagao, D. H., & Davis, J. H. (1980). Some implications of temporal drift in social parameters. *Journal of Experimental Social Psychology, 16,* 479-496.

Ornstein, N. J. (1985, May 7). Genesis of a 'gerrymander'. *Wall Street Journal,* p. 28.

Rapoport, A., Felsenthal, D., & Maoz, Z. (1986). *Sincere vs. sophisticated behavior in noncooperative four-person games* (IPDM Report No. 38). Haifa, Israel: University of Haifa.

Ringlemann, M. (1913). Recherches sur les moteurs animes: Travail de l'homme. *Annales de l'Institut National agronomique,* 2e serie-tomie XII, 1-40.

Ross, E. A. (1908). *Social psychology: An outline and a source book.* New York: Macmillan.

Ross, L. (1977). The intuitive psychologist and his shortcomings: Distortions in the attribution process. In L. Berkowitz (Ed.), *Advances in experimental social psychology* (Vol. 10, pp. 173-220). New York: Academic Press.

Schelling, T. C. (1978). *Micromotives and macrobehavior.* New York: Norton.

Schneider, W. (1985, October 31). U.S. supreme court enters thicket of gerrymander. *Los Angeles Times,* Part IV, p. 1.

Sen, A. K. (1970). *Collective choice and social welfare.* San Francisco: Holden-Day.

Shaw, M. E. (1932). A comparison of individuals and small groups in the rational solution of complex problems. *American Journal of Psychology, 44,* 491-504.

Smith, A. (1776/1976). *The wealth of nations.* Chicago: University of Chicago Press.

Smoke, W. H., & Zajonc, R. B. (1962). On the reliability of group judgments and decisions. In J. H. Criswell, H. Solomon, & P. Suppes (Eds.), *Mathematical methods in small group processes* (pp. 322-333). Stanford, CA: Stanford University Press.

Snyder, M. L., & Jones, E. E. (1974). Attitude attribution when behavior is constrained. *Journal of Experimental Social Psychology, 10,* 585-600.

Steiner, I. D. (1972). *Group process and productivity.* New York: Academic Press.

Stoner, J.A.F. (1961). *A comparison of individual and group decisions under risk.* Unpublished master's thesis, Massachusetts Institute of Technology, Cambridge, MA.

Swap, W. C., and associates. (1984). *Group decision making.* Newbury Park, CA: Sage.

Turner, R. H., & Killian, L. M. (1957). *Collective behavior.* Englewood Cliffs, NJ: Prentice-Hall.

Vinokur, A., & Burnstein, E. (1974). Effects of partially shared persuasive arguments on group-induced shifts: A group problem-solving approach. *Journal of Personality and Social Psychology, 29,* 305-315.

Wall Street Journal (1985, May 1). Gerrymander dynasty, p. 32.

Wallach, M. A., Kogan, N., & Bem, D. J. (1962). Group influence on individual risk taking. *Journal of Abnormal and social psychology, 65,* 75-86.

White, L. A. (1947). Cultural and psychological interpretations of human behavior. *American Sociological Review, 12,* 686-698.

Wilder, D. A. (1977). Perception of groups, size of opposition, and social influence. *Journal of Experimental Social Psychology, 13,* 253-268.

Winter, L., Uleman, T. S., & Cunniff, C. (1985). How automatic are social judgments? *Journal of Personality and Social Psychology, 49,* 904-917.

Wolfers, A. (1959). The actors in international politics. In W. Fox (Ed.), *Theoretical aspects of international relations* (pp. 83-106). Notre Dame, IN: Notre Dame University Press.

Worth, L. T., Allison, S. T., & Messick, D. M. (1986). *Impact of a group's decision on perceptions of one's own and others' attitudes.* Unpublished manuscript, University of California, Santa Barbara.

Yandrell, B., & Insko, C. A. (1977). Attributions of attitudes to speakers and listeners under assigned-behavior conditions: Does behavior engulf the field? *Journal of Experimental Social Psychology, 3,* 269-278.

5

Individual and Group Goals

DIANE M. MACKIE
GEORGE R. GOETHALS

Diane M. Mackie is Assistant Professor of Psychology at the University of California, Santa Barbara. Before receiving her Ph.D. in Social Psychology from Princeton University, she taught at the University of Auckland, Auckland, New Zealand. Her research interests include group processes, particularly the cognitive and motivational consequences of social categorization, and social influence, particularly the effects of factors like group membership on the extent and goals of processing persuasive messages.

George R. Goethals is Professor of Psychology and Acting Dean of the Faculty at Williams College. He received his Ph.D. from Duke University. His research interests include self-serving biases in attributional and social comparison, particularly in the role of self-esteem in social projection. He is coauthor of *Psychology* with Crider, Kavanaugh, and Solomon, and Coeditor of *Theories of Group Behavior*, with Mullen. He has served as Associate Editor of the *Journal of Experimental Social Psychology*.

Social psychology has traditionally been concerned with the nature of the social group and its relationship to the individual human beings who compose it (Allport, 1924; Allport, 1954; LeBon, 1895; McDougall, 1920). The thesis of this chapter is that groups have goals that are similar to those of individuals, that groups and individuals are interdependent for success in achieving their goals, though they sometimes face goal conflict, and that the key phenomena of intragroup life reflect tension between individual and group goals, and continued negotiation directed toward the satisfaction of both of them. In order for both individual and group goals to be simultaneously satisfied, an isomorphism between them must be forged, such that the same actions are perceived as leading to the simultaneous attainment of both individual and group goals.

We will consider first the goals of both individuals and groups, emphasizing their similarity in kind. Second, we will consider how the specific goals of individuals and groups can conflict. Third, we will

AUTHORS' NOTE: We would like to thank Clyde Hendrick, Eric Knowles, Brian Mullen, and two anonymous reviewers for their helpful comments on earlier drafts of this article.

consider how processes of social influence, cooperation and competition, and inclusion and exclusion are involved in resolving goal conflicts and forging goal isomorphism. Finally, we will discuss the key process of maintaining group identity and its role in facilitating goal isomorphism.

Before considering individual and group goals, we must ask whether the group can legitimately be said to have goals, needs, and purposes. To what extent is it philosophically sound to speak of group goals, group strategies, and group identities? Although the group does not have the empirical existence of the individual, we take the approach that for its members, and often for the members of other groups, it has a psychological reality equivalent to that of individuals. Following W.I. Thomas (see Coser, 1956), we believe that the perception of groups and group goals makes them real in their consequences. Thus in speaking of group goals we mean goals that group members perceive as having been consensually agreed upon or imposed by group members (Cartwright & Zander, 1968). We will also suggest in a later section of the chapter that the psychological reality of a group can be activated in ways that help ensure the achievement of group goals and the stability of group membership.

INDIVIDUAL AND GROUP GOALS

Theories of motivation have recognized a wide variety of human needs and goals (Cofer & Appley, 1964; Maslow, 1970; Murray, 1938). Groups can also be seen as having goals, and because a group's goals reflect the goals of its members, it is not surprising that they are of a similar kind. While there are a variety of goals that could be proposed as characteristic of both individuals and groups, there are three such goals that seem to be of special importance for understanding the ways groups and individuals strive for goal isomorphism. We will attempt to illustrate how individuals and groups resolve conflict and achieve isomorphism with respect to these goals, which we term utilitarian, knowledge, and identity goals. Utilitarian goals, especially the abilities of problem solving groups to organize for such goals, have received considerable emphasis in the experimental social psychological literature. The knowledge function was made explicit in social psychology by Festinger (1950), Kelley (1952), and Deutsch and Gerard (1955), but has faded from research significance. The identity function has been more prominent in sociology (e.g., Mead, 1934), but it has recently assumed considerable importance in the group literature of social psychology.

Utilitarian Goals

Most theories of motivation recognize needs for tangible outcomes, such as for food, water, shelter, and so forth, that must be satisfied for the organism to survive. The need for tangible outcomes produces what we refer to as utilitarian goals. In introducing the idea of *effect dependence,* Jones and Gerard (1967) indicated that many of these needs can be satisfied through social interaction among interdependent individuals. People generally join groups and stay in them because they perceive that belonging to the group will satisfy their needs for protection, money, achievement, or the like. Because of this general need for the group to achieve certain goals in order to obtain outcomes for its members, group goals can be a direct reflection of individual needs and goals. For example, union members define certain concessions from management as their goal and obtaining these concessions becomes a goal of the group as a whole. Similarly, the telephone company has the goal of making money for its stockholders. Festinger (1950) recognized that groups have goals by his concept of *group locomotion.* He also recognized that these goals must reflect the concerns and needs of individual group members.

Knowledge Goals

The companion concept to Jones and Gerard's (1967) idea of effect dependence, *information dependence,* presumes that individuals are dependent on other people for information or knowledge about how the world works. The concept of information dependence signals that obtaining knowledge and defining reality is an important goal for individual human functioning (Heider, 1944; Maslow, 1970; Murray, 1938). Festinger (1950) suggested that groups as a whole also strive to define reality. His concept of *social reality* embodies this notion. It suggests that reality construction or knowledge goals can arise in groups for two reasons: (a) so that individual group members can satisfy their needs to know through knowledge available and obtainable in the group (Wegner, 1987), and (b) so that the group as a whole can have a definition of social reality. Knowledge goals are closely related to utilitarian goals. The need to construct reality may emerge in groups out of a concern with group locomotion. The social reality that emerges in a group can define for its members what utilitarian goals are important and how they can be satisfied. Evidence of the need to define reality in a group comes from many studies that show group consensus seeking tendencies (Jones & Gerard, 1967, chap. 10; Schachter, 1959; Wrightsman, 1960).

Identity Goals

Many theories of personality and motivation assume that people have an active desire to understand themselves as well as reality more generally (Erikson, 1968; Festinger, 1954). Knowledge of the self as well as external reality is useful in functioning more effectively. Festinger's (1954) social comparison theory hypothesizes that people have drives to evaluate their opinions and abilities. Together these drives suggest a need to know both oneself and the world.

Erickson's (1968) closely related identity theory describes a need to know oneself and to form an ego-identity, a sense of who one is and the role one can play in society. The need for identity, however, is more than a desire to know and understand oneself. The desire simply to know implies a disinterested perspective on the object of knowledge; equally important is the desire to establish a positive sense of self. Erikson's concept of identity posits a positive sense of self and a positive sense of the productive role one can play in society. More recently, social identity theorists (Tajfel & Turner, 1986) explicitly discuss the individual's desire for a positive self-concept and the parallel need for groups to establish a positive social identity.

According to Tajfel and Turner (1986), individuals and the group as a whole desire to compare favorably to relevant comparison groups on socially desirable traits in order to carve out a positive social identity. This desire of groups to define themselves positively relative to other groups leads group members to allocate outcomes in ways that favor their own group and to compete with other groups, not so much for needed resources but for the positive social identity, the "bragging rights," that goes with besting the others. Research reviewed by Tajfel and Turner is impressive in showing that arbitrary division of individuals into groups leads to in-group favoritism and out-group hostility in the interest of achieving positive social identity. Thus the need for identity involves two things: a need to know oneself and one's place, and a need to have that self-knowledge be positive.

The above three goals, utilitarian, knowledge, and identity, are not an exhaustive list of human motives. We think they are primary in group and individual functioning, and we will use them to develop our main theme, that is, the pressures toward isomorphism between the concerns, needs, and goals of the individual and those of the group. Let us now turn to exploring the manifestations of seeking utilitarian outcomes, knowledge, and identity in group contexts.

CONFLICT BETWEEN INDIVIDUAL AND GROUP GOALS

Thibaut and Kelley (1959) characterized group interaction, especially initial interactions between groups and their members, as pervaded by an atmosphere of ambivalence. Such ambivalence reflects the recognition by both group and individual that although they are interdependent for mutual goal satisfaction, their interdependence will exact some price. For individuals, the costs include interaction with others who are hardly known (resulting in primary tension, Bormann, 1975; Thibaut & Kelley, 1959); personal investment of goods, services, time, and effort (often demanded by groups as means of assuring commitment, Aronson & Mills, 1959); increasing vulnerability to social rejection (Pepitone & Wilpinski, 1960; see Shrauger, 1975, for a review); and, most importantly, restrictions of individual freedoms in the service of group coordination and the necessary delay or redirection of individual goals. For the group, attainment of goals is hampered by individuals pursuing separate goals (creating process losses due to member motivation and coordination, Steiner, 1972), and by the necessity either of ensuring that individual goals are satisfied or of persuading individuals to pursue group goals.

Two cases of conflict over individual and group goals can be considered. First, both individual and group can be pursuing the same goal, but can wish for different manifestations of it. For example, both individual and group may be simultaneously concerned with establishing an identity but the identity they wish to establish may differ. Second, the goal most salient to the individual at any given time may not mesh with the goal that the group is pursuing. For example, conflicts can arise when individuals are more concerned with attaining social support from fellow group members than with task demands that ensure resources for the group. We will consider these two kinds of conflicts separately, as conflicts within goals and conflicts between goals.

Conflicts Within Goals

Conflicts within individual and group goals can arise in the pursuit of any of the three goals we have defined as primary. The common's dilemma (Hardin, 1968) or social trap (Platt, 1963; Dawes, 1980) are prime examples of cases in which an individual's short-term utilitarian goals conflict with the long-term best interest of the group. Similarly, the individual's view of reality may conflict with the group's view of reality, creating situations in which social influence from the group is opposed by the individual's attempt to wield minority influence to impress a new opinion on the group. The outcome of individual resistance to the group message has, of course, particularly high stakes for the group because of the possibility that other group members could become similarly rebellious (Allen, 1975).

The condition in which individual identity and group identity do not mesh has been studied mainly from the point of view of role conflict (Merton, 1948). One of the group's most important tasks for successful goal attainment is the organization of roles within the group so that utilitarian, informational, and identity needs can be met. Role strain (Secord & Backman, 1964) can occur when groups redefine roles while individuals retain old beliefs about the requirements of the role. For example, in an attempt to deal with reduced funding, a university might decide that faculty have to demonstrate productivity and accountability, requirements that conflict with faculty members' beliefs in a traditional model of academic freedom and repugnance for "punching the clock." Groups often assign role expectations by virtue of age, sex, race, or religion, and roles carry expectations about membership in such groups. These expectations are particularly hard on individual group members assigned roles that do not match personal characteristics. For example, consider the high frequency with which young female assistant professors are mistakenly thought to be secretaries, with resulting social pressure to cultivate sobersided, dignified, and intellectual behavior, what Ellis and Keedy (1960) referred to as the "wise man" role.

Conflict within goals may take the form of intragroup competition. Although intergroup competition may be more prevalent than intragroup competition (Krebs & Miller, 1985), the latter is an important manifestation of individuals seeking to achieve goals that conflict with those of other group members. Individuals within a group may compete to obtain limited resources, i.e., utilitarian goals. For example, members of a community may compete for scarce grazing land, water, or gasoline, often creating the typical "commons dilemma" noted above. Members of a community may also compete for well-paying jobs. In addition to competition among individuals, the larger group may compete with a single individual who is perceived as obtaining more than a fair share of resources, especially when success may have implications for relative status or ability that the group may not want to confer on that individual (Hoffman, Festinger, & Lawrence, 1954).

Competition for scarce resources in groups may be accompanied by competition for status, from which may derive an important component of identity. In fact, competition within groups may be a major manifestation of the need for identity. Furthermore, achieving recognized status within the group may be extremely useful in the pursuit of somewhat limited utilitarian resources. Although human beings may not establish dominance hierarchies that are as rigid as those of other species, people do compete for positions of power and leadership that confer status. The more status and power a person has in the group, the more the norms regarding the distribution of resources are likely to be favorable to that person, understandable in terms of distributive justice or equity. The more one contributes to a group, and high status implies large contributions, the more one is entitled to participate in its benefits. Thus people within groups may compete for status in order directly to satisfy identity needs and indirectly to satisfy utilitarian objectives (Adams, 1965).

Conflicts Between Goals

A second set of situations arise when the group is pursuing one goal while some members are pursuing another. This condition has been assumed to be the case in the bulk of research and theorizing on problem solving groups. The group goal of successfully achieving utilitarian goals is in conflict with individual members' concern with favorable interpersonal interactions. A supervisor's reluctance to ask others to fill a less desirable role, for example, may interfere with the efficient organization necessary to carry out a task. Similarly, an individual's desire for status within the group may create a situation in which the individual attempts to dominate task interactions, thereby jeopardizing utilitarian goal attainment.

What is the consequence of these conflict situations? Our view is that individuals and groups can forge goal isomorphism by engaging in social influence to achieve consensus, by engaging in varying degrees of competition and cooperation, or by including or excluding particular individuals in the group.

FORGING GOAL ISOMORPHISM

The central assumption in this chapter is that intragroup life is marked by the seeking of isomorphism between individual and group goals. Individuals join groups with the expectation that their individual goals can be better met through group action than through individual action; likewise, groups recruit and retain individuals with the expectation that their group goals can be better met with the participation of key individuals. This simultaneous activity of individuals and groups trying to reach their goals and forge goal isomorphism is not always smooth or easy. It will manifest itself in three classes of behavior: social influence, cooperation and competition, and inclusion versus exclusion. Mutual action of the individual toward the group and of the group toward the individual in these three areas underlies much of what we believe to be important in intragroup behavior. Furthermore, action by the group as a whole with respect to other groups in these same three domains accounts for a great deal of intergroup behavior.

Social Influence

Both individuals and groups who are concerned with reaching goals through concerted action will need to influence others so as to achieve consensus both about what goals should be pursued and about how to obtain them. These two kinds of influence are implicit in Festinger's (1950) concept of group locomotion. Group locomotion requires uniformity of opinion. The group must agree on where it wants to go (ends) and how it wants to get there (means) before it can actually locomote from one region to another in its life space (Lewin, 1935; Jones & Gerard, 1967, chap. 9). Thus influence will take place concerning what to do and how to do it. While Festinger presented group locomotion as something that generates pressures toward uniformity, another way of looking at it is to say that uniformity of needs and goals creates pressures toward group locomotion. In short, effect-dependent, interdependent individuals (Kelley & Thibaut, 1978) join groups to better achieve their ends in concert, and the ends they conjointly hold become goals of the group.

It is important to add that intragroup influences may flow in one of two ways, from the individual toward other group members, or from the group toward the individual. Festinger (1950, 1954) recognized that uniformity of opinion in a group can be achieved by changing self or changing other. Individuals may try to change others or find that they are the targets of influence, or both. Festinger's theoretical statements and other early treatments of social influence generally assumed that influence would flow in the direction of the minority member. The larger group would attempt to change the deviant individual or subgroup.

More recent treatments of social influence have highlighted the conditions under which an individual or a minority can move the majority (Moscovici, 1980).

Influence is implied by the need to establish consensus for the attainment of all three primary goals. The attainment of utilitarian goals demands agreement about the efficient coordination of abilities and resources. The goal of achieving a definition of reality also obviously demands social consensus. Often overlooked is the fact that influence is also an important factor in shaping an individual's identity within a group and the group's identity as a whole. As with influence regarding utilitarian objectives and influence regarding the nature of reality, influence regarding an individual's personal characteristics flows two ways. First, the larger group can convey its opinions regarding the individual's characteristics and thereby influence the individual's identity through the process of reflected appraisal (Cooley, 1902; Gergen, 1971; Jones & Gerard, 1967; Mead, 1934). Second, the individual can influence the group regarding his or her own personal traits. Such influence is usually done through the form of self-presentation known as *self-construction* (Baumeister & Hutton, 1987). Self-construction and reflected appraisal are closely related reciprocal processes. Most notions of identity (Cooley, 1902; Erikson, 1968; Mead, 1934) assume that people's self-concepts are inevitably influenced by what others think. As Goffman indicated, our face, that is, our positive identity, is "only on loan" to us from society. Thus the individual may attempt self-construction through various self-presentational influence strategies (ingratiation, intimidation, etc., see Jones & Pittman, 1982), but the success of the effort from the individual's point of view depends on other people's accepting the presented self and conveying that acceptance in a reflected appraisal.

One of the most effective strategies groups can utilize to influence their members and ensure the meshing of individual and group goals is the development and strict maintenance of norms. Norms are sets of expectations that govern group and individual beliefs and behavior. Although group members may conform to group norms because of fears of sanctions for transgressions, more often group norms are internalized through the process of socialization into the group and thus act as powerful internal determinants of group-relevant behavior (Sherif, 1936). The importance of norms as influence strategies in a group is reflected in the fact that group norms tend to develop particularly in relation to the three goals that we have characterized as central functions of group life. The types of norms most studied in social psychology are norms that govern the coordination of interpersonal action, in order that group tasks may be more efficiently completed. Interactional norms govern turn-taking and allocation procedures, situational norms determine appropriate behavior in a given situation, and roles establish group members' participation in coordinated actions. An important set of norms also serve informational uses (Kelley, 1952; Sherif, 1936), such as norms for judging success, recognition of beauty, and evaluation of family size. These norms give correct information about reality in the face of ambiguity, and may often seem so useful in this respect that they replace a more rational but exhaustive search for information.

Particularly powerful norms develop to help fulfill identity needs in groups, particularly needs for love, status, and esteem. Etiquette norms, for example, supervise routine exchanges between group members (such as ritual greetings and inquiries about personal health) that satisfy the desire to be noticed and accorded concern while protecting each person from unpredictability, uncertainty, and embarrassment (Goffman, 1959). Other norms also preserve the identity of the group as a whole, not only by encouraging joint commitment internally but by advocating preference for the in-group over other groups. Such preference is manifested in the allocation of highly valued commodities, including such things as praise. Thus norm formation relating to the pursuit of informational, identity, and utilitarian goals is clearly a central part of the group's action toward the individual.

The particular potency of norms in interpersonal situations was first pointed out by Thibaut and Kelley (1959), who realized that referring to shared norms rather than engaging in active and repeated influence attempts represented huge savings in personal power. The same argument can clearly be made at the group level: When consensually agreed upon norms can be used to modify, coordinate, intensify, or halt individual action, the group need not suffer the losses incurred by constant vigilance, influence attempts, and lack of coordination. Because norms short circuit the need for extensive information exchange and behavior calibration, they serve as persuasion heuristics of particular potency in the group situation. Instituting (and institutionalizing) norms are thus ways that groups can more efficiently attain their own goals while protecting individual goals.

Competition and Cooperation

If individuals and groups are to achieve their goals they must be prepared to compete, sometimes within the group, more often against others outside the group. At the same time, competition must be regulated. The unbridled use of power and competition within groups is disruptive to both group locomotion and the prevailing social reality, and unrestricted competition between groups, especially in modern times, can have devastating consequences to the advantage of no one.

We noted earlier that competition can be a feature of intragroup life. However, achieving goal isomorphism within the group requires countervailing pressures toward cooperation. On the most obvious level, if people in a group cannot get along and work together, it is hard to imagine that group surviving, let alone thriving. The need for the group to maintain cohesive working relations has been treated in a variety of ways by social scientists. In his seminal essay *On Face-Work* Goffman discussed society's need for people to get along well with each other and to maintain positive intragroup relations:

> Societies everywhere, if they are to be societies, must mobilize their members as self-regulating participants in social encounters. One way of mobilizing the individual for this purpose is through ritual; he is taught to be perceptive, to have feelings attached to self and a self expressed through face, to have pride, honor, and dignity, to have considerateness, to have tact and a certain amount of poise. These are some of the elements of behavior that must be built into the person if practical use is to be made of him as an interactant. (Goffman, 1967, p. 44)

In other words, societies require individuals who can cooperate and get along (and, interestingly, individuals who have positive feelings about themselves) if they are to function. Otherwise neither groups nor brief social encounters will work.

While the need to achieve goals and forge goal isomorphism may typically produce cooperation on the intragroup level, the result on the intergroup level is more often competition, both the real competition focused upon by Sherif and associates' (Sherif, Harvey, White, Hood, & Sherif, 1961) work and the social competition focused on in Tajfel and Turner's (1986) work. Groups compete for information, status, and resources at the expense of other groups. For example, a group might attain certain goals, such as the attainment of material prosperity for its members, by taking material resources from other groups in competitions, such as wars and struggles over tax reform. Similarly, the establishment of group realities may take place through competition about information, as when groups of scientists with opposing theoretical allegiances compete to provide proof for their particular views of reality, or compete for the right to try to prove their theories. The limited payload and personnel of manned spacecraft, for example, created a situation in which experimental proposals compete for the right to collect data. In a similar way, different theories about reality and the experiments designed to support them compete for finite research funds: To the extent that one version of the truth is funded, another will not have the chance to dominate.

Identity or status can also be an object of intergroup competition, as work within the framework of social identity theory (Tajfel & Turner, 1986) has emphasized. Research on biased allocation strategies focuses on ways in which one group can promote a sense of superiority over other groups by allocating resources associated with status, such as points or money, to the in-group. Groups make allocations that raise their relative outcomes, thus serving identity goals, even when doing so lowers their absolute outcomes, thus frustrating their utilitarian goals.

These examples point to situations in which one group actually gains information, identity, and resources at the expense of another group. A more central focus of social identity theory concerns one group's use of other groups as a biased comparison point. Comparisons are made or information is processed about one or more out-groups in such a way that the in-group's (and perhaps others') perception of the group will be changed, although objectively group attainments have remained the same. In the case of material outcomes, biased appraisal of the outcomes of other groups can be used to justify the achievements of the group to its members. Biased comparisons about resource states in the in-group may also be used to appeal to third bodies for a larger allocation of resources.

Establishment of group realities may occur only within the context of differentiation from and comparison to other groups. Thomas Szasz (1974), for example, argued that the perception of the majority as mentally healthy (sane) depends crucially on the presence of a dissenting minority that the majority can label mentally unhealthy or insane. Although definition of reality depends on consensus maintenance within the group, it may also depend on dissent between groups, and consequent intergroup differentiation. Taking a similar position, Kuhn (1962) argued that during periods of normal science, when one paradigm dominates and alternatives are not really considered, science makes little progress; real advances in our ability to know reality await the comparison of current versions of reality with new ones. Szasz goes so far as to suggest that when no reality alternative exists against which the validity of an accepted point of view can be tested, a deviant reality, and its adherents, will be produced. Thus persecution and execution of witches demonstrated the nonviability of their world view to adherents of the currently accepted religious views.

Finally, social comparison with other groups can be used to provide group members with a positive group or social identity by overvaluing the group product and devaluing other groups' products (see Hinkle & Shopler, 1979, for a review), by assigning moral worth and virility to the in-group and characteristics of the diabolical enemy to other groups (White, 1966, 1977), by making favorable comparisons to the in-group and unfavorable ones to the out-group (Mackie, 1983), and by maintaining negative stereotypes about out-groups (Tajfel, 1981; Tajfel & Forgas, 1983).

Inclusion and Exclusion

Individuals may seek to be included in groups where they perceive that their goals will be achieved. This is a primary source of initial group formation. Conversely, they may leave, if they can, groups in which their goals are not being met. Individuals may perceive that their utilitarian goals can be achieved in the company of other individuals in a group. For example, an individual may join a food cooperative or a babysitting pool in order to achieve specific utilitarian goals. Just as commonly, perhaps, individuals may join (or leave) groups in order to satisfy identity concerns. They may feel that being a member of a particular group gives them a desired identity. Simmel (1955) defined identity in terms of the totality of an individual's group memberships. For example, belonging to a history book club or the Republican Party may confer an important aspect of identity on an individual. People may also join groups to satisfy knowledge needs. A person might join a scientific organization, such as the Society of Experimental Social Psychology, for the benefits of knowledge to be derived.

Inclusion and exclusion can be just as important for satisfying the group's goals as the individual's. Individuals may be particularly helpful in a group's efforts to satisfy utilitarian goals. To the extent that they bring rewards to the group, individuals will be included and retained (even against their will). Hollander's (1958) concept of idiosyncrasy credit suggests that individuals will be retained in a group as long as the balance of the outcomes they bring to the group is positive. Those who bring substantial rewards to the group have a substantial positive balance, or "credit," which they may spend by acting in ways which the group finds negative. One way of doing so is by violating group norms, that is, being idiosyncratic or deviant. A person with lots of credit can afford to deviate and still maintain a positive balance.

The importance of inclusion and exclusion in reaching a group's utilitarian goals can also be seen in terms of Festinger's (1950) concept of group locomotion. Festinger noted that group locomotion requires opinion uniformity that can be achieved through rejection of deviants. Thus rejection of deviants, and perhaps the inclusion of those who support group consensus, is an important manifestation of group's attempts to reach utilitarian goals.

Inclusion and exclusion are obviously important for the group's attempts to reach its reality and identity goals. Festinger's theories of informal social communication and social comparison both make clear that rejection of deviants is, along with social influence, the primary means of obtaining the uniformity of opinion needed to establish a coherent social reality. Rejection of those who threaten a group's desired social identity has not been explored as much as the rejection of opinion deviants who threaten a group's social reality. However, it is easy to imagine inclusion being used equally in both cases. The process of inclusion in Greek-letter fraternities and sororities on college campuses illustrates inclusion in the service of identity needs. A fraternity or sorority will attempt to include individuals whom it perceives will enhance its social identity as determined by intergroup comparisons.

Finally, we should note that the processes of inclusion and exclusion that operate on an intergroup level are quite similar to those that operate within groups. Groups may seek to include other groups, such as in the case of corporate takeovers, annexations of small countries, and the formation of national alliances. More commonly on the intergroup level, however, the inclusion/exclusion process tilts toward the exclusion of other groups, in the form of biased social comparison and psychological rejection, verbal derogation, or overt harm-doing. The widespread phenomena of ethnic hostility and intergroup conflict so aptly addressed by social identity theory amply illustrate these intergroup exclusion processes.

GROUP IDENTITY AND GOAL ISOMORPHISM

In the previous sections we have pointed out the essential tension in the relationship between individual and group, the paradox of their necessary mutual interdependence for gain, and the simultaneous costs that such interdependence necessarily extracts. We have also suggested that the processes that characterize intragroup life reflect the attempt to resolve this tension through processes of social influence, cooperation and competition, and inclusion and exclusion, aimed toward establishing consensus, cooperation, and cohesion. In this section we review evidence that suggests a highly successful strategy for the achievement of just such ends: the fostering and maintenance of a group identity that transforms and, at least temporarily, replaces individual identity. The acceptance of group identity transforms individual concerns into group concerns, and makes group concerns inherently the concern of the individual. When such isomorphism of identity obtains, the same actions are perceived as leading to the simultaneous achievement of both individual and group goals.

What is meant by the psychological recognition of group membership or group identity? Tajfel (1978), and Tajfel and Turner (1986) characterize social situations as lying on a continuum from the extremely interpersonal to the extremely intergroup. Toward the intergroup extreme, interactions are based purely on the protagonists (most often individuals, not groups) perceiving themselves and acting in terms of group memberships. Individual features lose relevance, and the participants become representatives or exemplars of their group memberships. Turner (1982, 1986) has developed this idea even more explicitly. According to Turner, when in-group membership is salient, individual group members "self-stereotype," perceiving themselves (as well as other members) as embodying the common characteristics of the group, rather than as embodying unique combinations of qualities that identify them as individuals. An immediate consequence of such self and other classification is an enhancement of the perception of intragroup similarities and intergroup differences (Bruner, 1957; Tajfel, 1969; Tajfel & Wilkes, 1963; Wilder, 1981). According to Turner (1986), this perception of oneself and others primarily in terms of group-relevant characteristics leads to a psychological acceptance of interchangeability between group members. This interchangeability produces in turn the conditions for intragroup influence, cooperation, and attraction.

How does interchangeability have this effect? First, because the self is perceived as interchangeable with others and because one reality is assumed, there are implicit expectations that similar others will perceive reality in the same way. This increases both pressures toward consensus and the probability of its being reached (Asch, 1952; Festinger, 1950; Kelley, 1967). Second, to the extent that others are seen as similar to the self in terms of the defining characteristics of the group, mutual attraction, and thus group cohesion and longevity, will be enhanced. Lott and Lott (1965) conclude that explicit group membership and the similarity that is mediated by categorization are the major determinants of attraction. The minimal group experiments (Tajfel, Flament, Billig, & Bundy, 1971) demonstrated that a psychological in-group relationship alone produces positive attitudes toward and liking for other in-group members; factors that are concomitant to real group membership such as proximity, common fate, and shared outcomes only enhance this effect (Berscheid & Walster, 1978; Dion, 1979).

Third, and most important for our purposes, interchangeability of other group members and the self diffuses self-interest in interactions and increases cooperation to the extent that one's own and others' goals appear identical. Research on mixed motive games can be brought to bear as evidence for this proposition. One of the clearest concerns in this literature has been the low rate of spontaneous cooperation in such situations (approximately 30%, according to Eiser, 1978) even when spontaneous cooperation optimizes individual gains (Oskamp, 1971). The search for structural variables that increase this level of cooperation has inevitably turned to manipulating the degree of relatedness between the players, by increasing supraindividual concerns (Sherif, 1967), communication and interaction (Deutsch & Krauss, 1962; Edney, 1980), common fate (Pruitt & Kimmel 1977) and trust, empathy, and similarity between players (Dawes 1980; Pruitt & Kimmel, 1977). As Turner (1986) points out, these variables are all implicitly aimed at producing a collective or joint unit, a psychological group of the participants that, in turn, increases cooperation. The same consequences of group membership are as apparent in the applied domain. In studying the motivating factors of both assembly line workers and corporate executives, Zander (1971, 1977) concluded that "team spirit" was in many instances more important in determining productivity than striving for individual achievement.

Making group identity salient can thus both create isomorphism between individual and group goals and, concomitantly, increase the likelihood that the conditions necessary for goal attainment are produced. Social psychological research points to two clear sets of factors or conditions under which this occurs. The first incorporates all those factors and conditions that increase unit formation between individuals. These include the factors mentioned above as being manipulated to promote attraction and cooperation between co-acting individuals—perceived similarity, common fate, proximity, shared success and failure, social contact, and common designation (Cartwright & Zander, 1968; Dion, 1979; Heider, 1958; for a review, see Turner, 1981). The second set of factors promoting the salience of group identity are those that lead one group of individuals to distinguish themselves from others. Individuals categorize themselves as a group to the extent that the perceived similarities among them are greater than the perceived differences between them and other people in the social environment (Turner, 1986). This means that different group identities may be made salient by the presence of different comparison groups (Boyansky & Allen, 1973; McGuire, McGuire, Child, & Fujioka, 1978).

By far the most researched, and perhaps the most effective, condition for enhancing the salience of group identity by contrast to other groups is intergroup competition. The positive benefits of intergroup competition on intragroup relations were first noted by Coser (1956). His original proposal that intergroup competition would increase internal cohesion and strengthen group boundaries had led to research demonstrating the much more extensive effects of intergroup competition. In addition to increasing cohesion and unity, intergroup competition has beneficial effects on intragroup morale, cooperation, work motivation, attraction, and conformity pressures (Brewer, 1979; Blake & Mouton, 1961; Dion, 1979; Hensley & Duval, 1976; Hinkle & Schopler, 1979; Lanzetta, 1955; Ryan & Kahn, 1970, 1975; Sherif, 1967; Sherif et al., 1961; Stein, 1976; Stouffer et al., 1949; Turner, 1981, 1982).

This research, taken as a whole, suggests that the activation, salience, and acceptance of group identity fosters the conditions necessary not only for successful group achievement but also for maintenance of the group. Much of the research has focused particularly on strategies that help produce the conditions under which instrumental needs can be filled via utilitarian goal achievement. As evidence for the interdependence of the individual and the group, it suggests that groups that successfully mediate goals for their members are better able to retain their members than those that fail to do so (Lott & Lott, 1965). However, other research findings indicate that the relationship between group goal attainment and group cohesion is not so straightforward. Individuals sometimes adhere to groups that fail to attain material benefits (even when exit is possible, see Kennedy & Stephan, 1977). Such groups may, however, provide clear identity benefits for their members, an aspect of group goal attainment that has been relatively rarely considered in contrast to the pursuit of utilitarian goals. Rabbie and Horwitz (1969), for example, found that either group reward or group punishment increased group cohesion if it made the commonalities of group membership salient. Clearly one of the advantages of the social identity strategy is that it provides simultaneously for both expressive and instrumental needs by fulfilling identity and utilitarian goals.

A wide range of research therefore suggests that the fostering of group identity offers a viable solution to the essential problem of the relationship between individual and group. This is not to suggest that such a solution is an instant cure-all for the problems of group productivity and dislocation of individual and group goals. Clearly, the possibility of making salient, encouraging, and indeed imposing the acceptance of group identity may be more or less difficult for different groups under different circumstances, as the literature cited above testifies. In addition, some of the limitations and possible boundary conditions of the strategy need to be explored. For example, there is evidence that individuals resist any overwhelming attempts to make them identical to many others, and attempt themselves to reassert a sense of uniqueness (Codol, 1975; Snyder & Fromkin, 1980). However, this may not be as much of a problem for group interaction as it initially appears. One of the necessary aspects of organization for achievement of group goals is, after all, differentiation, particularly in terms of the task roles people must play to perform goal-relevant tasks. This often provides members with unique places in the social world, while not undermining the unity of the group. Interestingly, Kimberley (1984) has suggested that successful intragroup functioning depends on a balance between differentiation in instrumental or task structure and equivalence in what are termed equality structures (structures that reflect what we have called identity goals).

Nor are we suggesting that isomorphism is the only possible solution to the attainment of group goals. For example, exchange theories of group life suggest the ways in which activity that achieves a group goal (for example, work) can be exchanged for an individual goal (for example, money). Although such relationships can achieve both individual and group ends, our review of the literature suggests that the salience of individual goals to the group members under these circumstances will make the relationship between group and individual less stable. In extending Thibaut and Kelley's (1959) theory of interdependence to personal relationships, Kelley and Thibaut (1978) have in fact suggested that the way to maintain what might originally be an exchange relationship is to transform its nature into one of joint or mutual attainment of outcomes. This is clearly the function of group membership in the research cited above.

CONCLUSION

We have argued that key aspects of group life reflect negotiation between individuals and groups as they strive to establish isomorphism between their goals. Individuals and groups have goals for utilitarian outcomes, knowledge, and identity. They are frequently interdependent for the satisfaction of their goals, but when the concerns of the individual do not match the concerns of the group, they are at cross purposes. These instances of conflict can be resolved by forging isomorphism between group and individual goals. Isomorphism can be achieved by exerting social influence to achieve consensus, establishing norms for appropriate behavior, fostering cooperation within the group and competition outside the group, and, finally, by appropriately including or excluding group members. We have emphasized the importance of heightened salience of group membership as a factor that can facilitate conformity to group pressures, adherence to group norms, intragroup cooperation, intergroup competition, and the maintenance of group cohesion. In stressing the interdependence of individual and group, and asserting the similarity of individual and group goals, as well as the similarity of their means of achieving their goals, we have accorded the group a vibrant and independent status. The group is a psychologically real entity, and activating the concept of group membership modifies individual thought and action in ways that dramatically affect intragroup behavior. This psychological reality of the group for the individual underlines the similarity between the ways psychologically real groups and empirically real individuals pursue their goals.

REFERENCES

Adams, J. S. (1965). Inequity and social exchange. In L. Berkowitz (Ed.), *Advances in experimental social psychology* (Vol. 2, pp. 267-299). New York: Academic Press.

Allen, V. L. (1975). Social support for nonconformity. In L. Berkowitz (Ed.), *Advances in experimental social psychology* (Vol. 8, pp. 2-46). New York: Academic Press.

Allport, F. W. (1924). *Social psychology*. New York: Houghton Mifflin.

Allport, G. W. (1954). The historical background of social psychology. In G. Lindzey (Ed.), *The handbook of social psychology* (1st ed.). (Vol. 1, pp. 3-56). Cambridge, MA: Addison-Wesley.

Aronson, E., & Mills, J. (1959). The effect of severity of initiation on liking for a group. *Journal of Abnormal and Social Psychology, 59,* 177-181.

Asch, S. E. (1952). *Social psychology.* Englewood Cliffs, NJ: Prentice-Hall.

Baumeister, R. S., & Hutton, D. G. (1987). Self presentation theory: Self-construction and audience pleasing. In B. Mullen & G. R. Goethals (Eds.), *Theories of group behavior* (pp. 71-87). New York: Springer-Verlag.

Berschied, E., & Walster, E. H. (1978). *Interpersonal attraction* (2nd ed.). Reading, MA: Addison-Wesley.

Blake, R. R., & Mouton, J. S. (1961). Reactions to intergroup competition under win-lose conditions. *Management Science,* 420-435.

Bormann, E. G. (1975). *Discussion and group methods: Theory and practices* (2nd ed.). New York: Harper & Row.

Boyansky, E. O., & Allen, V. L. (1973). Ingroup norms and self-identity as determinants of discriminatory behavior. *Journal of Personality and Social Psychology, 25,* 408-418.

Brewer, M. B. (1979). Ingroup bias in the minimal intergroup situation: A cognitive-motivational analysis. *Psychological Bulletin, 86,* 307-324.

Bruner, J. S. (1957). On perceptual readiness. *Psychological Review, 64,* 123-151.

Cartwright, D., & Zander, A. (1968). *Group dynamics: Research and theory* (3rd ed.). New York: Harper & Row.

Codol, J-P. (1975). On the so-called "superior conformity of the self" behavior: Twenty experimental investigations. *European Journal of Social Psychology, 5,* 457-501.

Cofer, C. N., & Appley, M. H. (1964). *Motivation: Theory and research.* New York: John Wiley.

Cooley, C. H. (1902). *Human nature and the social order.* New York: Scribner.

Coser, L. A. (1956). *The functions of social conflict.* New York: Free Press.

Dawes, R. (1980). Social dilemmas. *Annual Review of Psychology, 31,* 169-183.

Deutsch, M., & Krauss, R. M. (1962). Studies of interpersonal bargaining. *Journal of Conflict Resolution, 6,* 52-76.

Deutsch, M., & Gerard, H. B. (1955). A study of normative and informational influences upon individual judgment. *Journal of Abnormal and Social Psychology, 51,* 629-636.

Dion, K. L. (1979). Intergroup conflicts and intragroup cohesiveness. In W. G. Austin & S. Worchel (Eds.), *The social psychology of intergroup relations* (pp. 211-224). Monterey, CA: Brooks/Cole.

Dovidio, J. F., & Morris, W. N. (1975). Effects of stress and commonality of fate in helping behavior. *Journal of Personality and Social Psychology, 31,* 145-149.

Edney, J. J. (1980). The commons problems: Alternative perspectives. *American Psychologist, 35,* 131-150.

Eiser, J. R. (1978). Cooperation and competition between individuals. In H. Tajfel & C. Fraser (Eds.), *Introducing social psychology* (pp. 151-175). London: Penguin.

Ellis, R. A., & Keedy, T. C., Jr. (1960). Three dimensions of status: A study of academic prestige. *Pacific Sociological Review, 3,* 23-28.

Erikson, E. H. (1968). *Identity: Youth and crisis.* New York: Norton.

Festinger, L. (1950). Informal social communication. *Psychological Review, 57,* 271-282.

Festinger, L. (1954). A theory of social comparison processes. *Human Relations, 7,* 117-140.

Gergen, K. (1971). *The concept of self.* New York: Holt, Rinehart & Winston.

Goffman, E. (1959). *The presentation of self in everyday life.* New York: Doubleday.

Goffman, E. (1967). *Interaction ritual.* Garden City, NY: Doubleday.

Hardin, G. (1968). The tragedy of the commons. *Science, 162,* 1243-1248.

Heider, F. (1944). Social perception and phenomenal causality. *Psychological Review, 51,* 358-374.

Heider, F. (1946). Attitudes and cognitive organization. *Journal of Psychology, 21,* 107-112.

Heider, F. (1958). The psychology of interpersonal relations. New York: John Wiley.

Hensley, V., & Duval, S. (1976). Some perceptual determinants of perceived similarity, liking, and correctness. *Journal of Personality and Social Psychology, 34,* 159-168.

Hinkle, S., & Schopler, J. (1979). Ethnocentrism in the evaluation of group products. In W. G. Austin & S. Worchel (Eds.), *The social psychology of intergroup relations* (pp. 160-173). Monterey, CA: Brooks-Cole.

Hoffman, P., Festinger, L., & Lawrence, D. H. (1954). Tendencies toward comparability in competitive bargaining. *Human Relations, 7,* 141-159.

Hollander, E. P. (1958). conformity, status and idiosyncracy credit. *Psychological Review, 65,* 117-127.

Jones, E. E. & Pittman, T. S. (1982). Toward a general theory of self-presentation. In J. Suls (Ed.), *Psychological perspectives on the self* (Vol. 1, pp. 231-262). Hillsdale, NJ: Lawrence Erlbaum.

Jones, E. E., & Gerard, H. (1967). *Foundations of social psychology.* New York: John Wiley.

Kelley, H. H. (1952). Two functions of reference groups. In G. Swanson, T. M. Newcomb, & E. L. Hartley (Eds.), *Readings in social psychology* (pp. 410-414). New York: Holt, Rinehart & Winston.

Kelley, H. H. (1967). Attribution theory in social psychology, In D. Levine (Ed.), *Nebraska symposium on motivation* (Vol. 15, pp. 192-238). Lincoln, NB: University of Nebraska Press.

Kelley, H. H. & Thibaut, J. W. (1978). *Interpersonal relationships: A theory of interdependence.* New York: John Wiley.

Kennedy, J., & Stephan, W. (1977). The effects of cooperation and competition on ingroup-outgroup bias. *Journal of Applied Social Psychology, 7,* 115-130.

Kimberly, J. C. (1984). Cognitive balance, inequality and consensus: Interrelations among fundamental processes in groups. In E. Lawler (Ed.), *Advances in group processes* (Vol. 1, pp. 95-126). New York: JAI Press.

Krebs, D. L., & Miller, D. T. (1985). Altruism and aggression. In G. Lindzey & E. Aronson (Eds.), *The handbook of social psychology,* (Vol. II, 3rd ed., pp. 1-72). New York: Random House.

Kuhn, T. (1962). *The structure of scientific revolutions.* Chicago: University of Chicago Press.

Lanzetta, J.T. (1955). Group behavior under stress. *Human Relations, 8,* 29-52.

LeBon, G. (1895). *The crowd.* London: Ernest Benn.

Lewin, K. (1935). *A dynamic theory of personality.* New York: McGraw-Hill.

Lott, A. J., & Lott, B. E. (1965). Group cohesiveness as interpersonal attraction: A review of relationships with antecedent and consequent variables. *Psychological Bulletin, 64,* 259-309.

Mackie, D. M. (1983). Social comparison in high and low status groups. *Journal of Cross Cultural Psychology, 15,* 379-398.

Maslow, A. H. (1970). *Motivation and personality* (2nd ed.). New York: Harper & Row.

McDougall, W. (1920). *The group mind.* New York: G. P. Putnam.

McGuire, W. J., McGuire, C. V., Child, P., & Fujioka, T. (1978). Salience of ethnicity in the spontaneous self-concept as a function of one's ethnic distinctiveness in the social environment. *Journal of Personality and Social Psychology, 36,* 511-520.

Mead, G. H. (1934). *Mind, self, and society.* Chicago: University of Chicago Press.

Merton, R. K. (1948). *Social theory and social structure.* New York: Free Press.

Moscovici, S. (1980). Toward a theory of conversion behavior. In L. Berkowitz (Ed.), *Advances in experimental social psychology* (Vol. 13, pp. 209-239). New York: Academic Press.

Murray, H. A. (1938). *Explorations in personality.* New York: Oxford University Press.

Newcomb, T. M. (1953). An approach to the study of communicative acts. *Psychological Review, 60,* 593-404.

Oskamp, S. (1971). The effects of programmed strategies on cooperation in the Prisoner's Dilemma and other mixed motive games. *Journal of Conflict Resolution, 15,* 225-259.

Pepitone, A., & Wilpinski, C. (1960). Some consequences of experimental rejection. *Journal of Abnormal and Social Psychology, 60,* 359-364.

Platt, J. (1963). Social traps. *American Psychologist, 28,* 641-651.

Pruitt, D., & Kimmel, M. J. (1977). Twenty years of experimental gaming: Critique, synthesis, and suggestions for the future. *Annual Review of Psychology, 28,* 363-392.

Rabbie, J. M., & Horwitz, M. (1969). Arousal of ingroup/outgroup bias by a chance win or loss. *Journal of Personality and Social Psychology, 13,* 269-277.

Ryan, A. H., & Kahn, A. (1970). Own-group bias: The effects of individual competence and group outcome. *Proceedings of the Iowa Academy of Science, 77,* 302-307.

Ryan, A. H., & Kahn, A. (1975). The effects of intergroup orientation on group attitudes and proxemic behavior: A test of two models. *Journal of Personality and Social Psychology, 31,* 302-310.

Schacter, S. (1959). *The psychology of affiliation.* Stanford, CA: Stanford University Press.

Secord, P. F., & Backman, C. W. (1964). *Social psychology.* New York: McGraw-Hill.

Sherif, M. (1936). *The psychology of social norms.* New York: Harper.

Sherif, M. (1967). *Group conflict and cooperation: Their social psychology.* London: Routledge & Kegan Paul.

Sherif, M., Harvey, O. J., White, B. J., Hood, W. R., & Sherif, C. W. (1961). *Intergroup conflict and cooperation.* Norman, OK: Institute of Group Relations.

Shrauger, J. S. (1975). Responses to evaluation as a function of initial self-perceptions. *Psychological Bulletin, 82,* 581-596.

Simmel, G. (1955). *Conflict.* New York: Free Press.

Snyder, C. R., & Fromkin, H. L. (1980). *Uniqueness: The human pursuit of difference.* New York: Plenum.

Stein, A. A. (1976) Conflict and cohesion: A review of the literature. *Journal of Conflict Resolution, 20,* 143-172.

Steiner, I. D. (1972). *Group process and productivity.* New York: Academic Press.

Stouffer, S. A., Lumsdaine, A. A., Lumsdaine, M. H., Williams, R.H., Jr., Smith, M. B., Janis, I. L., Star, S. A., & Cottrell, L. S., Jr. (1949). *The American soldier: Combat and its aftermath* (Vol. 2). Princeton, NJ: Princeton University Press.

Szasz, T. (1974). *The myth of mental illness* (rev. ed.). New York: Harper & Row.

Tajfel, H. (1969). Cognitive aspects of prejudice. *Journal of Social Issues, 25*(4), 79-97.

Tajfel, H. (1978). *Differentiation between social groups.* London: Academic Press.

Tajfel, H. (1981). *Human groups and social categories: Studies in social psychology.* Cambridge: Cambridge University Press.

Tajfel, H. & Forgas, J. P. (1983). Social categorizations: Cognitions, values, and groups. In J. P. Forgas (Ed.), *Social cognition: Perspectives on everyday understanding* (pp. 113-140). London: Academic Press.

Tajfel, H., & Turner, J. C. (1986). An integrative theory of intergroup relations. In S. Worchel & W. G. Austin (Eds.), *The psychology of intergroup relations* (pp. 7-24). Chicago: Nelson Hall.

Tajfel, H., & Wilkes, A. L. (1963). Classification and quantitative judgment. *British Journal of Psychology, 54,* 101-114.

Tajfel, H., Flament, C., Billig, M. G., & Bundy, R. F. (1971). Social categorization and intergroup behavior. *European Journal of Social Psychology, 1,* 149-77.

Thibaut, J. W., & Kelley, H. H (1959). *The social psychology of groups..* New York: John Wiley.

Turner, J. C. (1981). The experimental social psychology of intergroup behavior. In J. E. Turner & H. Giles (Eds.), *Intergroup behavior* (pp. 66-101). Oxford: Blackwell.

Turner, J. C. (1982). Towards a cognitive redefinition of the social group. In H. Tajfel (Ed.), *Social identity and intergroup relations.* (pp. 15-40). Cambridge: Cambridge University Press.

Turner, J. C. (1986). Social categorization and the self concept: A social cognitive theory of group behavior. In E. Lawler (Ed.), *Advances in group processes* (Vol. 2, pp. 77-122). New York: JAI Press.

Wegner, D. M. (1987). Transactive memory: Contemporary analysis of the group mind. In B. Mullen & G. R. Goethals (Eds.), *Theories of group behavior* (pp. 185-208). New York: Springer-Verlag.

White, R. K. (1966). Misperception and the Vietnam war. *Journal of Social Issues, 22*(3), 1-156.

White, R. K. (1977). Misperceptions in the Arab-Israeli conflict. *Journal of Social Issues, 33* (1), 190-221.

Wilder, D. (1981). Perceiving persons as a group: Categorization and intergroup relations. In D. L. Hamilton (Ed.), *Cognitive processes in stereotyping and intergroup behavior* (pp. 213-258). Hillsdale, NJ: Lawrence Erlbaum.

Worchel, S. (1979). Cooperation and the reduction of intergroup conflict: Some determining factors. In W. G. Austin & S. Worchel (Eds.), *The social psychology of intergroup relations* (pp. 262-273). Monterey, CA: Brooks/Cole.

Wrightsman, L. S. (1960). The effect of waiting with others on changes in level of felt anxiety. *Journal of Abnormal and Social Psychology, 61,* 216-222.

Zander, A. (1971). *Motives and goals in groups.* New York: Academic Press.

Zander, A. (1977). *Groups at work.* San Francisco: Jossey-Bass.

6

Attributions of Responsibility for Collective Endeavors

MARK R. LEARY
DONELSON R. FORSYTH

Mark R. Leary is Assistant Professor of Psychology at Wake Forest University. His current research interests include self-presentation, social anxiety, and the self. He is the author of *Understanding Social Anxiety* (1983) and *Social Psychology and Dysfunctional Behavior* (1986; with Rowland Miller).

Donelson R. Forsyth, an Associate Professor in the Department of Psychology at Virginia Commonwealth University, is currently investigating individual differences in ethical ideology and attributional reactions to success and failure. His books include *An Introduction to Group Dynamics* (1983) and *Social Psychology* (1987).

For the last two decades, social psychologists have been preoccupied with the study of causal attributions. Building on theoretical foundations erected by Heider (1958), researchers have studied the cognitive processes involved when people attempt to identify the causes of behaviors and events. The bulk of this effort has been spent on the study of intrapsychic processes: factors that instigate attributional processing, the impact of various types of information on attributional conclusions, and biases that distort perceptions of causality.

Interpersonal aspects of attributions have not been wholly ignored, however. Attributions are important not only because they form the basis of person and event perception, but also because they influence subsequent social behavior. Our reactions to others' compliments, insults, and arguments depend on our analysis of the cause of their actions. When two individuals disagree on the cause of a behavior, they must negotiate to reach an acceptable middle ground. Groups that fail

AUTHOR'S NOTE: The second author acknowledges the support provided him while on leave at Pennsylvania State University. Thanks are extended to Clyde Hendrick and three anonymous reviewers for the extremely helpful comments they offered in reaction to an earlier draft of this chapter.

must identify the causes of their difficulties if they are to improve in the future. And individuals, when explaining their successes, must choose between self-aggrandizing and self-effacing explanations. These examples all support Heider's original assumption that individuals' causal ascriptions influence their interpersonal behaviors.

This chapter examines one particular type of causal attribution: group members' attributions of responsibility for collective endeavors. People not only formulate attributions about the causes of their own behavior and behaviors performed by other individuals, but they often seek explanations of events or outcomes that involve several people. For example, members of the executive committee that made the decision to create "new Coke" have undoubtedly wondered why that venture failed so miserably. Similarly, players on athletic teams often discuss why they defeated an opponent, and married couples disagree regarding their relative responsibility for family problems. Even social psychologists, who study attributions, sometimes wrangle over responsibility for coauthored books or articles. In each of these examples, collaborative participants in an event seek to explain the occurrence or nonoccurrence of an outcome that affects them all.

Our review considers both the antecedents and consequences of responsibility attributions in groups. The first section of the chapter examines diffusion of responsibility, factors that focus responsibility on certain members of the group, and reactions to performance feedback. The second section deals with the impact of these attributional tendencies on group processes, including intragroup conflict, group performance, and the allocation of rewards among members. In reviewing and integrating the literature regarding attributions for joint endeavors, we focus primarily on attributions about the group and its outcomes rather than on attributions about individuals' behaviors. Thus, although the extensive literature on attributions about individuals is indirectly relevant throughout the chapter, we discuss this work only when essential. Further, we include research regarding attributions in close relationships only when it is clearly relevant to group process.

ATTRIBUTIONAL PROCESSES IN GROUPS

Group activity is often accompanied by attributional activity. When interacting in a group or working with others on a task, group members often identify the causes of the group's actions and outcomes and discuss their conclusions with others. They may review the group's reasons for choosing one course of action over another, ruminate over their part in the group's overall performance, ponder the factors that contributed to group success or failure, or consider the relative inputs of various members to the group outcome. Although the research literature on attributions in groups is significantly smaller than the literature on individual's attributions, researchers have succeeded in identifying several attributional processes that occur in groups, including diffusion of responsibility, focusing responsibility, and performance-linked attributional biases.

Diffusion of Responsibility

Diffusion of responsibility is one of the most basic attributional tendencies that occurs in groups. Put simply, feelings of personal responsibility decrease when people join groups. Latane and Darley (1970), for example, demonstrated that groups of bystanders are less helpful than single bystanders. A number of factors combine to generate this effect (see Cacioppo, Petty, & Losch, 1986), but Latane and Darley attributed this tendency to the fact that personal responsibility decreases when responsibility for helping is shared with other onlookers. For example, when Schwartz and Gottlieb (1976) exposed lone individuals and five-person groups to a bogus violent crime, they found that 62% of the single bystanders spontaneously reported thinking about their obligations to help whereas only 27% of the subjects in groups reported such thoughts. Also, on a subsequent questionnaire, 36% of the group members reported thoughts about reduced responsibility; none of the single subjects reported such thoughts.

This decrease in personal responsibility is not unique to bystander settings. In the area of group polarization, early studies of risky shifts found that individuals reported feeling less accountable for their decisions following group discussion (e.g., Vinokur, 1971). Zimbardo (1969), in his theory of deindividuation, argued that some groups instigate responsibility diffusion by refusing to identify individual members and their inputs. In a study of social traps, Fleishman (1980) found that responsibility for a collective outcome diminishes as the collective increases in size. Studies of social loafing conducted by Williams, Harkins, and Latane (1981) similarly indicate that group members feel less responsibility when working in a group than when working alone. Undoubtedly other factors play important roles in producing the bystander effect, polarization, deindividuation, selfishness in social traps, and social loafing, but diffusion of responsibility is a recurring theme underlying all these phenomena.

Focusing Responsibility

Joining a group tends to decrease feelings of personal responsibility, but a number of social and personal variables places limits on this effect. These variables work by focusing responsibility for the group's outcomes (Moriarty, 1975).

Leadership. The leader of a group often assumes special responsibility for performance. Zander (1971), for example, appointed one member of a group the leader: He made all decisions after consulting with the other group members. Zander found that individuals who made the decisions for their group took more responsibility for the group's product than did individuals in more peripheral positions. This tendency was even stronger when the group failed rather than succeeded.

Other studies also suggest that leaders, unlike followers, take as much credit for failure as they do for success. In one of the few studies to manipulate leadership and group outcome (Caine & Schlenker, 1979), ROTC cadets worked on tactical decision problems in three-man groups. Subjects in different groups were assigned to one of three roles: group leader, who made unilateral decisions that were binding on the group; followers, who provided input to the leader; or equals, whose inputs were combined in a majority-decision role. After working under one of these procedures, subjects learned that the group had performed well or poorly, and their reactions were assessed. Results showed that leaders accepted equal responsibility for success and failure. Followers and equals, in contrast, claimed more personal responsibility for group success than failure. As a result, after success, followers and equals claimed as much responsibility as leaders, even though leaders actually had considerably more responsibility. After failure, leaders accepted more responsibility than either followers or equals.

Two processes may induce leaders to accept more responsibility for group outcomes than other group members. First, in many settings leaders perform special tasks that are more essential to the group than the followers' tasks. Not only do leaders often make executive decisions on the group's behalf, but their handling of group discussions and decision making has direct implications for group performance. Beyond that, norms dictate that leaders should accept responsibility for the functioning of their groups, even if they were not directly involved in a particular decision. For example, field manuals for the armed services dictate that military leaders are ultimately responsible for all decisions that are made within their units. Most business and government organizations have similar norms, although they are often implicit.

Thus leaders tend to take more responsibility for their group's performance than do followers. Having a leader, however, does not necessarily reduce the other group members' responsibility. Diener, Fraser, Beaman, and Kelem (1976), for example, examined Halloween trick-or-treaters' reactions when anonymous versus identifiable. Although the children stole relatively more money and candy when they were anonymous, this difference was minimized when one member of the group was appointed leader. Diener and his colleagues explained that since the leader could have been apprehended had the experimenters discovered the transgression, the other group members still felt responsible for their actions.

Centrality. Zander (1971), in his extensive studies of motives and goals in groups, reported that individuals who occupy relatively central positions within the status hierarchy of the group take extra responsibility for their groups' activities and outcomes. In one study he arranged for 180 boys to work in three-person groups creating designs with dominos. Although one of the boys was selected to always put down the first domino, the task was such that his initial choice had no greater impact on the outcome than all subsequent choices. Nonetheless, the boys who went first reported feeling more responsible for the group's performance. Zander found similar tendencies in his studies of central and peripheral members of the governing boards of United Funds. Relative to peripheral members, those individuals who held an appointed office on the board or who played a more active role in group decision making reported feeling more responsible for their group's outcomes.

Performing particularly important tasks for the group also increases group members' feelings of responsibility. Pepitone (1952), after separating group members, asked them to sort abstract symbols. All subjects performed the same chore, but some were led to believe that their task was necessary for group success. Others were told that their task was not an important one for the group to complete, and a third group of subjects was told that their activity was as important as all other subjects' activities. Pepitone found that subjects felt more responsibility when working on the more important task, and that they also sorted more symbols in that condition. Similar findings were reported by Zander (1971), and Zander and Forward (1968).

Task competence. Responsibility is often focused on individuals who possess special competencies. In studies of helping, for example, bystanders are even less likely to get involved if they think someone with special training is also witnessing the emergency. Conversely, those with special expertise or knowledge are more likely to take responsibility for helping (Huston, Ruggiero, Conner, & Geis, 1981; Schwartz & Clausen, 1970).

In a related context, Zander and Wulff (1966) told some individuals that they were particularly proficient at the group task, while others were told that they lacked task-relevant skills. They found that individuals who thought they were more competent at the task took more responsibility than did those who felt less competent. Relative to the less proficient members, the more competent group members also thought their ability had a significant impact on the group's product, that the test was more valid, and that their teammates pressured them more.

Assigned responsibility. Maruyama, Fraser, and Miller (1982) found that feelings of responsibility can be heightened through direct assignment. They studied children who were trick-or-treating on Halloween. When the children visited one of the experiment-associated homes, an experimenter explained that she was collecting candy for hospitalized children. In the control condition, she pointed to a box on the table and told the children, "Please give them as many as you want by putting the candies in the white box on the table." In the one-child-responsible condition, she selected one child to be the leader: "I will put you in charge of the group here." In the each-child-responsible condition the experimenter made each child feel responsible: 'I am counting on you and you and you . . .'" As responsibility increased from none to one to each child, the trick-or-treaters donated more and more candy.

Attributions and Group Outcomes

As we have seen, studies conducted in a wide variety of social collectives indicate that group members often feel less personally responsible than single individuals. This general tendency, however, is muted by leadership position, centrality, personal competencies, and assignments of responsibility. Yet, as much as these structural factors influence feelings of responsibility, even they are overshadowed by the impact of feedback about the group's performance. Paralleling results obtained in individual performance settings, group members often display a *self-serving,* or egocentric bias: They claim personal responsibility for group successes, but disclaim responsibility for group failures. As an old saying aptly notes, "Success has many parents, but failure is a bastard." In other cases, however, individuals' attributions are *group-serving,* or sociocentric. Group members emphasize the entire group's responsibility after success, and the group's blamelessness after failure.

The self-serving bias in groups. In the prototypic experimental paradigm, subjects perform an additive or compensatory group task on which group performance ostensibly can be assessed, but individual performance cannot (Steiner, 1972). This setting parallels the structure of the tasks many naturally occurring groups face; the group's outcome is relatively clear-cut but the relative contributions of (at least some) group members in producing the outcome are ambiguous. After working together on these problems, subjects receive feedback indicating that their group performed very poorly or very well (occasionally, a "no feedback" condition is included). They then make attributions for the group's outcome. Field studies of attributions have also examined such groups as athletic teams and fund-raising organizations (see Brawley, 1984; Rejeski & Brawley, 1984; Zander, 1971).

Virtually without exception, these studies show that the members of successful groups take more personal responsibility for the group's performance than do members of failing groups (Beckman, 1970; Forsyth & Schlenker, 1977; Medow & Zander, 1965; Miller & Schlenker, 1985; Mynatt & Sherman, 1975; Norvell & Forsyth, 1984; Schlenker, 1975; Schlenker & Miller, 1977a, 1977b; Schlenker, Miller, Leary, & McCown, 1979; Schlenker, Soraci, & McCarthy, 1976; Streufert & Streufert, 1969; Wolosin, Sherman, & Till, 1973; Wortman, Costanzo, & Witt, 1973). Wolosin et al. (1973), for example, had subjects divide 100 "responsibility points" up among three sources: themselves, their partner, and the situation. After success, subjects gave themselves 39 points and their partner 33 points. After failure, the partner got 37 points while subjects gave themselves 33 points.

Schlenker and his colleagues have tested for self-serving biases directly by assessing subjects' perceptions of their responsibility relative to other group members (e.g., Forsyth & Schlenker, 1977; Miller, Goldman, & Schlenker, 1978; Schlenker, 1975; Schlenker & Miller, 1977a; Schlenker et al., 1979). In some cases, subjects were asked to estimate the responsibility of the best, worst, and average members.

Also, measures of relative responsibility were sometimes derived by subtracting subjects' ratings of personal responsibility from the responsibility they assigned to others. In general, these studies show that group members claim relatively more responsibility for success than they attribute to other members, while taking relatively less responsibility for failure.

A similar tendency to attribute failures to another member of the group has been documented using the so-called "teacher paradigm." In these studies a subject, acting as a teacher, tries to teach a student a concept. In most cases, subjects take credit when the student learns, but deny responsibility when the student fails (Beckman, 1970; Johnson, Feigenbaum, & Weiby, 1964). The opposite tendency—taking extra responsibility for a student's failure and sharing responsibility for success—has also been noted, but these exceptions occur primarily among professionals who are trained not to blame the learner (Ames, 1975; Beckman, 1973; Ross, Bierbrauer, & Polly, 1974).

Evidence indicates that group members also emphasize their responsibility for success and minimize their blame for failure in indirect ways. For example, members of failing groups tend to attribute their personal performance to distractions in the group setting, to the difficulty of the group's task, and to uncontrollable internal constraints, such as fatigue (Forsyth & Schlenker, 1977; Wortman, Costanzo, & Witt, 1973). Also, after success individuals evaluate their personal performance and the group's performance identically. After failure, however, group members often admit their group performed poorly, but that they did quite well (Roberts, 1978; Schlenker, Soraci, & McCarthy, 1976; Zander, 1971). Members of failing groups also claim that they exercised less influence over other group members than subjects in successful groups (Leary, 1978).

Group-serving biases. In the studies discussed above, group members attributed responsibility in ways that made them appear in a favorable light compared to other group members. However, in many instances group members make flattering attributions for the group as a whole. Rather than egocentrically claiming more responsibility for success than they attribute to the rest of the group, members of a successful group may make group-serving attributions that put the entire group in a good light (e.g., we all did well; we're a great group). Similarly, after failure, members may join together in blaming outside forces and absolving one another of responsibility. Indeed, some studies have shown that members of successful groups attribute more responsibility to the "average" member and the group as a whole than members of failing groups (Caine & Schlenker, 1979; Forsyth & Schlenker, 1977; Leary, 1978; Schlenker et al., 1976). In addition, the more positive the group's performance on the task, the more the group members (a) emphasize the validity of the feedback (Forsyth & Schlenker, 1977; Schlenker et al., 1976), (b) stress the importance of success on the particular task (Forsyth & Schlenker, 1977; Zander, 1971), (c) express commitment to the group (Zander, 1971), (d) emphasize their association to the group (Cialdini et al., 1976), (e) accurately recall their group's score (Dustin, 1966; Zander, 1971), and (f) exaggerate the degree of consensus present in the group (Schlenker & Miller, 1977b).

Self-serving and group-serving attributions are not necessarily mutually exclusive. Members of a failing group can maintain that they had little to do with the group's actions, and at the same time point out external factors that unfairly constrained the efforts of the other group members. Studies suggest, however, that group-serving attributions become more likely and self-serving attributions less likely in certain group situations. Cohesiveness, for example, increases group-serving attributional biases and decreases self-serving attributions (Dion, Miller, & Magnan, 1971; Schlenker & Miller, 1977b).

In one study, Schlenker and Miller (1977b) manipulated the cohesiveness of ad hoc groups by telling some subjects that a pretest indicated the members of their group would be highly compatible and other subjects that the members of their groups were incompatible. Self-serving attributions were obtained only in groups whose members thought they were not compatible, whereas the attributions of members of compatible groups did not differ as a function of performance. Further, members of cohesive groups were willing to accept more responsibility for failure than members of noncohesive groups. Put another way, the attributions of cohesive groups were more veridical than those of noncohesive groups. To the degree that this finding reflects a general phenomenon, egocentric attributions may be less prevalent in many real-world settings than they are in ad hoc laboratory groups. In most research, group members are strangers who are unlikely to be particularly beneficient in their attributions. As a result, they make self-enhancing attributions at the expense of other members. When members know and like one another, they should be less likely to be egocentric than when they dislike each other or do not know one another well at all.

As a result, self-serving attributions are less prevalent during intergroup conflict. During intergroup rivalries, internal cohesion increases along with the tendency to derogate the out-group (Brewer, 1979; Coser, 1956). White (1977) documented the pervasive tendency for group members to blame the conflict on the opposing group while praising their own group's values. During conflict, group members are also particularly likely to overestimate their group's capabilities, while derogating the prowess of the opponent. Janis (1982), in his studies of groupthink, identified similar tendencies in highly cohesive decision-making groups. His case studies revealed that the group members often insisted that their group was doing an outstanding job, and that failures were due to the out-group members' stupidity and lack of moral turpitude.

Sources of Attributional Biases in Groups

Studies of attributions for group performance lead to one clear conclusion: Group members tend to take credit for successes, but avoid blame for failure. As in the individual attribution literature, however, researchers continue to debate the relative merits of cognitive, motivational, and self-presentational explanations of these attributional biases (see Ross & Sicoly, 1979; Schlenker & Miller, 1977a).

Information-processing models. One explanation for attributional biases in groups emphasizes nonmotivational, cognitive processes. First, people may be more likely to encode, store, and retrieve memories of their own inputs to the group than the inputs of other members, leading them to see themselves as central figures in the group drama (Ross & Sicoly, 1979). In making attributions, group members presumably attempt to recall each participant's contributions to the final group product. For a variety of reasons, however, people's personal contributions are more available in memory than are the inputs of other group members: They possess more information regarding their own contributions than others' contributions (particularly "behind-the-scenes" work); they encode their own contributions more clearly due to greater salience or importance; they retrieve their contributions from memory more easily; and they may spend more time thinking (both prospectively and retrospectively) about their own inputs to the joint endeavor. As a result of these heuristics, people may claim more credit for group outcomes than they assign to other members (Nisbett & Ross, 1980; Ross & Sicoly, 1979; Thompson & Kelley, 1981). Second, people appear to perceive a stronger relationship between their behavior and positive outcomes than between their behavior and negative outcomes (Miller & Ross, 1975). As a result, positive outcomes are attributed to oneself, but negative outcomes to external factors. And third, Feather (1969) suggested that people are more likely to attribute expected than unexpected outcomes to themselves. To the extent that people expect that things generally go well (e.g., Weinstein & Lachendro, 1982), they accept more responsibility for group success than group failure.

In support of an information processing view, people remember more accurately their own contributions to the group than others' inputs (Ross & Sicoly, 1979). For example, individuals in romantic relationships tend to recall their personal contributions to the relationship more easily than their partner's contributions, leading them to overestimate their role in the relationship (Ross & Sicoly, 1979; Thompson & Kelley, 1981). In team sports, competitors tend to see the "turning points" in athletic contests as due to actions of their own team rather than to actions of the opposing team (Brawley, 1984; Ross & Sicoly, 1979). (Interestingly, this effect is independent of whether one's own team won or lost the contest.) Further, when asked to recall a single event from a sport competition, team members tend to report a play in which they were personally involved (Brawley, 1984). Brawley investigated coaches' and players' perceptions of their contributions to the players' activities and outcomes and found that both groups emphasized their own contributions more than the other group's. In addition, when asked to recall examples of one's own and the other's contributions to activities, personal contributions were named far more than other's contributions.

The impact of cognitive availability on attributions should be attenuated by inducing members to more carefully consider others' inputs. Ross and Sicoly (1979) manipulated information availability by focusing students on either their own or on their supervisor's contributions to their BA thesis. Subjects who were led to focus on their supervisor's contributions assigned him or her greater responsibility for the final outcome than those led to focus on their own contributions.

Self-esteem explanations. Other researchers have assumed attributional biases arise from people's motivation to protect and enhance their self-image (hence the label *self-serving* bias). By externalizing failure and internalizing success, group members can maintain their sense of confidence and self-worth (Streufert & Streufert 1969).

Some of the strongest support for an esteem-maintenance explanation comes from a study conducted by Schlenker and Miller (1977a). They led members of ad hoc groups to believe that they had sided with or against the majority opinion on a group decision. Logically, members in the minority are not as responsible for the group's decision as those in the majority. However, group members' attributions for success and failure were not affected by minority and majority status in a logical fashion. Majority members claimed more responsibility than minority members only when the group performed well or average. When the group performed poorly, members in the majority took no more responsibility than those in the minority! This pattern clearly reflects a nonological, self-serving bias and lends support to motivational explanations.

A motivational approach can also account for group-serving attributional biases. As Streufert and Streufert (1969) suggested, group members' attributional reactions to failure may be mediated by their desire to maintain group unity. If the cause of the failure is located within the group, then the group's cohesiveness will diminish. If, however, the group members blame external factors, then the group will avoid the pernicious consequences of failure. For example, Lerner (1965) found that intermember relations deteriorated when group members blamed one another for their failures. If groups blamed external factors, liking for the group actually increased, revealing a "joint misery" effect (Thibaut, 1950; Wilson & Miller, 1961).

Furthermore, Norvell and Forsyth (1984) found that when group members discussed their performance, they emphasized their group's responsibility more if the group succeeded and their leader was ostensibly a novice. Groups that failed, however, denied responsibility when they thought their leader was an expert. Presumably, members of failing groups with a novice leader had a plausible nonthreatening excuse for their difficulties—the leader's inexperience. However, failure under the guidance of an expert leader was more threatening, resulting in self-serving attributions.

Self-presentational explanations. A third view suggests that individuals' attributions serve to affect how they are perceived and evaluated by others. Being seen as highly responsible for a success enhances one's public image and social esteem, whereas being linked to a fiasco does not (Forsyth & Schlenker, 1977). Even self-deprecating attributions—publicly accepting responsibility for failure—may serve self-presentational goals by appearing magnanimous, modest, and fair (Bradley, 1978; Miller & Schlenker, 1985; Tetlock, 1985).

According to the self-presentational model, when members discuss the causes of past performance among themselves, they must balance their desire to be self-aggrandizing against the possibility of being seen as egotistical and immodest (Forsyth, Berger, & Mitchell, 1981). In one study that investigated how members resolve this dilemma, Miller and Schlenker (1985) found that subjects privately claimed more personal responsibility for a group success than they admitted to the rest of the group (the typical self-serving pattern). However, a reverse egocentrism effect emerged on ratings of relative responsibility when subjects' attributions would be seen by other group members; subjects in this condition claimed less relative responsibility for a success than for a failure. Thus, as in individual testing situations, egotistical patterns of attributions may arise under purely private conditions (e.g., Riess, Rosenfeld, Melburg, & Tedeschi, 1981). Further, subjects in this study were clearly sensitive to the interpersonal implications of their attributional statements (Forsyth, 1980) in that they were willing to appear to accept relatively more responsibility for failure than success (see Bradley, 1978).

An integrated viewpoint. While some argue that biased attributions serve to protect group members' sense of self-worth, others argue that cognitive mechanisms or self-presentational motives provide better accounts for self-serving and group-serving attributional tendencies. However, attributional biases may result from all three of these factors. Attributions serve a variety of functions for individuals: They make it possible to predict future events, provide explanations for puzzling outcomes, offer a way of protecting one's self-esteem, and convey information about one's self and one's group to other people (Forsyth, 1980; Tetlock & Levi, 1982). This functional view of attributions suggests that, depending on the circumstances, all three processes combine to determine attributions after success and failure.

Because the available empirical evidence is limited, the proper domain of application for each explanation cannot be specified clearly, so our discussion at this point is admittedly speculative. At the most general level, the degree to which attributions are biased in a self- or group-serving direction should reflect the relative importance of explanatory accuracy versus protection of self- or social esteem. For example, when groups work on important tasks they will face again in the future, a premium is placed on accuracy, and members' attributions should reflect relatively logical information processing strategies. Not only is an accurate appraisal of the group's strengths and weaknesses important for long-term success in such a situation, but biased attributions are held in check by the possibility that they may be invalidated in the future (Wortman et al., 1973).

On the other hand, biased attributions may be more likely in short-term groups in which the importance of accurate explanations is minimal and there are few risks associated with self-enhancement. Given that this is the context in most studies of group attributions, biases may be particularly prevalent. We also suspect that group members' attributions will be motivated by esteem concerns when the group has repeatedly failed a task that cannot be avoided. Under such circumstances, accurate attributions are likely to threaten members' self- and social esteem and there is little reason to be accurate. As a result, members may turn their attention from pursuing group success to simply avoiding failure (Zander, 1977), or at least to reducing the negative personal implications of failure.

EFFECTS OF ATTRIBUTIONS ON GROUP PROCESSES

We have seen that individuals generally feel less personal responsibility for outcomes when they join groups, that this reduction in responsibility is more pronounced after failure than success, and that certain situational and personal factors moderate the magnitude of these attributional tendencies. In this section we conclude our analysis of attributions in groups by considering the effects of attributions on group processes, including conflict, negative group processes, group performance, status allocations, and satisfaction.

Attributional Conflict

Horai (1977) dealt with the problems that arise when two parties disagree about the causes of events. Congruent with an interpersonal approach to attributions, Horai contended that "the social individual is not merely a passive information processor who ascribes causes to events, but is an active information provider who attempts to manage other parties' causal explanations" (p. 88). After considering some of the predominantly verbal strategies that individuals use to manage others' attributions, she concluded that "conflict rooted in disparate attributions concerning the cause of events appears to be prevalent in many situations" (p. 97).

Self-serving tendencies may promote attributional conflicts in groups. Not sharing one another's egocentric viewpoints, members may regard self-serving claims as unwarranted and obnoxious. Forsyth, Berger, and Mitchell (1981) illustrated this process by assessing group members' reactions to other members whose attributions were ostensibly self-serving (taking high responsibility for success or low responsibility for failure), equalitarian (attributing equal responsibility to oneself as to other members), or group-serving (claiming little personal responsibility for success, while accepting blame for failure). When the group had performed poorly, members who claimed low responsibility were evaluated less favorably than those who accepted medium or high responsibility. When the group had performed well, those who claimed high responsibility relative to the group were liked least. Interestingly, the self-abasing but group-serving members were not liked more than equalitarian members. In brief, group members who made egocentric attributions were not well liked by their fellow group members. In situations in which many group members make such attributions, group cohesion may be affected as each member derogates each of the others for blaming the group.

If attributional conflict is not resolved, members may ultimately leave the group, as evidenced by the exit of many disgruntled rock musicians, professional athletes, political associates, and business partners from their respective groups. Comparable processes may operate in failing groups as members disassociate themselves from the group's difficulties. To the degree that other members don't share these perceptions, they may feel they are being blamed unjustly for their part in the failure, leading them to dislike the group and shun future involvement. Shaw and Breed (1970) investigated the effect of attributional scapegoating by having two teams compete against one another. Certain members of each team were confederates of the researcher, and these confederates systematically blamed one of the actual subjects for the team's losses. Relative to others who had escaped blame, unfairly accused group members were less satisfied with their teams, belittled their teammates' abilities, and preferred to work with other groups on future tasks.

Attributional Bases of Negative Group Processes

Studies have found repeatedly that the reduction in personal responsibility that occurs in groups causes many undesirable effects. Zimbardo (1969), for example, argued that when individuals become submerged in groups, they lose their sense of personal identity and responsibility. Hence, they tend to engage in more extreme, and often more aggressive, behavior. In support of this assumption, Diener, Lusk, DeFour, and Flax (1980) found that as group size grows, feelings of self-consciousness and responsibility decrease. Diener et al. (1975) verified this assumption by manipulating group members' feelings of personal responsibility. They found that individuals who felt less responsibility were more likely to behave aggressively.

Similarly, Milgram (1974) blamed obedience to a malevolent authority on reductions of personal responsibility that occur in groups. Milgram argued that the individual who is part of an organized social group sometimes enters an agentic state in which "he sees himself as a agent for carrying out another person's wishes" (1974, p. 133). In such a state, destructive obedience becomes more likely. In support of his argument, Milgram found that obedient subjects assigned more responsibility for their antisocial behavior to the experimenter than to themselves. Defiant subjects, in contrast, attributed their behavior to themselves rather than to the experimenter. Also, relative to defiant subjects, obedient subjects blamed the learner for his own suffering.

Decreased personal responsibility in groups has also been linked to selfish refusals to contribute to a public good, and to individuals' exploitation of other group members in order to ensure their own rewards. Fleishman (1980) explained this selfish tendency to maximize personal gain at the expense of others as due to the reduction of personal responsibility that occurs when individuals join collectives. In a study of this process, Fleishman created a fictitious "union" and asked members to donate money either to a fund that would benefit everyone in the union or to a fund that would benefit only the individual. He found that the correlation between personal responsibility and donations to the union was .61. Moreover, as the size of the group increased, individuals' feelings of responsibility—and their contributions—decreased. They assumed others' donations would compensate for their own selfishness.

In brief, as we discussed above, decreased responsibility in groups is associated with a number of undesirable effects. Thus group process and performance should generally be enhanced by attempts to heighten members' feelings of responsibility. For example, delegating authority should increase personal responsibility, as should assigning all members to important tasks, assuring that all members feel competent to contribute to the group effort, and directly stressing individual responsibility. Research is needed on the effects of inducing responsibility on group process and performance.

Attributions and Performance

According to Zander (1971,1977), groups rely on feedback to plan future behavior. A group must gather information concerning the quality of its performance, assess the magnitude of the discrepancy between the desired performance and actual performance, and then revise the group's activities or reset group goals.

Attributions play a vital role in this process. If the group performs poorly, it must locate the cause of the problem. If the group members cannot identify the root of their difficulties, then changes can be made only on a trial-and-error basis. If individuals make self-serving attributions that lay the blame on other group members, the group may experience discord and reduction in productivity. Also, if the group members engage in group-serving attributions by blaming outside factors, the true source of the problem may remain unexcised. After success, if group members credit their personal ability or their group's prowess when the outcome resulted from external factors, then the group members may select unrealistic goals. By examining the link between attributions and performance, researchers may be able to make suggestions for improving productivity in groups.

Status, Reward Allocation, and Satisfaction

Research suggests that the allocation of rewards, power, and status in groups depends, in part, on perceptions of each individual's contribution to the group endeavor. Suchner and Jackson (1976) presented a social-exchange model of attributions of responsibility and status allocations in groups. According to their model, group members consider three key variables when allocating status: the individual's competence, contributions, and performance. To test their model, some group members were told that their leader was an expert on the task, whereas the remaining subjects thought the leader was incompetent. The group members then discussed three problems and passed on their recommendations to the leader. In some instances the group's solution was approved by the leader, in other instances it was disapproved. Last, the group either succeeded or failed. Surprisingly, Suchner and Jackson found that the leader's acceptance or rejection of the group's recommendation proved to be the critical determinant of responsibility attributions: Leaders were viewed as more responsible when they overturned the group's recommendation and inserted their own solutions. Through correlational analyses, Suchner and Jackson also found that responsibility and status were highly correlated. They could not determine, however, whether responsibility attributions mediated the allocation of status, or whether these two variables were only spuriously correlated.

Attributions also mediate the allocation of rewards in groups. Equity norms dictate that group members should be recognized and rewarded in terms of their contributions to the group's performance (Hatfield, 1983). However, when several group members privately claim more than their share of responsibility, bitter rivalries may emerge. Because several members' rewards do not match their perceived contributions, feelings of inequity and dissatisfaction with group membership may result. The tendency for group members to overestimate their responsibility for group successes may lead them to expect a disproportionate share of rewards, such as status, prerogatives, and power. If, in fact, the member's contributions are notable, the group usually provides additional compensation (Suchner & Jackson, 1976). However, to the extent that such perceptions are self-serving, a member may experience inequity and assert a right to the spoils. Thus, not only do attributions affect how members assign status and allocate rewards, but they mediate each member's reaction to the rewards received. Significant dissatisfaction and disunity results when members perceive that their contributions have not been fairly acknowledged and rewarded by others in the group.

CONCLUSIONS

Although a dominant force in social psychology, attribution theory has been criticized for being too esoteric and overconceptualized. Such criticisms can be met, however, by emphasizing the impact of attributions on social behavior. The research reviewed in this chapter suggests that individuals display predictable attributional reactions in group settings, and that these reactions affect group structure, performance, and conflict.

Many issues involving attributions in collectives need additional attention, but three seem paramount. First, diffusion of responsibility is a key concept in analysis of many social phenomena, including bystander intervention, deindividuation, and social loafing. Yet, in the vast majority of studies, diffusion of responsibility is only assumed to be the mediating process, but is not documented empirically. Future studies need to examine this reduction in personal responsibility directly and to examine how different group variables influence diffusion of responsibility.

Second, only a few studies have examined group-serving attributions. It is possible that many demonstrations of apparently self-serving attributions in group settings are, in fact, group-serving attributions. Unless attributions for both oneself and for other group members are assessed in such studies, it is difficult to distinguish self-serving from group-serving effects. Further, researchers need to investigate factors that determine when group members make group-serving versus self-serving attributions.

Finally, the mechanisms responsible for self-serving and group-serving attributional biases need more attention. Happily, the field has moved beyond debates regarding which of the three processes—information-processing, esteem-maintenance, or self-presentation—causes the effect, to a recognition that all three are probably involved. If so, however, researchers need to take seriously the task of determining when attributions serve each of these three functions.

REFERENCES

Ames, R. (1975). Teachers' attributions of responsibility: Some unexpected counter-defensive effects. *Journal of Educational Psychology, 67,* 668-676.

Beckman, L. (1973). Teachers' and observers' perceptions of causality for a child's performance. *Journal of Educational Psychology, 65,* 198-204.

Beckman, L. J. (1970). Effects of students' performance on teachers' and observers' attributions of causality. *Journal of Educational Psychology, 61,* 76-82.

Beckman, L. (1973). Teachers' and observers' perceptions of causality for a child's performance. *Journal of Educational Psychology, 65,* 198-204.

Bradley, G. W. (1978). Self-serving biases in the attribution process: A reexamination of the fact or fiction questions. *Journal of Personality and Social Psychology, 36,* 56-70.

Brawley, L. R. (1984). Unintentional egocentric biases in attributions. *Journal of Sport Psychology, 6,* 264-278.

Brewer, M. B. (1979). In-group bias in the minimal intergroup situation: A cognitive-motivational analysis. *Psychological Bulletin, 86,* 307-324.

Cacioppo, J. T., Petty, R. E., & Losch, M. (1986). Attributions of responsibility for helping and doing harm: Evidence for confusion of responsibility. *Journal of Personality and Social Psychology, 59,* 100-105.

Caine, B. T., & Schlenker, B. R. (1979). Role position and group performance as determinants of egotistical perceptions in cooperative groups. *Journal of Psychology, 101,* 149-156.

Cialdini, R. B., Borden, R., Thorne, A., Walker, M., Freeman, S., & Sloane, L. T. (1976). Basking in reflected glory: Three (football) field studies. *Journal of Personality and Social Psychology, 34,* 366-375.

Coser, L. A. (1956). *The functions of social conflict.* New York: Free Press.

Diener, E., Dineen, J., Endresen, K., Beaman, A. L., & Frasser, S. C. (1975). Effects of altered responsibility, cognitive set, and modeling on physical aggression and deindividuation. *Journal of Personality and Social Psychology, 31,* 328-337.

Diener, E., Fraser, S. C., Beaman, A. L. & Kelem, R. (1976). Effects of deindividuation on stealing among Halloween trick or treaters. *Journal of Personality and Social Psychology, 33,* 178-183.

Diener, E., Lusk, R., DeFour, D., & Flax, R. (1980). Deindividuation: Effects of group size, density, number of observers, and group member similarity on self-consciousness and disinhibited behavior. *Journal of Personality and Social Psychology, 39,* 449-459.

Dion, K. L., Miller, N., & Magnan, M. A. (1971). Cohesiveness and social responsibility as determinants of group risk taking. *Journal of Personality and Social Psychology, 20,* 400-406.

Dustin, D. S. (1966). Member reactions to team performance. *Journal of Social Psychology, 69,* 237-243.

Feather, N. T. (1969). Attributions of responsibility and valence of success and failure in relation to initial confidence and task performance. *Journal of Personality and Social Psychology, 13,* 129-144.

Fleishman, J. A. (1980). Collective action as helping behavior: Effects of responsibility diffusion on contributions to a public good. *Journal of Personality and Social Psychology, 38,* 629-640.

Forsyth, D. R. (1980). The functions of attributions. *Social Psychology Quarterly, 43,* 184-189.

Forsyth, D. R., Berger, R., & Mitchell, T. (1981). The effects of self-serving vs. other-serving claims of responsibility on attraction in groups. *Social Psychology Quarterly, 44,* 59-64.

Forsyth, D. R., & Schlenker, B. R. (1977). Attributing the causes of group performance: Effects of performance quality, task importance, and future testing. *Journal of Personality, 45,* 220-236.

Hatfield, E. (1983). Equity theory and research: An overview. In H. H. Blumberg, A. P. Hare, V. Kent, & M. Davies (Eds.), *Small groups and social interaction* (Vol. 2, pp. 401-412). New York: John Wiley.

Heider, F. (1958). *The psychology of interpersonal relations.* New York: John Wiley.

Horai, J. (1977). Attributional conflict. *Journal of Social Issues, 33,* (1) 88-100.

Huston, T., Ruggiero, M., Conner, E. R., & Geis, G. (1981). Bystander intervention into crime: A study based on naturally occurring episodes. *Social Psychology Quarterly, 44,* 14-23.

Janis, I. L. (1982). *Victims of groupthink* (2nd ed.). Boston, MA: Houghton Mifflin.

Johnson, T. J., Feigenbaum, R., & Weiby, M. (1964). Some determinants and consequences of the teacher's perception of causation. *Journal of Educational Psychology, 55,* 237-246.

Latane, B., & Darley, J. M. (1970). *The unresponsive bystander: Why doesn't he help?* New York: Appleton-Century-Crofts.

Leary, M. R. (1978). *Self-presentational components of leadership.* Unpublished thesis, University of Florida, Gainesville.

Lerner, M. J. (1965). The effect of responsibility and choice on a partner's attractiveness after failure. *Journal of Personality, 33,* 178-187.

Maruyama, G., Fraser, S. C., & Miller, N. (1982). Personal responsibility and altruism in children. *Journal of Personality and Social Psychology, 42,* 658-664.

Medow, H., & Zander, A. (1965). Aspirations of group chosen by central and peripheral members. *Journal of Personality and Social Psychology, 1.* 224-228.

Milgram, S. (1974). *Obedience to authority.* New York: Harper & Row.

Miller, R. S., Goldman, H. J. & Schlenker, B. R. (1985). Egotism in group members: Public and private attributions of responsibility for group performances. *Social Psychology Quarterly, 48,* 85-89.

Miller, D. T., & Ross, M. (1975). Self-serving biases in the attribution of causality: Fact or fiction? *Psychological Bulletin, 82,* 213-255.

Moriarty, T. (1975). Crime, commitment, and the unresponsive bystander: Two field experiments. *Journal of Personality and Social Psychology, 31,* 370-376.

Mynatt, C., & Sherman, S. J. (1975). Responsibility attribution in groups and individuals: A direct test of the diffusion of responsibility hypothesis. *Journal of Personality and Social Psychology, 32,* 1111-1118.

Nisbett, R. E., & Ross, L. (1980). *Human inference: Strategies and shortcomings in social judgment.* Englewood Cliffs, NJ: Prentice-Hall.

Norvell, N., & Forsyth, D. R. (1984). The impact of inhibiting or facilitating causal factors on group members' reactions after success and failure. *Social Psychology Quarterly, 47,* 293-297.

Pepitone, E. (1952). *Responsibility to group and its effects on the performance of members.* Unpublished doctoral dissertation, University of Michigan.

Rejeski, W. J., & Brawley, L. R. (1984). Attribution theory in sport: Current status and new perspectives. *Journal of Sport Psychology, 5,* 77-99.

Riess, M., Rosenfeld, P., Melburg, V., & Tedeschi, J. T. (1981). Self-serving attributions: Biased private perceptions and distorted public descriptions. *Journal of Personality and Social Psychology, 41,* 224-231.

Roberts, G. C. (1978). Children's assignments of responsibility of winning and losing. In F. Small & R. Smith (Eds.), *Psychological perspectives of youth sports* (pp. 145-171). Washington, DC: Hemisphere.

Ross, L., Bierbrauer, G., & Polly, S. (1974). Attribution of educational outcomes by professional and nonprofessional instructors. *Journal of Personality and Social Psychology, 29,* 609-618.

Ross, M., & Sicoly, F. (1979). Egocentric biases in availability and attribution. *Journal of Personality and Social Psychology, 37,* 322-336.

Schlenker, B. R. (1975). Group members' attributions of responsibility for prior group performance. *Representative Research in Social Psychology, 6,* 96-108.

Schlenker, B. R., & Miller, R. S. (1977a). Egocentrism in groups: Self-serving biases or logical information processing? *Journal of Personality and Social Psychology, 35,* 755-764.

Schlenker, B. R., & Miller, R. S. (1977b). Group cohesiveness as a determinant of egocentric perceptions in cooperative groups. *Human Relations, 30,* 1039-1055.

Schlenker, R. B., Miller, R. S., Leary, M. R., & McCown, N. E. (1979). Group performance and interpersonal evaluation as determinants of egotistical attributions in groups. *Journal of Personality, 47,* 575-594.

Schlenker, B. R., Soraci, S., Jr., & McCarthy, B. (1976). Self-esteem and group performance as determinants of egocentric perceptions in cooperative groups. *Human Relations, 29,* 1163-1176.

Schwartz, S. H., & Clausen, G. T. (1970). Responsibility, norms, and helping in an emergency. *Journal of Personality and Social Psychology, 16,* 299-310.

Schwartz, S. H., & Gottlieb, A. (1976). Bystander reactions to a violent theft: Crime in

Jerusalem. *Journal of Personality and Social Psychology, 34,* 1188-1199.

Shaw, M. E., & Breed, G. R. (1970). Effects of attribution of responsibility for negative events on behavior in small groups. *Sociometry, 33,* 382-393.

Steiner, I. D. (1972). *Group process and productivity.* New York: Academic Press.

Streufert, S. & Streufert, S. C. (1969). Effects of conceptual structure, failure, and success on attribution of causality and interpersonal attitudes. *Journal of Personality and Social Psychology, 11,* 138-147.

Suchner, R. W., & Jackson, D. (1976). Responsibility and status: A causal or only a spurious relationship? *Sociometry, 39,* 243-256.

Tetlock, P. E. (1985). Toward an intuitive politician model of attribution processes. In B. R. Schlenker (Ed.), *The self and social life* (pp. 203-234). New York: McGraw-Hill.

Tetlock, P. E., & Levi, A. (1982). Attribution bias: On the inconclusiveness of the cognitive-motivation debate. *Journal of Experimental Social Psychology, 18,* 68-88.

Thibaut, J. (1950). An experimental study of the cohesiveness of underprivileged groups. *Human Relations, 3,* 251-278.

Thompson, S. C., & Kelley, H. H. (1981). Judgments of responsibility for activities in close relationships. *Journal of Personality and Social Psychology, 41,* 469-477.

Vinokur, A. A. (1971). A review and theoretical analysis of the effects of group processes upon individual and group decisions involving risk. *Psychological Bulletin, 76,* 231-250.

Weinstein, N. D. & Lachendro, E. (1982). Egocentrism as a source of unrealistic optimism. *Personality and Social Psychology Bulletin, 8,* 195-200.

White, R. K. (1977). Misperception in the Arab-Israeli conflict. *Journal of Social Issues, 33* (1), 190-221.

Williams, K., Harkins, S., & Latané, B. (1981). Identifiability as a deterrent to social loafing: Two cheering experiments. *Journal of Personality and Social Psychology, 40,* 303-311.

Wilson, W., & Miller, N. (1961). Shifts in evaluation of participants following intergroup competition. *Journal of Abnormal and Social Psychology, 63,* 428-432.

Wolosin, R. J., Sherman, S. J., & Till, A. (1973). Effects of cooperation and competition on responsibility attribution after success and failure. *Journal of Experimental Social Psychology, 9,* 220-235.

Wortman, C. B., Costanzo, P. R., & Witt, T. R. (1973). Effects of anticipated performance on the attribution of causality to self and others. *Journal of Personality and Social Psychology, 27,* 372-381.

Zander, A. (1971). *Motives and goals in groups.* New York: Academic Press.

Zander, A. (1977). *Groups at work.* San Francisco: Jossey-Bass.

Zander, A., & Forward, J. (1968). Position in group, achievement motivation, and group aspirations. *Journal of Personality and Social Psychology, 8,* 282-288.

Zander, A., & Wulff, D. (1966). Members' test anxiety and competence: Determinants of a group's aspirations. *Journal of Personality, 34,* 55-70.

Zimbardo, P. G. (1969). The human choice: Individuation, reason, and order versus deindividuation, impulse, and chaos. *Nebraska Symposium on Motivation, 17,* 237-307.

7

The Influencing Process
in Group Decision Making

MARTIN F. KAPLAN

Martin F. Kaplan is Presidential Research Professor of Psychology at Northern Illinois University. He has been at NIU since 1965, with leaves as a Research Scientist at the University of California, San Diego, and the University of North Carolina. Present research interests include social judgment, the development of moral judgment, juror decision making, and small group decision and influence processes. He edited *The Impact of Social Psychology on Procedural Justice* (1986), and coedited *Human Judgment and Decision Processes* (1975), and *Human Judgment and Decision Processes in Applied Settings* (1977). His chapters in edited volumes deal with individual differences in social judgment, individual juror judgments, jury deliberation, group decision making, character testimony, and moral judgments. Unpublished activities—and to a small extent, talents—also lie in basketball and softball small group participation, and country and old-time fiddle music listening. He is a Fellow of the American Psychological Association (Divisions 8 and 41).

Decisions and judgments are often made by groups engaged in discussion. Members may enter discussion with a decision preference, which may change as a consequence of the arguments or decision preferences of other members. This chapter focuses on the influence processes that emerge when groups reach a judgment. Though interest in *how* group members influence one another has a long history (e.g., Bechterev & de Lange, 1924; Dashiell, 1935; Jenness, 1932), focused study on the influence process received its major impetus with the report of what has come to be known as *group polarization* or *choice shift* (Cartwright, 1973; Stoner, 1961). *Group polarization* describes the finding that the prediscussion tendencies of individuals toward a particular direction are enhanced following discussion. *Choice shift* refers to a related aspect—that the *group* decision may be more extreme in the same direction than the average of members' individual prediscussion preferences. For example, jurors who tended toward conviction before deliberation may favor conviction more strongly after discussion,

AUTHOR'S NOTE: The contributions of Charles E. Miller to some of the ideas discussed here are gratefully acknowledged.

both in private individual judgments and in the consensus group decision (Myers & Kaplan, 1976).

Three considerations ought to be made clear before going on. First, for purposes of analyzing influence processes, we need not distinguish between individual and group shifts because both require some sort of influence during discussion. Second, any model of group influence must account for shifts in either direction, e.g., toward conviction or acquittal. A lack of such generality eventually doomed several explanations of polarization (e.g., "risk as a value") that could only handle shifts in one direction, or that treated only one sort of decision (e.g., judgments involving risk) (Cartwright, 1973). Third, although our departure point is the polarization phenomenon, analysis of influence must be able to deal with shifts of *any* sort, whether toward a more extreme or a more moderate judgment. We search, then, for general models and conditions that help us to understand any actual or potential change due to discussion.

The lengthy story of the many theories that have been offered for polarization has been chronicled elsewhere (Burnstein & Sentis, 1981; Kaplan & Miller, 1983; Lamm & Myers, 1978). After a spirited period of theory construction and testing, two theories remained as general models of the influence process. Not coincidentally, these theories had been introduced earlier as explanations for social conformity (Deutsch & Gerard, 1955). They refer, respectively, to *normative* and *informational* influence.[1]

MECHANISMS OF NORMATIVE AND INFORMATIONAL INFLUENCE

According to normative influence, judgment shifts result from exposure to others' choice preferences and subsequent conformity to the implicit or explicit norms in these preferences. Informational influence attributes shifts to the incorporation of relevant arguments or information about the issue that are shared between discussants. The two models differ importantly in the mechanisms of influence they propose, the aspects of discussion they consider crucial, and their underlying assumptions about human nature. These differences will be considered in this section, and the next section will briefly describe comparative tests of their predictions.

Normative influence theory posits change in order to enhance one's position in the group and/or one's self-image, and to verify the adequacy of one's behavior (Pruitt, 1971; Sanders & Baron, 1977). The former goal is motivated by a desire to maximize social rewards, for instance, acceptance and status. By conforming to extreme and normatively preferred views reported by other members (and here, the norm may refer to either or both the discussion group or some outside referent group), the individual places his or her decision in the most favorable light. By being more extreme than the group average, one is presenting oneself as both similar to others and distinctive in the approved direction. This brings both social and intrinsic rewards. The latter goal, verification of behavioral adequacy, is motivated by a desire to gauge social reality; one assures the adequacy of one's choices by aligning them with those of others. The motivation for normative influence is clearly based on social rewards (acceptance, status, and adequacy) and their attainment by conformity.

Informational influence implies that judgments, whether before or after discussion, are based on information about the issue. If judgments shift, it is because one has incorporated new information that was provided during discussion. This information can be provided forcefully, through persuasive arguments (Burnstein & Vinokur, 1975), or passively, via information sharing (Kaplan, 1977). But there is a paradox that has been overlooked by most proponents of informational influence. How can shifts occur when a group shares facts, whether forcefully or passively, that have been previously available, or that are of the same extremity as those already used in individual decisions? We know that individuals will shift toward greater extremity even when all group members share the same extremity prior to discussion; this is the essence of the polarization phenomenon. If facts no more extreme than those already incorporated are being shared in discussion, how can people shift their judgments? Kaplan (1977, 1984; Kaplan & Miller, 1983) has elaborated the informational influence model to resolve this paradox by reference to information integration theory (Anderson, 1981; Kaplan, 1975), a general model of social judgment. Any judgment is an integration of separate pieces of information about the object or issue. Each piece of information has two quantitative attributes: scale value and weight. *Scale value* refers to the subjective position of a piece of information on the judgment dimension. For example, that "new Coke" tastes sweeter to subjects may have a high scale value on the dimension, "should (should not) replace 'old Coke.'" *Weight* represents the functional importance of that information, that is, its relative contribution to judgment. In the above example, for instance, the information that people don't like to depart from tradition (negative value) may have more weight for judgment than the fact that it tastes sweeter (positive value). By reducing information to its component scale values and weights, it is possible to combine qualitatively different information (e.g., price, taste, tradition, production costs, etc.) into a unitary judgment (e.g., "market 'new Coke'").

The weighted scale values are combined into a unitary judgment by means of an integration rule (e.g., market new Coke = f[weight $\times$ price, weight $\times$ taste preference, weight $\times$ tradition, weight $\times$ costs, etc.]. This rule takes the form of an empirically determined algebraic function linking the scale values, usually averaging. The integration equation also has an allowance for an *initial impression,* which gives the scale value of the judgment existing prior to having information about the issue. Initial impression may be likened to a preexisting bias toward a certain judgment. For example, prior to hearing evidence in a jury trial, the juror has a prejudgment or starting point based on judgments of people or defendants in general ("they're all probably guilty"), on legal norms ("innocent until proven guilty"), or on task instructions ("assume a neutral position") (Kaplan, 1982).

Prior to discussion, a preliminary judgment is made. It is based on an average of the scale values of the incorporated information *and* of the initial impression. Each value contributes to the average in proportion to its weight. Two points are critical. First, in many issues and with many judged objects, this initial impression will be neutral, or at least less extreme in value than the information that was given. The more moderate initial impression (judgment in the absence of information) has the effect of drawing the average toward neutral (Kaplan, 1975). Second, the prediscussion judgment is based on a limited subset of available and potential information. Some information is not represented in the preliminary judgment because it was overlooked, misunderstood, disbelieved, forgotten, or simply not integrated due to limited information processing capacity. Taken together, these points suggest that the preliminary judgments will not be as extreme as warranted by the information set.

During discussion, members share information that was salient to their preliminary judgments. Since the subset of information used and therefore shared by each member will not be identical, some shared information will be effectively novel for each member, that is, previously unintegrated. The subset of information utilized after discussion will be enlarged, shifting the response from the initial impression toward the more extremely valued information. The end result of this information-enlarging process is the polarization effect. Note that polarization would not be predicted from incorporating more information of the same value as that originally used (since the average would remain the same) without allowing for a moderating initial impression. This analysis of the mechanism of informational influence is similar to the treatment of the "set size effect" in social cognition (Anderson, 1981; Kaplan, 1981), which refers to the polarization of our impressions of others due to increases in the size of the set of similarly valued information.

A simplified numerical exercise can illustrate this crucial point about the role of increased information in the polarization process. Assume a response scale from "definitely innocent" (−10) to "definitely guilty" (+10). Jurors hear evidence during a trial that is uniformly strong in guilt appearance, that is, each of several pieces of evidence has a scale value of +8. Prior to deliberation, Juror X's preliminary judgment is based on three pieces of evidence, giving (of course) an average value of +8. In discussion, jurors communicate the evidence that was salient to them, and X incorporates three more pieces of evidence, each with scale values of +8. On the face of it, X's response should not change, since the average remains the same. But if we consider that X's judgment also incorporates a scale value for an initial impression, and furthermore that this value will be less extreme than that of the information (say, the neutral point, or 0), then we see that the prediscussion judgment will be $[(3)8 + 0]/4 = 6$. When the three additional pieces of evidence are incorporated, the postdiscussion judgment now becomes $[(6)8 + 0]/7 = 6.9$. The shift from 6 to 6.9 represents polarization. Had the discussed and incorporated information been more moderate in scale value (e.g., + 4) or of a different valence (e.g., −4) than the originally utilized information, we would have observed a moderation shift in X. Thus this analysis can apply to both polarization and moderation shifts.

In addition to different mechanisms of influence, the normative and informational models have other fundamental differences. They differ in their underlying conceptions of human nature. Normative influence implies that we seek approval and belongingness, and in our social relations we aim for harmony and communality. Informational influence suggests that centrality of being correct, of knowing and understanding our world, and therefore of needing and processing information.

The foregoing distinction suggests another difference. Normative influence, being centered on interpersonal relations, does not involve the assumption of an objectively "correct" judgment, whereas informational influence does seem to involve this assumption.

The models also differ in the psychological attributes considered central to social relations. Normative influence can be labeled a socioemotional model, concentrating on our emotional responses to differences and harmony. Informational influence is more cognitive, centering on the beliefs we have about our world, and their transformations.

Finally, the models differ in the aspect of group discussion considered crucial. For normative influence, it is the choices and preferences held by others, that is, the judgments *per se*. For informational influence, it is the facts, rationales, and arguments supporting the judgments, in short, the component parts of judgments. Lamm and Myers (1978) have labeled this last distinction a question of *source* versus *message* effects.

NORMATIVE *OR* INFORMATIONAL INFLUENCE: CONFRONTATION

The two modes of influence have generally been tested by confrontation. For example, Brown (1965) argued that the content of discussion is of no importance compared to interpersonal dynamics, whereas Burnstein and his coworkers (see, e.g., Burnstein & Vinokur, 1973) contended that the distribution and preponderance of arguments entirely accounts for shifts. The relevant literature has been thoroughly reviewed (see Burnstein & Sentis, 1981; Isenberg, 1986; Kaplan & Miller, 1983; and Lamm & Myers, 1978) and need not be repeated here. It is useful, though, to mention the types of confrontational tests that have been reported.

A tally of the relevant studies shows informational influence to be more prevalent than normative in instances of shifts, and to produce stronger shifts where both modes are introduced (Burnstein & Sentis, 1981; Kaplan & Miller, 1983). One type of test varies one mode of influence in the absence of the other. When people are provided with the preferences of others without being given relevant arguments, polarization is either weak or absent (Clark & Willems, 1969; Teger & Pruitt, 1967; Wallach & Kogan, 1965). Stronger polarization is found when arguments are shared without presenting the arguer's position (Burnstein & Vinokur, 1975; Clark, Crockett, & Archer, 1971; St. Jean, 1970). Of course, it is possible that people infer an arguer's position from the argument (c.f., Jones & Harris, 1967).

A second type of test involves covarying positions and informational content. The arguments ascribed to other members may be opposite in value to their alleged position; e.g., a discussant says he or she thinks the defendant is guilty but then shares exonerating facts about the case. In this instance, judgment shift is toward the information value of the arguments, and not the stated position (Burnstein & Vinokur, 1973; Kaplan, 1977).

The third type of test covaries the number of arguments and number of participants favoring different positions. When either one or five members give either one or five distinct arguments in total, the extent of polarization is determined by the number of distinct arguments, and not by the number of participants favoring a particular position (Vinokur & Burnstein, 1974; Kaplan, 1977).

The fourth test involves the novelty of the information shared in discussion. Informational influence requires that the information shared in discussion be novel or nonredundant for a given member, that is, shifts follow from the incorporation of previously unintegrated information. Normative influence predicts no differential effect for redundant versus nonredundant information, but ascribes shifts to the force of the number of people expressing some preference. Research supports the former prediction; shifts are larger when discussion includes a variety of facts or facts previously unincorporated by some members compared to facts known to all members (Kaplan & Miller, 1977).

NORMATIVE *AND* INFORMATIONAL INFLUENCE: RECONCILIATION

In sum, the research seems to favor informational over normative influence in hand-to-hand battle. However, it is difficult to abandon belief in the viability of normative influence, as witnessed by ongoing attempts to demonstrate the importance of interpersonal pressure (c.f., Kerr, MacCoun, Hall, & Hymes, in press). After all, there is a long history of normative conformity in situations involving minimal information (e.g., Asch, 1955). And, most of the studies supporting informational over normative influence have involved subjects with minimal interpersonal interactions discussing unengaging issues. Such studies are unlikely to arouse strong pressure to agree for agreement's sake or to value group harmony and others' opinions of oneself. Conditions in many studies may not be favorable for producing the motivation for acquiescence to norms.

In a broad sense, the normative and informational formulations appeal respectively to emotive and cognitive aspects of interpersonal relations and decision making. Their appropriateness as explanatory devices may depend on which aspect is elicited by conditions. Just as human nature is multifaceted, that is, emotive *and* cognitive, and just as a variety of elements exist in group settings, both forms of influence may operate in the same discussion, though to varying degrees. Both models strive for generality, but if each claims to be the sole descriptor of the influence process, generality is lost. It is suggested that shifts can and do occur through both modes of influence. Moreover, in addition to operating jointly during group discussion, the different modes may also "feed on one another" (Lamm & Myers, 1978, p. 186). For example, arguments may convey information about positions, and positions may imply arguments (Burnstein & Vinokur, 1975). Also, normative pressures may subtly determine the sorts of arguments one presents. It is reasonable to seek the conditions under which one or the other influence mode will be engaged rather than to pit one against the other to see which holds more "truth." By specifying and systematically testing controlling conditions, a unified model of influence in discussion should be obtainable. The remainder of this chapter explores likely conditions. These conditions are culled from a variety of paradigms and domains in social and personality psychology: group performance, persuasion, conformity, leadership, moral reasoning, distributive justice, and gender differences. Though these domains deal with conditions affecting influence, these conditions have not been systematically applied to group decision making, nor have they been considered as interrelated variables in a unitary model of normative/informational influence. For easy reference, Table 7.1 provides a summary of conditions that favor each influence mode.

Normative influence presupposes an emphasis on the *group* and its dynamics, and on one's position in it. Informational influence is driven by a desire to arrive at accurate or correct decisions. The distinction is between group and task/issue concerns. The first three conditions follow from the core concerns that produce the two influence modes, as well as a distinction between facts and values.

Type of Issue

We have characterized normative influence as centering on concerns about the group and one's position in it, and informational influence as flowing from concerns about decision accuracy. Certain issues may elicit more of one sort of concern than the other, and therefore be more

TABLE 7.1
Conditions Favoring Normative or Informational Influence

| | Emergent Mode of Influence | |
Conditions	Normative	Informational
Underlying motivation	maintain harmony acceptance by group self-presentation comparison with others	being correct knowing being informed about components of a decision
Type of issue	judgmental (value-laden)	intellective (factual)
Interactive goal	group set	task set
Personal orientation	communal, socio-emotionally oriented	agentic, task oriented
Mode of response	public	private
Decision rule	enhanced by unanimity rule	enhanced by unanimity rule

likely to engage one over the other influence mode. The crucial distinction is between facts and values. Broadly speaking, factual questions can be decided by reference to observable events; for validation of a decision, one need only "look up" demonstrations of an event or hear about them in discussion. Value questions on the other hand involve evaluative, "good-bad" preferences that can only be validated by consensus, or reference to other's expressions of values (Byrne, 1971). For example, choice of a given method of birth control can be supported by appeal to data or hearsay on cost, safety, effectiveness, etc., but whether birth control is "wrong" is validated by comparison to others' values, as expressed in norms. Knowing what alternative is factually correct requires gathering and being influenced by information, whereas knowing what value alternatives are to be preferred requires comparing one's values with the norms and values of others. Values and facts are not entirely separable, that is, facts can be value-determined, and they do require consensus in their definition and measurement. But with facts, consensus in their definition is more complete and is not a central issue, whereas with values, consensus *is* the issue. This distinction naturally favors the informational influence mode for questions of fact, and the normative mode for questions of values. Regarding the latter, it should be noted that normative comparison need not be limited to norms within the discussion group. Particularly with familiar and ego-involving issues, comparison may also be with outside referent groups or moral authorities, such as peers, religious groups, families, and the like.

Laughlin and Earley (1982) make a similar and useful distinction between *intellective* and *judgmental* issues. They suggest that issues can be placed on an intellective-judgmental continuum on much the same fact/value basis as discussed here. Intellective issues are factual in nature and have, in principle, demonstrably (i.e., empirically) correct solutions and factual ways to evaluate choice alternatives. They possess social consensus on the validity of key axioms and on what is or is not factual (e.g., there is agreement on what "miles per gallon" means, and on its relation to the issue of gas economy). Judgmental issues have no empirically correct solutions (in the sense of demonstrability within a shared conceptual system), and involve value-laden judgments such as proper conduct, ethics, and esthetics. There is no clear consensus on key axioms, and arguments are based on personal definitions of terms (e.g., there is relatively little agreement on what is meant by stylishness in a car). Thus the task with intellective issues is to reach the *correct* answer by unearthing facts, and the task with judgmental issues to decide the *proper* or *valued* position by reaching consensus or by appeal to logical consistency with other values, because facts do not inform about the alternatives in these instances (McGrath, 1984).

Intellective issues tend to be factually "argument rich" in that information can be marshalled to support one solution or another, and correctness can be assessed by appeal to empirical facts. Judgmental issues tend to be "argument poor"; few demonstrable facts are available for test of a value, and positions on value are more naturally supported or refuted by appeal to consensus or logic. Try convincing a "pro-lifer," for example, about the merits of abortion by sharing statistical information about birth rate, economics, etc.! Conversely, one is less likely to be convinced that some production method is cost-efficient because others think it is than by test-run data. To support the aligning of issues and influence modes, Laughlin and Earley (1982) report that the implicit voting rules emerging with each type of issue are consistent with the respective influence modes. For example, a "truth wins" rule is more likely to be adopted with an intellective issue.

Although differences in argument richness characterize the two types of issues, the number of potential factual arguments is a by-product of the more critical distinction between the empirical demonstrability of facts versus values. Whether the availability of facts or the nature of the issue is more important in determining influence mode is an empirical question. We may hypothesize, however, that intellective issues should lead to greater use and effect of informational influence, and judgmental issues to greater use and effect of normative influence.

Interactive Goal of the Group

The distinction between concerns with the group versus concerns with correctness leads to the second critical condition. The way the group views the goal of discussion and decision making can affect the emergent influence mode. Some tasks and conditions elicit social concerns with maintaining group harmony and cohesion, whereas others engage a concern with making a correct decision on a given issue. These concerns have been labeled, respectively, *group* and *task* sets (Thibaut & Strickland, 1956) in group problem solving. Where the former set is invoked normative influence should predominate, whereas the latter set should lead to accumulating information, and thus to greater use and effect of informational influence.

Groups that are in long-term relationships may elicit social concerns that predominate over reality-testing needs, and therefore adopt a group set. If, for example, the ongoing nature of the group elicits concerns about harmony and cohesion, or if the group will be involved in future decisions together, the focus will be on aligning one's judgments with those of other members. Groups for whom cohesion is important for attainment of other goals (e.g., people who must cooperate outside the particular decision context) will be interested in maintaining harmony, and thus will be sensitive to deviations from consensus or norms. On the other hand, short-term groups, assembled for a single decision (sometimes called "task forces"), should orient toward the issue at hand, and adopt a task set, maximizing informational influence. Thus conditions that vary the concern of the group should also vary the likelihood of a particular influence mode emerging.

As an illustration, the author is presently conducting a study in which fraternity and sorority members are discussing issues either with members of their own fraternity/sorority, or with strangers from other organizations. Moreover, they are being told either that they will discuss a second issue with the same group and that cohesion is important to proper discussion, or that they will discuss a second issue with a recomposed group, and that being correct is important to the task. It is expected that more normative influence will be found in naturally long-term groups and in those making multiple decisions under a cohesion set, and more informational influence will be found in unacquainted groups and in those making a single decision with the same members under a correctness set.

As a further example, juries in shorter trials should, other things equal, display more informational influence. But as the length of the trial or deliberation increases and juror interaction is enhanced, more normative influence should emerge.

Individual Orientation of Group Members

Just as groups may adopt a particular set toward the group or the task, individuals may also approach discussion with a particular orientation style. A common thread of individual differences in orientation toward social interactions runs through a number of diverse social psychological domains. These threads converge to suggest a dichotomy of orientation toward task (or agency), or toward harmony (or socio-emotional) needs. This dichotomy is highly reminiscent of the distinction in group set discussed above, and leads to a similar treatment with respect to influence modes.

In most instances, moderate relationships have been reported between orientation type and gender, but it is more important for present purposes to consider styles as a social orientation, and not as gender specific. Whether a style is "masculine" or "feminine" or is associated with biological sex are questions that can be argued elsewhere (see, e.g., Eagly, in press).

Influenceability. Individual differences in influenceability have been linked to sex and gender. Eagly (in press) proposes that sex differences in influenceability in both conformity and persuasion are governed by social relations orientations or styles that are stereotypically associated with sex roles. These orientations are labeled *agentic* and *communal* (Bakan, 1966; Eagly, in press). The former describes a social interaction goal that encompasses self-assertion, adherence to task demands, and concern with adequacy and correctness. The latter is an interaction goal centered on concern with others' welfare and feelings, and with harmonious and smoothly functioning social relations. The former is stereotypically associated with the masculine sex role, and the latter with the feminine, though it remains to be seen whether either gender roles or stereotypes primarily account for orientation type. It may be more useful to conceive of orientation as an individual difference rather than as a gender-linked variable. In the context of group processes, it seems reasonable to hypothesize that possession of one or the other orientation will produce different forms of susceptibility; that is, agency is more likely to lead to greater use and effect of informational influence, and communion to greater use and effect of normative influence. In terms of our preceding discussion of issues and group interactive goals, individuals oriented toward agency are concerned with the task and the correctness and adequacy of decisions and therefore will seek information toward that end, whereas communal individuals are attuned to interpersonal relations and maintaining harmony, and will therefore seek agreement and consensus. In short, a focus on the group, whether instilled by the nature of the issue, the imputed goal of discussion, or personal orientation, will make normative influence salient. Focus on the task will favor informational influence.

Moral decision making. A similar dichotomy is evident in treatments of moral decision making. Gilligan (1982) identifies two moral orientations: *morality of justice* and *morality of care.* The former orientation embraces intellective abstractions (e.g., "justice," "fairness") and is traditionally considered as the highest stage of moral functioning (Kohlberg, 1976). Gilligan suggests that this form of morality is tied to a masculine orientation, and is not the only type of morality. The morality of care emphasizes social care and responsibility as the highest form of morality, and is associated with a feminine gender orientation (Ford & Lowery, 1986; Gilligan, 1982). Note that Gilligan proposes a socioemotional versus intellective dichotomy in moral evaluation that aligns with the orientation dichotomy that has been suggested for influenceability. This strengthens the case for the existence of a broad individual difference dimension that should be related to differential use of normative and informational influence. "Care" persons should be communal and concerned with normative influence, and "justice" persons should be agentic and tend more to informational influence.

Distributive justice. Distributive justice studies are concerned with the allocation of rewards to task participants on the basis of such variables as work accomplished, effort, and need. A common distinction is made between allocating rewards among participants *equally* versus *equitably* (i.e., on the basis of deservingness, however defined). Systematic differences in implicit allocation rules appear on the basis of age, sex, and other variables. It has been suggested that equal sharing is motivated by a desire to maintain harmony, pleasantness, and cohesion among participants ("for the good of all"), and equitable sharing reflects concern for justice and fairness vis-á-vis the particular task (Kahn &

Gaeddert, 1985; Streater & Chertkoff, 1976). Different interaction goals are attained by equal and equitable allocations (Deutsch, 1975). Preferences for equity may reflect agentic (task- and problem-focused) goal orientations, and equality preferences may be related to communal (interpersonal- and harmony-focused) orientations. In this regard, Kahn, O'Leary, Krulewitz, and Lamm (1980) attribute the greater preference by females for equal allocations to an orientation toward interpersonal aspects of relationships. Males, on the other hand, are more likely to allocate equitably, a rule that Kahn et al. attribute to an orientation toward task aspects.

Once again we see the dichotomy between group and task concerns. Persons with a communal orientation would be more likely to allocate rewards equally, have a morality of care, and use normative influence. Persons with an agentic orientation would be expected to allocate rewards equitably, have a morality of justice, and be prone to informational influence.

Leadership in groups. Thus far we have seen that in widely different paradigms two individual orientations emerge: one *communal,* centering on the personal and group harmony consequences of actions, and the other one *task oriented,* emphasizing task and solution demands. These orientations align nicely with the major conditions for normative and informational influence discussed earlier.

Leadership studies provide another affirmation of these central styles. Bales and Slater (1955) identified two leader types: task specialists, who are oriented toward achieving the instrumental goals of a group, and socio-emotional leaders, whose concern is group cohesion and compatibility. A similar distinction was posed by Cartwright and Zander (1968), who labeled leader objectives as either goal achievement or group maintenance. Bales (1970) suggested that these interaction styles in groups are gender-linked. Indeed it is found that men give information and opinions more than women. That is, men engage in more task behavior, whereas women agree more and act friendlier than men, and thus engage in more social behavior (e.g., Piliavin & Martin, 1978; Wood & Karten, 1986). Reaffirming the leadership style dichotomy in a meta-analysis of studies of sex differences in group discussion, Carli (1982, reported in Eagly, 1987) found greater task contribution by men, and greater positive socio-emotional contribution by women.

The Leader Behavior Description Questionnaire (Stodgill, 1974) and Bales's (1970) Interaction Process Analysis were devised to assess relative goal orientation toward interpersonal relations versus tasks.

Both may serve as handy operationalizations of the orientation dichotomy.

Decision Rule

Some voting rule is necessary to aggregate the preferences of individual members into a group decision. It seems reasonable to expect that the nature of that rule, for instance, whether a decision requires unanimous or majority agreement, would affect the mode of influence employed. Although it is not clear on theoretical grounds what that effect may be (Hastie, Penrod, & Pennington, 1983), some speculations may be offered, subject to an empirical test to be described later in this chapter.

Groups given a unanimous rule take longer, and have more difficulty in reaching a decision (Miller, 1985; Nemeth, 1977). Does this allow more time to fully share information, or will information be exhausted soon and groups then resort to bare assertions of preference (i.e., normative pressure)? One possibility is that the type of influence enhanced by a unanimity rule depends on the "argument richness" of the issue. If few factual arguments can be made, groups will quickly exhaust information, and will default to normative arguments in the expanded time period.

The more general possibility is that decision rule moderates the effect of the issue on the mode of influence that is used. The use and effect of informational influence, which naturally flows from intellective, argument-rich issues, should be augmented by a unanimity requirement. Conversely, assignment of a unanimity rule in deciding a judgmental, argument-poor issue should augment the use and effect of normative influence. In short, unanimity rules should enhance the use of the influence mode that normally predominates an issue. These speculations call for content analyses of discussion to trace the predominance of one or the other influence mode over time. Research bearing on the proposed interaction between decision rule and issue type will be reported later in this chapter.

Public Versus Private Responses

Conformity pressure is greatest if responses are given publicly (Allen, 1965). Consequently, normative influence should be more likely to emerge, and be more effective, if the response mode is public than if it is private. Note that studies showing that polarization in individual members is primarily due to informational influence typically ask for private responses following discussion (Kaplan & Miller, 1983). This suggests that private responding favors informational, and public responding enhances the chance of normative influence.

Ego Involvement

Isenberg (1986) suggested that social comparison should be more likely in ego involving decisions, and informational influence should operate more strongly in less involving decisions. When members are highly involved, values are engaged, attention to the range of information and issues is narrowed, and the chance of new information being introduced in discussion is lessened if people have already integrated much of the information in such issues. Thus the combination of aroused values and less new information being available or attended to favors normative influence under ego involvement. On the face of it, though, it would be difficult to separate the condition of involvement from the question of type of issue; judgmental issues tend to be more involving by their very nature than intellective issues. The question is whether issues determine influence mode due to distinctions in demonstrability of preferences, potential number of factual arguments, or ego involvement. The three factors tend to be highly correlated in issues.

A STUDY OF SOME CONDITIONS
THAT DETERMINE INFLUENCE MODE

Kaplan & Miller (1987) tested the interactive effects of two of the conditions (issue type and decision rule) on influence mode attempted, member satisfaction, and decision outcome.

Issue type was varied by asking groups to decide on one of two possible awards in a civil damage trial. Some groups decided *compensatory damages,* which are monetary awards given to compensate the plaintiff for losses resulting from the defendant's wrongful actions. These losses include past and present physical and mental pain, permanent disability and disfigurement, medical care and treatment, and lost wages. Other groups decided *exemplary damages,* which are monetary awards in addition to compensatory damages, intended as punishment for the defendant and an example to others. Compensatory damages indemnify for documented losses that can be factually argued (i.e., supported, denied, or disputed in amount), and so constitute a predominantly intellective or factual issue. Exemplary damages relate to the perceived deviance of the defendant from community standards of conduct, and thus represent a judgmental or value-laden issue. To support our equation of award with issue-type, it was found in pretesting that the former elicited more factual arguments and support for positions than statements of normative values, and the latter elicited the reverse pattern.

In groups of six, subjects read a description of a case brought against a furnace manufacturer for injuries suffered when a furnace exploded. The case was written so that the manufacturer was clearly at fault, but there was dispute over the extent of injury to the plaintiff, and the costs of dealing with the injuries. Subjects were to assume that the verdict had been reached in favor of the plaintiff. Their task was to individually decide a monetary award for compensatory or exemplary damages (groups in the latter condition were told to assume that compensatory damages had been previously awarded), and then to discuss the award to arrive at a group figure. A unanimous decision rule was assigned to half the groups, and a majority rule (4-2 minimum) to the remaining half. After the group verdict, subjects again gave an individual, private recommendation. Finally, subjects completed a questionnaire regarding their feelings about the process and outcome of the discussion.

Three sets of dependent variables are of interest: damage awards and their changes due to discussion, normative and informational content of discussion, and subjective reactions to process and outcomes of discussion. The major concern here is with the second set: types of influence attempted as a function of issue type and decision rule.

Looking first at awards, the only significant shift from prediscussion individual to postdiscussion group decisions was for exemplary damages decided under unanimity rule. In this condition, there was a substantial increase in the amount of the award. Awards given privately after discussion were essentially the same as the group awards, except for the condition where exemplary damages were decided under majority rule; individuals preferred giving higher awards, on the average, than had been decided by the group. As we shall see, this condition also saw members reporting the least satisfaction with their group's discussion processes and decisions.

Discussion was taped and later coded according to the following scheme:

Testimony. Statements citing testimonial facts that were provided in the case description ("He was a heavy smoker.").

Inference. Statements of facts not given in the case description but inferred from those given. ("Just the hospital bills alone for five days would be enormous.")

Values. Statements of personal or societal norms of right or wrong in actions and outcomes; statements of appropriateness. ("It's wrong to put off repairs for so long.")

Verdict Preferences. Statements alluding to one's preference for the amount of the award, including both simple declarations ("He should get more than that.") and normative pressure to reach a specific verdict ("Do what the majority thinks is right.").

Nonspecific Pressure. Statements applying pressure on actions and decisions but *not* toward a particular decision. ("If we can get this done we can go home.").

Procedures. Statements about rules and procedures. ("Should we take a vote now?").

Legal Issues. Statements about pertinent law. ("If they give him the money, does it have to be used for that?").

Other. Statements not included in the other categories and irrelevant to the trial. ("What psych section are you in?").

Counts in these categories were further divided into direct assertions, references to others' assertions, agreement with others, disagreement with others, and questions. Excellent interrater coding reliability was obtained (mean agreement coefficient for discussions coded independently by two raters = .92).

Very few statements fell into the last four categories. *Testimony* and *inference* statements were considered to reflect informational influence, and statements of *values* and *verdict preferences* were taken to reflect normative influence. Since patterns were nearly identical for direct assertions alone and total number of statements within categories, the former counts were utilized.

Two main findings are important for the question of conditions affecting the emergency of influence modes. First, different issues elicited different influence modes. Normative influence appeared more often in discussions of the exemplary award (the judgmental issue) than in compensatory award discussions, and informational influence was attempted more often in groups discussing compensatory awards (the intellective issue) than in those deciding exemplary awards. Second, this tendency for an intellective issue to elicit more informational than normative influence, and for a judgmental issue to elicit more normative than informational influence was greater under a unanimity than a majority decision rule. In short, a unanimity requirement enhances the effect of issue on the type of emergent influence.

It may be that a unanimity rule makes it more difficult to reach consensus, and groups rely more on the influence mode natural to the particular issue to achieve this difficult consensus. Oddly though, the unanimous groups did not spend more time discussing than the majority groups, so we cannot conclude that, in the exemplary award condition, they ran out of things to argue and resorted to normative pressure. We did find that the differential effects of issue and decision rule were located in the second half of discussion, and not in the first half. Further research and careful monitoring of discussion is needed to detect why issue and rule should matter for influence attempts only in the later stages of discussion.

Turning last to postdecisional reactions, responses to the outcome and process of decision making showed a pattern whereby majority rule groups were most discontented, especially when deciding the judgmental issue. They reported the least satisfaction with the decision, the least thoroughness, fairness, and responsiveness by others, and the most pressure. These majority rule/judgmental issue groups also had the lowest count of facts discussed.

Several conclusions are worthy of mention. First, the intellective-judgmental nature of the issue is a determining condition for the type of influence people will attempt, especially later in discussion. It remains to be seen whether a particular type of influence will be more *effective* with its corresponding issue type. Research is underway on this question.

Second, when a group decision is harder to obtain because of the use of a unanimity rule, group members will make greater use of the type of influence that is naturally associated with the issue.

Third, the magnitude of choice shift is a joint function of issue and decision rule. This may be due to the peculiar conjunction here of a judgmental issue that provoked considerable variability in prediscussion preferences with a unanimity rule, which requires members to take extreme outliers into account in order to reach agreement (see Kaplan & Miller, 1987, for speculation on this point).

Fourth, if member satisfaction is important (and we can certainly think of many situations in which member perceptions and satisfaction are at least as important as the decision itself), it is wise to match the decision rule to the issue. Specifically, judgmental issues, which rely on social consensus for validation, provoked strong dissatisfaction when decided by majority vote. If an issue of values and norms is to be decided, the closer to unanimity the vote, the more satisfying the process and outcome will seem in retrospect.

CONCLUSIONS

I have argued that normative and informational influence, though associated with quite different sources, forms, processes, and conceptions of underlying social motivation, are not mutually exclusive, but can operate jointly in the group decision making process. The trick in reconciling the two influence modes is to identify the conditions that give rise to each, and, furthermore, to identify the theoretical principles that underlie these conditions.

In general, normative influence is in response to variables pertaining to group and interpersonal attributes; informational influence revolves more on variables related to the decision task and its successful resolution. Consequently, anything that focuses concern on the positions and preferences of others, their status, power, numbers, acceptance/rejection, harmony, and so on will enhance the use of normative influence. Anything that makes salient the task, the correctness/adequacy of the decision, and the need for gathering information, will facilitate the use of informational influence. This principle gives rise to the crucial conditions of type of issue being decided, orientation of the group, and personal orientation of individual members. Intellective or factual issues, task orientations, and agentic personal orientations provide fertile conditions for informational influence. Judgmental or value-laden issues, group orientations, and communal personal orientations enhance normative influence attempts.

Other conditions may play mediating roles as well. *Decision rule* appears to act as a moderator of issue effects. A unanimity requirement increases the use of the influence mode that normally follows from a particular type of issue. Normative influence may be more effective with *public* declarations of individual choices, and informational influence may have a stronger effect on *private* responding. *Ego involvement* in the issue may enhance the chance of normative influence. Finally, though initial preference distribution in the group is important to the degree of choice shift (see, e.g., Kerr, MacCoun, Hall, & Hymes, in press), its precise role in the induction of normative or informational influence is not readily apparent. It is likely that certain patterns of preference distribution will favor a particular influence mode more than another.

With attention turned away from antithesis and toward synthesis of influence modes, other controlling conditions will no doubt be identified in time. This chapter is intended as a suggestive impetus to this enterprise.

NOTE

1. Other typologies of social influence have been suggested, but these may be reasonably fit to the normative/informational dichotomy. Kelman (1958) identifies *compliance* (one behaves in the requested way to achieve some end with the influencer), *identification* (one is influenced because the group is liked and admired), and *internalization* (one is influenced on the basis of the content of the influence attempt). The first two appear to be consistent with normative influence as it is customarily defined, and the last with informational influence. French and Raven (1959) offer five types of influence or power: *referent* (a liked person has more influence), *reward* (a person with the ability to reward has more influence), *coercive* (a person with the ability to punish has more influence), *legitimate* (a person with ligitimized status has the right to prescribe behavior), and *expert* (the influencer has greater resources—knowledge—with respect to the issue). The first four sources of influence can be easily seen as a finer elaboration of normative influence, and the last as a restatement of informational influence.

REFERENCES

Allen, V. L. (1965). Situational factors in conformity. In L. Berkowitz (Ed.), *Advances in experimental social psychology* (Vol. 2, pp. 133-175). New York: Academic Press.

Anderson, N. H. (1981). *Foundations of information integration theory.* New York: Academic Press.

Asch, S. E. (1955). Opinions and social pressure. *Scientific American, 193,* 31-35.

Bakan, D. (1966) *The duality of human existence.* Chicago: Rand McNally.

Bales, R. F. (1970). *Personality and interpersonal behavior.* New York: Holt, Rinehart & Winston.

Bales, R. F., & Slater, P. (1955). Role differentiation in small decision making groups. In T. Parsons & R. F. Bales (Eds.), *Family, socialization, and interaction process* (pp. 259-306). New York: Free Press.

Bechterev, V. M., & de Lange, M. (1924). Die Ergebnisse des Experiments auf den gebieteder kollectiven Reflexologie. *Zeitschrift fur Angewandte Psychologie 24,* 305-344.

Brown, R. (1965). *Social psychology.* New York: Free Press.

Burnstein, E., & Sentis, K. (1981). Attitude polarization in groups. In R. E. Petty, T. M. Ostrom, & T. C. Brock (Eds.), *Cognitive responses in persuasion* (pp. 197-216). Hillsdale, NJ: Lawrence Erlbaum.

Burnstein, E., & Vinokur, A. (1973). Testing two classes of theories about group-induced shifts in individual choice. *Journal of Experimental Social Psychology, 9,*123-137.

Burnstein, E., & Vinokur, A. (1975). What a person thinks upon learning he has chosen differently from others: Nice evidence for the persuasive arguments explanation of choice shifts. *Journal of Experimental Social Psychology, 11,* 412-426.

Byrne, D. (1971). *The attraction paradigm.* New York: Academic Press.

Cartwright, D. (1973). Determinants of scientific progress: The case of the risky shift. *American Psychologist, 28,* 222-231.

Cartwright, D., & Zander, A. (1968). *Group dynamics: Research and theory.* New York: Harper & Row.

Clark, R. D., Crockett, W. H., & Archer, R. (1971). Risk-as-value hypothesis: The relation between perception of self, others, and the risky shift. *Journal of Personality and Social Psychology, 20,* 425-429.

Clark, R. D., & Willems, E. P. (1969). Where is the risky shift? *Journal of Personality and Social Psychology 13,* 215-221.

Dashiell, J. F. (1935). Experimental studies of the influence of social situations on the behavior of individual human adults. In C. Murchison (Ed.), *Handbook of social psychology* (pp. 1097-1158). Worchester, MA: Clark University Press.

Deutsch, M. (1975). Equity, equality, and need: What determines which value will be used as the basis of distributive justice? *Journal of Social Issues, 31,* 137-149.

Deutsch, M., & Gerard, H. G. (1955). A study of normative and informational social influences upon individual judgment. *Journal of Abnormal and Social Psychology, 51,* 629-636.

Eagly, A. H. (1987). *Sex differences in social behavior: A social role interpretation.* Hillsdale, NJ: Lawrence Erlbaum.

Ford, M. R., & Lowery, C. R. (1986). Gender differences in moral reasoning: A comparison of the use of justice and case orientations. *Journal of Personality and Social Psychology, 50,* 777-783.

French, J.R.P., & Raven, B. (1959). The bases of social power. In D. Cartwright (Ed.), *Studies in social power* (pp. 150-167). Ann Arbor, MI: University of Michigan Press.

Gilligan, C. (1982). *In a different voice.* Cambridge, MA: Harvard University Press.

Hastie, R., Penrod, S. D., & Pennington, N. (1983). *Inside the jury.* Cambridge, MA: Harvard University Press.

Isenberg, D. J. (1986). Group polarization: A critical review and meta-analysis. *Journal of Personality and Social Psychology, 50,* 1141-1151.

Jenness, A. (1932). The role of discussion in changing opinion regarding a matter of fact. *Journal of Abnormal and Social Psychology, 27,* 279-296.

Jones, E. E., & Harris, V. A. (1967). The attribution of attitudes. *Journal of Experimental Social Psychology, 3,* 1-24.

Kahn, A.S., & Gaeddert, W. P. (1985). From theories of equity to theories of justice: The liberating consequences of studying women. In V. E. O'Leary, R. K. Unger, & B. S. Wallston (Eds.), *Women, gender, and social psychology* (pp. 129-148). Hillsdale, NJ: Lawrence Erlbaum.

Kahn, A. S., O'Leary, V. E., Krulewitz, J. E., & Lamm, H. (1980). Equity and equality: Male and female means to a just end. *Basic and Applied Social Psychology, 1,* 173-197.

Kaplan, M. F. (1975). Information integration in social judgment: Interaction of judge and informational components. In M. F. Kaplan & S. Schwartz (Eds.), *Human judgment and decision processes* (pp. 139-171). New York: Academic Press.

Kaplan, M. F. (1977). Discussion polarization effects in a modified jury decision paradigm: Informational influences. *Sociometry, 40,* 262-271.

Kaplan, M. F. (1981). Amount of information and polarity of attraction. *Bulletin of the Psychonomic Society, 18,* 23-26.

Kaplan, M. F. (1982). Cognitive processes in the individual juror. In N. L. Kerr & R. M. Bray (Eds.), *The psychology of the courtroom* (pp. 197-220). New York: Academic Press.

Kaplan, M. F. (1984). How do people influence in deliberation? A social psychological view. *Behavioral Sciences and the Law, 2,* 1-6.

Kaplan, M. F., & Miller, C. E. (1977). Judgments and group discussion: Effect of presentation and memory factors on polarization. *Sociometry, 40,* 337-343.

Kaplan, M. F., & Miller, C. E. (1983). Group discussion and judgment. In P. Paulus (Ed.), *Basic group processes* (pp. 65-94). New York: Springer-Verlag.

Kaplan, M. F., & Miller, C. E. (1987). Group decision making and normative vs. informational influence: Effects of type of issue and assigned decision rule. *Journal of Personality and Social Psychology, 53.*

Kelman, H. C. (1958). Compliance, identification, and internalization: Three processes of attitude change. *Journal of Conflict Resolution, 2,* 51-60.

Kerr, N. L., MacCoun, R., Hall, C. A., & Hymes, J. A. (in press). Gaining and losing social support: Momentum in decision making groups. *Journal of Experimental Social Psychology.*

Kohlberg, L. (1976). Moral stages and moralization: The cognitive developmental approach. In T. Lickona (Ed.), *Moral development and behavior: Theory, research, and social issues* (pp. 31-53). New York: Holt, Rinehart & Winston.

Lamm, H., & Myers, D. G. (1978). Group-induced polarization of attitudes and behavior. In L. Berkowitz (Ed.), *Advances in experimental social psychology* (Vol. 11, pp. 145-195). New York: Academic Press.

Laughlin, P. R., & Earley, P. C. (1982). Social combination model, persuasive arguments theory, social comparisons theory, and choice shift. *Journal of Personality and Social Psychology, 42,* 273-280.

McGrath, J. E. (1984). *Groups: Interaction and performance.* Englewood Cliffs, NJ: Prentice-Hall.

Miller, C. E. (1985). Group decision making under majority and unanimity decision rules. *Social Psychology Quarterly, 48,* 51-61.

Myers, D. G., & Kaplan, M. F. (1976). Group-induced polarization in simulated juries. *Personality and Social Psychology Bulletin, 2,* 63-66.

Nemeth, C. (1977). Interactions between jurors as a function of majority versus unanimity decision rules. *Journal of Applied Social Psychology, 7,* 38-56.

Piliavin, J. A., & Martin, R. R. (1978). The effects of the sex composition of groups on style of social interaction. *Sex Roles, 4,* 281-296.

Pruitt, D. G. (1971). Conclusions: Toward an understanding of choice shifts in group discussion. *Journal of Personality and Social Psychology, 20,* 495-510.

Sanders, G. S., & Baron, R. S. (1977). Is social comparison irrelevant for producing choice shift? *Journal of Experimental Social Psychology, 13,* 303-314.

St. Jean, R. (1970). Reformulation of the value hypothesis in group risk taking. *Proceedings of the 78th Annual Convention of the American Psychological Association, 5,* 339-340.

Stodgill, R. M. (1974). *Handbook of leadership: A survey of theory and research.* New York: Free Press.

Stoner, J. A. (1961). *A comparison of individual and group decisions involving risk.* Unpublished master's thesis, School of Industrial Management, Massachusetts Institute of Technology.

Streater, A., & Chertkoff, J. (1976). Distribution of rewards in a triad: A developmental test of equity theory. *Child Development, 47,* 800-805.

Teger, A. I., & Pruitt, D. G. (1967). Components of risk taking. *Journal of Experimental Social Psychology, 3,* 189-205.

Thibaut, J. W., & Strickland, L. (1956). Psychological set and conformity. *Journal of Personality, 25,* 115-129.

Vinokur, A., & Burnstein, E. (1974). Effects of partially shared persuasive arguments in group-induced shifts. *Journal of Personality and Social Psychology, 29,* 306-315.

Wallach, M. A., & Kogan, N. (1965). The role of information and consequences in group risk taking. *Journal of Experimental Social Psychology, 1,* 1-19.

Wood, W., & Karten, S. J. (1986). Sex differences in interaction style as a product of perceived sex differences in competence. *Journal of Personality and Social Psychology, 50,* 341-347.

8

Categorization, Competition, and Collectivity

CHESTER A. INSKO
JOHN SCHOPLER

Chester A. Insko is a Professor of Psychology at the University of North Carolina at Chapel Hill. His primary interests are in attitudes, out-group rejection, and balance theory. He has published *Theories of Attitude Change, Experimental Social Psychology* (with J. Schopler), and *Introductory Statistics for Psychology* (with D. Schoeninger). He is also a member of the UNC Macintosh Users Group.

John Schopler is a Professor of Psychology at the University of North Carolina at Chapel Hill. He specializes in the study of interdependence in dyads and larger groups. He has coauthored *Experimental Social Psychology* (with C. Insko), and *Introduction to Psychology* (with C. Morgan, D. King, and J. Weisz), and published in the areas of helping, person perception, crowding, group-product evaluations, and interpersonal power. He is also the starting pitcher of the departmental co-rec baseball team.

THE MERE-CATEGORIZATION TRADITION

In recent years Tajfel and his associates (e.g., Billig & Tajfel, 1973; Tajfel, 1970; Tajfel & Billig, 1974; Tajfel, Billig, Bundy, & Flament, 1971; Turner, Brown, & Tajfel, 1979) have presented an abundance of evidence that has been interpreted as indicating that the mere-categorization of subjects into subsets ("groups") leads to an orientation of favoritism toward one's own category (see Brewer, 1979, for a review, and Tajfel, 1982; Tajfel & Turner, 1986, for more recent discussions).

AUTHORS' NOTE: This chapter owes much to many associates at the University of North Carolina, but most particularly to the late John Thibaut. What is summarized in this chapter, in fact, is a brief synopsis of John's final involvement with social psychology. John spent much of his professional career emphasizing the importance not just of individuals exposed to social stimuli, but of the interdependence of two individuals. In recent years, however, he increasingly recognized that two-on-two interdependence is very different from one-on-one interdependence. It will be obvious to the reader that this chapter raises as many questions as it answers. There is a sense in which that is characteristic of John, who never stopped asking questions, and certainly never lost either his enthusiasm for or his commitment to social psychology.

Although various categorization procedures have been used, the most common one involves dividing subjects into groups on the basis of their fabricated preferences for paintings by Klee relative to those by Kandinsky. Subjects first view and rate pairs of unidentified Klee-Kandinsky slides, and then go to separate rooms where they are subsequently told that they are members either of the Klee-preferring group or of the Kandinsky-preferring group. The dependent variable is assessed by subjects allocating money to unidentified members of own group (excluding self) and unidentified members of the other group. As previously indicated, the results of many such studies have been interpreted as indicating that subjects follow an orientation that favors own group relative to other groups in the relative allocation of money.

PERCEIVED COLLECTIVITY (ENTITATIVITY)

Although people may be assigned to many social categories, such as age, nationality, gender, and religion, common sense suggests that such categories may or may not be perceived as collectives or groups. Much common parlance, for example, assumes that only some women have the "raised consciousness" associated with the conception of themselves as members of a group rather than as instances of a mere demographic category. In 1958 Campbell coined the term "entitativity" to refer to the perception of an aggregate of people as possessing the characteristics of an entity. Horwitz and Rabbie (1982), however, credit Lewin (1948) with an even earlier interest in the importance of perceived collectivity or entitativity. Lewin attempted to "raise the consciousness" of Jewish adolescents by arguing that the important determinant of who belongs to what group in not the degree of similarity-dissimilarity among the involved individuals but "interdependence of fate" (1948, p. 184). According to Horwitz and Rabbie, Lewin had been influenced by his experiences in Europe, where some people were categorized and treated as Jews even though they had not previously considered themselves to be Jewish.

The issue of what necessary and sufficient conditions give rise to the perception of entitativity has received surprisingly little attention. Campbell's analysis applied Gestalt principles to define how perceptions of aggregates shift to perceptions of a collective entity. Thus he discussed such factors as continuous configurations over time (common fate), proximity, and similarity. Much of Campbell's discussion, however, was from the perspective of an external observer, while our current interest is in perceived entitativity from the perspective of the individual within the category or group.

Both Lewin and Campbell clearly believed that demographic categories *per se* do not create entitativity; however, the research of Tajfel and his associates was designed to show that they do. Tajfel did not use the term "entitativity," but he clearly believed that mere differential categorization was sufficient to induce "genuine awareness of membership in separate and distinct groups" (1978a, p. 35). What is the evidence for this dramatic theoretical position? It comes from a series of experiments following the above described procedure in which subjects allocate money between members of their own category (other than self) and members of the other category. To the extent that the money is allocated so as to maximize own category outcomes, there is evidence for self identification with own-category members, and to the extent that money is allocated so as to maximize the outcome difference between own- and other-category members, there is evidence for explicit social comparison between categories. And it is clear that identification with own-category members and social comparison between own and other categories provide compelling evidence for a sense of "being in it together" (entitativity).

Given the cognitive nature of the problem, one might question why Tajfel and his associates did not simply ask subjects whether they felt they were in a group. For example, why not ask subjects categorized as Kandinskys whether they conceived of the Kandinskys as a group or as separate individuals? Although Tajfel did not directly address this issue, it can be argued that there are two difficulties with this approach. The first difficulty resides in the lack of English words distinguishing aggregates from collective entities. The most frequently used term, "group," has different meanings in different contexts. Indeed, in many contexts "group" means nothing more than category or set. Thus for Tajfel's subjects to have reported that the Kandinskys were a "group" would be interesting, but certainly not definitive. The second difficulty with this approach is that it does not explicitly relate to the identification with own category and the relativistic social comparison between categories that are implied by Tajfel's conception of psychologically real groups. These latter processes are behaviorally assessed by the allocation of money between categories, and it is for that reason that such assessment provides a superior measure of entitativity.

All allocation tasks, however, are not equal. Tajfel and his associates have claimed that their results reflect the importance of maintaining one's social identity/esteem through belonging to a group that is seen to be better than other groups. This interpretation assumes a strong degree of entitativity and positively discrepant social comparisons. Our objection to Tajfel's evidence concerning the minimal conditions inducing entitativity and social comparison is based on his procedure for assessing the allocation of money. In our view, the Tajfel procedure does not permit subjects to express the full range of possible social orientations. Indeed, our alternative assessment procedure produces different results. With this alternative procedure, subjects appear to make allocation decisions that reflect minimal degrees of entitativity as well as some concern with the welfare of all subjects who are present (i.e., both Klees and Kandinskys).

Before describing the alternative assessment, we will briefly describe the Tajfel procedure. A more complete description of the Tajfel assessment procedure can be found in Turner (1978, pp. 112-115), and in Bornstein, Crum, Wittenbraker, Harring, Insko, and Thibaut (1983a, pp. 322-323), who also review the procedure devised by Brewer and Silver (1978), and by Ng (1981). A brief overview of Tajfel's system follows.

OVERVIEW OF THE TAJFEL ASSESSMENT PROCEDURE

The Tajfel assessment procedure requires subjects to select one column of payoff points from a matrix. Each column contains a payoff amount for an own-group member and another group-member. The matrices are designed to measure four between-group orientations. These are (1) maximum in-group profit or absolute in-group favoritism (MIP), (2) maximum difference or relative in-group favoritism (MD), (3) fairness (F), and (4) maximum joint profit (MJP). As is illustrated in Table 8.1, the Tajfel measurement procedure requires that any matrix be presented in both an own/other form and an other/own form. With an own/other matrix, own outcomes are in the top row and other outcomes in the bottom row, while with an other/own matrix the reverse is the case.

Tajfel matrices are arbitrarily scored in one unit intervals either from right to left or from left to right. The subtraction of such scores for the two forms of a matrix allows for the calculation of what are referred to as "pulls." Thus the own/other matrix with right-to-left scoring minus the other/own matrix with right-to-left scoring yields the pull of MD on

TABLE 8.1
An Example of Tajfel's Assessment Procedure

Own/Other Matrix Contrasting MD and MIP + MJP

	MD												MJP MIP
Own group	7	8	9	10	11	12	13	14	15	16	17	18	19
Other group	1	3	5	7	9	11	13	15	17	19	21	23	25
Right to left scoring	12	11	10	9	8	7	6	5	4	3	2	1	0
Left to right scoring	0	1	2	3	4	5	6	7	8	9	10	11	12

Other/Own Matrix Combining MD, MJP, and MIP

													MD MJP MIP
Other group	7	8	9	10	11	12	13	14	15	16	17	18	19
Own group	1	3	5	7	9	11	13	15	17	19	21	23	25
Right to left scoring	12	11	10	9	8	7	6	5	4	3	2	1	0

SOURCE: From Bornstein, Crum, Wittenbraker, Harring, Insko, and Thibaut, "On the measurement of social orientations in the minimal group paradigm," *European Journal of Social Psychology*, Vol. 13, p. 324. Copyright 1983 by John Wiley & Sons, Ltd. Reprinted by permission of John Wiley & Sons, Ltd.

NOTE: Suppose that a subject responds to the own/other matrix by selecting the 7/1 column, and responds to the other/own matrix by selecting the 19/25 column. The own-other resonse implies that the subject prefers a maximum own/other difference of 6 (7−1) to the combination of 19 for own group and 46 (19+25) for both groups implied by the 19/25 column at the right end of the matrix. On the other hand, the other-own response implies that the subject prefers the combination of an own-other difference of 6 (25−19), 25 for own group, and 46 (19+25) for both groups to the minimal values implied by the 7/1 column at the left end of the matrix. Calculation of the pull of MD on MJP + MIP is accomplished by subtracting the response to the other-own matrix scored right to left from the response to the own-other matrix scored right to left. For the hypothetical subject this would yield a pull of MD on MJP + MIP of 12 (12−0). On the other hand, for the pull of MJP + MIP to left. For the hypothetical subject the pull would be on MD the same procedure is used except that the own-other matrix is scored left to right. For our hypothetical subject the pull would be 0 (0−0).

217

MJP + MIP. On the other hand, the own/other matrix with left-to-right scoring minus the other/own matrix with right-to-left scoring yields the pull of MJP + MIP on MD. Matrices other than the ones in Table 8.1 enable the scoring of still other pulls, for example, the pull of F on MIP + MD. Because the operation required for the calculations of pulls is not intuitively obvious, a concrete scoring example is presented at the bottom of Table 8.1.

MULTIPLE ALTERNATIVE MATRICES (MAMs)

Bornstein, Crum, Wittenbraker, Harring, Insko, and Thibaut (1983a) developed a procedure for measuring seven social orientations, some of which are conceptually similar to MD, MJP, MIP, and F. Following Kelley and Thibaut (1978), these orientations, along with their abbreviations, are:

A. Orientations favoring own group.
   1. Maximizing own gain—max own.
   2. Maximizing relative own gain—max rel own.
   3. Maximizing joint gain, but favoring own group—max joint own.
B. Orientations favoring other group.
   4. Maximizing other's gain—max other.
   5. Maximizing relative gain of other—max rel other.
   6. Maximizing joint gain, but favoring other group—max joint other.
C. An orientation that favors neither group.
   7. Minimizing the difference in gain—min diff.

Each orientation implies distinctive interpersonal values or assumptions. In the context of the mere-categorization situation, consider, for example, the three orientations favoring own group. Max own means that the allocator chooses the alternative that gives own group the highest payoff. Use of this simple strategy implies that the allocator has identified with own group and is indifferent about the consequences to the other group. Max rel own, on the other hand, ignores the payoff that is best for own group in favor of the choice that maximizes the differences between own and other group. As such, it requires comparisons of own and other payoffs for each alternative and is satisfied by the choice that maximizes the difference between own and other group. Use of this strategy implies both identification and social comparison. Finally, max joint own is a strategy that attempts to maximize the amounts of the joint payoffs, as long as own payoff is higher. The meaning of this strategy is more ambiguous since it requires a concern for keeping the payoff to the other group at a relatively high level.

The seven social orientations include ones that are similar to those identified by Tajfel. Max own is similar to maximum in-group profit (MIP), max rel own is similar to maximum differences (MD), max joint other is similar to maximum joint profit (MJP), and min diff is similar to fairness (F). Bornstein et al.'s assessment procedure involves the use of multiple alternative matrices, or MAMs. The matrices that were used can be understood from the perspective of either a spatial model or a set of mathematical constraints. We will present the spatial model here. The mathematical constraints are described in the appendix.

The spatial model showing the relationships among the seven orientations is presented in Figure 8.1. Own-group outcomes are represented along the horizontal axis, and other-group outcomes along the vertical axis. In the derivation of the matrix values, both axes varied from 0 to 80.

Consider first the min-diff and max-joint lines. The min-diff line runs from the lower-left corner and consists of points in which own and other outcomes are exactly equal. The max-joint line runs from the upper-left to the lower-right corner and consists of points in which the sums of own and other outcomes are equal. Given the constraint that all outcomes lie to the left of the max-joint line, the intersection of the min-diff and max-joint lines represents the highest possible sum of outcomes for which there is complete equality of own and other outcomes. Points on the max-joint line *above* this intersection represent the highest possible sum of outcomes with an advantage to other (max joint other). Points on the max-joint line *below* this intersection represent the highest possible sum of outcomes with an advantage to own (max joint own). In order to obtain unconfounded assessments of these three orientations, Bornstein et al. moved two points from the intersection and selected the next five points. These areas of selected points are represented by heavy lines. For min diff, the five own/other values are 34/34, 35/35, 36/36, 37/37, 38/38; for max joint own, 42/38, 43/37, 44/36, 45/35, 46/34; for max joint other, 38/42, 37/43, 36/44, 35/45, 34/46.

Consider next the max-own line. Given that max own maximizes own outcomes and involves a smaller sum than max joint own, the max-own line should lie below the min-diff line, below the max-joint-own line, and further to the right than the selected max-joint-own points. The max-own line in Figure 8.1 is perpendicular to the

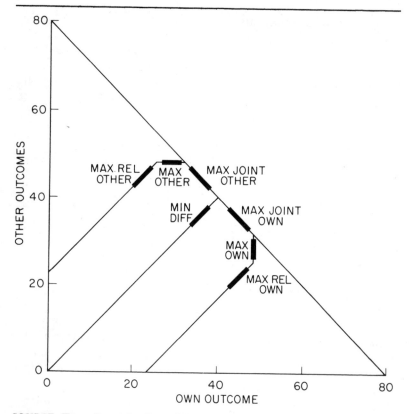

SOURCE: From Bornstein, Crum, Wittenbraker, Harring, Insko, and Thibaut, "On the measurement of social orientations in the minimal group paradigm," *European Journal of Social Psychology*, Vol. 13, p. 329. Copyright 1983 by John Wiley & Sons, Ltd. Reprinted by permission of John Wiley & Sons, Ltd.

Figure 8.1 Spatial Model Showing the Relationship Among the Seven Orientations

horizontal axis and intersects the max-joint line one unit below the selected max-joint points. The selected points on the max-own line are the first five values beginning one unit below the intersection. These own/other values are 47/32, 47/31, 47/30, 47/29, 47/28.

Given that max rel own maximizes the difference between own and other outcomes with an own advantage and is unconfounded with the previously selected orientations, the relevant line should lie below the min-diff line, below the max-joint-own line, and to the left of the max-own line. The max-rel-own line in Figure 8.1 is parallel to the min-diff line. The selected points on the max-rel-own line are the first five values beginning one unit below the intersection with the max-own line. These values are 46/26, 45/25/, 44/24, 43/23, 42/22. The simple reversal of the own-group and other-group values for max own and max rel own provides the values for max other and max rel other.

Using each of the five own-other values for each orientation twice enables construction of the 10 matrices contained in Figure 8.2. In actual use, each multiple alternative matrix is presented on a separate page and the subject is instructed to circle one box in each matrix. The values in the top of each box represent own outcomes and the values in the bottom of each box represent other outcomes. Each box, of course, represents a different one of the seven orientations; for example, 47/32 is max own, 44/24 is max rel own, etc.[1] Each subject receives seven scores, each score being the frequency with which each orientation is selected over the 10 matrices.

INITIAL RESEARCH WITH THE MAMs

Bornstein et al.'s (1983a) Three Experiments

Initial research revealed that in the mere-categorization situation the use of MAMs produces somewhat different results form those repeatedly obtained by Tajfel and his associates. Bornstein et al. conducted three mere-categorization experiments, two with undergraduates from the University of North Carolina and one with 14- and 15-year-old, 9th- and 10th-grade public-school students. The investigation of these two different subject populations was meant to parallel Tajfel's investigation of similar age groups in Europe. Tajfel and his associates have generally concluded that MD (maximum difference) is most important, although they have also reported evidence for MIP, MJP, and F. Thus, for example, Turner, Brown, and Tajfel (1979) summarized their results as indicating that "MD is the most powerful single determinant of responses, although it is only nonsignificantly more influential than MIP + MJP" (p. 200). It is, of course, MD that most explicitly implies the relativistic social comparison that is indicative of entitativity.

All three of the Bornstein et al. experiments followed the usual categorization procedure. Subjects in same-sex "groups" initially viewed and indicated their differential preference for pairs of unidentified Klee and Kandinsky slides, went to individual rooms where they were informed of their preference category, and finally allocated money

own	47	44	34	31	25	44	36
other	32	24	34	47	45	36	44

own	38	45	47	34	29	42	22
other	42	35	28	34	47	22	42

own	38	37	47	31	24	43	44
other	42	37	28	47	44	37	24

own	38	45	45	47	36	25	28
other	38	35	25	30	44	45	47

own	23	45	28	35	42	34	47
other	43	25	47	35	38	46	32

own	47	43	32	46	35	24	37
other	29	37	47	26	35	44	43

own	43	36	44	47	37	26	30
other	23	36	36	29	43	46	47

own	42	32	37	46	47	34	23
other	38	47	37	26	30	46	43

own	30	47	46	22	43	35	36
other	47	31	34	42	23	45	36

own	46	29	38	35	47	42	26
other	34	47	38	45	31	22	46

SOURCE: Adapted from Bornstein, Crum, Wittenbraker, Harring, Insko, and Thibaut, "On the measurement of social orientations in the minimal group paradigm," *European Journal of Social Psychology,* Vol. 13, p. 331. Copyright 1983 by John Wiley & Sons, Ltd. Reprinted by permission of John Wiley & Sons, Ltd.

Figure 8.2 Multiple Alternative Matrices

between members of the Klee-preferring category and members of the Kandinsky-preferring category (excluding self). Although Tajfel and his associates generally did not use cover stories, it was felt that for college subjects, at least, a cover story was advisable. Accordingly, in the first two experiments the college subjects were told that they were participating in a study of a possible payment procedure to be used in a larger, ongoing investigation of individual differences in people who have different artistic preferences. It was explained that the larger study subjects would evaluate paintings by Klee and Kandinsky, just as they had done, and then, unlike them, would complete an extensive and onerous battery of psychological tests. However, in order to maintain subjects' interests and involvement it was necessary to offer payment, and that it was hoped that interest and involvement would be further increased by letting subjects make decisions among themselves regarding the amount of payment. Since for obvious reasons each subject could not be allowed to determine how much he or she should receive, the experimenters had tentatively adopted a plan in which each subject would determine how much one or more other subjects received. Accordingly, the present study was designed simply as an investigation of this proposed payment procedure. Since the present subjects were not taking the psychological tests, the amounts of money were not as large as in the larger study but would be sufficiently large to maintain interest.

The first two studies both found significant amounts of max joint own and min diff with significantly more min diff for females than for males. Results for the second study are presented in Table 8.2. The tabled entries are the mean frequency of choice across the 10 matrices. With 7 orientations on each of 10 matrices, chance for any one orientation is (1/7) (10) or 1.43. Table 8.2 suggests the possibility that max joint own is greater for males than for females. While the sex difference in max joint own is not significant for either of the first two experiments, the pattern has occurred with sufficient regularity in later research to believe in its reliability.

An important result of the first two experiments relates to the low frequency of max rel own. Note that in Table 8.2 the mean is 0.86 for males and 0.58 for females. Each of these means is significantly *less* than chance, or 1.43. Max rel own, of course, is analogous to MD, and MD is supposedly one of the main distribution strategies evoked by mere-categorization.

After the subjects in the second experiment completed the MAMs, they were each given a colored pencil and asked to go back through the matrices and indicate a second preference on each matrix. Finally, they were given still a different colored pencil and asked to indicate a third preference. For the second preference there are, of course, only six

TABLE 8.2
Mean Frequency of First Preference

		Orientation					
	Max Own	*Max Rel Own*	*Min Diff*	*Max Other*	*Max Rel Other*	*Max Joint Own*	*Max Joint Other*
Males	1.83	0.86	2.83	0.34	0.20	3.14	0.80
Females	1.63	0.58	5.12	0.22	0.20	1.83	0.49

SOURCE: From Bornstein, Crum, Wittenbraker, Harring, Insko, and Thibaut, "On the measurement of social orientations in the minimal group paradigm," *European Journal of Social Psychology,* Vol. 13, p. 336. Copyright 1983 by John Wiley & Sons, Ltd. Reprinted by permission of John Wiley & Sons, Ltd.
NOTE: Since each subject chose among the seven orientations ten times, the scores have a possible range from 0 to 10.

alternatives and chance is thus $(1/6)(10)$ or 1.67. For the second-preference data, the only alternative, or orientation, to differ from chance is max joint own. Mean second preference frequency is 2.69 for males and 4.17 for females. The sex difference is significant. For the second preference, females responded more like males on the first preference, presumably because min diff was relatively unavailable for females as a possible second preference.

With the third preference, only five alternatives are available and chance is $(1/5)(10)$ or 2.00. For the third preference data, none of the orientations differs significantly from chance. The important implication of this result is that, even by the third choice and a reduced number of possibilities, subjects did not show a significant preference for max rel own (or for max own).

But if by the third preference subjects did not select max rel own, what were they selecting? Close examination of individual response patterns indicated that for the second preference, 11 of the 76 subjects selected five own-category-favoring orientations and five other-category-preferring orientations. Since such alternation is an alternative way of achieving min diff, it seems quite likely that some subjects adopted alternation among own-and other-favoring orientations as a conscious strategy. Beyond these 11 subjects there were many others who followed what appeared to be different alternation strategies. There were, for example, five subjects who selected own-favoring orientations six times and other-favoring orientations four times, four subjects who selected own-favoring orientations five times, other favoring orientations four times, and min diff once. Perhaps these and other similar alternation patterns were pursued by subjects who insisted upon achieving a max-joint-own result. To the extent that alternation was a strategy to achieve min diff, max joint own, or max joint other, the presence of these orientations as specific alternatives for the first preference should have reduced the number of alternations for the first-preference choices. At a purely descriptive level, that appears to have been the case. For example, for the first-preference selections there were only two subjects who selected five own-favoring orientations and five other-favoring orientations.

Whether or not the alternation patterns represented conscious strategies, it is abundantly clear that subjects were generally avoiding the max-rel-own response. Informal interviews with the subjects revealed that many of them believed that blatant discrimination between categories was unjustified or even silly.

It is, of course, possible that the difference between Bornstein et al.'s results and the results of Tajfel and his associates is not due to the differing measuring instruments, but to some other variable or variables, such as differing subject populations, experimenters, or procedures. In order to obtain evidence relevant to this possibility, Bornstein et al.'s second experiment included a condition in which subjects responded on the Tajfel matrices rather than on the MAMs. Analysis of the data revealed, as in many of Tajfel's experiments, significant effect for all pulls, including MD on MJP + MIP. Obviously the differing measuring instruments yield different results.

Bornstein et al.'s (1983a) third experiment was done with 9th- and 10th-grade junior-high school students from a middle-class suburb. No cover story was used. In terms of deviation from chance, the data indicated significant effects for min diff and max own. There is also a significant tendency for females to make a greater number of min diff responses than males. These MAM results with younger children are somewhat discrepant from expectations. Max rel own did not occur, but, unlike with college students, max own did occur.

Wittenbraker (1983) Experiment

Wittenbraker (1983) collected mere-categorization data from male and female 5th-, 9th-, and 12th-grade students from the same school system from which subjects were selected in Bornstein et al.'s (1983a) third experiment. In order to have somewhat greater assurance that the MAMs were understandable (particularly for younger subjects), Wittenbraker presented the matrices as an array of bar graphs, with bars of one color for Kandinsky outcomes and bars of another color for Klee outcomes. The numerical outcomes were recorded at the top of each bar.

Wittenbraker did not analyze his data by reporting overall deviation from chance tests for all subjects. Rather, these deviation from chance tests were done only within each of the six cells of the design. These tests revealed a significant effect for min diff within each of the six cells, a significant effect for max joint own for 5th- and 12th-grade males, and a significant effect for max own for 9th-grade males. The 5th- and 12th-grade students responded more like college students, and the 9th-grade students responded more like 9th-grade students in Bornstein et al.'s (1983a) third experiment. If 9th-grade students do differ from both younger and older students, the difference cannot plausibly be related to differential ability to understand the MAMs.

Bornstein et al. (1983b) Experiments

Turner (1983a, 1983b) has raised a major objection to Bornstein et al.'s (1983a) MAMs, and also two somewhat less important objections to some of Bornstein et al.'s procedural details. Initially we will focus on the two procedural objections. The first of these is that the Bornstein et al. cover story possibly distorted the results. The second is that Bornstein et al. erred when the MAMs were structured so that each subject allocated money to just one own-category member and one other-category member.

To investigate these matters, two different experiments were conducted. The first experiment compared the old cover story with a new cover story and also with a third condition where there was no cover story of any kind. The second experiment contrasted a procedure in which each subject allocated money to a single own-category member and a single other-category member with a procedure in which different matrices related to different own- and other-category members. In the first experiment, the three-level cover-story manipulation is not significant, and in the second experiment the two-level constancy-of-recipient manipulation is not significant. The only suggestion of an effect for the cover-story manipulation is a tendency for max joint own to decrease in the no-cover-story condition. In terms of deviation from chance, both experiments found the usual strong effects for min diff and somewhat weaker effects for max joint own.

A Fifth Replication and
Overall Summary of Initial Results

With the replication of Bornstein et al.'s (1983b) deviation from chance effects in a further (unpublished) experiment, there is considerable reason to believe in their reliability. Across a total of five studies with college students, there is a consistent tendency for only min diff and max joint own to occur. Also, there is evidence (sometimes nonsignificant, but always present) for min diff to occur more frequently for females and max joint own to occur more frequently for males. There is also evidence that a similar pattern occurs for 5th- and 12th-grade students. The one exception to the general pattern appears to be 9th-grade students, for whom max own is substituted for max joint own. All subjects have revealed effects for min diff, and none have revealed effects for max rel own. Thus, despite some discrepancy for 9th-grade students, the MAMs data from the initial research in the mere-categorization are reasonably consistent.

THE MAXIMIZATION ASSUMPTION

Turner's (1983a, 1983b) Questioning
of the Maximization Assumption

Bornstein et al. (1983a, 1983b) argued that multiple alternative matrices, unlike the matrices used by Tajfel and his associates, allow for the unconfounded measurement of social orientations. This unconfounding, however, is based on the assumption that subjects respond to the MAMs by selecting the pair of numbers that maximizes a specific orientation. For instance, the subject who is concerned with equality of outcomes should pick the pair of outcomes that are most nearly equal; the subject who is concerned with joint outcomes should pick the outcomes with the largest sum; the subject who is concerned with own outcomes should pick the outcomes with the largest own outcomes; the subject who is concerned with winning should pick the pair of outcomes with the largest own advantage.

As mentioned above, Turner (1983a, 19893b) has raised a major objection to the MAMs. This objection specifically relates to the maximization assumption. In Turner's own words, "Most preferred outcomes are not restricted to the maximal values of strategies" (1983b, p. 383). Turner's argument is most plausible as specifically applied to a strategy or orientation of winning. Suppose that a subject wishes to win, but does not wish to win to the extent that is possible through the selection of the max-rel-own possibility on the matrix. Such a subject accordingly might select max own, not because of a desire to max own, but because of a desire to win to a lesser extent than is possible through the selection of max rel own. Alternatively, the subject might select max joint own, not because of a desire to maximize the sum of own and other outcomes with an own advantage, but because of a desire to achieve a relative difference favoring own category/group to a lesser extent than is possible.

Aside from its bearing upon the possibility of achieving unconfounded measurement of orientations, the maximization issue has a direct bearing upon the theoretical issue concerning whether or not categories are collectives (psychologically real groups). Recall that research with adult subjects has revealed an abundance of evidence for max joint own, but no evidence for max rel own or max own. The absence of max rel own, in particular, is important because max rel own involves an explicit social comparison between categories/groups that provides the most compelling evidence for entitativity. Max own, likewise, could be interpreted as providing evidence for entitativity because the subject explicitly advantages one category/group (excluding self), thus suggesting self-indentification with that category/group. But, with adult subjects at least, evidence for neither of these orientations has been found.

What has been found, of course, is evidence for max joint own. Could max joint own be interpreted as providing evidence for entitativity? Max joint own certainly does involve an advantage for own category. If max joint own is taken at face value however, the own advantage occurs in the context of concern for the outcomes of both Klees and Kandinskys. Thus the evidence for entitativity is at best ambiguous, and the issue can only be settled through further research. On the other hand, Turner does not take max joint own at face value. His perspective is that many, or most, subjects select max joint own not because they want to maximize the sum of own and other outcomes with an own advantage, but rather because they want to win to a lesser extent than is possible through max rel own. Thus if the maximization assumption is rejected, max joint own and max rel own are not fundamentally different, and max joint own does indeed provide evidence for entitativity.

Insko et al. (1986) Questionnaire Study

Insko, Pinkley, Harring, Holton, Hong, Krams, Hoyle, and Thibaut (1986) conducted a questionnaire study that attempted to ascertain the subjects' own interpretations of the reason for their selection of max joint own and max own.

Male subjects were tested in the standard Klee-Kandinsky categorization procedure with some variation in the administration of the MAMs. Rather than giving the subjects all 10 of the matrices at once, they were delivered one at a time until any given subject selected either max joint own or max own. If and when max joint own or max own was selected, the subject was given a postexperimental questionnaire containing open- and close-ended assessments of the reason for the immediately previous choice. If the subject failed to select max joint own or max own, the postexperimental questionnaire was not given. Since females display a preference for min diff, male subjects were used to maximize the opportunity of obtaining usable data.

The open-ended question simply asked subjects to state the reason for their immediately prior selection, and the close-ended question forced subjects to choose between the Bornstein et al. rationale and the Turner rationale. For max own these rationales or alternatives were "To gain the most amount of money possible," and "To win by less than the biggest margin." For max joint own the rationales or alternatives were "To gain the highest combined amount of money for everyone, with my group receiving slightly more," and "To win by less than the biggest margin."

The results for both the open- and close-ended assessments of both max joint own and max own are very consistent—the vast majority of the subjects opted for the Bornstein et al. rationale. For example, of the 21 subjects who had previously chosen max joint own, the judges coded 18 as consistent with the Bornstein et al. rationale and 3 as consistent with the Turner rationale ($p = .0006$ by binomial test). Here is an example of a Bornstein et al. response: "I tend to favor the person that had the same opinion (choice of paintings) as I did; therefore, I awarded that person more points. However, I wanted to keep the distribution as even as possible between the two groups while also giving a maximum number of points to *each* group." On the other hand, Turner responses did occur, for example: "I picked the two numbers that were closest; I choose to win by less than the biggest possible amount." Thus it is clearly not the case that Turner-type rationales were never given, but it does appear that their frequency was relatively small. While such results certainly do not constitute definitive proof for the maximization assumptions, the fact that the subjects themselves believed the assumption to be correct clearly adds to its credibility.

Cross-Matrix Inconsistency of Responses

At the level of the single response to a single matrix, the maximization assumption has at least a degree of plausibility. There is a problem, however, in that not all subjects respond consistently to all matrices. Thus it could be argued that across all 10 matrices maximization does not occur. It should be recognized, however, that subjects may be attempting to maximize an orientation that is different from any one of the seven possibilities represented by a specific pair of numbers. Thus a subject may prefer a composite of min diff and max joint and accordingly alternate between max joint own and max joint other, or perhaps less astutely between max own and max other. Likewise, a subject may prefer a composite of max own and max rel own and alternate between these two orientations. Furthermore, it is quite likely that in a fairly ambiguous situation like the mere-categorization situation, some subjects may change their minds as repeated responses are made. Thus what was maximized early may be different from what was maximized late. Note further that the subject may make an error, and that the three possibilities of preferring an unrepresented orientation, change of mind, and error may occur in various combinations.

The seven orientations directly assessed by the MAMs obviously do not represent all of the possibilities for all situations. However, the measured orientations were at least partly based on empirical investigation, particularly the work of McClintock (1972) on social "motives." For example, in one study with Belgian and American college students, McClintock reports that various reasons were given for the choice of a particular cell in an MDG matrix, but that the most frequent reasons included maximizing own gain, maximizing joint gain, maximizing relative gain for self, and permitting others to maximize relative gain.

If one were interested in measuring orientations other than the seven represented in the MAMs, one could develop alternative matrices or could develop a scoring key to code for alternation patterns. It should be recognized, however, that an investigator's theoretical interest may make it important to measure orientations that are otherwise only preferred in a composite form. Thus, given an interest in entitativity, it is reasonable to assess max rel own and max own separately—even though the composite might be preferred. The reason is that it is max rel own that gives direct behavioral evidence for self-esteem-related social comparison and therefore gives the best evidence for entitativity. Likewise, given an interest in fairness it makes sense to measure min diff separately from other orientations, even though the subject might prefer a composite of min diff and max joint.

BEYOND CATEGORIZATION TO COMPETITION

Previous research with the MAMs has demonstrated that for most subjects mere-categorization does not produce either max rel own or max own, but does produce max joint own (a tendency to maximize outcomes for both categories with an advantage for own category). Such results suggest that mere-categorization primes subjects to be competitive without producing the more obvious forms of competitiveness associated with max rel own and max own. If entitativity can vary in degree, mere-categorization induces only minimal levels. What then is required, beyond categorization, to produce high levels of entitativity and more competitiveness? Insko et al. (1986) proposed that all that is required is the belief that competition between the categories is appropriate. They tested this fairly simple idea with two experiments.

Insko et al. (1986) Experiment 1

In Experiment 1, information regarding the appropriateness of competition was conveyed through social consensus from fellow-category members. Following the usual mere-categorization procedure, six subjects were individually told that three of them were Kandinsky-preferring and three were Klee-preferring. Before filling out the MAMs, however, they were given an initial "test of social interaction" that involved individually deciding how 100 pennies should be divided between the Klees and the Kandinskys. Manipulated feedback regarding the choices of fellow category members provided information as to the appropriateness of competition in the situation. In-category feedback was either cooperative (both fellow category members opting for a 50-50 division) or competitive (both fellow category members opting for more pennies for own category). To clarify those instances in which the feedback was inconsistent with each subject's own choice, all subjects were told that in the case of a "discrepancy" the majority would rule. In addition, for purposes of analysis each subject's own cooperative or competitive choice was treated as a factor.

To complement the manipulation of in-category action there was also a manipulation of out-category action. Thus there were a total of three factors (in-category action, individual differences, out-category action), each of which had two levels (cooperative and competitive). After receiving the in-category and out-category feedback, all subjects responded to the MAMs.

If a belief in the appropriateness of competition is sufficient to produce competitiveness in a between-category situation, then the manipulation of in-category action should have had an effect. But should this not also have been the case for the manipulation of out-category action? Yes, most certainly. However, any effect of out-category action on competitiveness could be the result of a reciprocation tendency, as well as a belief in the appropriateness of competitiveness. Thus, even though there were effects of out-category action on both max rel own and max own, for purposes of demonstrating a social consensus effect, the important results are those for in-category action. Both max rel own and max own were greater with competitive than cooperative in-category action.

A possible objection to the interpretation of the effect of in-category action on a belief in the appropriateness of competition is that the effect of the in-category action may be a conformity effect. Such an alternative interpretation is indeed possible. Recognize, however, that conformity itself is partially a result of a concern with being correct, right, or appropriate (Insko, Drenan, Solomon, Smith, & Wade, 1983; Insko, Smith, Alicke, Wade, & Taylor, 1985). This is particularly true when, as in the mere-categorization situation, subjects are physically isolated from each other and identified only by a code number—thereby minimizing self-presentational concerns.

A further result is that the subjects who initially choose to divide the 100 pennies with an own-category advantage selected both max own and max rel own to a greater extent than did the subjects who initially choose to divide the 100 pennies evenly between the categories. Two interpretations of this result are possible. The first is a generalized-individual-difference interpretation and the second is an entrapment-self-attribution interpretation.

The generalized-individual-difference interpretation is that for some, but not all, individuals mere-categorization does indeed produce tendencies toward both max rel own and max own, as Tajfel, Turner, and associates have been advocating. This phenomena, however, applies to only some individuals. Thus previous research with adult subjects had not revealed evidence for max rel own and max own as a function of mere-categorization because, when the data for those individuals responding with max rel own or max own were averaged together with the data for all individuals, the overall mean was lowered to a level at or below chance.

The entrapment-self-attribution interpretation is that some individuals were entrapped by the lack of max joint own into making a competitive division of the 100 pennies, and consequently made a competitive self-attribution that was reflected in the choice of max rel own and max own on the MAMs. Recognize that for the subject who does not wish to give the other category more pennies than own category, the choice is between min diff (a 50-50 division of the pennies) and a confound of max own and max rel own (more pennies to own than to other category). A max joint own response is not possible. Hence, it could be that those subjects who otherwise would have chosen max joint own were entrapped, as it were, into choosing the confound of max own and max rel own. However, as a result of this competitive choice they made a self-attribution that a competitive orientation was preferred. Hence max own and max rel own were selected (rather than max joint own) on the MAMs. Paraphrasing Bem (1967), it is as if the subjects said to themselves, "I responded competitively, therefore I believe in the appropriateness of competition."

Evidence that the manipulation of subjects' supposed, but not actual, prior belief responses can have an effect on subsequently reported belief responses has been obtained by Ross, Insko, and Ross (1971), and Schopler and Compere (1971). Still further evidence in support of the entrapment-self-attribution interpretation is that significantly more males than females opted for a competitive division of the 100 pennies and that in the usual mere-categorization situation it is primarily the males who select max joint own. Nonetheless it is clear that currently there is no convincing way of demonstrating that one interpretation is totally correct and the other totally incorrect. The generalized-individual-difference interpretation does receive circumstantial support from the apparent tendency of 9th-grade students to select max own in a situation in which there is no prior division of 100 pennies. Thus it is possible that there is a subset of individuals for whom awareness of membership in a category is sufficient to generate entitativity. It should be noted, however, that the finding that some subjects respond competitively as a function of mere-categorization involves a confound of mere-categorization and the responsibility for dividing outcomes between own and other category. Possibly this subset of individuals responds to the combination of categorization and outcome allocation. We are skeptical that there are any individuals for whom categorization, and categorization alone, is sufficient to generate entitativity, but this is an issue that can only be studied through the use of some alternative measure of entitativity.

To the extent that entrapment-self-attribution interpretation is correct, the results fit nicely with the general perspective that mere-categorization will lead to max rel own and max own if there is reason to believe in the appropriateness of competition. In the case of the individual-difference variable, the evidence comes from own behavior. In the case of the in-category-action variable, the evidence comes from the behavior of fellow-category members.

Insko et al. (1986) Experiment 2

The results of Experiment 1 are generally consistent with common sense expectations. Experiment 2 was designed to provide a more indirect and less obvious test of the idea that competition between categories of individuals will occur if there is reason to believe in the appropriateness of such competition. The experimental procedure involved two phases. The second phase simply involved the usual Klee-Kandinsky categorization procedure with the MAMs as the assessment instrument. The first phase involved play of the Prisoner's Dilemma Game (PDG) matrix either one-on-one or group-on-group. Previous research by McCallum, Harring, Gilmore, Drenan, Chase, Insko, and Thibaut (1985) has demonstrated that group-on-group play of the PDG is far more competitive than is one-on-one play. Hence the idea was to expose subjects to a situation in which competitiveness did or did not occur prior to their participation in the mere-categorization situation. If the group-on-group play of the PDG created a belief in the appropriateness of competitiveness, that belief should carry over to the mere-categorization situation where competitiveness less obviously occurs. Because subjects were informed that who was a Klee and who was a Kandinsky was unrelated to group assignment in the previous PDG situation, there was no reason for the subjects who had been in groups in the PDG situation to believe that their fellow category members were former allies.

The results for the first phase replicated the McCallum et al. (1985)

finding of more competitiveness between groups than between individuals. The results, in fact, were descriptively larger than those in the McCallum et al. experiment—possibly because three-person rather than two-person groups were used. The magnitude of the effect was sufficiently large to produce nonoverlapping distributions, that is, the most competitive pair of individuals were still more cooperative than the least competitive pair of groups.

The results for the mere-categorization phase indicated a significantly greater amount of max own for those subjects who had been in the group rather than the individual condition of the prior PDG situation. There was no comparable effect for max rel own. Apparently the two situations were not sufficiently linked so as to allow for a carryover of the more blatant form of competitiveness represented by max rel own. Nonetheless, the fact that there was carry over of max own is consistent with the general notion that competitiveness between categories will occur if subjects have any reason to believe in its appropriateness.

The evidence generally indicates that for most people categorization is not sufficient to generate max rel own or max own. The fact, however, that categorization (in the context of some responsibility for a division of outcomes) does generate max joint own suggests that such categorization draws attention to the possibility of more blatant competitiveness and that very little additional suggestion is required to produce such a response.

Toward a Reconceptualization of Entitativity

Does categorization (even in the context of outcome allocations) create entitativity? The answer to this question is not entirely clear. The evidence suggests that categorization alone does not generally produce max rel own. If entitativity implies an own-advantaging social comparison between own-group and other-group, the nonoccurrence of max rel own certainly creates uncertainty regarding entitativity in this relativistic sense. On the other hand, mere-categorization does produce max joint own, particularly with males. If entitativity implies identification with the tangible outcomes of own group, then perhaps the max-joint-own result does imply entitativity in this alternative sense. There is a problem, however, in that it is not clear whether the max joint own response implies identification with own category, identification with all the subjects who are present in the session (i.e., both Klees and Kandinskys), or, more plausibly, an attempt to compromise between both identifications. Thus the evidence linking mere-categorization with entitativity is unclear. Furthermore, the problem is compounded by uncertainty regarding the precise meaning of "entitativity."

An alternative way to conceptualize the problem is from the perspective of a group schema and the possibility that there are different types of group schemas. A group schema is a set of beliefs regarding expected behavior within own group and expected relations between own-group and some other group or groups. Since people have had extensive group experience, it is quite plausible that such schemas exist.[2] It also appears likely that there may be variation among such sets of group-related beliefs in the extent to which they involve between-group competitiveness. At the most competitive extreme, there may be beliefs relating to the importance of "being better," "winning at all cost," and, in general, providing social comparison evidence for pridefulness and high self-evaluation. At a less-competitive level, there may be beliefs relating to the importance of identification with a group achieving high, tangible outcomes. And, at an even lesser level of competitiveness, there may be beliefs regarding the importance of balancing high own-group outcomes against a concern that all groups achieve as much as possible. These three types of schemas, of course, correspond to max rel own, max own, and max joint own.

Since the concepts of group schema and entitativity are closely linked, the variation among different types of group schemas could be taken as implying a variation among different types of entitativity. From this perspective the allocation of outcomes among categories of subjects does create entitativity in a less competitive sense. It, furthermore, follows that the two above experiments, which demonstrated the importance of additional information regarding the appropriateness of competition, in fact revealed the minimal conditions for the production of entitativity in a more competitive sense. Since a belief in the appropriateness of competition is a central aspect of the more competitive group schema, it is quite reasonable that the creation of this belief should instantiate such a schema. What is needed to support this reconceptualization of entitativity is independent empirical evidence that group schemas do vary in the hypothesized manner.

INDIVIDUAL-GROUP DISCONTINUITY

An Old Problem with Contemporary Relevance

In the Insko et al. Experiment 2, the greater amount of competitiveness between groups than between individuals was used as a mechanism for suggesting a belief in the appropriateness of competition. Beyond this, however, there is a close conceptual linkage between the two phases of the experimental procedure. The first phase relates to the discontinuity between interindividual and intergroup behavior and generally suggests a question regarding the reason why individuals differ from groups. The second phase relates to the mere-categorization situation and generally suggests a question regarding when it is that an aggregate of individuals constitutes a psychologically real group. These two interrelated questions are closely related to an old problem in social psychology—the problem of the group mind.

There is a long historical tradition of concern with the apparent difference between individual and group behavior that can be traced back to Plato's *Republic*. In more modern times the discussion has related to crowd behavior and the group mind (e.g., Allport, 1924; Brown, 1954; Durkheim, 1898; LeBon, 1895; McDougall, 1920). LeBon argued that individuals who join groups regress to primitive mental states, become vulnerable to losing moral standards and inhibitions, and become prone to competitive, barbaric acts, including violence—all presumably because of the emergence of a group mind. Among American social scientists, Floyd Allport (1924) is well known for having rejected the concept of the group mind. It is, however, less well known that he cited the general problem of the relation of the individual and the group as the master problem of social psychology.

Roger Brown (1954) points out that the evidence for the group mind comes from the "discontinuity" (p. 843) between groups and individuals. Apparently, however, aversion to the metaphysical context of the problem led many social psychologists to avoid study of the behavioral discontinuity itself. Thus social psychology's master problem dropped out of mainstream social psychology. This is indeed unfortunate. Not only are the theoretical issues important, but also there is an obvious relation to social problems associated with various "group-isms" such as ethnocentrism, racism, sectionalism, patriotism, and so on. An appreciation of individual-group discontinuity provides an important correction against any attempt to view prejudice, or out-group projection, as a purely interindividual phenomenon.

Literature Overview

Despite the general neglect of the group-mind problem, there is a somewhat scattered literature relating to the comparison of interindividual and intergroup relations. This literature contains numerous suggestions of differences between interindividual and intergroup competitiveness, but the evidence is rarely as direct or as unambiguous as one would hope. For purposes of a brief overview, this literature can be divided into four categories.

The first category (e.g., Doise, 1969; Wilson & Kayatani, 1968) includes studies in which there is between-dyad play of a mixed-motive game followed by within-dyad play for division of winnings. These studies have all found between-dyad play to be more competitive than within-dyad play. To be sure, this is a comparison of groups and individuals, but the comparison is obviously confounded by the fact that the individuals are allies. As a result, these studies do not involve a direct test of the hypothesis that groups tend to be more competitive than individuals.

A second category includes studies which have examined the effects of varying degrees of negotiator "accountability" to the home group on the competitiveness of bargaining. To the extent that low accountability is similar to one-on-one bargaining and high accountability is similar to group-on-group bargaining, this literature is seemingly relevant to our present concern. Unfortunately, however, these studies appear to indicate that the effects of accountability are, at worst, inconsistent and, at best, complex. Thus, Gruder (1971) found an effect only for first concessions; Klimoski and Ash (1974) for randomly selected representatives, but not for elected representatives; and Carnevale, Pruitt, and Seilheimer (1981) for face-to-face negotiation, but not for non-face-to-face negotiation. Also, Druckman (1967) reported an effect for whether bargainers represented themselves or groups, and subsequently (Druckman, 1971) engaged in a controversy with Vidmar (1971) over this matter. Because of these inconsistent results, it is not clear that high accountability representatives will under all conditions be more competitive than low accountability representatives. Research generated by Adams's (1976) theory of boundary roles (see Holmes & Lamm, 1979, for a summary) appears to indicate that negotiator behavior can be influenced to be *either* more competitive or more cooperative by constituent expectations reinforced by trust, surveillance, and sanctions.

A third category includes studies in which either individuals or groups played against a programmed opponent (e.g., Rabbie, Visser, & van Oostrum, 1982; Pylyshyn, Agnew, & Illingworth, 1972). Rabbie et al. compared the play of individuals, dyads, and triads against a programmed opponent that responded in a cooperative, competitive,

competitive, cooperative sequence. Analysis of only the fourth trial data indicated that dyads were more competitive than individuals, but that, paradoxically, there was no difference at all between individuals and triads. Further trials with a tit-for-tat sequence revealed no difference, even with dyads. A tit-for-tat sequence does, however, encourage cooperation (Axelrod, 1984). A similar consideration applies to the Pylyshyn et al. experiment, which compared the play of individuals against a computer with groups against a computer and found that groups were *less* competitive than individuals. Because the computer had been programmed to respond so as to encourage cooperation, the experiment may demonstrate little more than that in a problem-solving situation "two heads are better than one."

A fourth category includes direct comparisons of interindividual and intergroup interaction (e.g., Komorita & Lapworth, 1982; Lindskold, McElwain, & Wagner, 1977). Komorita and Lapworth investigated the difference between interindividual and intergroup interaction in a situation in which there was no face-to-face contact, and Lindskold et al. investigated the difference between individuals and groups in a situation in which an individual played a group. In both studies more competition was found for groups than for individuals.

Of all this research, perhaps the studies in the fourth category are most encouraging. In general, however, it is interesting that until McCallum et al., (1985) no one had apparently investigated the simple difference between interindividual and intergroup relations in a face-to-face situation without programmed responses. Recall that the McCallum et al.'s research was the research used as a model for the first phase of what was referred to above as Insko et al. (1986) Experiment 2.

McCallum et al. conducted two experiments. The first experiment included two independent variables: individuals competing with individuals versus dyads competing with dyads, and sex of participants (all male or all female). Subjects were initially shown an example of a PDG matrix, played 3 practice trials, and then 10 "real" trials. Points in the matrices represented pennies, and the matrices varied somewhat from trial to trial. Competing individuals or teams were located in separate rooms. After examining the matrix for a given trial, individuals or team representatives went to a table in a central room to discuss possible action, and then returned to their home room, where a choice was actually made. It is important to recognize that the decision was not made by the representative, as in the accountability research, but by the group as a whole. The final decision or choice was written on a piece of paper and subsequently carried back to the central room. Upon the arrival of both subjects, the experimenter announced the choices and passed out whatever money was earned. This general procedure was continued for 10 trials. The results indicated significant and sizable main effects across a variety of assessments. Compared to individuals, groups made more competitive choices and fewer cooperative choices. Groups also earned less money. All of these effects were quite large. For example, out of 20 possible cooperative choices, groups made 7.57 and individuals made 13.67.

McCallum et al.'s second experiment was like the first except for the addition of a third variable relating to type of matrix. In one level of the type-of-matrix variable the matrix was a PDG, just as in the first experiment. In the other level, however, the matrix was what Kelley and Thibaut (1978) refer to as an MFC, or mutual-fate-control matrix. As is well known, the competitive response in a PDG may reflect either an attempt to increase own outcomes (max own) or an attempt to increase the differences between own and other outcomes (max rel own). With an MFC matrix, however, the competitive choice reduces other outcomes but does not increase own outcomes, and hence more obviously reflects max rel own than max own. In general, an MFC matrix provides less reason for being competitive.

The results of the second experiment indicate that dyads were more competitive and less cooperative than individuals, that both dyads and individuals were less competitive and more cooperative with the MFC than the PDG matrix, and, of most interest, that the magnitude of the difference between dyads and individuals was just as great for the MFC matrix as for the PDG matrix. The latter finding provides circumstantial support for the assertion that the difference between dyads and individuals relates to max rel own, for instance, to winning, being better, and, by implication, to self-esteem. On the other hand, the results of the experiment do not enable us to rule out the possibility that a max own orientation is also part of the difference. It is true that a single isolated competitive choice on the MFC matrix does not increase own outcomes. It is still possible, however, that over a series of trials a competitive choice might be motivated by a desire to encourage the opponent to act in a way that would increase own outcomes. Of course, this is also true for the PDG matrix. Thus the difference between the matrices is in the relative fostering of max own rather than in the presence or absence of max own.

As indicated in a previous section, the first phase of the Insko et al.

(1986) Experiment 2 included a replication of the first McCallum et al. experiment, except that three-person, rather than two-person, groups were used. Again, large effects were obtained—in fact, the effects were descriptively larger than those that McCallum et al. obtained with two-person groups. An additional study (Insko, Pinkley, Hoyle, Dalton, Hong, Slim, Landry, Holt, Ruffin, & Thibaut, in press) replicated the results with three-person groups. Thus there are all together four studies that have found large tendencies for intergroup relations to be more competitive than interindividual relations. In view of the inconsistency in the previous literature, such large effects are somewhat surprising.

Given the apparent difference between the four above studies and the rest of the literature, it might be thought that the finding of rather extreme intergroup competitiveness is due to the somewhat limited nature of the intergroup contact. Recall that the intergroup contact occurred through representatives. To investigate this matter, the Insko et al. (in press) study included a condition in which not just the representatives but all three members of each group entered the center room for discussion of each upcoming trial. The results indicated that this condition, termed group-all, did produce less competitiveness than the usual group-representative condition. However, there was still a descriptively large difference between the group-all condition and the usual individuals' condition. This difference is, in fact, descriptively larger than the one obtained by McCallum et al. with two-person groups.

A final matter relates to the possibility that the differences between intergroup and interindividual behavior are an artifact of the fact that, for the groups, less money is available for each individual than in the individuals' condition. To investigate this matter, two of the above studies manipulated the values in the PDG matrices so as to equate the two conditions on a money-available-for-each-individual basis. The results were comparable. There is no doubt that groups are more competitive than individuals, at least in some circumstances.

THREE HYPOTHESES

Altruistic Rationalization

In recent years, European social psychologists have written extensively on the differences between intergroup and interindividual behavior (e.g., Brown & Turner, 1981; Doise, 1978; Tajfel, 1978a; Tajfel &

Turner, 1979, 1986), and Tajfel (1978b, 1981, 1982), Turner (1981), and Tajfel and Turner (1979, 1986) have related the presumed competitive nature of intergroup behavior to attempts to maintain social identity. The basic idea behind social identity theory is that to the extent that the individual identifies with his or her group, a relative difference favoring own group bolsters, or is consistent with, positive self-evaluation. Thus the engine driving intergroup discrimination and competitiveness is self-esteem maintenance or bolstering.

The idea of a link between self-esteem and intergroup competitiveness is intuitively compelling and does fit with McCallum et al.'s (1985) finding that the difference between intergroup and interindividual competitiveness is just as large with an MFC as a PDG matrix. However, because individuals also obtain a self-esteem benefit from winning a competition, Tajfel's theorizing does not really explain why groups should be more competitive than individuals. McCallum et al. (1985) and Insko et al. (1986) proposed that the reason relates to the possibility of altruistic rationalization that exists in an intergroup situation, but not in an interindividual situation. In an intergroup situation, group members are able to act in a manner that is *both* helpful to fellow group members and selfish. Group members are thus able to rationalize their competitiveness as altruistic or on the behalf of fellow group members. The altruistic rationalization hypothesis bears some similarity to Snyder's concept of attribute ambiguity (Snyder, Kleck, Strenta, & Mentzer, 1979; Snyder, Smaller, Strenta, & Frankel, 1981; Snyder & Wicklund, 1981). Snyder has presented evidence that self-interested behavior is more likely to occur in those situations in which it is less clear that the behavior is self-interested, that is, in situations in which there is attributional ambiguity.

Unfortunately, the available evidence is not consistent with the altruistic-rationalization hypothesis. This evidence comes from the Insko et al. (in press) experiment that was described above as including a group-all condition with the group-representative and individuals' conditions. The group-all condition is a condition in which the intergroup contact on each trial involved all of the members in each group. In addition, the experiment includes a fourth condition, a so-called interdependence condition, that was designed to provide a test of the altruistic-rationalization hypothesis. This condition is like the individuals' condition in that individual subjects interacted, or bargained, with other individual subjects located in separate rooms. There were three subjects in separate rooms on one side of a suite who interacted with three different subjects located across a large center room in three additional "home" rooms. The three sets of one-on-one interaction occurred at separate tables in the center room. The interdependence condition differs from the individuals conditions in that the three subjects on each side of the suite shared their earnings. During the practice trials experimenters entered each subject's home room, took two-thirds of the earnings, and delivered one-third to each of the other subjects on the same side of the suite. Since such a procedure required that three different experimenters enter each subject's room during each trial, it was explained that during the actual trials the division of the money among the three subjects on each side of the suite would be delayed until all trials were completed. To the extent that the subjects took advantage of shared earnings to rationalize their competitiveness toward others, the interdependence condition should have produced more competitiveness than the individuals' conditions. In fact, the means for the two conditions are virtually identical. A further finding comes from postexperimental ratings of the extent to which the PDG choices reflected personal interests. According to the altruistic-rationalization hypothesis, group members rationalize their competitiveness as being altruistic. In fact, however, the subjects in the group-representative and group-all conditions reported that their personal choices were more self-interested than did the the subjects in the individuals' and interdependence conditions. Of course, such reports are consistent with actual behavior. From the perspective of the altruistic-rationalization hypothesis, such willingness to admit self-interest should not have been forthcoming.

Social Support for Shared Self-Interest

Consider again the four conditions of the Insko et al. (in press) experiment. The individuals' and interdependence conditions produced approximately equivalent amounts of minimal competitiveness, while the group-representative and group-all conditions produced much more marked competitiveness. What is it that differentiates the two conditions that are associated with competitiveness from the two conditions that are not associated with competitiveness? One obvious difference is the within-group contact that occurs in the group-representative and group-all conditions, but not in the interdependence condition or, of course, in the individuals' condition. Recall, however, the Insko et al. (1986) Experiment 1 finding that physically separated Kandinskys (Klees) would respond competitively on the MAMs if they were given feedback indicating that their fellow-category members had divided the 100 pennies in a competitive manner. Although within-group contact may contribute to between-group competitiveness, such competitiveness clearly can occur without within-group contact.

Another difference between the individuals' and interdependence conditions and the two groups' conditions is the exchange of within-group information that only occurs in the groups' conditions. From this perspective, what is important is not contact *per se,* but the exchange of information that is facilitated by contact. Furthermore, perhaps the crucial aspect of this exchange is social support for shared desires to obtain information indicative of superiority. Assuming that Tajfel is correct regarding the relationship between intergroup competitiveness and self-esteem, perhaps the group members in the group-representative and group-all conditions conformed to each other's implicit, but mutually shared, desires to behave in a self-interested manner. From the perspective of this hypothesis, all subjects wished to win or to demonstrate their superiority, but could only do so when reassured by their fellow group members that such self-aggrandizing behavior was socially acceptable. Subjects in the individuals' and interdependence conditions, of course, had no such social support.

The social-support-for-shared-self-interest hypothesis differs from the altruistic-rationalization hypothesis in that defensive denial is not involved, and also in that active social support, and not just the excuse for selfishness (as in the interdependence condition), is required. One appealing aspect of the social support hypothesis is that it dovetails very nicely with the Insko et al. (1986) Experiment 1 finding that such a simple matter as feedback regarding own-category members' competitiveness produced max own and max rel own in physically isolated individuals. People may be very quick to accept implicit suggestions to behave in a self-interested manner.

Group Schema

A third possibility is that some aspect of group experience may instantiate a group schema, or a set of learned beliefs regarding expected between-group competitiveness and within-group cooperativeness. The proposed group schema implies that own-group members are expected to be cooperative, friendly, loyal, helpful, courteous, and so on, while other-group members are expected to demonstrate such characteristics as competitiveness, unfriendliness, aggressiveness, and boastfulness. An interesting illustration of group schema-like expectations occurs in Plato's *Republic*, where Polemarchus defends a traditional maxim of Greek morality that "justice consists of helping one's friends and harming one's enemies" (1941, p. 12). The fact that this assertion has such a ring of familiarity despite the fact that it was written many centuries ago suggests that it may express something that is pervasive in social experience.

Although a cognitive perspective such as the group schema hypothesis might appear fundamentally different from the social-support-for-shared-self-interest hypothesis, we would prefer to regard the two hypotheses as involving related processes. Note that the possibility of receiving social support for shared self-interest may help explain why the group schema is initially learned, and that the instantiation of the group schema may serve self-interest.

Although both the social-support-for-shared-self-interest hypothesis and the group-schema hypothesis will be investigated in a future experiment or series of experiments, it would be naive to suppose that these two hypotheses represent the full and final explanation for what we regard as a provocative and important phenomena. We have been wrong enough in the past to realize that empiricism can deal harshly with our most prized ideas.

IMPLICATIONS FOR THE UNDERSTANDING OF OUTGROUP REJECTION

We initially indicated that individual-group discontinuity is of interest for two reasons. First, individual-group discontinuity relates fairly directly to the problem of the group mind, a problem of long-term general interest to social science. Second, individual-group discontinuity provides a different, but potentially helpful, perspective on the problem of outgroup rejection.

The latter point merits elaboration. It can be argued that the phenomenon of individual-group discontinuity implies that outgroup rejection is best understood as an intergroup, rather than an interindividual, phenomenon. To the extent that this is true, there is the further implication that the correct theoretical explanation for individual-group discontinuity will have implications for the understanding of outgroup rejection. Thus, if the social-support-for-shared-self-interest hypothesis proves to be correct, there is the strong implication that outgroup rejection is to be understood in terms of self-esteem serving social comparisons and within-group social support for such social comparisons. On the other hand, if the group-schema hypothesis proves to be correct, there is the equally interesting implication that outgroup rejection is to be understood in terms of the process of stereotyping.

There is a parallel between the concept of group schema and the concept of stereotype. Although stereotypes are frequently thought of as differing from outgroup to outgroup, Campbell (1967) has a provocative discussion of a universal stereotype, relating, for example, to untrustworthiness of the outgroup, and so on. Campbell's notion of a universal stereotype is very similar to the concept of group schema. Furthermore, Rokeach, Smith, and Evans (1960) are well known for having proposed that much outgroup rejection is to be understood as the result of attributed dissimilarities in belief (i.e., stereotyping), and the evidence is generally supportive of this assertion (see Insko, Nacoste, & Moe, 1983, for a review of the evidence, and Moe, Nacoste, and Insko, 1981, for an empirical study of 9th-grade students over a 13-year period). An obvious implication of such a conceptualization is that outgroup rejection can be ameliorated to the extent that there is prevention of or interference with instantiation of the group schema.

APPENDIX

MATHEMATICAL CONSTRAINTS FOR THE MAMs

In order for the seven orientations in a given multiple alternative matrix to be unconfounded, it is necessary that the values be selected according to mathematical constraints. These constraints, which provide mathematical definitions of these orientations, are listed in Table 8.3. Each time values are assigned to a cell to represent an orientation, there is a further constraint on the values that can be assigned to the other cell. Therefore the number of constraints should be equal to the number of orientations represented in the matrix.

Consider first the constraint for the max own orientation. To represent the max own orientation, one cell in the matrix (for example, cell 1) is set to a value of X greater than any other X in the matrix. In mathematical symbols,

$$X_1 > X_i, i \neq 1$$

This expression implies that the first own-group outcome is greater than the remaining six outcomes.

Max rel own reaches its maximum in the alternative or cell that has the greatest difference between own and other outcomes. Thus the difference

TABLE 8.3
Mathematical Definitions for the Seven Orientations
Where $\underline{X}$ = Own Outcomes, $\underline{Y}$ = Other's Outcomes,
and $\underline{i}$ = 1 . . . 7, Except as Indicated

(1) Max own = $X_1 > X_i$, $i \neq 1$

(2) Max rel own = $X_2 - Y_2 > X_i - Y_i$, $i \neq 2$

(3) Min diff = $|X_3 - Y_3| < |X_i - Y_i|$, $i \neq 3$

(4) Max other = $Y_4 > Y_i$, $i \neq 4$

(5) Max rel other = $Y_5 - X_5 > Y_i - X_i$, $i \neq 5$

(6) Max joint own = $X_6 + Y_6 > X_i + Y_i$, $i \neq 6$ or 7,

$$X_6 > Y_6, \ X_6 + Y_6 = X_7 + Y_7$$

(7) Max joint other = $X_7 + Y_7 > X_i - Y_i$, $i \neq 7$ or 6,

$$X_7 < Y_7, \ X_7 + Y_7 = X_6 + Y_6$$

SOURCE: From Bornstein, Crum, Wittenbraker, Harring, Insko, and Thibaut, "On the measurement of social orientations in the minimal group paradigm," *European Journal of Social Psychology*, Vol. 13, p. 328. Copyright 1983 by John Wiley & Sons, Ltd. Reprinted by permission of John Wiley & Sons, Ltd.

between X and Y in alternative 2 is set to be the greatest in the matrix,

$$X_2 - Y_2 > X_i - Y_i, i \neq 2$$

This expression implies that there is a particular difference between own-group and other-group outcomes involving the second alternative that is better than all other possible differences among the remaining six own-group and six other-group outcomes. Furthermore, since this second own-group outcome is not the largest outcome (X_1), as defined above, the orientation is unconfounded with the max own orientation.

The third constraint can be determined by using alternative 3 to specify the min-diff orientation, or the smallest absolute difference between X and Y in the matrix,

$$|X_3 - Y_3| < |X_i - Y_i|, i \neq 3.$$

This process is continued until all seven orientations are included in the matrix. The full set of constraints is presented in Table 8.3. Any matrix that satisfies simultaneously all these constraints is an unconfounded matrix with regard to these seven social orientations.

NOTES

1. The matrices in Figure 8.2 differ from those used in previous research in two respects. First, the rows were not labeled, and second, the order of the seven orientations on the first matrix were different. The order of the orientations on the first matrix in Figure 8.2 corresponds to the order in Table 8.2.

2. There is an interesting parallel between the concept of group schema and the concept of stereotype. Although stereotypes are frequently thought of as differing from group to group, Campbell (1967) argues that all stereotypes have universal characteristics, for example, attributed untrustworthiness of the out-group. The concept of group schema, furthermore, bears an obvious similarity to Tajfel's (e.g., 1970) concept of a "generic norm" concerning between-group competitiveness. Tajfel initially used the concept of a generic norm as his explanation of competition between categories/groups.

REFERENCES

Adams, J. S. (1976). The structure and dynamics of behavior in organization boundary roles. In M. D. Dunnette (Ed.), *Handbook of industrial and organizational psychology* (pp. 1175-1199). Chicago: Rand-McNally.

Allport, F. H. (1924). *Social psychology.* Boston: Houghton Mifflin.

Axelrod, R. (1984). *The evolution of cooperation.* New York: Basic Books.

Bem, D. J. (1967). Self-perception: An alternative interpretation of cognitive dissonance phenomena. *Psychological Review, 74,* 182-200.

Billig, M, & Tajfel, H. (1973). Social categorization and similarity in intergroup behavior. *European Journal of Social Psychology, 3,* 27-51.

Bornstein, G., Crum, L., Wittenbraker, J., Harring, K., Insko, C. A., & Thibaut, J. (1983a). On the measurement of social orientations in the minimal group paradigm. *European Journal of Social Psychology, 13,* 321-350.

Bornstein, G., Crum, L. , Wittenbraker, J., Harring, K., Insko, C. A., & Thibaut, J. (1983b). Reply to Turner's comments. *European Journal of Social Psychology, 13,* 369-382.

Brewer, M. B. (1979). In-group bias in the minimal inter-group situation: A cognitive motivational analysis. *Psychological Bulletin, 86,* 307-324.

Brewer, M. B., & Silver, M. (1978). Ingroup bias as a function of task characteristics. *European Journal of Social Psychology, 10,* 393-400.

Brown, R. (1954). Mass phenomena. In G. Lindzey (Ed.), *Handbook of social psychology* (Vol. 2, pp. 833-876). Cambridge, MA: Addison-Wesley.

Brown, R. J., & Turner, J. C. (1981). Interpersonal and intergroup behavior. J.C. Turner

& H. Giles (Eds.), *Intergroup Behavior* (pp. 33-65). Chicago: University of Chicago Press.

Campbell, D. T. (1958). Common fate, similarity, and other indices of the status of aggregates of persons as social entities. *Behavioral Science,3*, 14-25.

Campbell, D. T. (1965). Ethnocentric and other altruistic motives. In D. Levine (Ed.), *Nebraska symposium on motivation* (Vol. 13, pp. 283-311). Lincoln, NE: University of Nebraska Press.

Campbell, D. T. (1967). Stereotypes and the perception of group differences. *American Psychologist, 22*, 817-829.

Carnevale, P.J.D., Pruitt, D. G., & Seilheimer, S. D. (1981). Looking and competing: Accountability and visual access in integrative bargaining. *Journal of Personality and Social Psychology, 40*, 111-120.

Doise, W. (1969). Stratégie de jeu á lintérieu et entre des groupes de nationalités différentes. *Bulletin du Centre d'Études et Recherches Psychotechniques, 18*, 13-26.

Doise, W. (1978). *Groups and individuals: Explanations in social psychology*. Cambridge: Cambridge University Press.

Druckman, D. (1967). Dogmatism, prenegotiation experience, and stimulated group representation as determinants of dyadic behavior in a bargaining situation. *Journal of Personality and Social Psychology, 4*, 279-290.

Druckman, D. (1971). On the effects of group representation. *Journal of Personality and Social Psychology, 18*, 273-274.

Durkheim, E. (1898). Representations individuelles et representations collectives. *Revue de Metaphysique, 6*, 274-302.

Gruder, C. L. (1971). Relationships with opponent and partner in mixed-motive bargaining. *Journal of Conflict Resolution, 15*, 403-416.

Harring, K., Wittenbraker, J., Pinkeley, R., Insko, C. A., & Thibaut, J. (1984). *Inter-group versus inter-individual competitiveness and the measurement of social orientations with multiple alternative matrices: I*. Unpublished manuscript, University of North Carolina.

Holmes, J., & Lamm, H. (1979). Boundary roles and the reduction of conflict. In W. G. Austin & S. Worchel (Eds.), *The social psychology of intergroup relations* (pp. 241-274). Monterey, CA: Brooks-Cole.

Horwitz, M., & Rabbie, J. M. (1982). Individuality and membership in the intergroup system. In H. Tajfel (Ed.), *Social identity and intergroup relations* (pp. 241-274). New York: Cambridge University Press.

Insko, C. A., Drenan, S., Solomon, M. R., Smith, R. H., & Wade, T.J. (1983). Conformity as a function of the consistency of positive evaluation with being liked and being right. *Journal of Experimental Social Psychology, 19*, 341-358.

Insko, C. A., Nacoste, R. W., & Moe, J. L. (1983). Belief congruence and racial discrimination: Review of the evidence and critical evaluation. *European Journal of Social Psychology, 13*, 153-174.

Insko, C. A., Pinkley, R. L., Harring, K., Holton, B., Hong, G., Krams, D. S., Hoyle, R. H., & Thibaut, J. (1986). *Beyond categorization to competition: Expectations of appropriate behavior*. Unpublished manuscript, University of North Carolina.

Insko, C. A., Pinkley, R. L., Hoyle, R. H., Dalton, B., Hong, G., Slim, R. M., Landry, P., Holton, B., Ruffin, P. F., & Thibaut, J. (in press). Individual-group discontinuity: The role of intergroup contact. *Journal of Experimental Social Psychology*.

Insko, C. A., Smith, R. H., Alicke, M. D., Wade, J., & Taylor, S. (1985). Conformity and group size: The concern with being right and the concern with being liked. *Personality and Social Psychology Bulletin, 11,*, 41-50.

Kelley, H. H., & Thibaut, J. W. (1978). *Interpersonal relations.* New York: John Wiley.

Klimoski, R. J., & Ash, R. A. (1974). Accountability and negotiator behavior. *Organizational Behavior and Human Performance, 11,* 409-425.

Komorita, S. S., & Lapworth, C. W. (1982). Cooperative choice among individuals versus groups in an N-person dilemma situation. *Journal of Personality and Social Psychology, 42,* 487-496.

LeBon, G. (1895). *Psychologie des foules.* Paris: F. Olean. Translated, *The crowd.* London: Unwin, 1896.

Lewin, K. (1948). *Resolving social conflicts.* New York: Harper & Row.

Lindskold, S., McElwain, D. C., Wagner, M. (1977). Cooperation and the use of coercion by groups and individuals. *Journal of Conflict Resolution, 21,* 521-550.

McCallum, D. M., Harring, K., Gilmore, R., Drenan, S., Chase, J., Insko, C. A., & Thibaut, J. (1985). Competition between groups and between individuals. *Journal of Experimental Social Psychology, 21,* 301-320.

McClintock, C. G. (1972). Game behavior and social motivation in interpersonal settings. In C. G. McClintock (Ed.), *Experimental social psychology* (pp. 271-296). New York: Holt, Rinehart & Winston.

McDougall, W. (1920). *The group mind.* New York: Putnam.

Moe, J. L., Nacoste, R. W., & Insko, C. A. (1981). Belief versus race as determinants of discrimination: A study of Southern adolescents in 1966 and 1979. *Journal of Personality and Social Psychology, 41,* 1031-1056.

Ng, S. H. (1981). Equity theory and the allocation of rewards between groups. *European Journal of Social Psychology, 11,* 439-444.

Plato (1941). *The republic of Plato* (F. Cornford, trans.). New York: Oxford University Press.

Pylyshyn, Z., Agnew, N., & Illingworth, J. (1972). Comparison of individuals and pairs as participants in a mixed-motive game. *Journal of Conflict Resolution, 2,* 211-220.

Rabbie, J. M., Visser, L., & van Oostrum, J. (1982). Conflict behavior of individuals, dyads, and triads in mixed-motive games. In H. Brandstatter, J. J. Davis, & G. Stocker-Kreichgauer (Eds.), *Group decision making* (pp. 315-343). London: Academic Press.

Rokeach, M., Smith, P. W., & Evans, R. I. (1960). Two kinds of prejudice or one? In M. Rokeach (Ed.), *The open and closed mind* (pp. 132-168). New York: Basic Books.

Ross, M., Insko, C. A., & Ross, H. (1971). Self-attribution of attitude. *Journal of Personality and Social Psychology, 17,* 292-297.

Schopler, J. and Compere, J. S. (1971). Effects of being kind or harsh to another on liking. *Journal of Personality and Social Psychology, 20,* 155-159.

Snyder, M. L., Kleck, R. E., Strenta, A., & Mentzer, S. J. (1979). An attributional ambiguity analysis. *Journal of Personality and Social Psychology, 37,* 2297-2306.

Snyder, M. L., Smaller, B., Strenta, A., & Frankel, A. (1981). A comparison of egotism, negativity, and learned helplessness as explanations for poor performance after unsolvable problems. *Journal of Personality and Social Psychology, 40,* 24-30.

Snyder, M. L., & Wicklund, R. (1981). Attribute ambiguity. In J. H. Harvey, W. Ickes, & R. F. Kidd (Eds.), *New directions in attribution research* (Vol. 3, pp. 197-221).

Tajfel, H. (1970). Experiments in intergroup discrimination. *Scientific American, 223,* (5), 96-102.

Tajfel, H. (1978a). Interindividual behavior and intergroup behavior. In H. Tajfel (Ed.), *Differentiation between social groups: Studies in the social psychology of intergroup relations* (pp. 27-60). London: Academic Press.

Tajfel, H. (1978b). Social categorization, social identity, and social comparison. In H. Tajfel (Ed.), *Differentiation between social groups: Studies in the social psychology of intergroup relations* (pp. 61-76). London: Academic Press.

Tajfel, H. (1978c). The achievement of group differentiation. In H. Tajfel (Ed.), *Differentiation between social groups: Studies in the social psychology of intergroup relations* (pp. 77-98). London: Academic Press.

Tajfel, H. (1981). *Human groups and social categories: Studies in social psychology* Cambridge: Cambridge University Press.

Tajfel, H. (1982). Social psychology of intergroup relations. In M. R. Rosenzweig & L. R. Porter (Eds.), *Annual review of psychology* (Vol. 33, pp. 1-39). Palo Alto, CA: Annual Reviews.

Tajfel, H., & Billig, M. (1974). Familiarity and categorization in intergroup behavior. *Journal of Experimental Social Psychology, 10,* 159-170.

Tajfel, H., Billig, M., Bundy, R., & Flament, C. (1971). Social categorization and intergroup behavior. *European Journal of Social Psychology, 1,* 149-178.

Tajfel, H., & Turner, J. (1979). An integrative theory of intergroup conflict. In W. G. Austin, & W. Worchel (Eds.). *The social psychology of intergroup relations* (pp. 33-47). Belmont, CA: Wadsworth.

Tajfel, H., & Turner, J. C. (1986). The social identity theory of intergroup behavior. In S. Worchel & W. G. Austin (Eds.), *Psychology of intergroup relations* (pp. 7-24). Chicago: Nelson-Hall.

Turner, J. (1978). Social categorization and intergroup differentiation in the minimal group paradigm. In H. Tajfel (Ed.), *Differentiation between social groups: Studies in the social psychology of intergroup relations* (pp. 101-140). London: Academic Press.

Turner, J. C. (1981). The experimental social psychology of intergroup behavior. In J. C. Turner, & H. Giles (Eds.), *Intergroup behavior* (pp. 66-101). Chicago: University of Chicago Press.

Turner, J. C. (1983a). A second reply to Bornstein, Crum, Wittenbraker, Harring, Insko, and Thibaut on the measurement of social orientations. *European Journal of Social Psychology, 13,* 383-387.

Turner, J. C. (1983b). Some comments on . . . the measurement of social orientations in the minimal group paradigm. *European Journal of Social Psychology, 13,* 351-368.

Turner, J. C., Brown, R. J., & Tajfel, H. (1979). Social comparison and group interest in ingroup favoritism. *European Journal of Social Psychology, 9,* 187-204.

Vidmar, N. (1971). Effects of representational roles and mediators on negotiation effectiveness. *Journal of Personality and Social Psychology, 17,* 48-58.

Wilson, W., & Kayatani, M. (1968). Intergroup attitudes and strategies in games between opponents of the same or of a different race. *Journal of Personality and Social Psychology, 9,* 24-30.

Wittenbraker, J. (1983). *The etiology of intergroup discrimination: A developmental approach.* Unpublished doctoral dissertation, University of North Carolina, Chapel Hill.

9

Leadership Processes

INTRAPERSONAl, INTERPERSONAL, AND SOCIETAL INFLUENCES

MARTIN M. CHEMERS

Martin M. Chemers is Professor of Psychology at Claremont McKenna College. His primary research interests are in the area of leadership and cross-cultural organizational psychology. He is coauthor, with Fred Fiedler, of *Leadership and Effective Management* and *Improving Leadership Effectiveness: The Leader Match Concept,* and of *Culture and Environment,* with Irwin Altman.

It has been 20 years since the publication of Fiedler's (1967) *A Theory of Leadership Effectiveness* completely changed the direction of research on leadership and organizational effectiveness. The time is appropriate to ask what we have learned and where the field of leadership is headed. The purpose of this chapter is to provide an integrative perspective on contemporary leadership theory and to highlight productive areas for future development.

Any such review is affected by the author's biases. I will state mine early. As a social psychologist, I view leadership as a process of interpersonal influence. As the word *interpersonal* implies, this process includes persons, that is, people with values, thoughts, and emotions, relating to other people in a social and cultural milieu of norms and expectations. In order to understand the leadership process, we must approach it from the three levels of the person, the group or dyad, and the larger organization or society. If any of these levels is ignored, our understanding is necessarily flawed and incomplete.

AN HISTORICAL OVERVIEW

Although philosophers and social theorists have recognized the importance of leadership and have theorized about how people become and function as leaders, the scientific study of leadership dates only from the early part of the twentieth century. Early investigations were characterized by overly simplistic outlooks and were largely unproductive.

The first three decades of research were guided by the assumption of a trait that was unequivocally and universally associated with leadership emergence and effectiveness. Stogdill's (1948) comprehensive review of the trait literature sounded the death knell for this approach. He reported that while some traits, like intelligence, were often associated with leadership, the relationships were, overall, weak and inconsistent. He did not say, however, that personality has no role in leadership. Rather, he pointed out that personality must be considered within the interactional framework of the leadership situation, that is, the group composition, the tasks to be accomplished, the authority relations, and so on.

In the 1950s, the trait approach was replaced by an emphasis on behavior. The most productive studies attempted to define what leaders actually do. Observational studies of college students interacting in problem-solving groups identified two types of leaders, a task specialist and a socio-emotional specialist (Bales & Slater, 1945). In a similar vein, the Leader Behavior Description Questionnaire (LBDQ) was developed and tested on military and industrial leaders (Hemphill & Coons, 1957). Factor analysis of this 150-item scale indicated that most of the variance in leader behavior was accounted for by two factors: *Initiation of Structure*, which referred to the leader's directive, structuring, and goal-oriented behavior, and *Consideration*, which referred to leader behaviors relating to concern for followers, participation, and interpersonal warmth (Halpin & Winer, 1957).

Interviews with industrial workers about the characteristics of their supervisors yielded descriptions of a "production-oriented" foreman, who focused on getting the job done, and an "employee-oriented" supervisor, who was very concerned about the feelings and welfare of subordinates (Kahn & Katz, 1953). This growing consensus that leaders tend to exhibit two types of behavior, task-oriented and relationship- or morale-oriented, was encouraging for a time. The hopefulness was soon dashed by the reality that the behavioral factors were not consistently related to important organizational outcomes like group performance, follower satisfaction, or grievances (Fleishman & Harris, 1962; Korman, 1966). It is fair to say that by the early 1960s, the field of leadership was in disarray and disillusionment, a state that some scholars would argue exists to the present day.

Contingency Approaches

Stodgill's (1948) call for leadership theorists to bring together person and situation was not answered until the mid-1960s. Fred Fiedler and his colleagues and students at the University of Illinois had been engaged in an extensive program of research comparing the performance of leaders who differed in the ways in which they described a poor coworker. Subjects in these studies, some of which were conducted in laboratory groups and some in real-world organizations, were asked to describe "the one person in their experience with whom they had the hardest time getting a job done," that is, their least-preferred coworker, or "LPC."

Although the interpretation of the meaning of LPC has followed a sometimes torturous journey across the theoretical landscape, recent years have brought convergence. Researchers who work extensively with the measure (Chemers, Hays, Rodewalt, & Wysocki, 1985; Fiedler & Chemers, 1974; Rice, 1978) see LPC as a measure of motivational objectives in the leadership situation. Persons who rate their least-preferred coworker very negatively (low LPC leaders) derive a sense of self-esteem and personal satisfaction from successful task performance and are consequently distressed by anything or anyone (e.g., a poor coworker) who interferes with that goal. Low LPC leaders are extremely attentive to task-related aspects of the leadership situation, and when under pressure or stress tend toward more directive and structuring leadership behavior in an attempt to ensure success of this highly desired goal.

The leader who gives a poor coworker a relatively positive rating (high LPC) is more concerned with social acceptance and the positive regard of others than with task success. This leader is sensitive and responsive to the needs of subordinates, and when under pressure is likely to adopt a participative, considerate style of leadership.

Although Fiedler was relatively uncertain about the conceptual basis of the LPC measure, he did realize, early on, that it was a strong predictor of group performance. In a variety of military, business, and sports groups, the leader's LPC score significantly predicted performance on the group's assigned task. However, the superiority of the high or low LPC leader varied from one study to another. It was at this point that Fiedler (1964, 1967) began to examine the moderating effect of the situation on the relationship betwen LPC and performance.

Fiedler hypothesized that since leadership is a process of interpersonal influence, factors that affect the ease with which the leader can exert influence over followers should be important. Three such identified variables were (a) the loyalty and support the leader received from followers (*leader-member relations*), (b) the structure of the task in terms of goal and procedural clarity (*task structure*), and (c) the leader's formal authority (*position power*). These three variables are combined to form a continuum that Fiedler called *situational favorableness* and, more recently, *situational control* (Fiedler & Chemers, 1984).

By 1967, Fiedler had data on a considerable number of groups in a variety of settings. He assigned these groups to positions along the new dimension of situational favorableness. Figure 9.1 presents the resultant performance curve. According to this formulation, which Fiedler called the Contingency Model, no single style of leadership is effective in all situations. Rather, the directive, structuring approach of the low LPC leader is relatively more effective under conditions of very high control, in which the certainty of the situation provides the leader with the resources necessary to move forward, and in conditions of very low control, where the extreme problems of the leader's situation require decisive action. In the more ambiguous and delicate situations of moderate control, caused by a lack of follower commitment and support or by an unclear or creative problem, the more group-oriented, participative, and open style of the high LPC leader results in greater follower motivation and more creative problem solving behavior.

Problems with the Contingency Model

The Contingency Model burst into the vacuum of leadership theory and became the dominant explanatory approach to leadership performance. Today, when almost every topic in the organizational literature is explained via contingency principles, it is difficult to remember how innovative this person-situation perspective was at the time. It was not long, however, before the model began to attract its critics. Not only has dominant and singular status made the model attractive to critics, but a number of other features of its development and exposition contributed to its vulnerability.

First, there was the inductive manner of its development. The situational favorableness dimension was developed from studies already done rather than deductively from a well-articulated theoretical base. There was also the problem of the mysterious nature of the LPC construct itself. Its projective method of measurement and somewhat

THE CONTINGENCY MODEL

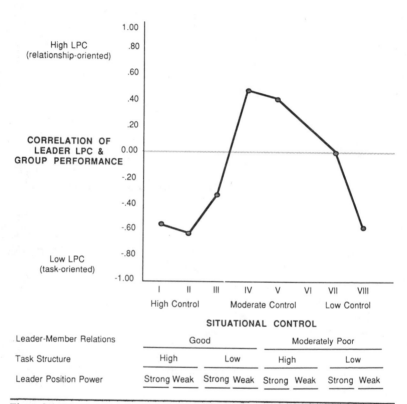

Figure 9.1 The Contingency Model of Leadership Effectiveness

vague interpretation made it a dubious answer to Stogdill's prayers. Finally, when Fiedler split his samples on the three measures of the situation, the number of groups available in each classification became quite small, resulting in probability levels below accepted standards.

These problems with the Contingency Model were dissected in a decade of controversy. External critics (Ashour, 1973; Graen, Alvares, Orris, & Martella, 1970) questioned the basic validity and utility of the model. Thoughtful analyses by members of Fiedler's research group

(Mitchell, Biglan, Oncken, & Fiedler, 1970) admitted problems, but argued that the model was, despite its shortcomings, a valid approach with high potential. Hindsight seems to favor Fiedler. Two recent meta-analyses (Peters, Hartke, & Phlomann, 1983; Strube & Garcia, 1981) collated the results of over 100 tests of the model's predictive validity. Both papers concluded that the basic tenets of the theory are well supported by the empirical evidence.

This is not to say that the theory is without problems. However, many of its weaknesses, (e.g., less than satisfactory treatment of the personality variable, a need for a more direct measure of the situation, and a clearer exposition of the behavioral processes that result in group performance, [Rice & Kastenbaum, 1983]), are exactly the problems that characterize the field of leadership as a whole.

Other Contingency Theories

Despite the controversy surrounding the Contingency Model, the potential of theories that integrate person and situation in the study of leadership did not escape researchers in the field. Several other contingency theories soon made their appearance. House (1971) presented the Path-Goal theory that related the leader behavior factors of *Initiation of Structure* and *Consideration* to subordinate motivation and satisfaction under varying task conditions. Structuring and directive behavior was seen as having its most positive effects when the subordinate needs direction by virtue of a lack of knowledge or experience with the job. Consideration is most beneficial when the subordinate's job situation is boring or aversive. Contrarily, when the subordinate knows how to do the job, structuring leader behavior is seen as overly close monitoring and reduces motivation and satisfaction, as does considerate behavior when the subordinate has an interesting and absorbing task.

Results from empirical tests of the predictive validity of the Path-Goal theory have been complex. Many studies have supported the model (House & Dessler, 1974; Schreisheim & DeNisi, 1981). Others have yielded more mixed results (Dessler & Valenzi, 1977; Downey, Sheridan, & Slocum, 1975). Path-Goal theory suffers from a lack of standardization in the specification of objective means for measuring key situational variables. Thus the means for specifying how unstructured or aversive a subordinate's job is vary greatly from one study to another. Recently, a study by Griffin (1981) indicates that subordinate characteristics, in this case desire for an interesting growth-promoting job, moderate the predictions of Path-Goal theory, adding further complexity to the theory.

Another very influential contingency theory is Vroom and Yetton's (1973) Normative Decision theory (NDT). Drawing on the work of Maier (1963) in the area of group processes, NDT develops a model for specifying what kind of decision strategy is most appropriate, given a number of situational contingencies. The theory describes a set of decision styles that range from autocratic to consultative to participitative. The effectiveness of each style in terms of decision quality, time utilization, and implementability is moderated by situational characteristics like subordinate support, task structure and information availability, and time pressure. Research testing the NDT has not been as extensive as that surrounding the Contingency Model or Path-Goal theory, but has been largely supportive (Jago & Vroom, 1977; Margerison & Glube, 1979).

By the mid 1970s, these three models of leadership were central in the research literature. A number of other research areas were developing, but the contingency theories with their major focus on the leader formed the core of the field. The three theories had much in common. Each had a leader variable that was related, directly or indirectly, to a dimension of direction-participation, and situational variables that related to the degree of structure and predictability in the task environment. Considerable overlap exists in the basic predictions of the theories, as well. Directive leader behavior is seen as most appropriate and most effective when the situation provides the leader with sufficient information and control to anticipate the outcomes of directive action. Considerate or participative behavior is considered most useful when the situation is more ambiguous or difficult. Each theory has a slightly different perspective, and differences between them do exist. Nonetheless, their similarities are real and provide a reasonable platform for examining and perhaps eventually integrating contemporary research and theory.

CONTEMPORARY LEADERSHIP RESEARCH

The field of leadership is an extensive one with investigators in a variety of disciplines: psychology, sociology, business, political science, and others. By drawing on selected research and theory from other fields, especially organizational behavior and management, one may hope to move toward an integrated perspective that will be the base for a more general theory of leadership.

I will consider three general areas of research as background for developing an integrative framework. The three areas are (a) leader-oriented approaches, particularly those that emphasize the role of individual differences, (b) exchange approaches that focus on the relationship between the leader and follower, with special emphasis on leader behavior, and (c) cognitive approaches that may help to provide an intrapersonal basis for understanding leadership behavior.

Leader-Oriented Approaches

Although the last 10 to 15 years have spawned many alternative approaches to the study of leadership, the leader-oriented contingency paradigms continue to be productive. Fiedler and his associates have developed a training program referred to as LEADER MATCH that is based on the contingency model (Fiedler & Chemers, 1984; Fiedler, Chemers, & Mahar, 1976). A number of empirical tests of the program have indicated that trained managers perform more effectively than untrained or alternatively trained leaders (Fiedler & Mahar, 1979; Leister, Borden, & Fiedler, 1977).

The Contingency Model has generated two recent approaches to the study of the intrapsychic aspects of leadership, focusing particularly on the experience of stress. In an extension of the model, Chemers et al., (1985) demonstrated the utility of the theory for explaining the etiology of job stress. Fiedler and Chemers (1984) used the term "match" to refer to the degree to which a leader's style is appropriate to the situational demands. Thus, task-oriented leaders in high control situations and relationship-oriented leaders in moderate control situations (Figure 9.1) are "in-match" and perform effectively. Chemers et al. (1985) hypothesized that leaders who are in-match would experience much less job stress and stress-related consequences than would out-of-match leaders. In a survey of university administrators, the hypotheses were strongly confirmed. Out-of-match department chairs reported significantly higher levels of job stress, stress-related illnesses, and days missed from work. Recent data with a large sample of public school administrators (Chemers, Hill, & Sorod, 1986) replicated the original results.

The role of stress in leadership dynamics has been integrated into a promising model relating intelligence to leadership effectiveness. Fiedler and his associates (Fiedler & Garcia, 1987; Fiedler & Leister, 1977;

Fiedler, Potter, Zais, & Knowlton, 1979; Frost, 1983) proposed a Cognitive Resources theory. Fiedler and Garcia report a considerable body of data indicating that when leaders are under stress, their intelligence is uncorrelated or even negatively correlated with group performance, but it is highly correlated with performance when they are not stressed. Conversely, under high stress conditions, it is the leader's job-relevant experience that predicts performance.

Path-Goal theory has not stimulated a great deal of research in the last few years. However, its perspective has influenced another productive line of research. The Path-Goal perspective predicts that the effects of leader behavior will have much weaker impact on subordinate motivation in some situations than in others. This view had led to a body of work classifying conditions under which organizational or technological factors will inhibit the effects of the leader's actions. Kerr and Jermier (1978) have discussed "substitutes for leadership" in which situational factors such as rigid technology, organizational policies, or subordinate experience moderate the importance of leader behavior.

More recently, Yukl (1979) and Hunt (1984) categorized a broad range of factors that influence the efficacy of leader behavior. An understanding of the situational variables that both enhance and diminish leadership effects holds promise for the development of a more general and inclusive definition of the situation in leadership studies.

Of the three major contingency theories, only the Contingency Model places importance on individual differences or personality aspects of the leader. Path-Goal theory and Normative Decision theory specify appropriate leader behaviors for a particular situation, as though the actual behavior is independent of any characteristics of the individual leader. A considerable amount of research belies that assumption.

For example, Jago (1978) reported that higher-level managers have a general bias toward the more participative decision styles. Hill and Schmitt (1977) reported that individuals will consistently tend toward a more participative or more autocratic set of styles. In a similar line of research, Bass and Valenzi (1974) identified a set of managerial styles (directive, manipulative, consultative, participative, and delegative) analogous to the directive-participative dimension discussed earlier. Empirical studies of these managerial styles by Shapira (1976), and Chitayat and Venezia (1984) indicated that subsets of the styles were correlated in a manner that would suggest some underlying dimension of personality (or values). Specifically, the more directive styles (direction and manipulation) were highly correlated with each other but were distinct from the more participative styles (consultation, participation, and delegation).

In recent years, there has been a resurgence of interest in the role of individual differences in leadership. Kenny and Zaccaro (1983) reanalyzed data from a study by Barnlund (1962) in which a group of 30 individuals participated repeatedly in task groups of changing task and member composition. Kenny and Zaccaro found that the percentage of variance in emergent leadership nominations attributable to individual characteristics was 49%.

Such a finding supports the assertion (House & Baetz, 1979) that failure to identify the specific trait associated with emergent or effective leadership does not mean that traits, or stable aspects and dispositions of the leader, have no relevance to performance when examined in the appropriate situational context. For example, McClelland and Boyatzis (1982) have shown that personality differences in the need for power and affiliation can predict managerial success up to 16 years later. These studies make a strong case for personality influences in leader behavior and performance.

Transactional and Exchange Approaches

The contingency approaches address the importance of follower support by including it as an aspect of the leadership situation. However, the seminal work of Hollander (1958) made clear how much of leadership status is dependent on the followers' views of the leader. In recent years the work of Graen and his associates (Dansereau, Graen, & Haga, 1975; Graen, 1976) has stimulated considerable interest in the relationship between leader and follower.

The Vertical Dyad Linkage Model proposes (a) that managers set up unique exchanges with each of their subordinates in the specification of their respective roles, and (b) that the quality of these exchanges has a profound influence on subordinate satisfaction, motivation, and organizational commitment. By and large, the empirical evidence supports the basic premises of the model (Graen & Ginsburgh, 1977; Graen & Schiemann, 1978).

However, what is missing from the Vertical Dyad Linkage model is any suggestion of what factors are responsible for the development of high quality exchanges. Here again, as in much of the organizational psychology literature, the person is missing from the role. Other researchers have not overlooked this problem.

In early studies, Haythorn, Couch, Haefner, Langham, and Carter (1956), and Sanford (1952) examined the role of follower authoritarianism in response to leaders. More recently, Weed, Mitchell, and Moffitt (1976) found that dogmatic followers like directive leaders. Likewise, Abdel-Halim (1983) found that followers' reactions to participative decision making depended on their view of the use of power within their organization and individual differences in the desire for participation. Pulakos and Wexley (1983) found that excellent manager-subordinate dyads were frequently composed of same-sex pairs who also saw themselves as similar to one another in important ways. In a review of both laboratory and field studies of leader behavior and subordinate performance, Sims and Manz (1984) concluded that the relationship between leader behavior and subordinate performance is reciprocally determined. Leaders' decisions regarding the use of reward and punishment are affected by both subordinate performance and subordinates' previous reactions to sanctions.

The literature on follower personality is not particularly well organized and does not provide a coherent picture of which traits are most useful to measure. It does, however, show that the personality, attitudes, and values of followers play an important role in their relationships with and reactions to their leaders. The systematic study of these effects is called for.

Cognitive Approaches

Thoughts, attitudes, and expectations comprise an important intrapersonal aspect of leadership. These cognitive factors have been approached from two perspectives, the leader's and the follower's. The follower's reactions to leader behavior have already been touched upon in the preceding section.

We know that followers' personality, values, and expectations influence their judgments of the leader. A further complication in the process of social judgments revolves around the ambiguity inherent in such judgments. Research indicates that people hold implicit theories about what leadership is and how it is manifested (Calder, 1977). These implicit theories of leadership may cause us to see what we expect to see. For example, when followers or observers believe that a group has performed well, they attribute to the leader behaviors that they believe are associated with effective leadership (Eden & Leviatan, 1975; Lord, Binning, Rush, & Thomas, 1978; Phillips & Lord, 1981).

One reason for the susceptibility of leader behavior ratings to bias and distortion is that the behavioral measures tend to be fairly general and global. Yukl and Nemeroff (1979) tried to answer this problem by the development of more extensive, articulated, and carefully developed rating scales. Another approach is to focus on more specific and concrete behavioral categories with higher reliability of observation. Komaki, Zlotnick, and Jensen (1986) argued that such an approach can be useful if it is guided by a clear theory about which discrete behaviors ought to be measured. They argued from an operant conditioning perspective that reward and punishment behavior is critical, at least to supervisory effectiveness. Komaki (1986) reported that managers identified as effective by their superiors did, in fact, spend more time monitoring specific samples of their subordinates' work, in order to deliver more informed reinforcement. While still in the early stages, this work may be useful in at least some areas of leadership study.

Komaki's study of leader monitoring behavior is premised on the assumption that leaders' actions are based on their perceptions of subordinate behavior and the causes of that behavior. A voluminous literature in social psychology addresses the manner in which people make attributions about the causes of others' behavior (e.g., Jones & Davis, 1965; Kelley, 1967). The study of leader attributions has been heavily influenced by that work.

Mitchell and his associates (Green & Mitchell, 1979; Mitchell, Green, & Wood, 1981) have examined the attributions leaders make about poor performers. Studies have shown that supervisors make more negative judgments about a poorly performing subordinate when the failure is the result of lack of effort rather than lack of ability (Knowlton & Mitchell, 1980) and supervisors make more negative and personal (i.e., dispositional) attributions when the outcomes of the performance have more serious implication for organizational functioning (Mitchell & Kalb, 1981; Mitchell & Wood, 1980).

A key issue in the attribution of causality is whether the responsibility for a behavior (or performance level) is assigned internally (to ability or effort) or to external causes (a difficult task or bad luck). Two of the most important determinants of the locus of causal attribution are (a) the source of the attribution, that is, actor or observer, and (b) the degree of ego involvement of the supervisor. Actors tend to make more situational attributions than do observers (the *actor-observer discrepancy,* Jones & Nisbett, 1972). When superiors are potentially held responsible for subordinate performance, they are also more likely to assign responsibility for failure externally (the *self-serving bias*, Weary, 1979).

Brown (1984) argued that both biases are likely to be strongly active when a manager is assigning responsibility for a subordinate's failure. He highlighted the role of *reversible perspective,* that is, the superior is an observer when viewing the behavior of a subordinate and an actor when assessing his or her own potential responsibility for the subordinate's failure. Since the actions of a subordinate usually have implications for the evaluation of the boss, the boss is likely to make strong, dispositional (self-serving) attributions, placing the blame for poor performance on subordinates.

The question of causal attribution becomes even more meaningful in the context of decisions about corrective action. Mitchell, Green, and Wood (1981) have shown that the action a manager proposes to take with regard to a poorly performing subordinate depends on the attribution of causality. For example, an attribution to a lack of subordinate effort might result in sanctions or dismissal while an attribution to task difficulty would yield a recommendation for more task-related training. This "attribution-to-action" relationship probably plays a central role in the kinds of leader-follower exchanges described in the Vertical Dyad Linkage model.

Recently, Dobbins (1985) found that women appear to use different norms than men when deciding on corrective action, even when responding to similar causal attributions. For example, men are more likely to use punitive sanctions when poor performance is the result of a lack of effort, while women are more likely to use supportive actions regardless of the cause. This finding suggests that both individual and cultural differences may be an important part of the leader-follower relationship.

TOWARD INTEGRATION

Most reviews of the leadership literature end on a sour note, concluding that the field has made minimal progress and is in a chaotic condition. From a historical perspective of the last 20 years, let alone the last 50, we reach a different conclusion. While there is diversity, there are also several promising commonalities that augur well for the future.

With respect to group productivity and performance, most theorists agree on a contingency perspective in which leader behavior, style, or decision-making strategy interacts with situational demands. There is also considerable agreement that the leader behavior dimension of interest is the degree to which the leader involves subordinates in planning and decision making. Similarly, there is considerable agreement on the elements of the situation that are crucial. Factors that contribute to the leader's sense of predictability and control over group processes seem to be the prime candidates, for example, follower support, information availability, task structure, and formal and informal authority.

It is also becoming evident that the leader's behavior is not independent of values and personality. Repeatedly we see that certain individuals are more prone to use a set of related strategies in interacting with subordinates. Subordinate reactions and their reciprocal effects on leader actions also arise out of consistent patterns of expectation and desire on the part of those followers. The roles that develop between leader and led subsequently give rise to relationships that determine motivation, satisfaction, effort, and, ultimately, performance and effectiveness.

While these general principles would elicit agreement from most leadership scholars, the empirical investigations and the mini-theories and models that guide them tend to be more fragmented and unrelated.

An Integrative Model

In a recent chapter (Chemers, 1983), I described an integrated systems-oriented model that has guided the research of my colleagues and myself. Figure 9.2 provides a graphic representation of a research hueristic that we have found to be helpful both in hypothesis generation and research strategy. The model diagrams the process of leadership within the social context. The top and bottom layers of the figure denote the parameters of that context. At the bottom is the more immediate group in which the leader and followers are embedded. The key situational variables that affect the perceptions of both leaders and followers are considered to be the interpersonal, task, and authority relations in the group. Most contemporary contingency theories incorporate some variant of a situational dimension reflecting the leader's perceived control. Aspects of follower support and loyalty, task clarity, and power or authority are the typical contributors to that dimension of control.

At the top of the figure, the same general factors are highlighted at the level of the larger society or culture. The immediate group, the leader and followers, that is addressed at the bottom of the figure, can be

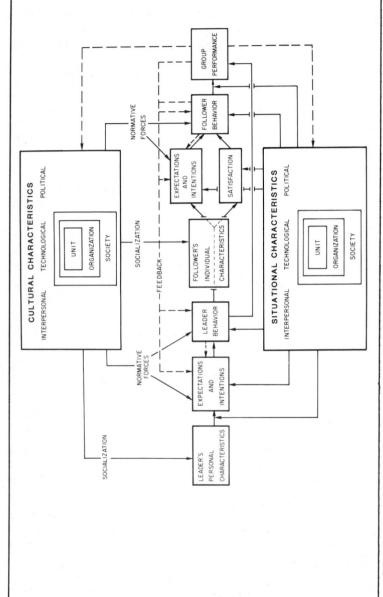

Figure 9.2 A Systems Process Mode of Leadership

thought of as surrounded by the more encompassing societal milieu represented at the top of the figure. The effects of the society are seen as long-term and stable, but are manifested in the small group on an immediate basis. For example, a society that places high value on harmonious interpersonal relations will instill such values in its members. When people interact in a small group, those values will guide perceptions of appropriate behavior and reactions to the behavior of others.

Within the social context, leaders and followers interact and react to one another based on their views of the demands and expectations of the situation, tempered by their own values and personalities. Thus the leader forms beliefs and expectations based on a perception of the situational demands and on personal dispositions, that is, values or traits. These expectations lead to actions. The relationship between expectancies and actions is shown with bidirectional arrows. The intent is to recognize the possibility that rather than guiding behavior, cognitive representations like expectancies are simply post-hoc explanations of actions. Behavior may be driven by more powerful emotional forces or habits. Weick (1969) has argued that groups are primarily emotional, and cognitions about behavior are retrospective attempts to make sense out of what has already happened.

The leader's behavior will have an impact on the expectations and emotions of followers. That impact is determined by the followers' individual characteristics, such as their values, needs, and perceptions of what is appropriate. The figure depicts that process by dotted lines passing through the filter of follower characteristics. The resultant behavior of leaders and followers affects the environment, through productivity, organizational change, and so on. These changes in the environment then provide feedback to the actors, affecting their causal attributions and future expectations.

For example, a highly task-oriented leader might perceive a situation as being unstructured and ambiguous, and given his expectations, begin to closely direct the work of a subordinate. If the subordinate values independence and autonomy, he or she may react negatively to this leader behavior, becoming hostile. The resultant performance might be low, and the leader will experience a sense of frustration and stress. The dyadic exchange will suffer, and both leader and follower satisfaction will be low.

The figure represents the process of leader and follower thought and action as linear, giving the impression of a unidirectional causality. This is not the case. Reciprocal influence exists between leader and follower. Also, the processes of leadership are temporarily cyclic. Thoughts and actions of the moment are influenced by past history and expectations of future outcomes.

To a degree, this model merely systematizes and organizes the various perspectives extant in the leadership literature. It also, however, emphasizes some key features of our approach. One of these features is the strong emphasis on the effects of stable individual differences. Values, personality, and cognitive styles affect our perceptions of social demands and appropriate action. Second, cultural differences hold a central role in the model. In the long term, socialization practices help to instill the values and personality traits that people carry into social interaction. More immediately, the normative expectations held by relevant actors guide both social reality and behavioral expression. Finally, the model makes very salient the need to tie together the various aspects of the process rather than treating leader behavior, leader-follower exchanges, and cognitive processes as separate phenomena.

Research with the Systems-Process Model

In collaboration with Roya Ayman, I have employed this model in the study of leadership cross-culturally. Our objectives in this research program are twofold. We would like to test the generalizability of leadership theories and constructs developed in the United States and Western Europe. Second, we want to gain an understanding of how unique and particular cultural norms and values contribute to a society's views of leadership. To this end, we have conducted a number of studies in Iran and Mexico and are beginning projects in Thailand, Korea, and Japan. Some of our recent findings illustrate the utility of an integrative approach.

In an earlier study conducted in Iran (Chemers, 1969), ratings of leader behavior completed by Iranians yielded a factor structure quite different from that found with Western samples. *Initiation of Structure* and *Consideration* loaded on a single factor, rather than emerging as independent factors, as is usually the case. In a more recent study, Ayman and Chemers (1983) administered a leader behavior scale containing two additional items. They replicated the single factor structure found earlier by Chemers; loading heavily on that factor were two new items, "My leader is a good leader" and "My leader is like a kind father to me." This factor, named *Benevolent Paternalism*, correlated very highly with subordinate satisfaction and superior ratings of group and leader performance.

The groups in the Chemers (1969) study were composed of American leaders and Iranian followers in a laboratory setting. In Ayman and Chemers (1983), both leaders and followers were Iranian managers in an industrial organization. The fact that Iranian followers rated leader behavior similarly when the leaders were Americans and when they were Iranians indicates that the raters held implicit theories about what a good leader does. Those theories guided their ratings independently of the leader's actual behavior. Much of the research on cognitive factors in leadership concerns the source and nature of implicit theories and prototypes influencing perceptions of leadership (Lord, Foti, & Phillips, 1982). The Ayman and Chemers study illustrates the strong impact of culture on implicit leadership theories, as well as the degree to which leader behavior ratings may reflect global evaluations of leaders rather than descriptions of specific behaviors.

The importance of individual differences as moderators of many leadership phenomena was shown in two studies addressing the relationship between performance and satisfaction. The inconsistency in findings relating performance and satisfaction has bothered organizational researchers for a long time (see Iaffaldano & Muchinsky, 1985, for a review). However, two studies using leadership style as a moderator variable yielded extremely powerful and clear results (Chemers & Ayman, 1985; Rice, Marwick, Chemers, & Bentley, 1982). Task-motivated (low LPC) leaders, who derive a sense of personal satisfaction and self-esteem from successful task performance, exhibit very strong positive correlations between their job satisfaction and job performance. Relationship-motivated leaders, on the other hand, exhibit weak or negative relationships between these two variables. The studies on perceptions of leader behavior and the studies on the congruence between performance and satisfaction reflect the importance of individual differences moderators in the complex relationships between people and their social environment.

The model also directs our attention to the fact that the interaction between leader and follower is embedded in a larger social context that provides norms and standards for appropriate action. An interesting finding generated by the model relates to the interaction of internal dispositions and social expectations. Ayman (1984) hypothesized that internal dispositions, such as task versus relationship motivation or work-related values, might be inhibited at the behavioral level by strong normative expectations for certain leader behaviors, especially in cultures where role expectations are clearly prescribed and rigid. In a study of Mexican middle managers, we included Snyder's (1974) Self-Monitoring Scale, a measure of the individual's sensitivity and responsiveness to normative expectations. We predicted that individuals who were less responsive to social expectations would show stronger relationships between their internal disposition and their overt behavior.

Indeed, we found that managers who were low self-monitors and less responsive to social expectations, showed clear and theoretically consistent relationships between their leadership style (LPC) and their behavior. All leaders, regardless of LPC, were high on consideration behavior, a strong cultural expectation. However, high levels of task-oriented, directive behavior was observed only for low LPC (task-oriented) leaders who were also low self-monitors.

The results for leader performance followed a similar pattern. For low self-monitors, the interaction of leadership style and situational control follows theoretical predictions. That is, low LPC leaders perform best in high control situations, and high LPC leaders do well in moderate control situations. However, for high self-monitors, the predicted interaction does not occur or is reversed, that is, the high self-monitoring leaders perform best in the situations where the *contingency model* predicts that they would be "out-of-match." The high self-monitoring leaders may be inhibiting their own personal inclinations in an attempt to respond to the expectations of others.

Chemers and Ayman (1986) followed up this study with a qualitative analysis of the construct validity of the LPC and self-monitoring scales. A new sample of 100 Mexican managers completed the two scales and were subsequently interviewed on their personal beliefs about leadership. The low self-monitors showed a very clear relationship between their leadership style and their views of leadership. Task-motivated leaders said that they valued decisive, directive, and adaptable leadership and were bothered by coworkers who interfered with their work or didn't follow orders. Relationships-motivated leaders valued leadership that was participative, tolerant, and trustworthy, and had difficulty with subordinates who caused conflict. On the other hand, the protocols of the task- and relationship-oriented leaders who were high self-monitors were indistinguishable from each other and seemed to reflect some general stereotypes, such as leaders as knowledgeable, open-minded and honest.

In addition to clarifying the nature of leadership style among Mexican managers, the inclusion of the self-monitoring construct provides an opportunity for enhancing the salience of personality factors in situations that Mischel (1977) would call "strong," that is, those in which strong behavioral norms wash out individual differences. The systems-process model enhances attempts to bring together individual difference, social, and cultural aspects of group process.

While each of the studies described above makes only discrete and limited contributions to our understanding of leadership processes, they offer the potential to be woven together into a fabric of understanding. By adopting an integrative perspective one can begin to ask, for example, how leadership style might affect the role-making transactions and exchanges between leaders and followers, or how individual differences affect the processes of attribution and corrective action.

An integrative perspective led to a recent study attempting to unite two lines of research. A study by Chemers et al. (1985), described earlier, found that leaders whose style and situation were in-match reported less stress and stress-related illness. That finding and the just-described results incorporating self-monitoring into the contingency model led Chemers, Sorod, and Akimoto (1987) to investigate cognitive and affective consequences of being in-match. They found that leaders of three-person laboratory groups who were in-match reported significantly higher levels of positive affect (on an affective adjective checklist), greater perceptions of control over group process, and more personal responsibility for performance outcomes. The followers of these leaders exhibited the same effects. However, the effects on followers was moderate by the leader's level of self-monitoring. The high self-monitoring leaders elicited more positive responses from their followers when the leaders were out-of-match than when they were in-match. Just as in the Mexico study, high self-monitors masked their internal states when dealing with other group members, even though they responded very positively to being in-match in their self reports.

Chemers, Sorod, and Akimoto concluded that the phenomenological experience of being in-match is one of alertness, enthusiasm, and control, and that a component of effective leadership is the communication of this positive experience to followers. The psychological "gestalt" created by the leader may be more important than the specific behaviors or decision strategies the leader uses. Recently, European researchers have been experimenting with much more phenomenologically oriented paradigms, emphasizing the ways in which the leader views the environment and self (Hunt, Hosking, Schriesheim, & Stewart, 1984). Such approaches may offer an exciting alternative to our present emphasis on behavioral ratings.

An integrative approach combining multiple perspectives seems useful. The field of leadership has amassed a considerable body of reliable findings. Promising new directions are appearing. What is important is that each successive theoretical or research strategy be meshed with previous knowledge rather than replace earlier work in an endless succession of fads and one-ups-manship. Leadership research can drive toward a bright future, if only the perennial mourners would move the hearse out of the road.

REFERENCES

Abdel-Halim, A. A. (1983). Power equalization, participative decision-making, and individual differences. *Human Relations, 36,* 683-704.

Ashour, A. S. (1973). Further discussion of Fiedler's contingency model of leadership effectiveness: An evaluation. *Organizational Behavior and Human Performance, 9,* 339-355.

Ayman, R. (1984, August). The effects of leadership characteristics and situational control on leadership effectiveness. In M. M. Chemers (Chair), *Leadership effectiveness in Mexico.* Symposium conducted at the International Congress of Psychology, Acapulco.

Ayman, R., & Chemers, M. M. (1983). The relationships of supervisory behavior ratings to work group effectiveness and subordinate satisfaction among Iranian managers. *Journal of Applied Psychology, 68,* 338-341.

Bales, R. F., & Slater, P. E. (1945). Role differentiation in small decision making groups. In T. Parsons & R. F. Bales (Eds.), *Family, socialization, and interaction process* (pp. 259-306). New York: Free Press.

Barnlund, D. C. (1962). Consistency of emergent leadership in groups with changing tasks and members. *Speech Monographs, 29,* 45-52.

Bass, B. M., & Valenzi, E. R. (1974). Contingent aspects of effective management styles. In J. G. Hunt & L. L. Larson (Eds.), *Contingency approaches to leadership* (pp. 130-156). Carbondale, IL: Southern Illinois University Press.

Brown, K. A. (1984). Explaining group poor performance: An attributional analysis. *Academy of Management Review, 9,* 54-63.

Calder, B. J. (1977). An attribution theory of leadership. In B. M. Staw & G. R. Salancik (Eds.), *New directions in organizational behavior* (pp. 179-204). Chicago, IL: St. Clair.

Chemers, M. M. (1969). Cross-cultural training as a means for improving situational favorableness. *Human Relations, 22,* 531-546.

Chemers, M. M. (1983). Leadership theory and research: A systems-process integration. In P. B. Paulus (Ed.), *Basic group processes* (pp. 9-39). New York: Springer-Verlag.

Chemers, M. M., & Ayman, R. (1985). Leadership orientation as a moderator of the relationship between job performance and job satisfaction for Mexican managers. *Personality and Social Psychology Bulletin, 11*, 359-367.

Chemers, M. M., & Ayman, R. (1986, August). *Emic/etic approach to leadership orientation and job satisfaction of Mexican managers.* Paper presented at the meeting of the International Association of Applied Psychology, Jerusalem.

Chemers, M. M., Hays, R. B., Rhodewalt, F., & Wysocki, J. (1985). A person-environment analysis of job stress: A contingency model explanation. *Journal of Personality and Social Psychology, 49*, 628-635.

Chemers, M. M., Hill, C. A., & Sorod, B. (1986). Personality-environment match and health: Support for the contingency model. Paper presented at the meeting of the American Psychological Association, Chicago, IL.

Chemers, M. M., Sorod, B., & Akimoto, S. A. (1987). [The phenomenology of leadership effectiveness]. Unpublished raw data.

Chitayat, G., & Venezia, I. (1984). Determinants of management styles in business and nonbusiness organizations. *Journal of Applied Psychology, 69,*

Dansereau, F., Jr., Graen, G., & Haga, J. (1975). Vertical dyad linkage approach to leadership within formal organizations: A longitudinal investigation of the role making process. *Organizational Behavior and Human Performance. 13*, 46-78.

Dessler, G., & Valenzi, E. R (1977). Initiation of structure and subordinate satisfaction: A path analysis test of path-goal theory. *Academy of Management Journal, 20*, 251-259.

Dobbins, G. H. (1985). Effects of gender on leaders' responses to poor performers: An attributional interpretation. *Academy of Management Journal, 28*, 587-598.

Downey, H. K., Sheridan, J. E., & Slocum, J. W., Jr. (1975). The path-goal theory of leadership: A longitudinal analysis. *Organizational Behavior and Human Performance, 16*, 156-176.

Eden, D., & Leviatan, U. (1975). Implicit leadership theory as a determinant of the factor structure underlying supervisory behavior scales. *Journal of Applied Psychology, 60*, 736-741.

Fiedler, F. E. (1964). A contingency model of leadership effectiveness. In L. Berkowitz (Ed.), *Advances in experimental social psychology* (pp. 150-190) New York: Academic Press.

Fiedler, F. E. (1967). *A theory of leadership effectiveness.* New York: McGraw-Hill.

Fielder, F. E., & Chemers, M. M. (1974). *Leadership and effective management.* Glenview, IL: Scott-Foresman.

Fiedler, F. E., & Chemers, M. M. (1984). *Improving leadership effectiveness: The Leader Match concept* (2nd ed.). New York: John Wiley.

Fiedler, F. E., Chemers, M. M., & Mahar, L. (1976). *Improving leadership effectiveness: The Leader Match concept.* New York: John Wiley.

Fiedler, F. E., & Garcia, J. E. (1987). *Cognitive resource theory.* New York: John Wiley.

Fiedler, F. E., & Leister, E. F. (1977). Leader intelligence and task performance: A test of a multiscreen model. *Organizational Behavior and Human Performance, 20*, 1-14.

Fiedler, F. E., & Mahar, L. (1979). The effectiveness of contingency model training: A review of the validation of Leader Match. *Personnel Psychology, 32*, 45-62.

Fielder, F. E., Potter, E. H., III, Zais, N. M., & Knowlton, W. A. (1979). Organizational stress and the use and misuse of managerial intelligence and experience. *Journal of Applied Psychology, 64*, 635-647.

Fleishman, E. A., & Harris, E. F. (1962). Patterns of leadership related to employee grievances and turnover. _Personnel Psychology, 15,_ 43-56.

Frost, D. E. (1983). Role perceptions and behavior of the immediate superior: Moderating effects on the prediction of leadership effectiveness. _Organizational Behavior and Human Performance, 31,_ 123-142.

Graen, G. (1976). Role-making processes with complex organizations. In M. D. Dunnette (Ed.), _Handbook of industrial and organizational psychology_ (pp. 1202-1245). Chicago: Rand-McNally.

Graen, G., Alvares, K. M., Orris, J. B., & Martella, J. A. (1970). Contingency model of leadership effectiveness: Antecedent and evidential results. _Psychological Bulletin, 74,_ 285-296.

Graen, G., & Ginsburgh, S. (1977). Job resignation as a function of role orientation and leader acceptance: A longitudinal investigation of organizational assimilation. _Organizational Behavior and Human Performance, 19,_ 1-17.

Graen, G., & Schiemann, W. (1978). Leader-member agreement: A vertical dyad linkage approach. _Journal of Applied Psychology, 63,_ 206-212.

Graen, S. G., & Mitchell, T. R. (1979). Attributional processes of leaders in leader-member interactions. _Organizational Behavior and Human Performance, 23,_ 429-458.

Griffin, R. N. (1981). Relationships among individual, task design, and leader behavior variables. _Academy of Management Journal, 23,_ 665-683.

Halpin, A. W., & Winer, B. J. (1957). A factorial study of leader behavior descriptions. In R. M. Stogdill & A. E. Coons (Eds.), _Leader behavior: Its description and measurement_ (pp. 39-51). Columbus, OH: Bureau of Business Research.

Haythorn, W., Couch, A., Haefner, D., Langham, P., & Carter, L. F. (1956). The effects of varying combinations of authoritarian and egalitarian leader and follower. _Journal of Abnormal and Social Psychology, 53,_ 210-219.

Hemphill, J. K., & Coons, A. E. (1957). Development of the leader behavior description questionnaire. In R. M. Stogdill & A. E. Coons (Eds.), _Leader behavior: Its description and measurement_ (pp. 6-38). Columbus, OH: Bureau of Business Research.

Hill, P. E., & Schmitt, N. (1977). Individual differences in leadership decision-making. _Organizational Behavior and Human Performance, 19,_ 353-367.

Hollander, E. P. (1958). Conformity, status, and idiosyncrasy credit. _Psychological Review, 65,_ 117-127.

House, R. J. (1971). A path-goal theory of leadership. _Administrative Science Quarterly, 16,_ 321-338.

House, R. J., & Baetz, M. L. (1979). Leadership: Some empirical generalizations and new research directions. In B. M. Staw (Ed.), _Research in organizational behavior_ (Vol. 1, pp. 341-423). Greenwich, CT: JAI Press.

House, R. J., & Dessler, G. (1974). The path-goal theory of leadership: Some post hoc and a priori tests. In J. G. Hunt & L. L. Larsen (Eds.), _Contingency approaches to leadership_ (pp. 29-62). Carbondale, IL.: Southern Illinois University Press.

Hunt, J. G. (1984). Organizational leadership: The contingency paradigm and its challenges. In B. Kellerman (Ed.), _Leadership: Multidisciplinary perspectives_ (pp. 113-138). Englewood Cliffs, NJ: Prentice-Hall.

Hunt, J. G., Hosking, D. M., Schreisheim, C. A., & Stewart, R. (1984). _Leaders and managers: International perspectives on managerial behavior and leadership._ New York: Pergamon.

Iaffaldano, M. T., & Muchinsky, P. M. (1985). Job satisfaction and job performance: A meta-analysis. *Psychological Bulletin, 97,* 251-273.

Jago, A. G. (1978). A test of spuriousness in descriptive models of participative leader behavior. *Journal of Applied Psychology, 63,* 383-387.

Jago, A. G., & Vroom, V. H. (1977). Hierarchical level in leadership style. *Organizational Behavior and Human Performance, 18,* 131-145.

Jones, E. E., & David, K. E. (1965). From acts to dispositions: The attribution process in person perception. In L. Berkowitz (Ed.), *Advances in experimental social psychology* (Vol. 2, pp. 220-26). New York: Academic Press.

Jones, E. E., & Nisbett, R. E. (1972). The actor and the observer: Divergent perceptions of the causes of behavior. In E. E. Jones, D. Kanouse, H. H. Kelley, R. E., Nisbett, S. Valins, & B. Weiner (Eds.), *Attribution: Perceiving the causes of behavior* (pp. 79-94). Morristown, NJ: General Learning Press.

Kahn, R. L., & Katz, D. (1953). Leadership practices in relation to productivity and morale. In D. W. Cartwright & A. Zander (Eds.), *Group dynamics* (pp. 554-570). New York: Harper & Row.

Kelley, H. H. (1967). Attribution theory in social psychology. In D. Levine (Ed.), *Nebraska symposium on motivations* (Vol. 15, pp. 192-240). Lincoln: University of Nebraska Press.

Kenny, D. A., & Zaccaro, S. J. (1983). An estimate of variance due to traits in leadership. *Journal of Applied Psychology, 68,* 678-685.

Kerr, S., & Jermier, J. M. (1978). Substitutes for leadership: Their meaning and measurement. *Organizational Behavior and Human Performance, 22,* 375-403.

Knowlton, W. A., Jr., & Mitchell, T. R. (1980). The effects of causal attributions on supervisor's evaluations of subordinate performance. *Journal of Applied Psychology, 65,* 459-466.

Komaki, J. L. (1986). Toward effective supervision: An operant analysis and comparison of managers at work. *Journal of Applied Psychology, 71,* 270-279.

Komaki, J. L., Zlotnick, S., & Jensen, M. (1986). Development of an operant-based taxonomy and observational index of supervisory behavior. *Journal of Applied Psychology, 71,* 260-269.

Korman, A. K. (1966). "Consideration," "initiating structures," and organizational criteria: A review. *Personal Psychology, 19,* 349-362.

Leister, A. P., Borden, D. F., & Fiedler, F. E. (1977). Validation of contingency model leadership training: Leader Match. *Academy of Management Journal, 20,* 464-507.

Lord, R. G., Binning, J. F., Rush, M. C., & Thomas, J. C. (1978). The effect of performance cues and leader behavior in questionnaire rating of leadership behavior. *Organizational Behavior and Human Performance, 21,* 27-39.

Lord, R. G., Foti, R. J., & Phillips, J. S. (1982). A theory of leadership categorization. In J. G. Hunt, U. Sekaran, & C. Schriesheim (Eds.), *Leadership: Beyond establishment views* (pp. 104-121). Carbondale, IL: Southern Illinois University Press.

Maier, N.R.F. (1963). *Problem solving discussion and conferences: Leadership methods and skills.* New York: McGraw-Hill.

Margerison, C., & Glube, R. (1979). Leadership decision-making: An empirical test of the Vroom and Yetton model. *Journal of Management Studies, 16,* 45-55.

McClelland, D. C., & Boyatzis, R. E. (1982). The leadership motive and long term success in management. *Journal of Applied Psychology, 67,* 737-743.

Mischel, W. (1977). On the future of personality measurement. *American Psychologist, 32,* 246-254.

Mitchell, T. R., & Kalb, L. S. (1981). Effects of outcome knowledge and outcome valence in supervisors' evaluations. *Journal of Applied Psychology, 66,* 604-612.

Mitchell, T. R., & Wood, R. E. (1980). Supervisors' responses to subordinate poor performance: A test of an attributional model. *Organizational Behavior and Human Performance, 25,* 123-128.

Mitchell, T. R., Biglan, A., Oncken, G. R., & Fiedler, F. E. (1970). The contingency model: Criticisms and suggestions. *Academy of Management Journal, 13,* 253-267.

Mitchell, T. R., Green, S. G., & Wood, R. E. (1981). An attributional model of leadership and the poor performing subordinate: Development and validation. In L. L. Cummings & B. M. Staw (Eds.), *Research in organizational behavior* (Vol. 3, pp. 197-234). Greenwich, CT: JAI Press.

Peters, L. H., Hartke, D. D., & Pohlmann, J. T. (1985). Fiedler's contingency theory of leadership: An application of the meta-analytic procedures of Schmidt and Hunter. *Psychological Bulletin 97,* 274-285.

Phillips, J. S., & Lord, R. G. (1981). Causal attributions and perceptions of leadership. *Organizational Behavior and Human Performance, 28,* 143-163.

Pulakos, E. D., & Wexley, K. N. (1983). The relationship among perceptual similarity, sex, and performance ratings in manager-subordinate dyads. *Academy of Management Journal, 26,* 129-139.

Rice, R. W. (1978). Construct validity of the least preferred co-worker score. *Psychological Bulletin, 85,* 1199-1237.

Rice, R. W., & Kastenbaum, D. R. (1983). The contingency model of leadership: Some current issues. *Basic and Applied Social Psychology, 4,* 373-392.

Rice, R. W., Marwick, N. J., Chemers, M. M., & Bentley, J. C. (1982). Least preferred co-worker (LPC) score as a moderator of the relationship between task performance and satisfaction. *Personality and Social Psychology Bulletin, 8,* 534-541.

Sanford, F. (1952). Research on military leadership. In J. Flanagan (Ed.), *Psychology in the world emergency* (pp. 17-74). Pittsburgh, PA: University of Pittsburgh Press.

Schreisheim, C. A., & DeNisi, A. S. (1981) Task dimensions as moderators of the effects of instrumental leadership: A two sample replicated test of path-goal leadership theory. *Journal of Applied Psychology, 66,* 589-597.

Shapira, Z. (1976). A facet analysis of leadership styles. *Journal of Applied Psychology, 61,* 136-139.

Sims, H. P., Jr., & Manz, C. C. (1984). Observing leader verbal behavior: Toward reciprocal determinism in leadership theory. *Journal of Applied Psychology, 69,* 222-232.

Snyder, M. (1974). Self-monitoring of expressive behavior. *Journal of Personality and Social Psychology, 30,* 526-537.

Stogdill, R. M. (1948). Personal factors associated with leadership: A survey of the literature. *Journal of Psychology, 25,* 35-71.

Strube, M. J., & Garcia, J. E. (1981). A meta-analytical investigation of Fiedler's contingency model of leadership effectiveness. *Psychological Bulletin, 90,* 307-321.

Vroom, V. H., & Yetton, P. W. (1973). *Leadership and decision-making.* Pittsburgh, PA: University of Pittsburgh Press.

Weary, G. (1979). Self-serving attributional biases: Perceptual or response distortions? *Journal of Personality and Social Psychology, 37,* 1418-1420.

Weed, S. E., Mitchell, T. R., & Moffitt, W. (1976). Leadership style, subordinate personality, and task type as predictors of performance and satisfaction with supervision. *Journal of Applied Psychology, 61,* 58-66.

Weick, K. E. (1969). *The social psychology of organizing.* Reading, MA: Addison-Wesley.

Yukl, G. A. (1981). *Leadership in organizations. Englewood Cliffs, NJ: Prentice-Hall.*

Yukl, G. A., & Nemeroff, W. F. (1979). Identification and measurement of specific categories of leadership behavior: A progress report. In J. G. Hunt & L. L. Larson (Eds.), *Cross-currents in leadership* (pp. 164-200). Carbondale, IL: Southern Illinois University Press.

10

A Person-Niche Theory of Depersonalization

IMPLICATIONS FOR LEADER SELECTION, PERFORMANCE AND EVALUATION

PHILIP M. SMITH
ANNA SABINE FRITZ

Philip M. Smith is a Management Consultant with the firm of C. Kiddy and Partners, Bristol, England. He has held academic appointments at the London School of Economics, the University of Bristol, England, and, most recently, the University of British Columbia, Canada. His major interests are group processes, language, and communication. Formerly Associate Editor of the *Canadian Journal of Behavioral Science,* he is an Editorial Consultant for the *Journal of Personality and Social Psychology*, the *Journal of Language and Social Psychology,* and Blackwell's of Oxford.

Anna Sabine Fritz is a graduate student in Psychology at the University of British Columbia. Her major areas of research interest are depersonalization, leadership, and gerontology.

> The leader role is not of one piece but rather is multifaceted and variegated. Still it is narrowly conceived predominantly as the direction of activity through the exercise of influence or power. More attention is needed to the wider range of behaviors that the leader role represents and the meanings these have for leaders and followers in context. (Hollander, 1985, p. 527)

A social group, like any class or category, exists only insofar as it can be distinguished from other groups, or in a few simpler cases, to the extent that members can be distinguished from nonmembers: In brief, no group stands alone. Many groups are convened more or less exclusively on the basis of explicit comparative agenda, where the group's primary objectives are measured in terms of performance relative to

AUTHORS' NOTE: The preparation of this article was supported by a grant from the Social Sciences and Humanities Research Council of Canada to the first author, who would also like to thank Howard Giles and two anonymous reviewers for comments on earlier drafts of this article, and the Department of Psychology at the University of Bristol, England, for sabbatical facilities.

some other group or groups, or to some superordinate organizational goal. Among numerous examples that come to mind are sports teams, combat units, political parties, commercial enterprises, and departments or divisions within complex organizations. The comparative, or intergroup, impetus may be less prevalent for other kinds of groups, such as families and surgical teams, but seldom, if ever, is it entirely absent. The induction of intergroup tendencies, and the transition between states of intense and attenuated intergroup comparison, exerts a pervasive influence on virtually every facet of group members' thoughts, feelings, and actions, including, we argue, the selection, performance and evaluation of leaders.

Turner and his colleagues (Turner, 1985; Turner, Hogg, Oakes, Reicher, & Wetherell, 1987) have recently presented a sophisticated theory and extensive data concerning the processes underlying group formation and variations in the salience of group membership, processes referred to by the term *depersonalization*. One of the central components of this theory is an assimilation-contrast model of how group membership affects the perception and evaluation of in-group and out-group members. In this paper, we extend Turner's theory to the domain of leadership, and find that the assimilation-contrast model fails to account for leadership phenomena in some kinds of groups. We offer an alternative, which we call the *person-niche model*, that provides a more general account of the effects of depersonalization. While the thrust of this article is mainly theoretical, we will illustrate with empirical examples throughout.

SELF-CATEGORIZATION THEORY

It might seem as if little of a general nature could be said about the consequences of shifts between states of high and low intergroup comparison, given the almost endless variety of groups to which we belong. However, the comparative nature of groups, and the possibility that the intergroup impetus varies over time, suggest the operation of processes that supercede the idiosyncracies of particular groups. Tajfel and Turner (1979) employed the concept of an interpersonal-intergroup continuum to describe variations in the cognitive prepotence of group membership in interpersonal relations:

> At one extreme . . . is the interaction between two or more individuals which is fully determined by their interpersonal relationships and

individual characteristics and not at all affected by various social groups
or categories to which they respectively belong. The other extreme
consists of interactions between two or more individuals (or groups of
individuals) which are fully determined by their respective memberships
of various social groups or categories, and not at all affected by the
interindividual personal relationships between the people involved.
(Tajfel & Turner, 1979, p. 34)

The Assimilation-Contrast Model

Tajfel (1969, 1978) was concerned mainly with the effects of
transitions from the interpersonal to the intergroup pole of the
continuum on intergroup relations and the perception of out-group
members. He proposed that the processes of stereotyping, prejudice,
and discrimination could be illuminated with reference to a psychophysical model, according to which the classification of simple stimuli
into categories or groups causes the perceptual accentuation of within-
class similarities and between-class differences. In the domain of social
relations, Tajfel postulated that these principles of judgmental contrast
interact with a need for positive self-evaluation, imbuing the assimilation-contrast process with attitudinal consequences. These are, furthermore, directed toward enhancing the *relative* prestige of the in-group, at
the expense of the out-group (Tajfel & Turner, 1979).

Turner and colleagues (Turner, 1982, 1985; Turner et al., 1987) have
elaborated and extended this theory to embrace the topics of group
formation and intragroup processes more generally. According to
Turner (1985), the effects of social categorization on group processes
originate with the cognitive redefinition of the self in terms of the
characteristics that define the group, a process that he calls *self-
categorization*. These characteristics then become the criteria for
inferring, by deduction, the group membership of unknown others, and
by induction, the characteristics of people whose group membership is
already known. Turner considers that the process of judgmental
contrast and self-evaluation described by Tajfel provide a good account
of the cognitive, attitudinal, and behavioral consequences of self-
categorization. Factors that contribute to the salience of a particular
group membership cause the individual increasingly to think of self and
others in terms of dimensions and attributes that define the group. That
is, people tend to *depersonalize* the basis of social cognition, and initiate
a chain of inference based increasingly on stereotypical group characteristics, and less and less on individuating personal characteristics.[1]

Turner (1985) derived a large number of important hypotheses from this formulation that have become the subject of much empirical attention. The most fundamental is that depersonalization will be expressed as an increase in uniformity of thought, feeling, and action toward in-group members and outgroup members, and increased differentiation between groups in directions consistent with positive self-evaluation (Brewer, 1979; Turner, 1976, 1981). The induction of perceived similarities among in-group members should also lead to mutual attraction or social cohesion within groups, and conversely, to ethnocentrism between groups (Billig & Tajfel, 1973; Brown, 1984; Turner, Hogg, Turner, & Smith, 1984). Hogg and Turner (1985a, 1985b) predict that depersonalization will cause the basis of interpersonal attraction to shift from individual differences among group members, to the relative status of the group itself, implying the homogenization of in-group evaluation. Other hypotheses pertain to the effects of depersonalization on cooperation: Depersonalization will result in the perception of identity of needs, goals, and motives within the group, causing increased cooperation within the group and competition between groups. Finally, the theory embraces the phenomena of social influence: Confidence in one's opinions, abilities, beliefs, and so on, is a function of agreement (real or imagined) among similar others, and therefore factors that promote self-categorization and subsequently depersonalization will enhance the pressure for uniformity of thought, feeling, and action among members of the group (Hogg & Turner, in press; Mackie, 1986).

Leadership

The significance of self-categorization theory is that it draws attention to the generic cognitive foundations of social groups in a manner that distinguishes them from specific conditions and variables that characterize particular groups. The theory has major implications for the whole domain of social relations, as is evident from the scope of group phenomena that it addresses, and the volume of research that it and its predecessors have generated (e.g., Hogg & Abrams, in press; Tajfel, 1978, Pt. I; Tajfel, 1981; Turner & Giles, 1981; Turner et al., 1987). Extending this theoretical framework to the domain of leadership results in important hypotheses about the relation between depersonalization and leader selection, performance, and evaluation. Considering first the choice of a leader, depersonalization-induced uniformity of thought, feeling, and action within the group, resulting in the homogenization of group goals and interchangeability among group members, would be predicted to reduce discrimination among group members in candidacy for the role of leader. As the salience of group membership increases—due to intergroup comparison for example—the distribution of "votes" and other indicators of leader preference ought to become more variable and less centered on any particular group member. With respect to performance, leaders selected by depersonalized groups, or leaders who find themselves in depersonalizing circumstances, ought to display increased uniformity in the treatment and evaluation of other group members in comparison to leaders of more personalized groups. Finally, the assimilation-contrast model generates a monotonic hypothesis regarding leader evaluation: Leaders will be better liked and more influential as a simple, direct function of depersonalization.[2]

Depersonalization in Structured and Unstructured Groups

We find that these derivations, while consistent with much of the experimental evidence reported to date on related topics, are in many cases not sufficient to account for the relation between depersonalization and group processes. Informal observation indicates that the predicted homogenization of perception and evaluation within groups sometimes does not obtain under circumstances where depersonalization ought to be at its highest. In fact, circumstances that elicit the comparative, intergroup agenda seem often to result in functional, judgmental, and evaluative discrimination among people in groups, albeit discrimination that is geared to the achievement of a shared group goal. Members of sports teams, combat units, and musical orchestras, for example, become less, not more, interchangeable at the point of intergroup competition. So, it might be expected, do members of functionally complex industrial work units become less interchangeable when their output as a group is under the scrutiny of management, or when the organization of which they are a part is threatened in some way.

It is noteworthy that the kinds of groups to which these observations seem to apply are all structurally complex, involving a division of group labor usually captured by the concepts of position and role, while the great majority of experimental evidence adduced in support of Turner's theory is based on experimental procedures that involve unstructured, or functionally undifferentiated, groups. Many experiments employ variants of the so-called social categorization procedure, in which subjects are categorized into groups but constrained from interacting and developing interdependencies with other group members (Turner, 1978, 1982). In some of these, "minimal" groups are created, using trivial and *ad hoc* criteria such as the toss of a coin or the drawing of a slip of paper. While perhaps not so deliberately, group process research in several other major areas pertinent to the theory also tends to employ structurally simple groups. While some experiments employ groups that are convened on the basis of transient experimental criteria, and others capitalize on long-standing, stable criteria, such as enthnicity and sex, group structure in the sense of role differentiation and division of labor is often controlled out of research designs. Furthermore, when individuating information is made available, it is usually in the form of personality traits, interests, attitudes, and behaviors that have an internal, dispositional locus, rather than information that describes externally designated role differences and functional status within the group.

The intuition that group structure plays a mitigating role in the appearance of assimilation-contrast effects is also supported by several pieces of experimental evidence. For example, Brown (1984) described an unpublished experiment (Turner & Brown, 1976) in which status hierarchies were created both within and between five-person groups, by means of feedback on ability tests. Assimilation-contrast effects were not observed; rather, "evaluations, whether of groups or group members, corresponded in a near perfect linear fashion to the objectively established status relations" (Brown, 1984, p. 616). Wilder (1978) reported three experiments in which information about out-group members indicating a heterogeneity of opinion and value orientation in the group resulted in the reduction of favoritism to the in-group. Fraser (1978, p. 214) speculated that the failure to observe group polarization effects in field studies of teams of civil servants evaluating job performance, academic faculty deliberating over student grades, health professionals discussing case reports, and student council committees, may be due in part to role differences between members.

The Person-Niche Model of Depersonalization

In light of these observations, we will make two elaborations to the theory in order to account for the effects of depersonalization in both structured and unstructured groups. The first elaboration takes the form of an assumption: We assume that the mental representation of a self-category comprises not only concrete instances of other members with whom one may be familiar, but also abstract generalizations concerning characteristic behaviors, activities and products, goals and the needs that fuel them, and the spatio-temporal settings in which these goals are pursued. We call this abstract, impersonal generalization the group *niche*. The reason for introducing this term will be described below.[3]

The second elaboration concerns the model on which both Tajfel's and Turner's predictions are based, in which assimilation-contrast effects are caused by the imposition of a discrete classification (often dichotomous in the case of social groups) on a series of continuous stimuli. The effect is predicted only where the classification is correlated with a focal attribute of the continuous series, suggesting that the classification acts as a cue focusing attention on intraclass similarities and interclass differences. The more salient these cues are, the more the underlying continuity between the categories is ignored.

This model appears to work fairly well with unstructured social groups. However, members of structured groups by definition share an aspect of group membership that actively encourages, even demands, within-group differences. Furthermore, the divisions of rights and responsibilities that define structured groups have often been developed precisely in response to intergroup competition and other factors that would be expected to lead to the reduction of within-group differences.

This paradox is more apparent than real if we relax the mechanistic constraints imposed on the perceptual side of Tajfel's and Turner's models caused by extrapolating too literally from the domain of simple psychophysical judgment. The more general idea at the root of their theorizing is that depersonalization reorients attention away from concerns related exclusively to individual welfare toward factors influencing the welfare of the group as a whole. Phrased in another way, depersonalization channels the information processing resources of the naive scientists away form intuitions (scripts, schemata, implicit theories, etc.) about individual, dispositional causes of behavior, and toward intuitions about influences that supercede the individual, such as shared attributes, purposes, settings, and other properties of the group niche. Depersonalization literally *de-personalizes* social inference, transforming the "naive psychologist" into a "naive sociologist!"

The primary implications of this hypothesis are that (1) among members of groups in a relatively interpersonal state, social judgment and decision making (including person perception, causal attribution, attraction, cooperation, and social influence) will be motivated by egocentric considerations, based on the degree to which others satisfy the requirements of personal self-esteem; and (2) among members of groups in a relatively intergroup, depersonalized state, the criteria of social judgment and decision making will be ethnocentric, based on one's evaluation of the group's comparative status, on one's beliefs about the importance of various positions and roles within the group in achieving positive group status, and on the degree to which individuals fulfill the obligations of these positions.

According to this hypothesis, depersonalization will result in assimilation effects only where groups are structurally undifferentiated, and where there are constraints on the emergence of structure. Under such conditions, the group niche is "holographic" (Albert & Whetten, 1985), and every member is assumed to have the same rights and obligations in the group as every other member. But among members of groups in which functional differentiation is imposed by custom, code, or law, intragroup relations will be guided by intuitions about the importance of various roles to the satisfaction of the group's needs, and the extent of individuals' conformity to the demands of these roles. While this argument implies the emergence of a common purpose among group members, especially vis-à-vis the out-group, it does not imply increasing similarity or interchangeability among them, or a uniformity of evaluation or action. In the following section we apply these ideas specifically to the topic of leadership.[4]

DEPERSONALIZATION AND LEADERSHIP

Leader Selection

The person-niche model yields the following prediction. *The person selected as leader will tend to be the one who is judged to be most likely to satisfy the requirements of positive self-evaluation, according to the state of depersonalization of the selectors at that time.*

This hypothesis predicts that the requirements of leadership vary systematically, depending on the relative priority of egocentric and ethnocentric needs. This simple idea furnishes the basis for predictions about the variability of leadership criteria both within and between groups at different points along the depersonalization continuum. The person-niche model predicts depersonalization-induced concern for the predicament of the group, and thus differentiation among group members on dimensions that are perceived relevant to group security. Only when the bases for discriminating among members on such dimensions are minimal do our predictions and those of the assimilation-contrast model converge. In such cases, depersonalization ought to induce more diffuse patterns of choice.

The leadership literature does not provide many examples of studies that directly manipulate intergroup comparison or other variables that can be translated into these terms. However, Jennings's (1950) study of sociometric choice among the inmates of a correctional training school for juvenile girls is relevant. The subjects lived in self-catered "cottages" of between 20 and 28 residents, and were occupied in vocational training at other sites in the institution during the day. They were asked to nominate, from among the other inmates, lists of those whom they would choose, and those they would reject, in the contrasting contexts of (a) loosely organized, informal leisure time, (b) living together in somewhat more formal cottage arrangements, and (c) working together on even more structured vocational projects. The former task, argues Jennings, elicited an image of what she calls the *psychegroup*, a "fluid, informal, relatively uninstitutionalized setting, where concerns and obligations of life are . . . at the command of the individual's wants and wishes," and in which sociometric choice has "*a largely personalized* base." The latter tasks, especially vocational training, elicited the *sociogroup*, and "collective, more or less formalized setting, where concerns must be shared and obligations held in common," in which choice has "*a largely impersonalized* base" (pp. 276, 278, emphasis in original). The descriptive affinities between this and our own formulations are obvious.

The varied yet highly predictable circumstances in which the girls lived make this an excellent location in which to study the dynamics of egocentric and ethnocentric preference. That the tasks really did elicit different representations is attested to by the fact that only 36% of the leisure nominations overlapped with the living/working choices. Several measures indicated that the formal settings elicited more rather than less complex patterns of sociometric choice, as the person-niche model would predict. For example, although there were more positive than negative choices in all settings, the distribution between positive and negative was more symmetrical in both the living and working settings (in the ratio of roughly 2:1), than in the leisure setting (4:1). Furthermore, there were twice as many reciprocated choices in the leisure setting, indicating greater dispersion of interpersonal preference, than in the other two settings. This pattern was also expressed in the finding that the distribution of choices was much more centralized on a few individuals in the sociogroup setting than in the psychegroup setting.

In contrast to the rich niche explored by Jennings, Gibb (1950) convened unstructured groups of 10 previously unacquainted men to work on cooperative tasks over several sessions. At several points, subjects were asked to nominate from among members those they would choose as personal friends (psychegroup), those they would like to remain in the group for subsequent activities (the sociogroup, according to Gibb), and the member they would judge to have been the leader on one of the tasks.

Not surprisingly, in this personalized, structurally undifferentiated group niche, egocentric (psychegroup) and ethnocentric (sociogroup) choices overlapped considerably (more than 50% on average), and this overlap increased over sessions. More importantly, leader nominations were more closely correlated with psychegroup choices than with sociogroup choices, as were leadership ratings made by two independent observers on three out of four occasions. In spite of the rather weak measure of depersonalized preference employed in this experiment, and modest correlations between the sociometric questions and leader nominations, it is significant that leader selection should have been better predicted by a measure of personal liking.

Our theory indicates that a careful analysis of group niche, and the modal working state of the group, ought to precede predictions about who will be selected as leader. Where group salience is low, choice patterns will be determined by intuitions about others' dispositions, and the prospect of personal welfare. Where salience is high, the role requirements of group success, and intuitions about how well group members can fulfill these requirements, will dominate.

Leader Performance

The idea that variations in the calculus of leader selection will be reflected in leaders' behaviors and styles is stated in the following hypothesis.

Other things being equal, leaders' competencies, and perceptions of their rights and obligations, will correspond most closely to the state-dependent criteria by which they are selected.

More specifically, one would expect leaders chosen by groups in a relatively personalized state to be either interpersonally adept, and/or influential in the distribution of individual reward and punishment. Leaders of depersonalized groups, on the other hand, would be expected to show strength in executive and strategic skills related to the group's success and failure. While the assimilation-contrast model predicts increasing uniformity of leaders' behavior toward members with increasing depersonalization, the person-niche model predicts that depersonalization will cause leaders to react to members according to the ethnocentric importance of the roles that they occupy, and whether or not they fulfill the demands of these roles. Again, the predictions of the two models converge only in the case of unstructured groups. Leaders themselves are expected to strive to maintain or recapture the state of depersonalization that led to their selection.

Within the enormous literature on leader behavior, bipolar and two-dimensional models are ubiquitous (see, for example, Bass, 1981, chaps. 18-22). Some of the more influential bipolar models, which are based on the idea of a continuum of leadership styles running between two antagonistic poles, contrast democratic with autocratic (Lewin & Lippitt, 1938), participative with directive (Tannenbaum & Schmidt, 1958), Theory X with Theory Y (MacGregor, 1960), and relations-oriented with task-oriented (Fiedler, 1967) leaders. In spite of differences among these models in terms of origins and emphases, they all capitalize on the distinction between "follower-focused" or "group maintenance—oriented" leadership on one hand, and "task-focused" or "goal achievement-oriented" leadership on the other (Bass, 1981; Cartwright & Zander, 1960). Whereas in the bipolar models these are mutually exclusive "styles," in other models they are conceived of as independent "dimensions" of leader behavior that can be manifest in varying combinations. The most important of these, evolving from the Ohio State Leadership Studies (e.g., Stogdill & Coons, 1957) is the distinction between consideration (the degree of concern shown by a leader for the welfare of group members) and initiation of structure (the degree to which the leader initiates, organizes, and directs group activity; see for example, Schreisheim, House, & Kerr, 1976; Blake & Mouton, 1978).

Parallels can easily be drawn between our concepts of personalized and depersonalized leadership, and the constellations of attitudes and behaviors that characterize group maintenance-oriented and goal achievement-oriented leadership. In fact, our theory provides a powerful unifying framework for predicting the relative prevalence on one type of leadership over the other. It also points the way to predictions concerning the interrelation between indices of personalized and depersonalized leadership in different groups. In groups that convene for a variety of purposes along the whole range of the depersonalization continuum, such as sports teams that meet for practice games with other teams and on informal social occasions, a very diverse set of skills is required of leaders who hope to be highly regarded in all corners of the group niche, and thus positive correlations between measures of consideration and initiation of structure (for example) are predicted. In groups that meet specifically for purposes at one or the other extreme of the continuum, such as hobby clubs (personalized) or emergency police tactical units (depersonalized), the requirements of leadership are specialized and circumscribed. In these cases, follower-focused and task-focused behavior will tend to be negatively correlated, insofar as the presence of niche-inappropriate behavior is antagonistic to niche-appropriate goals. In groups whose normal working mode is semiformal, neither highly personalized nor depersonalized, as is the case for many kinds of occupational groups, the two aspects of leadership skill will be uncorrelated, since niche-inappropriate behavior will tend to be seen simply as irrelevant or superfluous, rather than as antagonistic.

Leader Evaluation

The major hypothesis concerning leader evaluation follows directly from the preceding sections.

> *Group members' evaluation of and satisfaction with the leader are a direct function of (a) the similarity between the conditions under which the leader was selected, and the modal working state of the group; and (b) the leader's ability to adjust to the demands of new circumstances.*

This hypothesis provides the basis for specifying the conditions under which leaders will be applauded or challenged, as well as those in which the leader can expect to exert maximal social influence. The person-niche model, unlike the assimilation-contrast model, is nonmonotonic in this regard: Evaluation is not a function of selection state, leader performance, or evaluation state alone, but of all three in interaction.

Up to this point, we have considered the implications of the theory only for leaders who are selected by the group. Of course, leaders are often imposed on groups by external processes and authorities. Hollander (1985) makes the case that the election of a leader in itself "creates in followers a greater sense of responsibility and higher expectations for the leader's success" (p. 508). Certainly, the conscious selection of somebody from among one's numbers to fill a named position would be expected to evoke an explicit image of the group and its niche, and increase the likelihood of a match between the self-perceived needs of the group and the qualities of the leader. On the other hand, when a leader is appointed by an authority whose perceptions of the group's needs and goals (in depersonalization terms) are the same as those already established by the group, or one that is accepted by the group to have the right to set the group's agenda, the differences between election and appointment will be diminished, possibly even eradicated.

CONCLUDING REMARKS

Leadership is one of those rare topics in psychology that has sustained a tremendous intensity of research and scholarly interest despite drastic changes in the zeitgeist of our science. In fact, students of leaders and leadership have always been quick to respond to new theoretical trends in the discipline as a whole, and one finds in the vast and venerable leadership literature a virtual recapitulation of the most significant debates and developments that have shaped modern social psychology.

Contemporary developments, influenced by a mood of peacetime pragmatism, revealed a preoccupation with business leadership (e.g., Hunt, Sekaran, & Schriesheim, 1981). Leader effectiveness is the watchword of this trend, with group productivity and satisfaction considered two of its most important indicators. These priorities have quite naturally led to the tendency to equate leadership with the executive/managerial function, and to narrow the range of contexts in which leadership is studied primarily to those involving instrumental and often material goals.

This pragmatic thrust, while not wrong, is incomplete for two reasons. First, it bypasses the priorities of social psychology, inasmuch as it reifies the position and function of leadership in a named managerial role. Leadership does not inhere in a person, or in the position that person occupies or the role script attached to the position. Persons, positions, and roles may potentiate or constrain the form of interpersonal relations, but in the final analysis leadership is an *enacted* property of relationships among people in groups. It is the determinants, mediators, and consequences of such enactments, rather than of positions or roles in themselves, that have been the targets of examination in this article.

Second, the overwhelming emphasis on executive management has resulted in a concentration of leadership research at the "cutting edge" or "sharp end" of organizational practice, where group success and failure are measured against externally defined, usually competitive, standards of performance on instrumental tasks. The possibility that group survival and welfare hinges as much on group maintenance and cohesiveness as on standardized competitive performance, even for the most externally oriented and formal of organizations, is one that is sometimes underemphasized. Attempts to reconcile these apparently incompatible views of organizations and the functions of leadership are not new (Argyris, 1961; Blake & Mouton, 1978; Hersey & Blanchard, 1977; Likert, 1967; MacGregor, 1960; Reddin, 1977). What is new about our approach is that we have attempted to move from an intuitive and prescriptive stand on the suitability of different kinds of leaders and leadership to an explanatory theory based on the generic origins of group formation and comparison. Research is now being conducted to test this theory directly.

NOTES

1. Depersonalization should be distinguished from deindividuation at the outset. According to deindividuation theorists, group membership results in the loss of personal identity, ultimately leading to a diminished sense of responsibility, irrationality, and a regression to socially primitive forms of behavior. Depersonalization, on the other hand, simply entails variations in the relative priority of individual and group responsibilities. Indeed, insofar as group membership is often compatible with, and sometimes essential for, the satisfaction of personal needs, we argue that depersonalization results in the augmentation of responsibility, and the adoption of additional criteria for rational conduct, above and beyond those that are specific to the individual. The focus of this article is on the process and consequences of depersonalization, rather than on the various factors that cause groups to form and make group membership salient. The reader is referred to Reicher (1982) and to Turner (1985) for excellent discussions of these matters.

2. It might be thought possible to make the opposite case from the assimilation-contrast perspective: The homogenization of group goals should result in a high degree of consensus about the requirements of group leadership and hence in the convergence of leadership choices upon the individual thought to be most capable of fulfilling them. However, this convergence would be predicted by the same model to be offset by the tendency for group members to become more interchangeable.

3. This may seem contrary to the intuition that when one speaks or writes abstractly of a group, one tends to think only of people and their qualities. We suggest that people use

the term "group" in ordinary discourse mainly as a shorthand way of referring to people, rather than in the technical sense meant here. As a group member actively engaged in group activity, the features that will come most easily to mind will depend on what one is doing.

4. As far as the implications of the person-niche model for *inter*group relations go, we predict that homogenizing effects due to imminent intergroup comparison will occur mainly when knowledge about the out-group is very limited. Whenever there is knowledge (or belief) about the structure of roles and divisions of labor within the out-group, we predict differentiation among out-group members on the same basis as that among in-group members, that is, according to one's estimate on the potential impact of a particular out-group member on the group's ethnocentric aims.

REFERENCES

Albert, S., & Whetten, D. A. (1985). Organizational identity. In L. L. Cummings & B. M. Staw (Eds.), *Research in organizational behavior* (Vol. 7, pp. 263-295). Greenwich, CT: JAI Press.

Argyris, C. (1961). Organizational leadership. In L. Petrullo & B. M. Bass (Eds.), *Leadership and interpersonal behavior* (pp. 326-354). New York: Holt, Rinehart & Winston.

Bass, B. M. (1981). *Stogdill's handbook of leadership.* New York: Free Press.

Billig, M. G., & Tajfel, H. (1973). Social categorization and similarity in intergroup behavior. *European Journal of Social Psychology, 3,* 27-52.

Blake, R. R., & Mouton, J. S. (1978). *The new managerial grid.* Houston: Gulf.

Brewer, M. (1979). In-group bias in the minimal intergroup situation: A cognitive-motivational analysis. *Psychological Bulletin, 86,* 307-324.

Brown, R. J. (1984). The role of similarity in intergroup relations. In H. Tajfel (Ed.), *The social dimension: European developments in social psychology* (pp. 603-623). Cambridge; Cambridge University Press.

Cartwright, D., & Zander, A. (1960). *Group dynamics-research and theory* (2nd ed.). Evanston, IL: Row Peterson.

Eiser, J. R., & Stroebe, W. (1972). *Categorization and social judgment.* New York: Academic Press.

Fiedler, F. E. (1967). *A theory of leadership effectiveness.* New York: McGraw-Hill.

Fraser, C. (1978). Small groups II: Processes and products. In H. Tajfel (Ed.), *Introducing social psychology* (pp. 201-228). London: Penguin.

Gibb, C. A. (1950). The sociometry of leadership in temporary groups. *Sociometry, 13,* 226-243.

Hersey, P., & Blanchard, K. H. (1977). *Management of organizational behavior: Utilizing human resources.* Englewood Cliffs, NJ: Prentice-Hall.

Hogg, M. A., & Abrams, D. (in press). *Social identity.* London: Methuen.

Hogg, M. A., & Turner, J. C. (1985a). Interpersonal attraction, social identification and psychological group formation. *European Journal of Social Psychology, 15,* 51-66.

Hogg, M. A, & Turner, J. C. (1985b). When liking begets solidarity: An experiment on the role of interpersonal attraction in psychological group formation. *British Journal of Social Psychology, 24.*

Hogg, M. A., & Turner, J. C. (in press). Social identity and conformity: A theory of referent informational influence. In W. Doise & S. Mascovici (Eds.), *Current issues in European social psychology* (Vol. 2). Cambridge: Cambridge University Press.

Hollander, E. P. (1985). Leadership and power. In G. Lindzey & E. Aronson (Eds.), *Handbook of social psychology* (3rd ed., pp. 485-537). New York: Random House.

Hunt, J. G., Sekaran, U., & Schriesheim, C. A. (Eds.). (1981). *Leadership: Beyond establishment views.* Carbondale, IL: Southern Illinois University Press.

Jennings, H. H. (1950). *Leadership and isolation* (2nd ed.). New York: Longmans, Green.

Lewin, K., & Lippitt, R. (1938). An experimental approach to the study of autocracy and democracy: A preliminary note. *Sociometry, 1,* 292-300.

Likert, R. (1967). *The human organization.* New York: McGraw-Hill.

MacGregor, D. (1960). *The human side of enterprise.* New York: McGraw-Hill.

Makie, D. M. (1986). Social identification effects in group polarization. *Journal of Personality and Social Psychology, 50,* 720-728.

Reddin, W. J. (1977). An integration of leader-behavior typologies. *Group and Organization Studies, 2,* 282-295.

Reicher, S. (1982). The determination of collective behavior. In H. Tajfel (Ed.), *Social identity and intergroup relations* (pp. 41-83). Cambridge: Cambridge University Press.

Schriesheim, C. A., House, R. J., & Kerr, S. (1976). Leader initiating structure: A reconciliation of discrepant research results and some empirical tests. *Organizational Behavior and Human Performance, 15,* 297-321.

Stogdill, R. M., & Coons, A. E. (1957). *Leader behavior: Its description and measurement.* Columbus: Ohio State University, Bureau of Business Research.

Tajfel, H. (1969). Cognitive aspects of prejudice. *Journal of Social Issues, 25,* 79-97.

Tajfel, H. (1978). *Differentiation between social groups.* New York: Academic Press.

Tajfel, H., & Turner, J. C. (1979). An integrative theory of intergroup conflict. In W. G. Austin & S. Worchel (Eds.), *The social psychology of intergroup relations* (pp. 33-47). Monterey, CA: Brooks/Cole.

Tannenbaum, R., & Schmidt, W. H. (1958). How to choose a leadership pattern. *Harvard Business Review, 36,* 95-101.

Turner, J. C. (1978). Social categorization and social differentiation in the minimal group paradigm. In H. Tajfel (Ed.), *Differentiation between social groups* (pp. 101-140). New York: Academic Press.

Turner, J. C. (1981). The experimental social psychology of intergroup behavior. In J. C. Turner & H. Giles (Eds.), *Intergroup behavior* (pp. 66-101). Oxford: Blackwell.

Turner, J. C. (1982). Towards a cognitive redefinition of the social group. In H. Tajfel (Ed.), *Social identity and intergroup relations* (pp. 15-40). Cambridge: Cambridge University Press.

Turner, J. C. (1985). Social categorization and the self-concept. In E. E. Lawler (Ed.), *Advances in group processes* (Vol. 2, pp. 77-121). Greenwich, CT: JAI Press.

Turner, J. C., & Brown, R. J. (1976). *Hierarchies.* Unpublished manuscript, University of Bristol.

Turner, J. C., & Giles, H. (1981). *Intergroup behavior.* Oxford: Blackwell.

Turner, J. C., Hogg, M. A., Oakes, P. J., Reicher, S. D., & Wetherell, M. (1987). *Rediscovering the social group: A self-categorization theory.* Oxford: Blackwell.

Turner, J. C., Hogg, M. A., Turner, P. J., & Smith, P. M. (1984). Failure and defeat as determinants of group cohesiveness. *British Journal of Social Psychology, 23,* 97-111.

Wetherell, M., & Turner, J. C. (1984). *Social identification, differentiation and opinion shifts.* Unpublished manuscript, University of St. Andrews.

Wilder, D. A. (1978). Reduction of intergroup discrimination through individuation of the out-group. *Journal of Personality and Social Psychology, 36,* 1361-1374.

Available in this series . . .

REVIEW OF PERSONALITY AND SOCIAL PSYCHOLOGY

Group Processes and Intergroup Relations
Volume 9 **edited by CLYDE HENDRICK**
ISBN 0-8039-3090-9 cloth   ISBN 0-8039-3091-7 paper

Group Processes
Volume 8 **edited by CLYDE HENDRICK**
ISBN 0-8039-3071-2 cloth   ISBN 0-8039-3072-0 paper

Sex and Gender
Volume 7 **edited by PHILLIP SHAVER and CLYDE HENDRICK**
ISBN 0-8039-2929-3 cloth   ISBN 0-8039-2930-7 paper

Self, Situations, and Social Behavior
Volume 6 **edited by PHILLIP SHAVER**
ISBN 0-8039-2507-7 cloth   ISBN 0-8039-2508-5 paper

Emotions, Relationships, and Health
Volume 5 **edited by PHILLIP SHAVER**
ISBN 0-8039-2358-9 cloth   ISBN 0-8039-2359-7 paper

REVIEW OF PERSONALITY AND SOCIAL PSYCHOLOGY

Volume 4 **edited by LADD WHEELER & PHILLIP SHAVER**
ISBN 0-8039-2102-0 cloth   ISBN 0-8039-2103-9 paper

Volume 3 **edited by LADD WHEELER**
ISBN 0-8039-1854-2 cloth   ISBN 0-8039-1855-0 paper

Volume 2 **edited by LADD WHEELER**
ISBN 0-8039-1667-1 cloth   ISBN 0-8039-1668-X paper

Volume 1 **edited by LADD WHEELER**
ISBN 0-8039-1457-1 cloth   ISBN 0-8039-1458-X paper

NOTES